2nd Edition

Car Memorabilia
Price Guide

Ron Kowalke and Ken Buttolph

Published by

 **krause
publications**

700 E. State Street • Iola, WI 54990-0001
Telephone: 715/445-2214

Please call or write for our free catalog of automotive publications. Our toll-free number to place an order or obtain a free catalog is 800-258-0929 or please use our regular business telephone 715-445-2214 for editorial comment
and further information.

Library of Congress Catalog Number: 95-77318
ISBN: 0-87341-522-1
Printed in the United States of America

Contents

Introduction

Judging by the feedback we received, the first edition of the *Car Memorabilia Price Guide,* published in 1995, was a success. Reader feedback to the book most often took the form of leading with words of encouragement, segueing into constructive criticism and ending with a request that we do a follow-up edition. Foremost among the encouraging words, we were applauded for taking an "overall" approach to listing automobilia/automobilia values in a single source as opposed to keying on just one or two areas of collectibles, as is the format of many other price guides devoted to car memorabilia. We knew going in to the project that it would be an ongoing challenge to attempt to master this comprehensive approach, as the field of automobilia is large and diverse. But at the same time, it also made no sense to do it any other way as that "narrow" approach has been tried before many times – some successful, others not!

With that said, we feel the original *Car Memorabilia Price Guide*, flaws and all, showcased its potential and was a solid starting point. As with any first effort, especially one such as this trying to "do it all" and do it correctly, there is room for improvement. This second edition of the *Car Memorabilia Price Guide* addresses those areas of concern found – or pointed out – in the original as well as introduces changes that we feel will make this book a better tool for its readers.

Beyond the well-researched pricing updates, the most obvious change is size. We've added almost 100 pages to this second edition, including expanded or totally new listings of automobilia and new photo pages (eight of these pages are grouped into a first-ever color section). Also, we've expanded on the amount of direct-from-the-expert tips, including: 1) Where to start in a particular field of automobilia collecting; 2) Automobilia "bargain hunting"; and 3) How to spot overpriced or fraudulent automobilia. These experts tell all on "hot" collectibles such as motorcycle memorabilia and ceramic vehicles to "undiscovered" automobilia such as big rig collectibles and auto racing decals. Words of wisdom from authorities Roger Pribbenow (motorcycles), Phil Hall (decals), Andy Hill, Jr. (big rigs) and Ken Collins and Joel Dunford from Carllectibles! (ceramics) give you, the reader, proper background to buy or sell automobilia with confidence.

As was stated in the introduction of the first edition of *Car Memorabilia Price Guide*, to complete a book that covers the scope of material such as this undertaking can never be the work of a single author – or in this case, two authors. Many people contributed to this project and without their guidance and willingness to answer endless questions posed by the authors, this book would not have become a reality. The authors would like to take this opportunity to express our appreciation to each and every one of these individuals, ever so generous with their time and knowledge.

We believe the *Car Memorabilia Price Guide* reflects the professionalism and wealth of knowledge that can be found among the dealers and collectors of automobilia. Users of this book can also help us to make this product even better by taking the time to write us and tell us what you would like to see in future editions.

On page 6 there is a list of our "Panel of Experts" whom we encourage readers to contact if they have questions concerning any of the collectible items listed. Please patronize their businesses where listed or look them up in person in the vendor area at the next big collector vehicle show you attend. And when attending that show, make sure you don't forget to bring your copy of *Car Memorabilia Price Guide* to help you in your search for that desired item of automobilia.

Ron Kowalke
Ken Buttolph

On the cover:

Front: An assortment of automobilia including a Metalcraft Shell stake bed truck, Texaco Fire Chief tin sign, Around The World motor oil two-gallon can, Fisk tire patch kit, GM Polishing Cloth kit, Cross Country oil pitcher, AC Spark Plug set, Smith-Miller Mobiloil truck, Standard ISO VIS 30-weight oil quart glass container, Purity transmission grease five-pound tin can, Marathon handy oiler, Non-skid tire ashtray and Golden Shell bank.

Back: White Pepper gas globe, 1948 Tucker model and 1950 Steelcraft Comet F-350 pedal car.

Pricing

The range of values for the automobilia pictured in this book is listed as close to the item(s) pictured as the layout would allow. Estimated values for each item in **Good**, **Very Good**, and **Excellent** condition are given. Items in "Good" condition are better than average for their age and are restorable. "Very Good" items reflect minimal wear and tear or an amateur restoration. "Excellent" means like-new or restored to like-new condition.

Items in conditions too poor to be restored correctly are not appraised. A uniform system for pricing automobilia items in lesser conditions seems impossible to devise. Toys and license plates can be restored and, therefore, retain more value when in "poor" condition. Clothing, literature, and photographs are virtually worthless after a certain amount of wear and tear occurs. This is why we use only three conditions.

This second edition of *Car Memorabilia Price Guide* was created in the fall of 1997. The values for the items were determined by asking the advice of dozens of dealers and collectors who specialize in various types of automobilia. Pricing collectible items is always an "inexact science." Therefore, the values presented should always be used only as a guide.

We welcome any information that would help to refine future editions of this price guide and make it more useful to collectors. Contact: Old Cars Books Dept., 700 E. State St., Iola, WI 54900.

A special thank you to Sharon Korbeck, editor of Krause Publications' *Toys & Prices 1998,* for allowing us to use portions of that book for the toy vehicle section of *Car Memorabilia Price Guide.*

Also, a big thank you to Stacy "Rookie" Hilscher of Krause Publications' book production staff. Her page design expertise is greatly appreciated.

Cover photography: Ross Hubbard.
Cover artist: Tom Dupuis.
Color section designer: Christopher Pritchard.

Panel Of Experts

Petroliana
Jim Hummel
W8921 U.S. Hwy. 10
Hortonville, WI 54944
ph: (920)779-6259
FAX: (920)779-6230

E. Virgil Hackett
Virgil's Antiques
Pennsylvania
ph: (717)232-2575

Motorcycle Collectibles
Roger Pribbenow
c/o Motorcycle Chums Memorabilia
P.O. Box 160
DeForest, WI 53532

Barry Brown
H.D. Garage
18 Dumas St.
Hull, Quebec, CANADA
J8Y 2M6

Auto Racing Literature
Phil Hall
c/o Old Cars Book Dept.
700 E. State St.
Iola, WI 54990-0001

John & Enola Powell
Books & Bunque
6744 E. 49th St.
Indianapolis, IN 46226
ph: (317)562-1627

Auto Racing Decals
Phil Hall
c/o Old Cars Book Dept.
700 E. State St.
Iola, WI 54990-0001

Big Rig Collectibles
Andy Hill, Jr.
c/o Old Cars Book Dept.
700 E. State St.
Iola, WI 54990-0001

License Plates
Keith Marvin
c/o Old Cars Book Dept.
700 E. State St.
Iola, WI 54990-0001

Wayne Tyler
c/o Wayne's Auto Parts
14548 Mill Creek Drive
Montpelier, VA 23192
ph: (804)749-4641

Plastic Model Kits
Gerald Geiger
The Model Museum/Model Empire
7116 W. Greenfield Ave.
West Allis, WI 53214
ph: (920)453-4610
FAX: (920)453-8180

Stuart A. Lenzke/B. Mitchell Carlson
c/o Old Cars Book Dept.
700 E. State St.
Iola, WI 54990-0001

Hood Mascots
Charles Schalebaum
Allentown, Pennsylvania
ph: (610)435-4440
FAX: (610)435-3388

Hudson Collectibles
Jim and Sandy Boyle
c/o Old Cars Book Dept.
700 E. State St.
Iola, WI 54990-0001

John O'Halloran
8153 S. Homan Ave.
Chicago, IL 60652

Literature
Ron Ladley Literature
1850 Valley Forge Road
Lansdale, PA 19446
ph: (610)584-1665

Ceramics
Ken Collins/Joel Dunford
c/o Carllectibles!
P.O. Box 252
Highland, CA 92346
ph: (909)884-1474

Toys
Bill Hill Old Toys
8105 Crabb Road
Temperance, MI 48182
ph: (313)847-7783

Rick and Karie Watson
P.O. Box 132
Smithfield, ME 04978
ph: (207)362-6211

Buddy L
Al Kasishke
4661 S. St. Louis
Tulsa, OK 74105

Corgi
Mark Arruda
P.O. Box P44
South Dartmouth, MA 02748

Dinky
Dan Casey
Olympia, Washington

Hot Wheels
Bob Chartain
479 Sequoia
Redwood City, CA 94061

Miscellaneous
Collectors Auction Services
RR 2, Box 431, Oakwood Road
Oil City, PA 16301
ph: (814)677-6070
FAX: (814)677-6166

Big Rig Collectibles

By Andy Hill, Jr.

Today, there are memorabilia collectors of all kinds. Areas of interest for these collectors include antique cars, motorcycles and airplanes as well as one area that has gained a large following in recent years, the collecting of antique truck memorabilia.

The popularity of antique trucks – in this case, tractor-trailers or "big rigs" – and their associated memorabilia has experienced rapid growth over the years, especially since the American Truck Historical Society was founded in 1971. This is the first known organization that deals only with the preservation and restoration of old trucks and big rig memorabilia.

The American Truck Historical Society has 72 chapters throughout the United States, Canada and Australia, and holds a national truck show every year in a different part of the U.S., displaying well over 500 old big rigs. The chapters supporting the American Truck Historical Society also have separate, smaller shows throughout the year.

Other organizations with similar goals of preservation and restoration of old trucks have also evolved through the years. One such organization is the Antique Truck Club of America, supported by 11 chapters from the northeastern U.S. The Antique Truck Club of America has its own annual truck show in Macungie, Pennsylvania, with one of the best flea markets for collectible literature.

Literature

If your knowledge of trucks isn't what you would like it to be, there are magazines you can subscribe to, such as *Heavy Duty Trucking, Fleet Owner, Fleet Equipment, Owner - Operator* and *Overdrive*. In these magazines you will find the addresses of truck manufacturers that you can write to for free literature. Different truck builders are changing or discontinuing truck models every year, so this is a good starting point in collecting truck literature.

If you are interested in purchasing back issues of truck magazines, you will find it difficult to get the really old issues through the companies that publish these magazines. Back issues can sometimes be found at truck shows or flea markets for a reasonable price of $4.00 each on down to a $1.00 depending on condition.

Overdrive is one of the favorite old magazines to collect since its publisher pulled no punches when it came to the articles printed. This is also evident in the magazine's subtitles: 'The Price Of Truth $1.00' and 'The Voice Of The American Trucker'.

(Left) June 1972 and (Right) November 1973 issues of *Overdrive* magazine. Each is worth $4.00 in excellent condition.

Overdrive has been in print since 1962 and has undergone a change of publishers within the past seven years. This has made it difficult to acquire back issues such as *Overdrive*'s May 1968 or May 1971 issues. These two magazines featured stories on visits to Brockway's assembly plant, and are valued at $10.00 each in excellent condition. That coverage by *Overdrive* was responsible for Brockway's slogan: "The Most Rugged Truck In The World." The value of other magazines depends both on what articles appear within as well as condition.

Two excellent magazines based on old trucks and trucking companies are *Wheels of Time*, available through the American Truck Historical Society and *Double Clutch*, available through the Antique Truck Club of America. Both magazines are printed bi-monthly and cost $25.00 per year, which includes club membership.

To receive these magazines contact:

Wheels Of Time
American Truck Historical Society
P.O. Box 531168
Birmingham, AL 35253-1168

Double Clutch
Antique Truck Club Of America
P.O. Box 291
Hershey, PA 17033

When you've gotten as much information on a particular truck as you think you're going to find in old or new truck magazines, the next step is to try to collect the original sales literature pertaining to that truck. This literature was once easily accessible through the dealerships and ranges from one-page or multiple-page specification sheets to pamphlets, booklets, owner's manuals, reprints from old magazines, anniversary booklets, etc. A majority of this literature can be easily obtained for a reasonable price at truck shows, depending mainly on the make and year of the truck you have interest in.

For instance, one-page spec sheets of later year, "common" name trucks, will cost anywhere from $1.00 to $3.00. The older and harder-to-find one-page spec sheets can run up to $10.00 each, such as the 1920s and 1930s Brockway spec sheets.

(Left) 1920s or 1930s Brockway Model 90 spec sheet worth $10.00 in excellent condition. (Middle) 1950s Brockway Model 255W one-page spec sheet worth $5.00 in excellent condition. (Right) 1972 Brockway Model U360TL one-page spec sheet worth $3.00 in excellent condition.

These prices pertain only to original literature, not to the color photocopies that some vendors sell, so be aware of what you are buying. Collectors may knowingly buy these photocopies only for the information contained on them until they can find an original piece of literature.

If you are unsure of what you are buying, look for the following items that will help to distinguish a color copy from an original.

The first hint would be the texture of the paper. Originals are a little stiffer paper and sometimes smoother, whereas copy paper is not.

Second, look for a small white border around the outside of the paper that photocopier machines will leave. Finding the white border is made easier when an old, slightly discolored or stained spec sheet is copied. Color copiers will pick up the discolor giving a yellow-brown tint to the page.

Third, some spec sheets came originally with three-ring binder holes punched into them. Vendors may not take the time to punch holes into the photocopied spec sheets to try to make them look authentic.

The last and most obvious hint is when you have two pages stapled together, when there should be only one page with print on the front and back.

Original owner's manuals can range from $20.00 for the most recent to $125.00 for manuals from the 1920s and 1930s. It mainly depends on who has the manuals to sell and how much you're willing to spend. The same guidelines also hold true with instruction and shop manuals.

Old magazine ads with trucks in them, from magazines such as *Saturday Evening Post, Commercial Car Journal* or *Life*, have also made their way onto vendors' tables. The old magazine ads are usually on pages too big to be color copied. The ads will cost you $5.00 to $8.00 apiece.

A 1957 magazine ad valued at @ $8.00 in excellent condition.

Not only are truck sales literature and magazine ads collectible, but also the newsletters or magazines that truck builders send out to their employees and others. Examples of these publications would be Brockway's *Brock-caster*, Peterbilt's *First Class* or Mack's *Bulldog Bulletin*.

These newsletters or magazines describe the behind-the-scenes life of the truck builder and offer a Who's Who of the team that builds the trucks. They contain information you can't always get from other magazines or sales literature, and give you a feel for the truck company and why it made the decisions it did.

(Left) January/February 1977 (Right) July/August 1976 *Brock-caster* magazines worth $8.00 each in excellent condition.

Prices for these kinds of magazines range from $4.00 to $8.00. The more pages and information inside, the more the publication is worth. Expect to pay more money for Mack's *Bulldog Bulletin* because of the larger number of people who collect this magazine.

Peterbilt's Fall 1989 "First Class" 50th Anniversary issue worth $22.00 in excellent condition.

Publications that are special issues will cost more money, such as Peterbilt's Fall 1989 *First Class* Special 50th Anniversary issue, which is worth $22.00. Mack's December 1986 *Bulldog Bulletin* featuring Australia is worth $18.00. Any magazine or piece of literature that is a special issue or an anniversary issue will command a higher price than a "regular" issue.

It was once said that a picture is worth a thousand words, and that still holds true today. Truck photos are appreciated by all truck memorabilia collectors. Every photo tells a different story and to some collectors they are considered priceless. Vendors will sell photos from $2.00 up to $10.00, while other truck memorabilia collectors may trade, give away, or be willing to make copies of their photos for you – especially if you have the same areas of interest as them.

Another source for photos may be your area commercial photographer, especially if he has been in business a number of years. The photographer may have negatives of old truck photos he can reprint for you. Be aware, though, that you may pay a high price since photography is his business.

Apparel

Everybody wears clothing, so what a better way of advertising a brand name of a truck than on a piece of clothing, be it a hat, T-shirt, jacket or even a belt buckle.

Hats, found at truck shows, with old truck names on them such as Brockway, Federal, Sterling, etc., usually are not authentic. Vendors have embroidering companies create patches that look original and have them sewn onto hats more-than-likely produced cheaply overseas. These hats have a tag attached inside identifying the country of origin. Some vendors tear out this tag in an attempt to hide the fact that the hat is not genuine. Hats with Mack, Kenworth, Freightliner or Peterbilt on them may be authentic because they're still available through the truck company identified on the hat.

If you're looking for a specific value assigned to old truck clothing, there really isn't any. Clothing gets worn out, torn, fades or gets outgrown; plus, no one likes to buy someone else's hand-me-downs. Embroidered clothing is just a way for companies to advertise their trucks and allow enthusiasts to show off what are their favorite trucks by what they wear.

Belt buckles, on the other hand, are collectible and can have a value placed on them since they are more durable than apparel fabrics. New belt buckles from companies such as Mack will run about $12.95 to $18.95. Older belt buckles, especially ones featuring trucks that are no longer being produced, are worth more.

(Left) Early 1970s GMC Astro 95 belt buckle worth $21.00 in excellent condition. (Right) Canadian Mack belt buckle from the 1980s worth @ $30.00 in excellent condition.

An early 1970s belt buckle with a truck featured on it is valued at $20.00-$25.00 whereas it probably sold new for $3.00-$5.00.

Other belt buckles such as Mack's Maple Leaf buckle are worth more money than Mack's "normal" buckles from that era. The reason for this is that the Maple Leaf symbolizes Canada, where Mack once had an assembly plant (it closed in the early 1990s). Not as many of these buckles were made compared to the other buckles Mack offered. This Maple Leaf belt buckle with the name Mack in the middle and the bulldog on top of the name is worth a minimum of $30.00 in excellent condition.

Back before the no-smoking regulations ruled the country, truck manufacturers took advantage of smoking paraphernalia such as matchbooks, lighters and ashtrays to promote or advertise their trucks. Although smoking is now frowned upon in many parts of the country, smoking paraphernalia has made its mark as memorabilia, even to non-smokers. A book of matches that was once given away by truck dealerships is now worth $4.00 unused; generally, the value of a lighter that is no longer available has doubled from its original price.

Advertising on ashtrays was tried, with great success, by Brockway and Mack, both of which had their mascots mounted majestically on the ashtray rim. One of the popular Brockway ashtrays is the nine-inch diameter chrome version with a 6-1/4-inch gold husky mounted on it. It could be bought new through a dealership for $20.00 in the early 1970s. The same style ashtray is now worth at least $150.00, and if you find it any cheaper, buy it! In fact, at the 1994 American Truck Historical Society's National Truck Show in Buffalo, New York, an auction was held where the aforementioned ashtray sold for $300.00.

A Brockway nine-inch diameter chrome ashtray with a 6-1/4-inch gold Husky worth @ $150.00 in excellent condition.

Since Brockway went out of business in 1977, this makes it harder to find these ashtrays as compared to the ashtrays produced by Mack. Mack's ashtrays were discontinued when the 1995-1996 no-smoking laws went into effect. Because Mack is no longer offering ashtrays to the public, the value has increased.

In 1985, Mack sold its 5-1/2-inch diameter chrome ashtray with a three-inch chrome bulldog for $6.95. It is now worth $20.00. That same year, Mack also sold a seven-inch diameter chrome ashtray with a 4-1/2-inch chrome bulldog for $16.00 or with a 4-1/2-inch gold bulldog for $23.00. The ashtray with the chrome bulldog is now worth $50.00 and the gold bulldog version is worth $65.00.

(Left) A 5-1/2-inch diameter chrome ashtray with a three-inch chrome bulldog worth $20.00 in excellent condition. (Right) A seven-inch diameter chrome ashtray with a 4-1/2-inch chrome bulldog worth $50.00 in excellent condition.

Mack has rumored that it may re-introduce its ashtray line in 1998 because of popular demand. If that happens, this would decrease the value of the aforementioned existing Mack ashtrays.

Emblems and Hood Ornaments

Vehicle emblems and hood ornaments are popular not only with car enthusiasts but also with truck enthusiasts. Some emblems are still available through companies that deal in truck parts. Brockway hood and grille emblems are still available through Cook Bros. of Binghamton, New York, or J. Thomas Ltd. of Lancaster, Pennsylvania. The big chrome name emblems for Brockway will cost about $35.00 and the small ones will cost $22.00. These businesses also have new, gold Husky hood ornaments for $120.00.

The old Brockway name emblems or plates, shaped like the profile of a flying saucer, are not available through parts departments and were not used by Brockway after 1959.

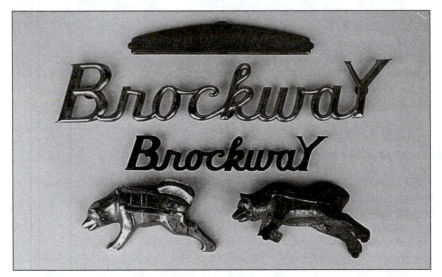

(Top) Brockway hood nameplate pre-1959. (Middle) Brockway grille or hood-side name emblem, smaller version for 1975-1977 dashboard. (Below left) Half chrome Husky for the hood. (Below right) Old Husky hood ornament from a Brockway 361.

The considerate and serious collectors don't steal emblems off junked trucks. This makes it harder for restorers to complete their projects when they have to hunt down a hood ornament because someone decided it would look neat on a garage wall. Be considerate and take these items off of trucks that are going to be cut up for scrap metal, not trucks that have a chance of being restored.

As this article points out, there is all sorts of memorabilia to be collected involving big rigs, and a lot of it is easily obtainable. Keep your eyes open and hold on to the materials truck dealers give away today, because someday it will have value to collectors.

Values of Select Brockway Truck Collectibles

1) Reprint of Brockway 25th Anniversary book (original price $12.00). EXC-$50.00.

2) Original Brockway 75th Anniversary book. EXC-$35.00.

3) Original May 1971 issue of *Overdrive* magazine. EXC-$10.00.

4) First book about Brockway trucks by Herman Sass. EXC-$20.00.

5) Photo (five-by-seven inch) of Brockway Model K361TL. EXC-$6.00

6) Brockway watch fob. EXC-$10.00.

7) Brockway logo pin. EXC-$2.50.

8) Brockway matchbook. EXC-$4.00.

9) Brockway bar of soap. EXC-$26.00.

10) Brockway Model 257TL truck pin. EXC-$5.50.

11) Brockway chrome ink pen. EXC-$28.00.

12) Photo (eight-by-ten inch) of Brockway Model U360TLY. EXC-$10.00.

Collecting Motorcycle Memorabilia

By Roger Pribbenow

Collecting motorcycle memorabilia gives us a glimpse into the past, and helps us visualize what life was like for the early motorcyclist. Many of the materials described here are also invaluable to the historian and the old motorcycle restorer. The sheer number and variety of items in this collector specialty has helped feed collector interest in the past few years. The relative rarity of these items when compared to similar items in the wider automotive category has also resulted in rapidly rising prices. Competition for these items is currently fierce!

History

The motorcycle was invented in the late 19th century and wasn't really widely available to the public until the early 20th century. The early motorcycle was more closely related to the bicycle and was co-promoted in the magazines and advertisements of the period. Motorcycle advertising and promotional items soon followed, representing the earliest collectible items, dating from around 1902 through the early 1920s.

From the mid-1920s through the late-1930s, motorcycles developed into the form which remained relatively unchanged until the late-1960s. Many collectors believe that this period represents the most interesting collectible period – the golden age of motorcycling.

Motorcycling suffered a blow during World War II, when the efforts of most motorcycle manufacturers (both foreign and domestic) turned to wartime production. Collectors will not find a great deal of items available from the war years.

After the war, motorcycling was revived as a popular pastime, and there were again large amounts of items produced, many of which are quite common. Many collectors relate to this period, dating from the late-1940s through the 1950s.

Most collections I've seen are based on items from one of the periods mentioned above, or a combination of all, from 1900-1965 or so. Items dating from the late-1960s through the 1970s are just starting to be more heavily collected. This trend will increase as larger numbers of younger collectors (especially those who do not remember the 1950s and relate more to items produced in their lifetimes) enter the market. Remember that many of the earliest items have by now been discovered and are now in the hands of antique and collectible dealers or collectors.

I have been recently putting away currently available items, such as new motorcycle brochures which don't cost anything to collect. At some time in the future, you can be sure that these will become collectible!

Categories of Collecting

Many collectors have found it easier to specialize in a particular group of items, reflecting their interest in a particular facet or time of motorcycle history. You may chose to collect only motorcycle oil cans or racing trophies, for example, or only Harley-Davidson items from 1930-1939. Or you may find it easier to build your collection at first from any motorcycle items that come your way and later specialize when you recognize where your interests lie. The following is a list of the types of items available, by category.

FAM/MATA/AMA/Other Club Materials

Motorcycling has always been a social sport, and many early motorcyclists were members of touring or fraternal clubs. The Fraternal Association of Motorcyclists (FAM) was formed in 1903 to serve the interests of early sport riders and racers and continued until 1918.

The Motorcycle and Auto Trade Association (MATA) replaced the FAM in 1919 through 1924 and in 1925 was replaced by the American Motorcycle Association (AMA), which continues to serve the motorcyclist today. All of these organizations produced numerous items of collector interest.

Early FAM and MATA items are mostly restricted to watch fobs (awarded to tour participants), membership pins and club identity tags. You may also find porcelain signs used to identify registered repair shops. The AMA items produced for so many years are the most common in this category.

The AMA presented different "gypsy tour" awards to all tour participants each year from 1925 to the present day. It's quite a challenge to put together a full set. The items

A group of FAM/MATA/AMA watch fobs and pins dating from 1917 through 1925. Prices vary greatly. $175-$400 each.

range from ladies earrings and makeup compacts to men's belt buckles and rings. Collectors have also found awards presented to individual motorcycle clubs for patriotic service or safety, in the form of trophies, plaques and large wall pennants.

Paper Items

This category is large and varied! Collectors may want to specialize in brochures produced by their favorite motorcycle manufacturer. Indian Motorcycle, for instance, produced its first brochure in 1902 and continued through 1953.

Along with brochures for each individual motorcycle model each year (as well as a general full line catalog), Indian produced posters, postcards, confidential dealer franchise booklets, parts and accessories catalogs, dealer newsletters and service bulletins and even a booklet on how to ride a motorcycle. Collectors also look for its newsletter for riders, *Indian News*. When you consider that every manufacturer produced similar materials, you are looking at a large number of items.

A large number of non-manufacturer items, such as motorcycle magazines, juvenile novels and even games with motorcycle themes were also distributed, capitalizing on the motorcycle craze.

Pins and Dealer Advertising Smalls

Almost any advertising medium you can name was used to promote the motorcycle. This category includes all small items produced by manufacturers, dealers and clubs for advertising purposes.

A group of early motorcycle flyers and brochures dating from 1912 through 1917. Manufacturers represented here include Dayton, Flying Merkel, Reading Standard, New Era and Yale. Prices on these items can range from $75-$350 each.

Collectors will find hat or jacket pins (still popular today), watch fobs, coin purses, rulers, key chains, knives, pens, pencils, tie clips, match safes, matchbooks, cigar cutters and more! Especially hard to find are employee service pins and dealer convention items such as party favors and identity pins.

This is a popular collector's specialty – many items can be displayed in a small space. You could also choose to combine this specialty with the aforementioned AMA awards smalls.

A grouping of Harley-Davidson watch fobs and other smalls, dating from the 1920s through the 1950s. The watch fobs in the top row range in price from $150-$250 each. The items in the lower row are as follows: hat pins, lower left, $100 each; "V" (for victory) pin, $90; figural bottle opener, $200-$350; lucky coin, $75-$100.

Toys and Models

Motorcycle toys can add real charm to your memorabilia collection! This is a large category, spanning the entire history of the motorcycle sport. This category crosses over into general toy collector territory, so you'll find competition from toy collectors as well as motorcycle memorabilia collectors.

Literally hundreds of different toys were produced. Early clockwork or wind-up motorcycle toys are the most difficult to locate as well as among the most expensive. This is also a category of specialization. Many collectors choose to collect only cast iron or only tin wind-up toys. Some collectors choose to collect only those toys made by a certain toy manufacturer, because of the style of design or color. An example of this would be tin wind-ups produced by Marx that exist in great numbers and variations.

You could also choose to collect only examples of Harley-Davidson toys, since so many were produced, from the earliest examples (1920s) in cast iron to 1950s plastic toys to lithographed tin toys from the 1960s.

Current die-cast models and model kits (representing vintage and current motorcycles) will probably be sought after by future generations.

Clothing and Accessories

Collectible motorcycle clothing is limited to items produced and sold by various motorcycle manufacturers and items specifically produced by motorcycle clubs. Most motorcycle manufacturers offered clothing items for sale at one time or another. These items include hats (men's and women's), caps, boots, sweaters, gloves, goggles, support belts and riding costumes.

Harley-Davidson marked almost all of its gloves and belts with its logos, so they are easy to identify. Many other clothing items worn by early motorcyclists came from other sources, such as sport aviation or the military.

The most common clothing item you'll find are hats produced by Harley-Davidson. I'd guess that every Harley rider from the 1920s through the 1950s wore a hat of some sort. Many of these 1940s-1950s examples have survived, many with their original pins or other decoration. Sweaters and racing togs from the teens through the 1930s are hard to find, especially those advertising more obscure manufacturers, such as Excelsior-Henderson. Some collectors specialize in heavily decorated leather back support belts or felt patches.

Many motorcycle clubs of the 1930s-1950s required their members to wear uniforms when traveling together to motorcycle events. The American Motorcycle Association encouraged this practice and awarded trophies for "best dressed" clubs, "most colorful" ladies auxiliary, etc., as this promoted the upstanding and respectable type of rider.

The so-called "outlaw" type of clubs, as immortalized in the 1954 movie "The Wild One", created their own style of identification. Painted leather jackets, hats and imprinted T-shirts from this period are all collectible. Some collectors have more recently sought out examples of the "colors" worn by "1%" or outlaw clubs of the 1960s and 1970s. I'd like to point out that nonmember possession of some of these items (if the club is still in existence) is taken seriously and has been acted upon by club members.

Signage/Store Displays

Signage items can range from small dealers' window decals to entire billboards. This category requires the largest display area and many times, the largest wallet! Rarest items in this category are dealers' signs, such as tin embossed examples and large neon building units.

Motorcycle manufacturers also produced interior advertising pieces in great numbers. Collectors are seeking cardboard displays (advertising motorcycles, motorcycle oil, and accessories), sales posters, neon advertising clocks, blackboards (where dealers chalked in prices of used machines and store specials) and banners.

Another item in this category is the shop demonstration or display unit. For example, Indian Motorcycle produced a horn demo unit that shop visitors used to compare the tone of the Indian accessory double horn to the stock horn. I'll bet this

These four items were meant for display at dealerships: (l to r) Indian dealer sign, 1940s, $300-$600; Harley-Davidson blackboard, 1940s, $500-$900; Harley-Davidson cardboard Chain Saver Display, 1940s, $100-$250; Harley-Davidson small outside dealer sign, 1940s, $400-$800.

was a favorite item with the salesman! Harley-Davidson built a large black and orange display to hold its line of genuine batteries, as well as a special advertising mirror promotion its cycle hats.

Containers and Packaging

The most popular items within this category are liquid containers, used for oil or cleaning products. This category crosses over into the popular petroliana field. The rarest containers are among the largest ones made such as Harley-Davidson's five-gallon oil cans and those that enjoyed a short production run, like Harley's single quart glass oil bottle with paper label produced during World War II.

This is a challenging category to collect, since new items are still being found. Look for containers that held motorcycle oil, paint, polish, chain oil, transmission oil, penetrating oil and cleaners.

Collectors also collect the boxes that originally held motorcycle parts. Manufacturers such as Harley-Davidson went to great lengths to standardize its packaging and package a great variety of items in matching containers.

Motorcycle Parts

Many collectors have a few examples of motorcycle parts or accessories in their collections. Early gasoline tanks with original paint and hand striping are considered by many to be works of art! Unusual or rare accessories are also coveted, and are of special interest in their original packaging.

Three Indian Motorcycle containers from the 1940s: (l to r) "Color Brite", $90; spray enamel, $120; chain oil, $125.

Motorcycling Images

Of great historical interest to many collectors are images of motorcycling in past days. Most commonly found are postcards (produced in the thousands by the larger

A Pope gasoline tank from 1913. Prices on this sort of item can range from $300-$1,000.

manufacturers), and individual "real photo" examples, produced as personal photos in the teens and 1920s. Collectors with a little more money to spend will seek out larger photos – 8 x 10s and larger are rare – especially if hand colored. Of special interest are "yard-longs", those three- to four-foot wide panoramic images, usually records of motorcycle tours.

Examples in all format sizes are valued by restorers because of the information they contain. Many of these photos have been used as reference when completing a difficult restoration. Some of these old photos are so sharp that you can read the brand name on the tires and even the machine's engine number! Almost all examples are interesting because of the special look they allow us into a time long passed.

A large hand-colored photo of four Detroit motorcycle policemen, 1909, $150-$250.

Reproductions

A few motorcycle items have recently appeared that are quite suspect. Two of the most recent are the "laughing Indian" pin and the Indian Motorcycle watch fob in the shape of an arrowhead. The reproductions are so good that many of these have been passed off as originals.

Also reproduced many times in the past are various Harley-Davidson and Indian signs, some clothing items, and various cast iron toys. When in doubt, do a little research – ask a fellow collector or refer to one of the motorcycle memorabilia books on the market.

Where To Find It

You can probably find some motorcycle memorabilia in your area. Many collectors travel hundreds and thousands of miles each year from auction to auction or to shows and swap meets throughout the country.

Motorcycle toys are available at many antique and toy shows held across the country. Attend as many antique motorcycle swap meets as you can, where you will find items for sale or trade. Auto shows, flea markets, antique shops and even garage sales are also a good source!

Spend some time seeking out and talking to other collectors who may sell or trade their duplicate items. Items are often offered for sale in collector publications, such as *The Antique Motorcycle* or *Old Cars Weekly News & Marketplace*. Be sure to do some networking – get a business card printed that you can hand out letting people know what you are looking for.

Antique Motorcycle Club of America

P.O. Box 333

Sweetster, IN 46987

For information on the Antique Motorcycle Club of America, publisher of *The Antique Motorcycle*.

Motorcycle Chums Memorabilia

P.O. Box 160

DeForest, WI 53532

Publisher of *Motorcycle Memorabilia, a Guide to Motorcycle-Related Collectibles*, picturing over 1,200 items in full color. Single copies are available for $20.00 plus $3.00 shipping.

Krause Publications

700 E. State Street

Iola, WI 54990

Publisher of *Old Cars Weekly News & Marketplace*.

Pricing

Prices are listed here for representative items with their pictures. If you're new to this hobby, you'll probably be surprised at the high prices asked for some items. While many items are rare and expensive, others are common and affordable if you're patient. Attend as many shows as you can and get a feel for pricing. If you're new to memorabilia collecting, my advice to you is to select only the items that really interest you and spend your money on those.

Collecting Auto Racing Decals

By Phil Hall

A glance at the front fenders of most of today's NASCAR Winston Cup stock cars reveals a population of stickers of various products and services that is so large that it overflows onto other parts of the body. Other forms of racing, from Formula One to local drags and short tracks, also find their race cars adorned with an endless variety of stickers.

In the bigger leagues of auto racing, the stickers are used to qualify a race vehicle for a contingency program, which pays dollars or products to drivers who do well and have the stickers of the paying companies on their machines. There are also other uses for stickers. These include the sticker as a symbol of approval from the sanctioning body for a vehicle to compete, or to promote a sponsor or other racing events.

Collecting today's racing stickers presents a problem – deciding which ones to obtain. There are so many to choose from. Acquiring them is usually not difficult as most companies that issue racing stickers are only too glad to get this free advertising out one way or another.

Uses for the stickers today are as endless as the variety. You can put them on your street-driven car or truck, toolbox or, if you are a youngster, your bike or coaster wagon. They make nice displays, look good encased in plastic in a loose-leaf binder or are just fun to stack up and save for use down the road.

The Early Years

Like most things, the auto racing sticker phenomenon wasn't always with us. Early race cars didn't have any adornments at all.

Using a race car for a billboard was not a priority early in this century. The closest race cars came to this was to letter the name of the car, in paint, so the fans could see that it was a Stutz or Studebaker or Miller Special, in addition to the car's numbers.

Though there likely were isolated prior users, the earliest examples of today's sticker ancestors started showing up in the 1930s. This is when the decalcomania process made it possible to put logos of products on small signs of all shapes. The transfers started with the message printed on a thin film that was on treated paper. To apply it to your race car, or whatever, you soaked the paper in warm water, then slid the film off onto the place where you wanted the transfer, smoothed it out and let it dry. They were called decals, for short, and the process was popular before and after World War II. It is still used today. Building scale model kits will often net you a decal sheet.

The companies active in early decal promotion were not many. They mainly were those producing items used in the race cars, such as Champion spark plugs, Perfect

A single decal, for Perfect Circle piston rings, adorned the side of the Marchese Special that Harry McQuinn drove in the 1938 Indianapolis 500.

Circle piston rings, Wynn's Friction Proofing oil, Mobilgas, Mobiloil and Bear wheel alignment service. Early contingency programs rewarded the drivers who carried these stickers. For some it was cash, for others the rewards were products or services.

There was no uniform size or placement for the stickers. On an Indy Championship car, small decals were usually carried low on the sides, between the wheels, but the Mobil 'Flying Red Horse' logo was on the nose or hood with reversed copies for the right and left sides.

After World War II, stock car racing leapfrogged in popularity, both of the new car and jalopy variety. Both were slow to attract stickers.

The new cars, NASCAR Grand National being the most organized and popular, did not attract contingency programs. Many a new model was covered with masking tape instead of decals to protect the glass headlights and finish. The reason being that plans were to sell these "race" cars later as used cars (only driven on Sundays, no doubt).

Once in awhile a point of purchase sticker appeared for Bardahl or some other product the car owner was likely selling. First to show up with the knowledge of the manufacturer included Champion, Wynn's and Purelube/Pure Sanitized gasoline. Air Lift suspension boosters also got involved around 1952.

Even more than those stickers found on the Indy cars, there was a wide variety of sizes and placement. Pure had large, near fender-length decals, Champion small ovals, and Wynn's small circles. The numbers increased slowly until 1957, when contingency stickers were all over the cars. From then on, numbers increased, sizes became more uniform and a slow gravitation to the front fenders began.

A major boost in the decal design came with the advent of vinyl-based material in the 1950s. It was tougher, easier to apply (just peel off the backing paper) and

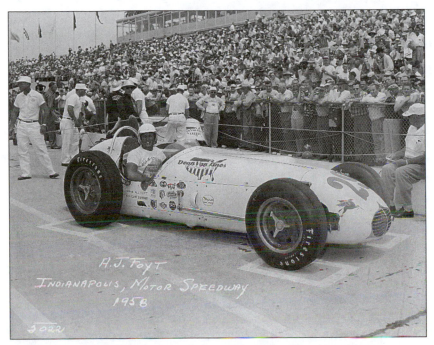

In 1958, second year driver A.J. Foyt may have worn just a T-shirt for protection, but his Dean Van Lines Special had the full range of the latest decals on its side. It also carried the Mobil 'Flying Red Horse' logos on nose and tail.

Still a bit sparse in the sticker department, this 1964 view of Richard Petty's NASCAR Plymouth shows the migration to the front fender. The odd-shaped one without writing is a Plymouth logo.

Drag racers joined their circle track counterparts in the sticker parade, as evidenced by this circa 1962 photo of Chris Karamesines, his 'Chizler' dragster and the track trophy queen.

could be die-cut to nearly any shape. By the 1960s, NASCAR stickers (still called decals) were nearly all vinyl. By the end of the decade they pretty much took the form and placement we know today.

Drag racing, midgets, sprints, sports cars and even motorcycles followed the decal evolution with the 1950s being the formative years. By decade's end, all had them to varying degrees.

Thrill of the Hunt

Collecting early racing decals today has all the fun of the hunt of most other automotive/racing memorabilia, but with one big difference, *price*. Though there are exceptions, for the most part decals are not expensive. Their prices have not taken off for the moon like those of most models, toys, programs, yearbooks and other remnants of bygone eras.

Like anything else, condition is important. Well preserved examples bring in more dollars, especially of the decalcomanias, which are fragile. Vinyls and later mylars are much tougher. In fact, getting an old decal to come off the paper intact and adhere to anything is chancy at best. They tend to fall apart with age. Early vinyls may lose their stickiness, but that can be remedied with adhesive or two-sided tape if need be.

Some early decals are today being reproduced on mylar. While of course these are not of true vintage, they have the advantage of being useable – and replaceable.

If you decide to collect decals of a specific era, type of car or year, take your time and research what was used on the racers at that time. Many decals come in several versions and the differences may be small.

If you are restoring a race car and want the exact decals it had when it ran, check old auto racing programs, magazines, yearbooks, photographs and today's excellent history volumes to see what decals it used and where they were placed. Also remember, in the course of a season, several different combinations could have been used.

Sources of Decals

Sources for decals today include automotive and auto racing memorabilia swap meets and even old-time garages still operating. If you're lucky, you'll unearth a set of decals that were tossed aside and never put on the car.

There are also sellers of new and vintage decals, but be careful to distinguish between what is original and what is reproduced. Costs range from a few cents from an uninformed swap vendor to $25-$30. Paying more means you really found something rare or you absolutely have to have it to complete your race car restoration or your decal collection.

Not all decals are pure product/service commercials. Some may depict race cars sponsored by a company. They also could be from a sanctioning body such as USAC, NASCAR or NHRA, for a race track or race event or even a generic souvenir decal depicting a non-specific race car or checkered flags.

An example of a race car decal that stands out is one issued by Wynn's after the Leslie-Kenz streamliner it sponsored hit 270.473 mph at the Bonneville Salt Flats in Utah in 1957. It's over 11 inches wide and seven inches deep (see color section of this book). It easily rises to the top of the price spectrum.

On the other hand, a United States Auto Club (USAC) decal (pre-vinyl) used on race cars, pace cars and service vehicles, should go for no more than a dollar or two.

Vinyls of the 1960s are generally lower priced, but a few such as Parnelli Jones' 1967 STP turbine Indy car can net $15 in nice shape. Sanctioning body-approved stickers always bring more than the commercial ones. Look for AAA or USAC registered car or NASCAR race car on the sticker.

Auto manufacturer's racing stickers are also interesting. They can range from a logo only, to a commemoration of a win or championship. Rare in the 1950s, they are common today. They are likely to be used on street-driven cars by enthusiasts of a given make.

While we have covered a few basic types of stickers/decals here, there are many others that have appeared. Some are little more than printed paper with a backing. These are nice to display – but keep them out of the weather. Reverse stickers on plastic or mylar sheets have been popular a long time. They stick to the inside of a window and the adhesive is on their face. Some stickers look like aluminum foil, are reflectorized or have metalflake in the design. Of course today there are holograms, spectrographics and other neat things to dazzle the beholder, but it will be a long time before serious collector status is debated.

Like everything else we collect, early racing decals are out there. They are a part of the history of the sport. Chase them now before somebody pushes the hot button.

Decal Prices

Description	Good	Very Good	Excellent
Wynn's logo with flags, late 1950s decal, 11" x 6".	8	12	15

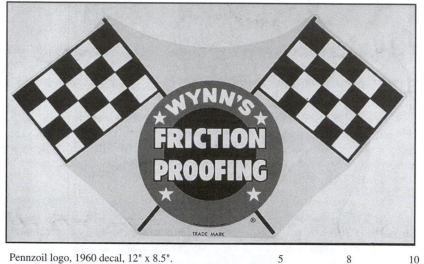

	Good	Very Good	Excellent
Pennzoil logo, 1960 decal, 12" x 8.5".	5	8	10

Description	Good	Very Good	Excellent
Generic crossed flags, pot helmet, 1950s decal, 9" x 4.5".	5	7	10

Generic midget, flags, pot helmet, Oilzum logo on hood, 1950s decal, 5" x 4".	9	12	15

Description	Good	Very Good	Excellent
Wynn's Don Garlits' Swamp Rat III, early 1960s decal, 5.5" x 2.5".	10	12	15

| Wynn's Joie Chitwood Thrill Show with 1958 Chevrolets decal, 4" x 2.5". | 4 | 7 | 10 |

| O'Hare Stadium (Chicago), early 1960s decal, 5" x 3.5". | 8 | 12 | 15 |

Description	Good	Very Good	Excellent
Rockford (Ill.) Speedway, early 1960s decal, 5" x 4.5".	3	5	7

Bob-Jo Speedway (Sycamore, Ill.), mid-1960s decal, 5" x 3.5".	2	3	5

Description	Good	Very Good	Excellent
D-A oil logo, 1960s decal, 2.75" circle.	1	2	3

Generic souvenir midget with flag, early 1950s decal, 4" x 3".	5	9	12

Description	Good	Very Good	Excellent
USAC shield, 1959 decal 3" x 3".	2	3	4

Generic souvenir Ford jalopy with flag, early
1950s decal, 4" x 2.5".   5   9   12

Description	Good	Very Good	Excellent
Road America steering wheel logo, 1960s decal, 2.75" circle.	2	3	4

| Air Lift early 1960s vinyl sticker, 9" x 5". | 5 | 8 | 10 |

Description	Good	Very Good	Excellent

Hot Rod Shop of Milwaukee, early 1960s decal,
3" x 3.5". 2 3 4

Castrol Brands Hatch Grand Prix, 1964 decal,
3.5" x 2.75". 2 3 5

Description	Good	Very Good	Excellent
Goodyear mid-1960s vinyl sticker, 10" x 5".	4	6	8

Leader Card Racer (Indy Championship cars), 1960s vinyl sticker, 4" circle.	10	12	15

Description	Good	Very Good	Excellent
STP 1967 Parnelli Jones Turbine, vinyl sticker, 7" x 2".	8	12	15

| American Motors Javelin (Trans Am) racing team, 1968 vinyl sticker, 3.5" circle. | 2 | 4 | 6 |

Description	Good	Very Good	Excellent
STP Novi reversible window sticker on plastic, mid-1960s, 3.5" x 2".	6	10	12

| Triumph champions, late 1960s vinyl sticker, 3" circle. | 1 | 2 | 3 |

Description	Good	Very Good	Excellent
USAC 1968 registered car, vinyl sticker, 4.5" x 2.5".	5	7	10

NASCAR Race Car, 1970s mylar sticker, 5.25" x 2.75".	4	6	8

IMCA registered car, 1970s mylar sticker, 5" x 3.5".	1	1	2

Collecting Ceramic Automobilia

By Ken Collins and Joel Dunford

The ceramic top fuel dragster shown with this feature as well as the Willys ceramic banks pictured in the color section of this book are the products of Carllectibles! of Highland, California (P.O. Box 252, Highland, CA 92346, 1-800-431-4522 or 909-884-1474). These intricate ceramic creations are part of the exciting – and expanding – hobby of collecting ceramic automobilia.

For anyone interested in getting involved in this area of collecting, or even for those who already have started their collection of ceramic cars and trucks, the following is an overview of this fun hobby area.

Sculpture

The creation of any ceramic piece begins with a sculpture. This sculpture is a completely detailed rendition of the finished piece in clay that will be used as the "master" in the moldmaking process. The amount of detail and realism included in this master sculpture will determine the amount of detail and realism in the finished piece. For a ceramic car, the collector should determine if an attempt has been made at realism or is a caricature or "cartoon" version of the car represented? Does the sculpture possess the smaller, more difficult to achieve details that would be found on the real hot rod, such as deep wheels, or are the wheels shallow and simplified? When evaluating a roadster or other open-top piece, the interior of a good sculpture should contain several details such as seats, steering wheel, dashboard, and gearshift as opposed to a completely undetailed interior that might be used for a potted plant or candy.

Glazing and Firing

Once the molds have been made from the master sculpture and the ceramic cars have been poured, these pieces, called "greenware", are fired in a kiln at a high temperature to reduce and harden the piece. At this point, they are coated with glaze and fired again to get their finished, glossy look. When evaluating the gloss quality of a piece, the collector should hold the piece at different angles and see how the light is reflected. When light is reflected unevenly or "ripply" this indicates a thin coating of glaze. A thick coat will reflect the light more evenly giving the piece a richer look. Another area to check on a ceramic car is the bottom of the tires. If they are not glossy and appear rough, they were dry-foot fired. This simply means that the glaze was left off the places on the piece that would touch the bottom of the oven and make them stick there. The more high quality pieces will have a smooth consistent coat of glaze over the entire car.

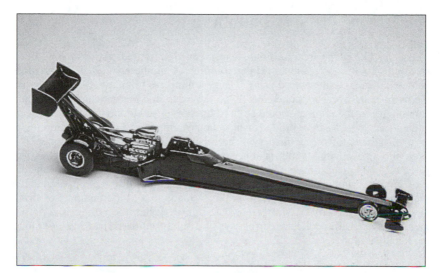

How a Carllectible! is made. We start with a block of clay and hand craft it into the desired shape. The clay car is allowed to dry about two weeks and then is hand sanded. Next, a five piece mold is made from the sculptured car from which a master mold is made. From this master the production molds are poured. Your car (as clay slip), is now ready to be poured into the production mold. After setting up it is removed and allowed to cure for three days before it is hand sanded and kiln fired Next the cars are glazed with color, hand numbered and kiln fired a second time. To finish, the wheels, windows and trim work are hand painted and the piece is ready for delivery.

To care for your Carllectible!, clean with glass cleaner or a mild liquid soap, dry and polish with a clean soft cotton cloth. Windows, wheels, tires and trimwork can be touched up with enamel paint and small brush.

Finishing

Once the piece has been gloss-fired it is ready for detail finishing. There are two types of detail painting that can be used together on the same piece. The first kind is hobby paint, which is applied to the top of the glazed piece to add details such as interior color, chrome colored rims, bumpers, etc. The main drawback to the use of paint is that it is not permanent and tends to wear off over time. Hobby paint can be scratched off during any rough treatment of the piece. It will also oxidize like any other paint. When used sparingly it can add to the details of a piece but the more it appears on a piece, the more it could lose value over time.

The best, highest quality pieces have their details fired onto the piece using different glazes at different stages of production. Glazes make a more permanent finish and can include lusters that actually contain precious metals in their mixtures, which, after being heated to 1,000 degrees, have a shine and durability much like the chrome on a real car. These gold and silver coatings, as well as other fired-on colors will not scratch off or lose their gloss over time. This allows the piece to hold its value.

Numbering

It seems like even cereal boxes are being printed in limited editions today! But a true limited edition is a numbered limited edition. A numbered piece is always more valuable then an unnumbered piece. The best numbered limited edition piece has the number stamped or painted clearly on the piece in a permanent fashion. On a ceramic piece, the number should be fired-on as opposed to having a certificate of authenticity, which can be printed on most home computers. Often, the edition size, or total number of pieces made will be included with that piece's number. For example, a piece with 10/8000 stamped on the bottom indicates that this is the 10th piece of 8,000 pieces made. Generally, the smaller the edition, the more valuable each piece is. Many collectors seek lower numbers in the edition as opposed to the higher numbers. This is different from pieces made in a limited number of firing days, since actual edition size is not determined. When the edition size is not included, the curious collector can always find out the edition's true size by calling the manufacturer.

Value

All of the above would be the main points to consider when collecting ceramic cars. Each collector must decide which of these is really important to him or her. The real value in any piece however, is in what it means to the collector. Don't pass up a "cartoon" car, or any other piece for that matter, just because the only value it may have is the smile it puts on your face.

PETROLIANA

Visible Gasoline Pumps

Description	Good	Very Good	Excellent
Visible pump, Butler, Model 61, 10-gal. "square" model, circa 1924	1310	2185	3220
Visible pump, Fry, Model 17, 5-gal. model, circa 1920	975	1650	2740
Visible pump, Fry, Model 87, 10-gal. model, circa 1926	1025	1850	2875
Visible pump, Fry, Model 117, 10-gal. model, circa 1923	1100	1925	3060
Visible pump, Tokheim, 620, 10-gal. model, circa 1926	890	1175	1750
Visible pump, Gilbert & Barker, T-8, self-measuring w/ 5-gal. attachment, 1912	1500	2275	3750
Visible pump, Correct Measure, "lighthouse" 10-gal. model, circa 1928	880	1340	1975
Visible pump, American, 360-V, 10-gal. model, circa 1923	645	1270	2130
Visible pump, Wayne, 452, 5-gal. model, twin cylinders, circa 1923	815	1420	2410
Visible pump, Wayne, 519-C, 10-gal. model, circa 1919	1230	2080	3150

Gasoline Pumps

Description	Good	Very Good	Excellent
Erie pump, Gulf brand gasoline, 72 inches tall, no globe	600	1000	1400
Frye pump, Atlantic brand gasoline, 73 inches tall, glass globe	750	1125	1500
Tokheim pump, Sky Chief brand gasoline, 57-1/2 inches tall, no globe	800	1200	1600
Tokheim Volumeter pump (Model 950), Gulf brand gasoline, clock-face, circa 1932, glass globe	750	1125	1500
Wayne pump, clock face, 78 inches tall, no globe	220	395	600
Milwaukee pump, clock face, no globe, circa 1932	275	430	745
Gilbert & Barker pump, clock face, circa 1937	105	165	350

Description			
Bennett pump, digital computing pump, glass globe, circa 1958	135	215	435
1970s Gulf dual digital computing gas pump (No-nox and Gulftane brands)	350	500	800

Gasoline Pump Globes

Description	Good	Very Good	Excellent
Globe, AAA-1 Ethyl brand gasoline, glass body, circa 1941	300	400	575
Globe, Acme Regular brand gasoline, plastic body, circa 1953	95	135	210
Globe, Aetna A-Plus brand gasoline, plastic body, circa 1961	175	280	440
Globe, Aetna Ethyl brand gasoline, glass body, circa 1935	260	350	475
Globe, Aetna Motor Gas brand gasoline, glass body, circa 1932	260	350	475
Globe, Aladdin brand gasoline, red glass body, circa 1941	490	650	1000
Globe, American brand gasoline, metal body, circa 1940	175	280	440
Globe, American Ethyl brand gasoline, metal body, circa 1933	290	375	550
Globe, American Liberty brand gasoline, plastic body, circa 1948	300	400	575
Globe, Amlico Premium brand gasoline, plastic body, circa 1955	95	130	210
Globe, Amoco brand gasoline, metal body, circa 1925	300	400	575
Globe, Amoco brand gasoline, glass body, circa 1959	175	280	440
Globe, Ashland A-Plus brand gasoline, plastic body, circa 1965	95	130	210
Globe, Ashland Ethyl brand gasoline, glass body, circa 1949	175	280	440
Globe, Atlantic Capitol brand gasoline, metal body, circa 1932	300	400	575
Globe, Atlantic Ethyl brand gasoline, metal body, circa 1930	290	375	550

Globe, Atlantic Imperial brand gasoline, plastic body, circa 1965	135	230	350
Globe, Atlantic Hi-Arc brand gasoline, metal body, circa 1940	290	375	550
Globe, Atlantic Polarine brand gasoline, one-piece glass body w/ chimney top, circa 1917	1375	2180	2900
Globe, Atlantic White Flash brand gasoline, metal body, circa 1946	300	400	575
Globe, Badger 60-62 brand gasoline, glass body, circa 1936	290	375	550
Globe, Barnsdall Be Square brand gasoline, one-piece etched glass body, circa 1922	1055	1605	2050
Globe, Barnsdall Motor Fuel brand gasoline, glass body, circa 1933	290	375	550
Globe, Barnsdall Super Gas brand gasoline, one-piece etched glass body, circa 1922	1055	1605	2050
Globe, Beeline Gasoline brand, plastic body, circa 1953	300	400	575
Globe, Bell Ethyl brand gasoline, rippled glass body, circa 1938	350	480	750
Globe, Bell Regular brand gasoline, plastic body, circa 1960	290	375	550
Globe, Ben Franklin Premium Regular brand gasoline, red rippled glass body, circa 1935	850	1300	1750
Globe, Bonded 68 brand gasoline, glass body, circa 1941	300	400	575
Globe, Bonded 98 brand gasoline, glass body, circa 1950	300	400	575
Globe, Bonded Ethyl brand gasoline, glass body, circa 1946	300	400	575
Globe, Calso Supreme brand gasoline, plastic body, circa 1955	105	145	250
Globe, Carter Extra brand gasoline, blue plastic body, circa 1955	175	280	440
Globe, Champlin Presto brand gasoline, glass body, circa 1936	175	280	440
Globe, Chevron Supreme brand gasoline, metal body, circa 1950	315	445	700
Globe, Chief Anti-Knock brand gasoline, metal body, circa 1922	1375	2180	2900
Globe, Cities Service Premium brand gasoline, metal body, circa 1949	290	375	550

Globe, Clark Super 100 brand gasoline, glass body, circa 1938	260	350	475
Globe, Cloverleaf brand gasoline, red plastic body, circa 1955	260	350	475
Globe, Colonial Eagle brand gasoline, plastic body, circa 1958	175	280	440
Globe, Colonial Ethyl brand gasoline, metal octagon body, circa 1927	370	525	850
Globe, Col-Tex Ethyl brand gasoline, plastic body, circa 1954	135	230	350
Globe, Comet Ethyl brand gasoline, glass body, circa 1948	175	280	440
Globe, Conoco Ethyl brand gasoline, glass body, circa 1935	290	375	550
Globe, Conoco Minuteman brand gasoline, metal body, circa 1915	1375	2180	2900
Globe, Conoco Triangle brand gasoline, metal body, circa 1940	315	445	700
Globe, Consolidated Ethyl brand gasoline, oval glass body, circa 1953	290	375	550
Globe, Coryell 70 Super brand gasoline, plastic body, circa 1954	135	230	350
Globe, Cosden Ethyl brand gasoline, glass body, circa 1935	135	230	350
Globe, Crownzol brand gasoline, glass body, circa 1938	175	280	440
Globe, Crown Ethyl brand gasoline, metal body, circa 1922	300	400	575
Globe, Crown Gold brand gasoline, glass body, circa 1959	290	375	550
Globe, Crown Silver brand gasoline, glass body, circa 1959	290	375	550
Globe, Dance Genuine Ethyl brand gasoline, glass body, circa 1953	370	525	850
Globe, Dance Super Hi-Test brand gasoline, glass body, circa 1955	370	525	850
Globe, Deep Rock Ethyl brand gasoline, glass body, circa 1940	175	280	440
Globe, Deep Rock Super brand gasoline, glass body, circa 1940	175	280	440
Globe, Derby Super Ratio Motor Fuel brand gasoline, metal body, circa 1923	565	860	1250

Globe, Diamond Nitro Gasoline brand, one-piece etched glass body, circa 1925	850	1300	1750
Globe, Dixie Blue brand gasoline, glass body, circa 1931	290	375	550
Globe, Dixie Ethyl brand gasoline, yellow plastic body, circa 1947	175	280	440
Globe, Dixie Ethyl brand gasoline, glass body with rippled edge, circa 1935	850	1300	1750
Globe, Dixie Nevernox brand gasoline, red one-piece glass oval, circa 1929	1055	1605	2050
Globe, Dixie Power To Pass brand gasoline, white one-piece glass oval, circa 1929	1055	1605	2050
Globe, Dixie Power To Pass brand gasoline, yellow plastic body, circa 1950	175	280	440
Globe, Dixie Premium brand gasoline, yellow plastic body, circa 1953	135	230	350
Globe, Dixolene brand gasoline, glass body, circa 1937	175	280	440
Globe, D-X Ethyl Lubricating Motor Fuel brand gasoline, banded glass body, circa 1939	290	375	550
Globe, Eason Ethyl brand gasoline, metal body, circa 1934	290	375	550
Globe, Elreco Premium brand gasoline, glass body, circa 1935	290	375	550
Globe, Empire Ethyl brand gasoline, one-piece baked glass body, circa 1923	490	650	1000
Globe, Esso Extra brand gasoline, metal body, circa 1947	290	375	550
Globe, Esso Plus brand gasoline, glass body, circa 1962	135	230	350
Globe, Essolene brand gasoline, metal body, circa 1937	290	375	550
Globe, Exxon Extra brand gasoline, plastic body, circa 1975	95	130	210
Globe, Falcon Ethyl brand gasoline, red plastic body, circa 1960	300	400	575
Globe, Flashlike Ethyl brand gasoline, metal body, circa 1929	290	375	550
Globe, Fort Pitt brand gasoline, metal body, circa 1928	490	650	1000
Globe, Frontier Ethyl brand gasoline, glass body, circa 1953	175	280	440

Globe, Frontier Rarin' To Go brand gasoline, plastic body, circa 1960	175	280	440
Globe, Fyre Drop brand gasoline, metal body, circa 1924	350	480	750
Globe, General Ethyl brand gasoline, metal body, circa 1930	370	525	850
Globe, General Violet Ray brand gasoline, metal body, circa 1930	850	1300	1750
Globe, Gilmore Ethyl brand gasoline, metal body, circa 1934	850	1300	1750
Globe, Gilmore "Roar With Gilmore" brand gasoline, metal body, circa 1933	1870	2645	3450
Globe, Golden Rule brand gasoline, glass body, circa 1941	135	230	350
Globe, Green Pepper Anti-Knock brand gasoline, metal body, circa 1932	315	445	700
Globe, Gulf brand gasoline, one-piece baked glass body, circa 1933	315	445	700
Globe, Gulf brand gasoline, glass body, circa 1947	175	280	440
Globe, Gulf No-Nox Motor Fuel brand gasoline, one-piece glass body, circa 1927	750	1125	1500
Globe, Hi-Speed Ethyl brand gasoline, glass body, circa 1938	175	280	440
Globe, Hi Tower Ethyl brand gasoline, glass body, circa 1941	175	280	440
Globe, Hi-Way brand gasoline, plastic body, circa 1955	95	130	210
Globe, Hood's Flo-Power Ethyl brand gasoline, red plastic body, circa 1952	175	280	440
Globe, Hoosier Pete 100 brand gasoline, glass body, circa 1955	290	375	550
Globe, Hornet brand gasoline, plastic body, circa 1954	95	130	210
Globe, Hudson brand gasoline, glass body, circa 1940	370	525	850
Globe, Hudson Ethyl brand gasoline, red plastic body, circa 1958	315	445	700
Globe, Humble brand gasoline, metal body, circa 1934	315	445	700
Globe, Husky brand gasoline, glass body, circa 1950	370	525	850

Globe, Husky Hi-Power brand gasoline, metal body, circa 1957	850	1300	1750
Globe, Husky Hi-Power brand gasoline, glass body, circa 1957	370	525	850
Globe, Idaho Ethyl brand gasoline, plastic body, circa 1940	370	525	850
Globe, Imperial Ethyl brand gasoline, glass body, circa 1952	175	280	440
Globe, Imperial Premium brand gasoline, plastic body, circa 1970	95	130	210
Globe, Indian Gas brand gasoline, metal body, circa 1929	370	525	850
Globe, Indian Gas Havoline brand gasoline, one-piece etched glass body, circa 1929	850	1300	1750
Globe, Johnson Time Tells Gasolene brand, metal body, circa 1935	850	1300	1750
Globe, Johnson Time Tells Ethyl Gasolene brand, glass body, circa 1935	315	445	700
Globe, Kendall brand gasoline, one-piece etched glass body, circa 1925	370	525	850
Globe, Kendall brand gasoline, glass body, circa 1938	175	280	440
Globe, Kendall Ethyl brand gasoline, glass body, circa 1935	290	375	550
Globe, Kerr McGee brand gasoline, plastic body, circa 1966	95	130	210
Globe, Keystone Ethyl brand gasoline, glass body, circa 1938	175	280	440
Globe, Keystone Ethyl brand gasoline, plastic body, circa 1951	95	130	210
Globe, Liberty Blue brand gasoline, metal body, circa 1935	1055	1605	2050
Globe, Linco brand gasoline, one-piece etched glass body, circa 1925	565	860	1250
Globe, Linco Ethyl brand gasoline, glass body, circa 1936	175	280	440
Globe, Lion Knix Knox brand gasoline, glass body, circa 1950	315	445	700
Globe, Litening brand gasoline, metal body, circa 1936	290	375	550
Globe, Loreco Ethyl brand gasoline, metal body, circa 1930	290	375	550

Globe, Lorex Motor Fuel brand gasoline, metal body, circa 1930	300	400	575
Globe, Magnolia Anti-Knock brand gasoline, metal body, circa 1924	1055	1605	2050
Globe, Magnolia Ethyl brand gasoline, metal body, circa 1930	370	525	850
Globe, Magnolia Maximum Mileage brand gasoline, metal body, circa 1930	850	1300	1750
Globe, Marathon Ethyl brand gasoline, metal body, circa 1932	850	1300	1750
Globe, Marathon Mile Maker brand gasoline, glass body, circa 1950	300	400	575
Globe, Marathon Multipower brand gasoline, metal body, circa 1936	1190	1825	2450
Globe, Marathon Super M brand gasoline, glass body, circa 1959	300	400	575
Globe, Marland Hi-Test brand gasoline, glass body, circa 1928	300	400	575
Globe, Martin Ethyl Premium brand gasoline, glass body, circa 1952	175	280	440
Globe, Martin Purple Martin brand gasoline, glass body, circa 1960	290	375	550
Globe, Martin Super Regular brand gasoline, plastic body, circa 1966	95	130	210
Globe, Martin Xtra Special brand gasoline, glass body, circa 1952	175	280	440
Globe, Meteeor 80 brand gasoline, glass body, circa 1941	290	375	550
Globe, Metro brand gasoline, metal body, circa 1929	260	350	475
Globe, Mileage Not A Nox brand gasoline, metal body, circa 1932	300	400	575
Globe, Mileage Plus brand gasoline, metal body, circa 1928	290	375	550
Globe, Mobilgas brand gasoline, metal body, circa 1932	290	375	550
Globe, Mobilgas brand gasoline, plastic body, circa 1959	135	230	350
Globe, Mobilgas Ethyl brand gasoline, metal body, circa 1932	290	375	550
Globe, Mobilgas Special brand gasoline, glass body, circa 1950	175	280	440

Globe, Monarch Ethyl brand gasoline, glass body, circa 1934	175	280	440
Globe, Mutual Ethyl brand gasoline, glass body, circa 1962	290	375	550
Globe, Mutual Ethyl brand gasoline, metal body, circa 1940	300	400	575
Globe, North Star brand gasoline, one-piece baked glass body, circa 1923	565	860	1250
Globe, Numex Ethyl brand gasoline, glass body, circa 1952	290	375	550
Globe, O'Day Anti-Knock brand gasoline, metal body, circa 1925	350	480	750
Globe, O'Day Crystal White brand gasoline, metal body, circa 1923	315	445	700
Globe, Oklahoma White brand gasoline, one-piece painted glass body, circa 1933	565	860	1250
Globe, Old Dutch brand gasoline, glass body, circa 1935	370	525	850
Globe, Old Dutch brand gasoline, plastic body, circa 1958	300	400	575
Globe, Olixir Lubricated Gas brand gasoline, metal body, circa 1935	300	400	575
Globe, Omar Ethyl brand gasoline, glass body, circa 1935	175	280	440
Globe, Onyx Ethyl brand gasoline, plastic body, circa 1954	95	130	210
Globe, Osceola Ethyl brand gasoline, one-piece plastic body, circa 1963	135	230	350
Globe, Oval-E Extra brand gasoline, blue plastic body, circa 1948	290	375	550
Globe, Pan-Am Economy brand gasoline, metal body, circa 1940	300	400	575
Globe, Pan-Am Ethyl brand gasoline, metal body, circa 1930	315	445	700
Globe, Panhandle Noxless brand gasoline, metal body, circa 1941	490	650	1000
Globe, Paraland Ethyl brand gasoline, plastic body, circa 1950	105	145	250
Globe, Pate Challenge brand gasoline, plastic body, circa 1957	135	230	350
Globe, Penn Drake Ethyl brand gasoline, glass body, circa 1941	300	400	575

Globe, Penn Valley brand gasoline, metal body, circa 1930	350	480	750
Globe, Pennzoil brand gasoline, one-piece etched glass body, circa 1925	1055	1605	2050
Globe, Pennzoil Ethyl brand gasoline, one-piece baked glass body, circa 1927	490	650	1000
Globe, Peoples Ethyl brand gasoline, plastic body, circa 1955	95	130	210
Globe, Pep-88 Ethyl brand gasoline, glass body, circa 1938	175	280	440
Globe, Phillips 66 brand gasoline, three-piece plastic body, circa 1956	175	280	440
Globe, Phillips 66 Ethyl brand gasoline, metal body, circa 1929	850	1300	1750
Globe, Phillips 66 Ethyl brand gasoline, glass body, circa 1929	370	525	850
Globe, Polly Gas brand gasoline, metal body, circa 1932	1475	2300	3150
Globe, Power "G" brand gasoline, banded glass body, circa 1941	290	375	550
Globe, Premier Ethyl brand gasoline, glass body, circa 1940	290	375	550
Globe, Progressive brand gasoline, glass body, circa 1956	175	280	440
Globe, Pure brand gasoline, glass body, circa 1957	300	400	575
Globe, Purol brand gasoline, metal body, circa 1918	490	650	1000
Globe, Purol Ethyl brand gasoline, glass body, circa 1935	175	280	440
Globe, Red Crown Gasoline brand, one-piece etched glass body, circa 1916	1375	2180	2900
Globe, Red Crown Gasoline brand, one-piece etched glass body, circa 1921	1475	2300	3150
Globe, Red Crown Ethyl brand gasoline, metal body, circa 1927	300	400	575
Globe, Red Head Ethyl brand gasoline, glass body, circa 1948	175	280	440
Globe, Red Pepper brand gasoline, one-piece etched glass body, circa 1926	850	1300	1750
Globe, Republic Hi-Way brand gasoline, plastic body, circa 1948	95	130	210

Globe, Republic Power Pak'd brand gasoline, plastic body, circa 1965	95	130	210
Globe, Richfield Ethyl brand gasoline, metal body, circa 1928	350	480	750
Globe, Richfield Ethyl brand gasoline, metal body, circa 1934	850	1300	1750
Globe, Rock Island Anti-Knock brand gasoline, metal body, circa 1941	290	375	550
Globe, Rock Island Ethyl brand gasoline, plastic body, circa 1955	175	280	440
Globe, Rock Island Nunbetter brand gasoline, metal body, circa 1936	350	480	750
Globe, Royal 400 Red Hat brand gasoline, glass body, circa 1934	400	655	1015
Globe, Save More Ethyl brand gasoline, glass body, circa 1953	175	280	440
Globe, Seaside Grade Plus brand gasoline, metal body, circa 1940	370	525	850
Globe, Seaside Silver Gull Tetraethyl brand gasoline, metal body, circa 1938	490	650	1000
Globe, Shell brand gasoline, glass body, circa 1952	750	1125	1500
Globe, Shell brand gasoline, one-piece etched "shell-shaped" glass, circa 1923	490	650	1000
Globe, Shell brand gasoline, plastic "shell-shaped" body, circa 1956	260	350	475
Globe, Super Shell Ethyl brand gasoline, one-piece "shell-shaped" body, circa 1935	565	860	1250
Globe, Silver King brand gasoline, metal body, circa 1931	370	525	850
Globe, Sinclair brand gasoline, one-piece etched glass body, circa 1923	565	860	1250
Globe, Sinclair Dino Supreme brand gasoline, plastic body, circa 1965	95	130	210
Globe, Sinclair Ethyl brand gasoline, glass body, circa 1947	300	400	575
Globe, Sinclair H-C brand gasoline, one-piece etched glass body, circa 1930	565	860	1250
Globe, Skelly brand gasoline, metal body, circa 1924	565	860	1250
Globe, Skelly brand gasoline, glass body, circa 1941	175	280	440

Globe, Skelly Premium brand gasoline, plastic body, circa 1952	95	130	210
Globe, Skelly Supreme brand gasoline, glass body, circa 1955	175	280	440
Globe, Socony Ethyl brand gasoline, metal body, circa 1930	300	400	575
Globe, Socony Motor Gasoline brand, metal body, circa 1920	370	525	850
Globe, Socony Special brand gasoline, metal body, circa 1924	350	480	750
Globe, Sohio Supreme brand gasoline, glass body, circa 1947	175	280	440
Globe, Southern brand gasoline, plastic body, circa 1956	95	130	210
Globe, Speedway 79 brand gasoline, glass body, circa 1957	175	280	440
Globe, Speedway Extra brand gasoline, glass body, circa 1957	175	280	440
Globe, Spur brand gasoline, oval plastic body, circa 1967	135	230	350
Globe, Standard brand gasoline, metal body, circa 1925	300	400	575
Globe, Stanocola In This Pump brand gasoline, metal body, circa 1921	565	860	1250
Globe, Sun Glo brand gasoline, plastic body, circa 1960	135	230	350
Globe, Sunoco brand gasoline, metal body, circa 1925	490	650	1000
Globe, Blue Sunoco brand gasoline, glass body, circa 1951	315	445	700
Globe, Blue Sunoco Knockless brand gasoline, metal body, circa 1924	300	400	575
Globe, Sunray brand gasoline, orange rippled glass body, circa 1935	1055	1605	2050
Globe, Sunray Ethyl brand gasoline, red plastic body, circa 1952	315	445	700
Globe, Super Kant Nock brand gasoline, glass body, circa 1934	175	280	440
Globe, Super Pepper brand gasoline, metal body, circa 1937	300	400	575
Globe, Super Senco brand gasoline, glass body, circa 1955	135	230	350

Globe, Superior 400 brand gasoline, glass body, circa 1939	175	280	440
Globe, Superior Ethyl brand gasoline, plastic body, circa 1955	95	130	210
Globe, Texaco brand gasoline, one-piece cast "chimney top" body, circa 1918	1190	1825	2450
Globe, Texaco Ethyl brand gasoline, one-piece cast body, circa 1928	750	1125	1500
Globe, Texaco Sky Chief brand gasoline, glass body, circa 1941	260	350	475
Globe, Texaco Sky Chief brand gasoline, plastic body, circa 1958	95	130	210
Globe, Thrift Premium brand gasoline, glass body, circa 1955	260	350	475
Globe, Thriftane brand gasoline, metal body, circa 1941	290	375	550
Globe, Tidex brand gasoline, metal body, circa 1938	290	375	550
Globe, Tower brand gasoline, glass body, circa 1941	315	445	700
Globe, Trackside Super Ethyl brand gasoline, glass body, circa 1960	175	280	440
Globe, Tri-Star Red Hat brand gasoline, one-piece etched glass body, circa 1928	1475	2300	3150
Globe, Tri-Star Red Hat brand gasoline, metal body, circa 1928	850	1300	1750
Globe, Tri-State Ethyl brand gasoline, glass body, circa 1935	260	350	475
Globe, Tri-State Super Motor brand gasoline, glass body, circa 1931	290	375	550
Globe, Tulsa Hi-Test brand gasoline, plastic body, circa 1960	135	230	350
Globe, Tydol Ethyl brand gasoline, glass body, circa 1946	260	350	475
Globe, Tydol Flying A Ethyl brand gasoline, glass body, circa 1952	260	350	475
Globe, Tydol With Ethyl brand gasoline, metal body, circa 1929	290	375	550
Globe, United Ethyl brand gasoline, glass body, circa 1941	175	280	440
Globe, United Hi-Test brand gasoline, glass body, circa 1941	290	375	550

Globe, United Regular brand gasoline, plastic body, circa 1970	95	130	210
Globe, Valvoline Ethyl brand gasoline, plastic body, circa 1934	260	350	475
Globe, Valvoline Red Star brand gasoline, metal body, circa 1926	370	525	850
Globe, Vickers Ethyl brand gasoline, red plastic body, circa 1941	135	230	350
Globe, Wadhams Ethyl brand gasoline, metal body, circa 1930	300	400	575
Globe, Wadhams Giant brand gasoline, glass body, circa 1933	175	280	440
Globe, Wasatch Ethyl brand gasoline, plastic body, circa 1940	490	650	1000
Globe, White Rose Enarco brand gasoline, metal body, circa 1916	300	400	575
Globe, White Rose Ethyl brand gasoline, glass body, circa 1931	370	525	850
Globe, White Rose No-Knock, one-piece baked glass body, circa 1927	1190	1825	2450
Globe, White Eagle brand gasoline, cast "eagle" body, circa 1927	490	650	1000
Globe, White Eagle brand gasoline, cast "eagle" body, circa 1932	850	1300	1750
Globe, White Pepper brand gasoline, metal body, circa 1930	300	400	575
Globe, White Star brand gasoline, metal body, circa 1921	850	1300	1750
Globe, White Star Ethyl brand gasoline, metal body, circa 1928	350	480	750
Globe, Wolf's Head Ethyl brand gasoline, glass body, circa 1955	290	375	550
Globe, Wolf's Head Ethyl brand gasoline, plastic body, circa 1965	175	280	440
Globe, Zephyr brand gasoline, glass body, circa 1941	175	280	440
Globe, Zephyr Ethyl brand gasoline, glass body, circa 1941	175	280	440
Globe, Zephyr Hi Octane brand gasoline, oval plastic body, circa 1958	135	230	350

Tire Valve Caps

Description	Good	Very Good	Excellent
Red Crown valve cap (original; set of 4)	5	10	20
Gold Crown valve cap (original; set of 4)	5	10	20

Harley-Davidson Motorcycle Petroliana

Description	Good	Very Good	Excellent
H-D Silver Heat Resistant Finish, pint, full, circa 1940	10	20	50
H-D touch-up paint, glass jar, full, circa 1958	10	20	50
H-D Gunk Motorcycle Cleaner, full, 4-1/2 inches tall, circa 1955	35	85	100
H-D standard piston (part 253-29A) in 3-5/8 x 4-1/4-inch box with original wrapper, with instruction sheet	25	50	75
H-D Pre-Luxe Motorcycle Oil tin can, quart, full, 5-1/2 inches tall	50	90	125
H-D Genuine Harley-Davidson Motor Oil can, one-gallon, circa 1938	315	445	700
H-D Genuine Harley-Davidson Motor Oil can, five-gallon, round w/ pour spout, circa 1925	490	650	1000
H-D (AMF) Pre-Luxe Motorcycle Oil cardboard can, quart, full, 5-1/2 inches tall	25	50	75
H-D Two-Cycle Motor Oil cone top tin can, full, 5-3/4 inches tall	50	90	125

Car Care Products/Parts/Tools

Description	Good	Very Good	Excellent
AC spark plug bird cage, 6 x 14-inch metal promotional display, circa 1938	100	150	200
Americo Grease, 10-pound tin can, full	5	15	25
Benford's Monarch Golden Giant spark plug, 24-k gold plated, in box	15	35	55
Buick Oil for Dynaflow Drive, five-gallon can, full	50	75	100
Cadillac Chromium Cleaner, quart tin can, full	10	20	30

Camel Tube Gum tire tube repair kit, 3-3/4 x 6-5/8-inch cardboard can, contents complete	5	15	25
Champion (Commercial) Spark Plug (part J-10), in box	3	7	15
Conoco Transmission Grease, 10-pound tin can, circa 1920	70	110	225
Delco Hydraulic Shock Absorber Fluid, quart tin can	10	20	30
Fiebing's Auto Mohair Dye, 3-1/2 x 7-1/2-inch tin can with paper label	15	40	80
Film-Fyter Windshield Wash service station cabinet, tin, in box	10	35	75
Firestone tire tube repair kit, 3-1/2 x 9-1/4-inch tin can, contents complete	5	15	25
Ford Body Polish (M-230-F), 32 fluid ounces	15	40	80
Huffman one-quart oil jar with baked-on logo, 13-1/2 inches tall	20	30	45
Huffman embossed one-quart oil jar, 13-1/2 inches tall	10	18	30
Peak Anti-Freeze, one gallon tin can	5	15	25
Sears Premium gasoline can, two-gallon tin can, empty	10	20	30
Shell embossed one-quart oil jar, 14-1/2 inches tall	50	75	100
Signal-Stat Flarestat emergency flasher kit, 7 x 3-inch cardboard box, circa 1950	15	35	55
Sinclair bulk oil dispenser	125	195	250
Tagolene (Skelly) Pressure Gun Grease, 25-pound tin can	11	22	35
Thermo Anti-Freeze, quart tin can, circa 1946	3	7	15
Vitrolin rain dispeller, pint tin can	40	65	90
Weed tire chain metal display rack, 30 x 40 inches, metal wire w/ tin sign, circa 1935	75	110	225
Westinghouse/Mazda Automobile Lamp Kit, 3 x 3-inch tin can	10	15	20
Whiz Motor Rythm engine tuning fluid, one-gallon tin can	6	14	25
Wonder Mist Cleanser Polisher, quart tin can	12	30	45

Motor Oil Cans/Quart

Description	Good	Very Good	Excellent
Ace High Motor Oil, quart tin can	25	35	45
Cen-Pe-Co Super Racing Oil, quart tin can	10	20	30
D-A Speed-Sport Motor Oil, quart cardboard can	10	20	30
Exceloyl Motor Oil, quart tin can	5	10	15
Indian Premium Motorcycle Oil, quart tin can	145	180	210
Oilzum Special Motor Oil, quart cardboard can	25	35	45
Texaco Marine Motor Oil, quart tin can	25	40	75
Wanda Paraffin Motor Oil, quart tin can	5	15	25

Motor Oil Cans/One-Gallon

Description	Good	Very Good	Excellent
Agalion Motor Oil, one-gallon tin can	125	175	210
Bull Dog Motor Oil, one-gallon tin can	50	90	125
Dearco Motor Oil, one-gallon tin can	40	75	100
Excelsior Motor Oil, one-gallon tin can	135	185	220
Gold Crest Motor Oil, one-gallon tin can	15	30	60
Mona Motor Oil, one-gallon tin can	225	290	335
Opaline (Sinclair) Motor Oil, one-gallon tin can, circa 1921	50	90	125
Permalube Motor Oil, one-gallon cardboard can, circa 1965	25	55	75
Pioneer Motor Oil, one-gallon tin can	40	75	100
Pure As Gold SAE 40 Motor Oil, one-gallon tin can	10	25	50
Russolene Brand Motor Oil, one-gallon tin can	15	30	60
Sterling Motor Oil, one-gallon tin can, circa 1925	40	75	100
Sun Ray Heavy Motor Oil, one-gallon tin can	35	65	85
Tiolene Motor Oil, one-gallon tin can	15	30	60
Veedol Motor Oil, one-gallon tin can	10	25	50

Motor Oil Cans/Two-Gallon

Description	Good	Very Good	Excellent
Bonded Motor Oil, two-gallon tin can	60	90	115
Booster Motor Oil, two-gallon tin can	15	35	45
Bull Dog Motor Oil, two-gallon tin can	130	175	225
Defender Motor Oil, two-gallon tin can	60	90	115
Golden Flash Motor Oil, two-gallon tin can	15	35	45
Grand Champion Motor Oil, two-gallon tin can	80	105	135
Lord Calvert Auto Oil, two-gallon tin can	15	35	45
Lucky Star Motor Oil, two-gallon tin can	15	35	45
Many Miles Motor Oil, two-gallon tin can	115	160	210
Marathon Motor Oil, two-gallon tin can	60	90	115
Penn Stag Motor Oil, two-gallon tin can	15	35	45
Polarine Motor Oil, two-gallon tin can	15	35	45
Ravenoyl Motor Oil, two-gallon tin can	45	60	75
Red Bell Motor Oil, two-gallon tin can	15	35	45
Road Boss Motor Oil, two-gallon tin can	15	35	45
Rocket Motor Oil, two-gallon tin can	15	35	45
Silver Shell Motor Oil, two-gallon tin can	40	75	100
Sturdy Motor Oil, two-gallon tin can	25	45	55
Tomahawk Hi-Speed Motor Oil, two-gallon tin can	60	90	115
Traffic Motor Oil, two-gallon tin can	15	35	45
Your Friend Motor Oil, two-gallon tin can	15	35	45

Motor Oil Cans/Other

Description	Good	Very Good	Excellent
Ace High Motor Oil, five-quart tin can	20	35	50
Admiral Penn Motor Oil, five-quart tin can	20	35	50
Bolivar Motor Oil, five-quart tin can	30	50	75
8 Motor Oil, half-gallon tin can, circa 1918	35	65	85
En-ar-co National Motor Oil, five-gallon tin can	30	50	75

Description	Good	Very Good	Excellent
Freedom Perfect Motor Oil, five-quart tin can	30	50	75
Invader Motor Oil, five-quart tin can	20	35	50
Jay-Bee Motor Oil, half-gallon tin can, circa 1915	30	50	75
Keystone Condensed Oil, 10-pound tin can	25	40	65
Parapride Motor Oil, five-quart tin can	30	50	75
Quaker State Medium Oil, five-gallon tin can	30	50	75
Trop-Artic Motor Oil, half-gallon tin can, circa 1917	100	150	250
Veedol Motor Oil, five-quart tin can	20	35	50

Petroliana And Related Advertising Signs

Description	Good	Very Good	Excellent
Atlantic White Flash gasoline sign, porcelain, 13 x 17 inches, 1949, red-white-blue	75	120	175
Authorized United Motors Service/Harrison Radiators combination sign, tin, circa 1925	220	325	575
Auto-Lite Spark Plug sign, tin, 12 x 30 inches,	120	250	475
Carburetor Specialists Hygrade System sign, tin, (round), yellow and blue	75	120	175
Champion Spark Plug sign, tin, white and red	95	150	225
400 Pacer with Ethyl gasoline sign, porcelain, 8-1/2 x 14 inches, black-red-yellow-white	100	200	375
Havoline Motor Oil sign, tin, red, white and blue	40	75	100
Humble Gasoline sign, porcelain	30	50	75
India Gasoline sign, porcelain	30	50	75
Mapco Speedway Coils sign, tin, 8 x 15 inches, circa 1932	75	120	175
Mobil flying horse sign, red, 30 x 45 inches, circa 1935	315	520	800
Oilzum Motor Oil building mount sign, tin, 20 x 12 inches (oval-shaped)	75	110	180
Olixir Supreme Top Cylinder Oil sign, tin, 16 x 8 inches, circa 1932	35	60	80
Penno Motor Oil building mount sign, tin	100	200	375
Royal Triton (Union 76) 10-30 motor oil sign, tin (oil can shaped)	75	120	175

Description	Good	Very Good	Excellent
Sinclair gasoline sign, tin, white/red/black/green	100	200	375
Sinclair H-C Gasoline sign, porcelain, green/red/white	220	375	575
Standard Oil Co. sign, porcelain, with Donald Duck "Knockouts for Winners" sales promotion	90	195	300
Texaco Diesel Chief sign, porcelain, 12 x 18 inches, 1966, red-white-black-green	75	120	175
Texaco distributor sign, porcelain, black letters on white background	85	175	275
Texaco "Fire Chief" gasoline pump sign, circa 1935	45	70	95
Topps Super Pyro Anti-Freeze outdoor mercury thermometer, 7 x 18 inches, circa 1950	30	50	75
Vico Motor Oil/Pep 88 Gasoline, black and orange, porcelain	75	120	175
Waverly Motor Oil maintenance record sign, tin, 36 x 24 inches	75	120	175
Willard Batteries sign, tin, circa 1935	30	50	75
Willard Starting Service building mount sign, tin, 20 x 22 inches, circa 1948	150	200	300

Paper/Cardboard/Cloth Petroliana

Description	Good	Very Good	Excellent
Clason's Touring Atlas of U.S. and Canada, 1930, softcover	15	40	65
Derby Anti-Freeze wall banner, cloth with stitched edges, blue	70	130	180
Goodyear hose and belt sign, cardboard, 1930s, with logoed brown paper storage wrapper	45	75	100
Gulf "Check Up Today" lubrication reminder card, 4 x 3 inches	1	2	3
Mobiloil "Fresh Start For Spring" two-way indoor sign, cardboard, transition period for company with oil can showing both gargoyle and pegasus logos, 30 x 44 inches, circa 1937	100	200	300
Montgomery Ward retail auto center tire sales display, composition board and plastic, 36 x 40 inches, circa 1965	60	110	140
Personal Budget Book from The Cities Service, 1930, softcover	2	4	6
Pure road map of Michigan, 1956	2	5	10

Description	Good	Very Good	Excellent
Quaker State Motor Oil wall banner, paper, white and green	15	35	55
Richfield road map of New Jersey, 1934	20	40	70
Standard Oil Eastern U.S. Interstate Map, 1957	10	15	35
Standard Oil Co. Stanolind Almanac, 1928-29, red and blue	20	35	50
Sunoco road map of Ohio-Indiana, 1950	4	7	10
Texaco Dealers Profit Computer, cardboard sleeve with paper insert, 1956	15	25	45
Texaco Premium Type Anti-Freeze wall banner, cloth with stitched edges, aqua	40	55	75
Tydol Veedol road map of Minnesota, circa 1943	5	10	15
Wadhams road map of Wisconsin, 1920s	15	25	45
Washington, D.C. map, compliments of Capital Sight-Seeing Automobiles, circa 1920s	10	15	20
Tropic-Aire (in-car heating system) product brochure, 1930, 8-page fold-out	10	20	40

Service Station Premiums

Description	Good	Very Good	Excellent
Atlantic Premium gas pump bank, tin litho, 2-1/4 x 5 inches, red-white-blue	20	40	65
Blakely's America's Finest Gasoline matchbook, w/ race car and rocket graphics	4	7	10
Blue Sunoco cigarette lighter, 1-1/2 inches tall, chrome-plated metal	10	25	35
Cities Service bottle opener, 6-1/2 inches long, plastic handle, white and green	3	7	10
Esso salt & pepper shaker set, 1 x 2-1/2 inches each, plastic, red-white-blue	15	30	45
Mobil Flying Horse tie clip, metal with red enameled horse	25	50	75
Skelly logoed playing cards (two-decks) in plastic display case	15	30	45
Standard Oil Checkers game with checkerboard, cardboard base with wood checkers	35	75	100
Sunoco gas pump AM/FM portable radio, 2-1/2 x 4-1/8 inches, plastic, blue and yellow	20	40	65
Texaco serving tray with picture of 1910 Ford Torpedo, 1940s, tin, black edge	15	30	45

Atlantic Imperial brand gas globe, gold-yellow-white, plastic body. EXC-$550

Bell Ethyl brand gas globe, blue-orange with rippled glass body. EXC-$750

Signal-Stat Flarestat emergency flasher kit, cardboard box. EXC-$55

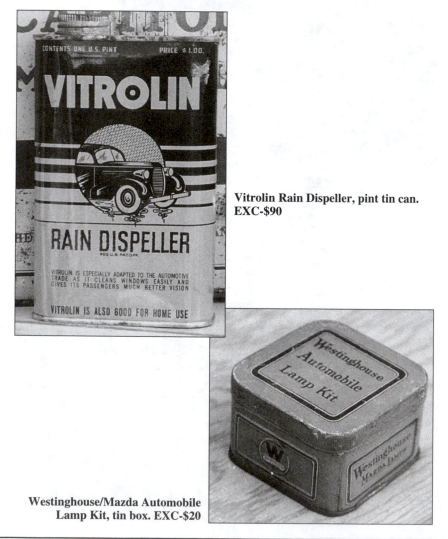

Vitrolin Rain Dispeller, pint tin can. EXC-$90

Westinghouse/Mazda Automobile Lamp Kit, tin box. EXC-$20

AC Spark Plug bird cage promotional display, wire cage with tin sign. EXC-$200

Buick oil for Dynaflow Drive, five-gallon tin can. EXC-$100

Weed tire chain display rack, wire rack with tin sign. EXC-$225

Topps Pyro Anti-Freeze mercury thermometer, tin, yellow-red. EXC-$75

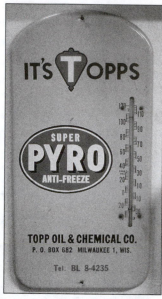

Waverly Motor Oil maintenance record sign, tin with chalkboard overlay. EXC-$175

(Note: The excellent (EXC) condition value of each item pictured is provided in the photo captions. Each item pictured may or may not be in excellent condition, but is shown to give visual representation of that item)

Mapco Speedway Coils sign, tin, orange-black. EXC-$175

Penno Motor Oil building mount sign, tin, black-white. EXC-$375

Willard Starting Service building mount sign, tin, white-black. EXC-$300

Olixir Supreme Top Cylinder Oil sign, tin, yellow-red-black. EXC-$80

Montgomery Ward retail auto center worn tire display sign, composition board and plastic, blue-black-yellow. EXC-$140

(Note: The excellent (EXC) condition value of each item pictured is provided in the photo captions. Each item pictured may or may not be in excellent condition, but is shown to give visual representation of that item)

Mobiloil oil change reminder indoor sign, two-way cardboard (transition period for Mobil as sign shows both gargoyle and pegasus logos), sky blue-red-white. EXC-$300

Petroliana

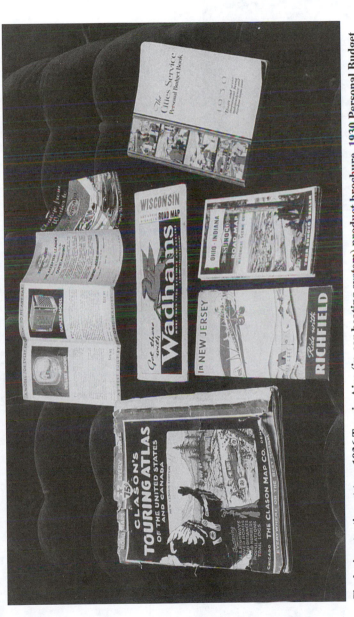

Clockwise starting at top: 1936 Tropic-Aire (in-car heating system) product brochure; 1930 Personal Budget Book from The Cities Service; 1950 Ohio-Indiana road map from Sunoco; 1934 New Jersey road map from Richfield; 1931 Clason's Touring Atlas; a 1920s Wisconsin road map from Wadhams (later Mobil). Respectively: EXC-$40; EXC-$6; EXC-$10; EXC-$70; EXC-$65; EXC-$45

Blue Sunoco three-piece gasoline pump globe from the late 1940s. EXC-$700

A rare Badger 60-62 three-piece gasoline pump globe from the late 1930s. This was a brand distributed by the Badger Petroleum Co. of McFarland, Wis. EXC-$550

Porcelain Texaco distributor sign from 1937. EXC-$275

A 1960s windshield wash cabinet made for
use at a service station but never taken out of
the box. EXC-$75

(Note: The excellent (EXC) condition
value of each item pictured is provided
in the photo captions. Each item pictured may or may not be in excellent
condition, but is shown to give visual
representation of that item)

Huffman 13-1/2-inch tall one-
quart oil jar with baked finish
from the 1930s. EXC-$45

Omar Ethyl brand gas
globe, yellow-black-red,
glass body. EXC-$440

(Note: The excellent (EXC) condition
value of each item pictured is provided
in the photo captions. Each item pictured may or may not be in excellent
condition, but is shown to give visual
representation of that item)

Dixie Ethyl brand gas globe,
blue and yellow, glass body
with rippled edge. EXC-$1,750

Skelly Premium gas globe, red-white-blue, plastic body. EXC-$210

Shell gas globe, white and red, one-piece glass shaped like shell. EXC-$1,000

Harley-Davidson Pre-Luxe Motorcycle Oil, quart tin can. EXC-$125

Harley-Davidson (AMF) Pre-Luxe Motorcycle Oil, quart cardboard can. EXC-$75

Texaco Marine Motor Oil (The Texas Co.), quart tin can. EXC-$75

Wanda 100 percent Paraffin Motor Oil, quart tin can. EXC-$25

Exceloyl Motor Oil (H.K. Stahl Co., St. Paul, Minn.), quart tin can. EXC-$15

Oilzum Special Motor Oil, quart cardboard can. EXC-$45

Cen-Pe-Co Super Racing Oil (Central Petroleum Co., Cleveland, Ohio), quart tin can. EXC-$30

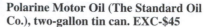

Polarine Motor Oil (The Standard Oil Co.), two-gallon tin can. EXC-$45

Penn Stag 100 Percent Pure Pennsylvania Motor Oil, two-gallon tin can. EXC-$45

(Note: The excellent (EXC) condition value of each item pictured is provided in the photo captions. Each item pictured may or may not be in excellent condition, but is shown to give visual representation of that item)

Keystone Condensed Oil (Keystone Lubricating Co., Philadelphia, Pa.), 10-pound tin can. EXC-$65

Americo Grease (American Oil Co., Troy, N.Y.), 10-pound tin can. EXC-$25

Whiz Motor Rythm Tune-Up Formula (R.M. Hollingshead Corp.), one-gallon tin can. EXC-$25

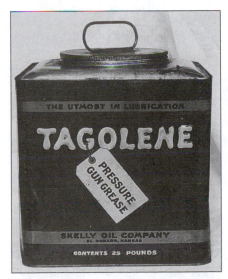

Tagolene Pressure Gun Grease (Skelly Oil Co., El Dorado, Kan.), 25-pound tin can. EXC-$35

Peak Anti-Freeze, one-gallon tin can.
EXC-$25

Sears Premium two-gallon gasoline
storage can. EXC-$30

Delco Hydraulic Shock Absorber Fluid
(Delco Products, Dayton, Ohio), quart
tin can. EXC-$30

Permalube Motor Oil (Product of
American Oil Co., Chicago, Ill.), one-
gallon cardboard can. EXC-$75

Cadillac Exclusive Accessories
Chromium Cleaner, quart tin can.
EXC-$30

Benford's Monarch Golden Giant
Spark Plug, 24-karat gold plated,
in box. EXC-$55

Champion Commercial Spark Plug (part J-10), in
box. EXC-$15

Firestone tire tube repair kit,
tin can. EXC-$25

Union 76 Royal Triton 10-30
motor oil wall sign, tin. EXC-$175

(Note: The excellent (EXC) condition
value of each item pictured is provided
in the photo captions. Each item pictured may or may not be in excellent
condition, but is shown to give visual
representation of that item)

Sinclair bulk oil dispenser. EXC-$250

Champion Spark Plugs wall sign, tin. EXC-$225

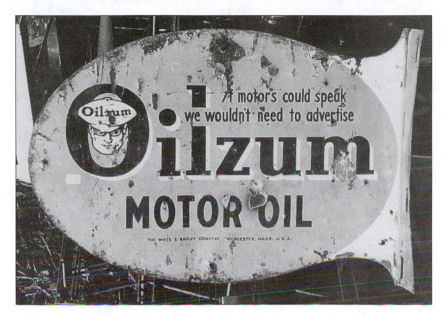

Oilzum Motor Oil (The White & Bagley Co., Worcester, Mass.) building-mount sign, tin, oval shaped. EXC-$180

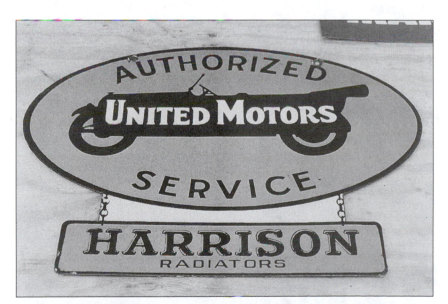

Authorized United Motors Service/Harrison Radiators combination sign, tin with porcelain finish, yellow-black-white, c. 1920s. EXC-$575

Mobil flying horse sign, red, 1930s. EXC-$800

(Note: The excellent (EXC) condition value of each item pictured is provided in the photo captions. Each item pictured may or may not be in excellent condition, but is shown to give visual representation of that item)

Auto-Lite Spark Plug sign, tin, blue-yellow-red-white. EXC-$475

Texaco Premium Type Anti-Freeze wall banner, cloth with stitched edges, aqua. EXC-$75

Quaker State Motor Oil wall banner, paper, white and green. EXC-$55

Gulf "Check Up Today" lubrication reminder card. EXC-$3

Skelly logoed playing cards (two decks) in plastic display case. EXC-$45

Blakely's Finest Gasoline book of matches with race car and rocket graphics. EXC-$10

Derby Anti-Freeze wall banner, cloth with stitched edges, blue-red-white-glitter. EXC-$180

Pure road map of Michigan, 1956. EXC-$10

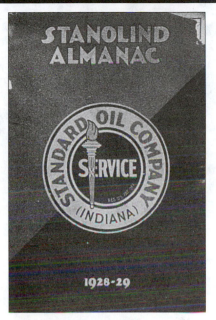

Standard Oil Co. Stanolind Almanac, 1928-29, red and blue. EXC-$50

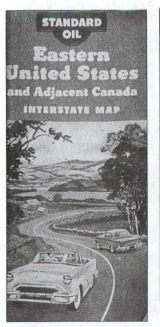

Standard Oil Eastern U.S. and Canada Interstate Map, 1957. EXC-$35

Capital Sight-Seeing Automobiles map of "Beautiful Washington" (D.C.), circa 1920s. EXC-$20

Tydol Veedol road map of Minnesota, circa 1943.EXC-$15

LITERATURE

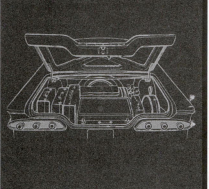

QUICK FACTS
ABOUT THE
1959 EDSEL

*Exciting new kind of car
that makes history
by making sense*

Automobile Literature

Description	Good	Very Good	Excellent
1904 ALAM Hand Book of Gasoline Automobiles (original)	50	85	125
1905 ALAM Hand Book of Gasoline Automobiles (original)	60	100	150
1906 ALAM Hand Book of Gasoline Automobiles (original)	50	85	125
1907 ALAM Hand Book of Gasoline Automobiles (original)	40	65	100
1908 ALAM Hand Book of Gasoline Automobiles (original)	40	65	100
1909 ALAM Hand Book of Gasoline Automobiles (original)	40	65	100
1910 ALAM Hand Book of Gasoline Automobiles (original)	33	55	85
1911 ALAM Hand Book of Gasoline Automobiles (original)	33	55	85

NOTE: Several editions of the ALAM Hand Book of Gasoline Automobiles have been reprinted by Floyd Clymer and Dover Press. These are now getting old and have appeal to collectors, although they are far less valuable than original editions.

Description	Good	Very Good	Excellent
1912 Automobile Board of Trade Hand Book (original)	30	50	75
1913 Automobile Board of Trade Hand Book (original)	30	50	75
1914 NACC Hand Book (original)	27	45	70
1915 NACC Hand Book (original)	27	45	70
1916 NACC Hand Book (original)	27	45	70
1917 NACC Hand Book (original)	25	42	65
1918 NACC Hand Book (original)	25	42	65
1919 NACC Hand Book (original)	23	40	60
1920 NACC Hand Book (original)	20	33	50
1921 NACC Hand Book (original)	20	33	50
1922 NACC Hand Book (original)	20	33	50
1923 NACC Hand Book (original)	20	33	50
1924 NACC Hand Book (original)	20	33	50
1925 NACC Hand Book (original)	20	33	50

1926 NACC Hand Book (original)	20	33	50
1927 NACC Hand Book (original)	23	40	60
1928 NACC Hand Book (original)	25	42	65
1929 NACC Hand Book (original)	27	45	70
1906 MoToR's Directory of Motor Cars	14	23	35
1907 MoToR's Directory of Motor Cars	14	23	35
1908 MoToR's Directory of Motor Cars	14	23	35
1909 MoToR's Directory of Motor Cars	14	23	35
1910 MoToR's Directory of Motor Cars	14	23	35
1911 MoToR's Directory of Motor Cars	14	23	35
1912 MoToR's Directory of Motor Cars	14	23	35
1913 MoToR's Directory of Motor Cars	14	23	35
Hartford's Golden Automobile Jubilee 1897-1947, program, 8-1/2 x 11 inches	20	35	45
1911 *The Motor Boys Over The Rockies*, fiction, Clarence Young, hardcover	12	18	26
1913 *The Automobile Girls at Washington*, fiction, Laura Dent Crane, hardcover	12	18	26
1913 *The Outdoor Girl's in a Motor Car*, fiction, Laura Lee Hope, hardcover	12	18	26
1915 Official Automobile Blue Book, 5-1/2 x 9-1/4 inches	25	45	100
1933-1934 Penn-Jersey Auto Stores parts catalog, 8-1/2 x 11 inches	20	30	40
1935 Texaco in Australia book, hardcover, 8-1/2 x 11 inches	75	100	150
1939 Chicago Automobile Show souvenir booklet *An Age of Wheelprints*, 8-1/2 x 11 inches	45	65	75
1942 Ward's Automotive Year Book, 8-1/2 x 11 inches, hardcover	25	45	100
1944 *How Dear to My Heart*, fiction, Emily Kimbraugh, hardcover	12	18	26
1957 "From Pencil to Proving Ground," 8-page fold out booklet of Ford's Rouge assembly plant	6	12	22
"How A Modern Compact Car Is Built" (1960, published by Rambler), 12-view fold-out (vertical format), 3-1/2 x 8-1/2 inches	5	10	15
"Buyer's Digest of New Car Facts for 1960" (published by FoMoCo), 96 pages, 7 x 10 inches	8	15	25

Description			
1973 Kenworth 50th Anniversary booklet, 8 pages, 8-1/2 x 11 inches	5	10	15
"Home for a day" Kaiser-Frazer Willow Cottage at Willow Run hospitality brochure, 3-page fold-out, 8-1/2 x 11 inches	15	25	50

Automobile Sales Literature

Description	Good	Very Good	Excellent
1911 Locomobile, sales catalog, hard cover	56	100	150
1912 Locomobile, sales catalog, hard cover	56	100	150
1910 Lorraine-Dietrich, sales pamphlet, soft cover	40	65	100
1912 Ford sales literature	30	50	75
1920s Chandler sales booklet	20	30	45
1930 Pierce-Arrow sales catalog, full color (standard version)	60	100	150
1930 Pierce-Arrow, all-line, "jumbo" sales catalog, 35 pages, 10-1/4 x 16-3/4 x 30 inches	300	500	750
1954 Kaiser Manhattan sales catalog, folio edition, 10 color plates	20	33	50
1919 Packard, Twin Six, hard cover presentation album, 39 pages, 8-3/4 x 12 inches	370	620	950
1927 Packard, "jumbo" sales catalog, 23 pages, 10 x 13-1/2 x 28 inches	140	230	350
1928 Packard, "jumbo" sales catalog, 23 pages, 10 x 13-1/2 x 28 inches	165	280	425
1914 Rolls-Royce sales catalog (Percy Northey color photos)	90	150	225
1938 Rolls-Royce, Phantom I sales catalog, 44 pages, 9-1/2 x 13 inches	90	150	225
1939 Rolls-Royce, Phantom I sales catalog, 44 pages, 9-1/2 x 13 inches	90	150	225
1928 Bentley Six, 6.5 liter sales catalog No. 27	350	600	900
1930s Flewitt Coachwork album, Rolls-Royce Phantom I and 20 horsepower	150	245	375
1930s Swallow side car sales literature	80	130	200
1932 Chevrolet sales booklet	20	30	45
1933 Plymouth, sales catalog	20	33	50
1934 Plymouth, sales catalog	20	33	50

1933 Packard Twelve, sales catalog	600	1000	1500
1934 Packard Twelve, sales catalog	600	1000	1500
1936 Packard 12, deluxe sales catalog	115	200	300
1938 The Phantom Corsair sales catalog, 8-1/2 x 11 inches	60	85	100
1939 DeSoto sales catalog	22	36	55
1948 Gatso Type 4000 (Holland) sales brochure, 2 pages, 9-1/2 x 6 inches	6	10	15
1949 Jaguar Type XK sales catalog, 8 pages, 14-1/2 x 10 inches	30	50	75
1951 Nash all-line sales catalog, 10 pages, 11 x 7-1/2 inches	8	15	22
1954 Anglia (English Ford) De Luxe sales catalog, shaped as Anglia tailfin	6	10	15
1955 Buick all-line sales catalog, 32 pages, 15 x 7-1/2 inches	14	23	55
1955 Chevrolet sales catalog	12	20	30
1955 Chrysler Windsor Deluxe sales catalog, 16 pages, 12 x 12 inches	14	23	55
1955 DeSoto all-line sales brochure, 12-view fold-out, 11 x 9-1/4 inches	14	23	55
1955 Hillman Husky sales brochure, 8-view fold out, 11-1/2 x 8-1/2 inches	6	10	15
1955 Nash all-line sales brochure, 8-view fold out, 14 x 11 inches	7	11	17
1955 Ford Thunderbird, color sales folder	10	17	25
1957 Ford Skyliner (retractable) sales folder	6	10	15
1957 Jaguar SS sales literature, four separate pieces	390	650	1000
1957 Opel all-line sales catalog, 12 pages, 11-1/4 x 8 inches	7	11	17
1958 Fiat 600D sales brochure, 4 pages, 11 x 8 inches	7	11	17
1958 Plymouth all-line sales catalog, 16 pages, 11-1/2 x 8 inches	12	20	30
1958 Volkswagen all-line sales catalog, 10 pages with centerfold pull-out, 8-1/4 x 12 inches	6	10	35
1959 Checker Model A-9 taxicab sales catalog, 8 pages, 12 x 9 inches	8	12	22

1959 Edsel all-model sales catalog, 10 pages, 5 x 8-1/2 inches	6	15	30
1960 Cadillac all-line sales catalog, 16 pages, 10 x 8-1/2 inches	7	11	17
1960 Citroen Ami 6 sales catalog, 28 pages, 10-1/2 x 7 inches	6	10	15
1960 Porsche 356B sales catalog, 8 pages, 8-1/2 x 11 inches	10	16	25
1960 Triumph/Herald sales brochure, 8-view fold-out, 8-1/2 x 11 inches	6	10	15
1962 Buick sales catalog, 16 pages	4	6	12
1962 Goggomobil TS 300 Coupe sales brochure, one page, 11-1/2 x 8 inches	8	12	18
1962 Sunbeam Rapier sales brochure, 12-view fold-out, 11-1/2 x 8-1/2 inches	7	11	17
1963 Checker 40th Anniversary all-line brochure, 8-view fold-out, 8-1/2 x 12-1/2 inches	7	11	17
1963 Lancia sales catalog, 20 pages, 11-3/4 x 8-1/4 inches	6	10	15
1963 Austin Healey Sprite MK II sales catalog, 12 pages, 11 x 8 inches	7	11	17
1963 BMW 1800 sales brochure, one page, 11-1/2 x 8 inches	7	11	17
1964 Cadillac all-line sales catalog, 24 pages, 9 x 8 inches	6	10	15
1964 Cadillac sales brochure, 24 pages	8	13	20
1964 American Motors sales folder	3	5	8
1965 Corvair Sprint sales catalog, 8 pages, 8-1/2 x 7 inches	9	13	22
1965 Imperial (Chrysler Corp.) sales catalog, 8 pages, 10 x 10 inches	6	10	15
1966 Mercedes-Benz all-line sales brochure, 24 pages, 8-1/4 x 4 inches	6	10	15
1966 MGB sales catalog, 16 pages, 11 x 8-1/4 inches	6	10	15
1969 American Motors AMX sales catalog	5	8	10
1970 Cadillac, all-line sales catalog	4	6	10
1971 Trabant 601 sales brochure, 8-view fold-out, 11-1/4 x 8 inches	8	12	18
1974 Chevrolet Corvette sales catalog	8	13	20

1975 Mercedes-Benz Passenger Car Program, all-line, 52 pages, 8-1/2 x 11 inches	4	6	10

Concept Car Literature

	Good	Very Good	Excellent
Buick Wildcat brochure, 8 x 8 inches, circa 1953	35	50	65
Buick XP-300 brochure, 8 x 6 inches, circa 1951	25	40	55
Chevrolet Biscayne brochure, 9 x 5 inches, circa 1955	25	40	55
Chrysler K-310 brochure, 8 x 4 inches, circa 1951	35	50	65
General Motors Firebird II brochure, 8 x 5 inches, circa 1957	25	40	55
General Motors LeSabre brochure, 8 x 6 inches, circa 1951	35	50	65
General Motors XP-21 Firebird brochure, 8 x 6 inches, circa 1954	35	50	65

Truck Sales Literature

Description	Good	Very Good	Excellent
1920s Clark of Oshkosh One-Ton Motor Truck sales catalog (body builder), 40 pages, 4-1/4 x 7 inches	20	35	70
1963 GMC truck sales catalog No. TSP63-6-20M, 7000 series fire trucks	2	4	8
Mack B-Series trucks and tractors brochure, 8-1/2 x 11 inches, circa 1954	50	75	125
Mack truck products brochure, full color, 14 x 12 inches, circa 1956	75	100	150

Accessory Catalogs

Description	Good	Very Good	Excellent
1935 Graham accessories booklet, 8 pages, 8-1/2 x 11 inches	10	20	35
1938 Graham accessories booklet, 8-view fold-out, 11 x 8-1/2 inches	10	20	35
1939 Graham accessories booklet, 8 pages, 11 x 16 inches	10	20	35

1939 Nash accessories booklet, 16 pages, 6 x 9 inches	10	20	35
1941 Oldsmobile accessories booklet, 24 pages, 4 x 7-1/4 inches	11	22	40
1942 Chrysler/Mopar accessories catalog, 6-view fold-out comprising 12 pages, 3-1/2 x 6-1/4 inches	10	20	37
1949 Chrysler/Mopar accessories catalog, 16 pages, 8-1/2 x 11 inches	9	18	35
1949 Pontiac accessories catalog, 24 pages, 8-1/2 x 11 inches	9	18	35
1950 Kaiser Vagabond/Traveler accessories booklet, 8-view fold-out	8	15	32
1951 Mopar accessories booklet, 28 pages, 8-1/2 x 5-1/2 inches	6	9	20
1951 Nash accessories booklet, 8-view fold-out, 10 x 8 inches	7	11	24
1951 Nash Rambler Airflyte accessories booklet, 8-pages, 11 x 7-1/2 inches	7	11	24
1952 Mercury accessories catalog, 34 pages, 8 x 8 inches	8	15	32
1954 Ford accessories booklet, 32 pages, 5 x 8-1/2 inches	8	15	32
1955 Cadillac accessories booklet, 20 pages, 7 x 7 inches	8	15	32
1955 Chevrolet accessories catalog, 32 pages, 9 x 6 inches	9	17	37
1955 Plymouth accessories brochure, 12-view fold-out, 7 x 9 inches	7	13	26
1955 Pontiac accessories catalog, 16 pages, 6 x 9 inches	8	15	32
1955 Studebaker accessories catalog, 22 pages, 12 x 8-3/4 inches	9	16	34
1956 DeSoto optional equipment catalog, 8 pages, 10 x 8 inches	7	13	26
1956 Dodge accessories booklet, 12 pages, 6-1/4 x 8-1/2 inches	7	13	26
1957 Imperial accessories pocket directory, 12 pages, 4-1/4 x 7 inches	8	15	32
1958 Chevrolet accessories catalog, 30 pages, 9 x 6 inches	9	17	37

1958 Dodge Swept-Wing accessories booklet, 24 pages, 8-1/2 x 5-1/2 inches	8	15	32
1958 Mopar accessories and car care material catalog, 36 pages, 8-1/2 x 11 inches	6	12	25
1958 Pontiac accessories catalog, 14 pages, 14 x 5-1/4 inches	7	13	26
1958 Rambler accessories booklet, 12 pages, 6-3/4 x 7-3/4 inches	5	10	22
1960 Buick Turbine Drive engineer approved accessories booklet, 16-view fold-out, 7 x 4 inches	3	6	11
1960 Corvair Custom Features catalog, 12 pages, 9 x 6 inches	5	10	22
1960 Plymouth accessories booklet, 20 pages, 8-1/2 x 6 1/4 inches	5	10	22
1961 Buick Engineer Approved Accessories Catalogue, 22 pages, 8-1/2 x 11 inches	7	13	26
1961 Cadillac accessories booklet, 18-view fold-out, 8 x 5 inches	8	15	32
1961 Oldsmobile accessories booklet, 30 pages, 7 x 5 inches	8	15	32
1961 Rambler American accessories booklet, 6 pages, 8 x 6 inches	5	10	22
1962 Ford accessories brochure, 12-view fold-out, 7-1/2 x 11 inches	7	13	26
1963 Buick Accessories Catalog, 4 pages, 8-1/2 x 11 inches	7	13	26
1963 Dodge options & accessories booklet, 12-view fold-out, 8-1/4 x 5-1/4 inches	5	10	22
1963 Mercury Comet accessories booklet, 18-view fold-out, 9 x 4 inches	5	10	22
1963 Mopar accessories booklet, 20 pages, 8-1/2 x 11 inches (spiral bound vertical format)	5	10	22
1964 Cadillac accessories booklet, 8 pages, 8 x 5 inches	7	13	26
1964 Chevrolet Feature Accessories catalog, 28 pages, oval-shaped 11-3/4 x 6-1/4 inches	8	15	32
1964 Pontiac Wide-Track accessories catalog, 24 pages, 8-1/2 x 11 inches	7	13	26
1964 Studebaker accessories catalog, 20 pages, 8-1/2 x 5-1/4 inches	6	12	25

	Good	Very Good	Excellent
1966 American Motors approved accessories booklet, 34 pages, 8-1/4 x 5 inches	5	10	22
1966 Ford Total Performance accessories catalog, 30 pages, 8-1/2 x 11 inches	7	13	26
1967 Camaro Custom Feature Accessories catalog, 12 pages (vertical format), 10-1/2 x 6 inches	8	15	32
1967 Lincoln Continental accessories and optional equipment booklet, 28 pages, 4-3/4 x 8-3/4 inches	7	13	26
1968 American Motors optional equipment and accessories booklet, 24 pages, 7-1/2 x 5-3/4 inches	5	10	22
1970 Chevelle, Monte Carlo, and Nova Custom Feature Accessories catalog, 28 pages, 6 x 10-1/2 inches	8	15	32
1970 Ford Maverick accessories brochure, 2 pages, 11 x 9 inches	5	10	22
1970 Lincoln-Mercury accessories booklet, 28 pages, 11 x 9 inches	5	10	22
1971 Buick "Are You Sure You Didn't Forget Something?" accessories brochure, 12-view fold-out, 3-3/4 x 8-1/2 inches	4	8	18
1972 Chevrolet truck accessories brochure, 16 pages, 8-1/2 x 4-1/2 inches	5	10	22
1976 Pontiac accessories catalog, 24 pages, 8-1/2 x 11 inches	4	8	18

Automotive Technical Literature

Description	Good	Very Good	Excellent
1915 Ford reference book	12	20	30
1916 Ford reference book	12	20	30
1917 Ford reference book	12	20	30
1918 Ford reference book	12	20	30
1919 Ford reference book	12	20	30
1920 Ford reference book	10	16	25
1921 Ford reference book	10	16	25
1922 Ford reference book	10	16	25
1923 Ford reference book	10	16	25
1924 Ford reference book	10	16	25

1925 Ford reference book	10	16	25
1926 Ford reference book	10	16	25
1927 Ford reference book	10	16	25
1928 Ford reference book	26	43	65
1929 Ford reference book	26	43	65
1930 Ford reference book	26	43	65
1931 Ford reference book	27	45	70
1932 Ford reference book	16	26	40
1933 Ford reference book	16	26	40
1934 Ford reference book	16	26	40
1915 Chevrolet reference book	20	32	50
1916 Chevrolet reference book	20	32	50
1917 Chevrolet reference book	20	32	50
1918 Chevrolet reference book	20	32	50
1919 Chevrolet reference book	20	32	50
1920 Chevrolet reference book	18	30	45
1921 Chevrolet reference book	18	30	45
1922 Chevrolet reference book	18	30	45
1923 Chevrolet reference book	16	26	40
1924 Chevrolet reference book	16	26	40
1925 Chevrolet reference book	14	23	35
1926 Chevrolet reference book	14	23	35
1927 Chevrolet reference book	12	20	30
1928 Chevrolet reference book	12	20	30
1929 Chevrolet reference book	12	20	30
1930 Chevrolet reference book	12	20	30
1931 Chevrolet reference book	12	20	30
1932 Chevrolet reference book	14	23	35
1933 Chevrolet reference book	10	16	25
1934 Chevrolet reference book	10	16	25
1934-1941 Chilton's Repair Manuals	16	26	40
1934-1941 MoToR's Repair Manuals	16	26	40

Description	Good	Very Good	Excellent
1934-1941 Audel's Repair Manuals	14	23	35
1934-1941 Glenn's Repair Manuals	16	26	40
1916 Ford Times, single issue	5	10	15
1916-1928 Chevrolet Four-Cylinder Model Parts catalog	12	20	30
1929 Oakland, master parts catalog	18	30	45
1931-1933 Ditz-Lac paint color chart with color samples and mix formulas	4	6	10
1931 Ford News, (single issue and supplement)	15	25	35
1949 Oldsmobile Hydra-matic Drive history manual	16	27	40
1951 Kaiser-Frazer special service tool update, 4 pages, 8-1/2 x 11 inches	12	20	32
1951 Kaiser-Frazer shop manual with 1952-1953 supplement	18	30	47
1955-1960 Chevrolet heavy-duty truck parts catalog, for 2nd series and 2- and 2-1/2-ton trucks	15	25	37
1956 Ford Truck, shop manual	15	25	37
1958 Dodge, paint chart, spring colors	5	7	12
1959 Cadillac shop manual	15	25	37
1961 Oldsmobile color selection chart	5	10	22
Pontiac Service Craftsman News, June 1963	1	3	7
1963 Corvette, shop manual, ST-21	12	20	32
1963 Ford color selection chart	4	6	14
1964 Mercury, paint chart	3	5	10
1964 Corvair Valve Servicing booklet, 10 pages, 4 x 9 inches	5	10	22
1968 Corvette, shop manual Supplement ST-34, 100 pages	8	12	24

Automobile Owner's Manuals

Description	Good	Very Good	Excellent
1915 Hudson Super Six owner's manual, 32 pages, 6 x 8 inches	12	22	34
1936 Dodge owner's manual, "Maintaining Dodge Dependability"	14	23	35

Description	Good	Very Good	Excellent
1946 Buick owner's manual, 100 pages, 5-1/2 x 8-1/2 inches	10	20	32
1949 Dodge operation and maintenance manual, 36 pages, 9 x 6 inches	10	20	32
1949 Frazer instruction book with cover sleeve, 48 pages, 6 x 9 inches	12	24	38
1952 Chevrolet owner's manual, 32 pages, 5-1/4 x 8-1/4 inches	10	20	32
1953 Anglia (Ford of England) instruction book, 88 pages, 5-1/2 x 8-1/2 inches	8	10	14
1956 Chevrolet owner's manual, 228 pages, 7-3/4 x 4-3/4 inches	12	22	36
1966 Chevelle owner's manual, 8 x 6 inches	12	22	34
1968 Ford owner's manual, 56 pages, 8-1/2 x 4 inches	10	20	32
1978 Mercury Owner Maintenance and Light Repair manual	6	10	17

Truck Owner's/Operator's Manuals

Description	Good	Very Good	Excellent
1952 Dodge truck driver's manual, 56 pages, 5-1/2 x 8-1/2 inches	6	9	16
1953 Ford truck operator's manual, 64 pages, 4-1/2 x 6 inches	6	9	16
1969 Ford truck operator's manual, 500 through 1000 series, 96 pages, 8 x 5 inches	5	8	12
1974 GMC truck owner's and driver's manual, models 1500 through 3500, 84 pages, 8-1/4 x 5-1/4 inches	5	8	12

Automobile Sales Catalog Art

Description	Good	Very Good	Excellent
1909 Reo sales catalog, one- and two-cylinder cars, 24 pages, 8 x 9-3/4 inches	45	75	110
1913 Renault sales catalog, 54 pages, 9-3/4 x 12-1/2 inches	50	85	125
Circa 1925 Elcar sales catalog, 15 pages, 8 x 10 inches, fours and sixes	15	25	40

Description	Good	Very Good	Excellent
1938 Chrysler Imperial (Canadian) 22 pages, 8-1/2 x 11, plastic spiral binding	30	50	75
1912 Rolls-Royce sales catalog	60	100	150
1930 Willys-Knight sales catalog	20	30	45
1920 Cole sales catalog	33	55	85
1926 Packard "Attributes of Packard," eight-page specialty sales catalog, 8-1/2 x 11 inches, color art work	40	65	100
1926 Packard, "The Packard," auto company magazine	30	50	75
1926 Packard "Passenger Transportation," corporate magazine	30	50	75
Circa 1920s Dodge catalog, with pen-and-ink sketches (possibly by artist Norman Bel Geddes)	25	42	65
1928 Oldsmobile sales catalog, size approximately 7-3/4 x 11-1/2 inches	14	23	35
1929 Oldsmobile, "Details of Construction," sales catalog, approximately 24 pages, size 9-3/4 x 15-1/2 inches, covers F-29 and F-30 models	14	23	35
1930 Oldsmobile, "Details of Construction," sales catalog, approximately 24 pages, size 9-3/4 x 15-1/2 inches, covers F-29 and F-30 models	18	30	45
1919-1920 Cadillac, Open Cars, sales catalog with folio, size 7 x 11 inches sepia-and-ink sketches	80	130	200
1935 Studebaker, President, sales catalog, 16 pages, 10 x 12 inches	20	33	50
1917 Oakland Model 34, sales catalog	25	40	60
1929 Ford Model A, showroom poster, factory issued original	25	40	60
1929 Ford Model A, showroom poster, reproduction by Autographics	60	100	150
1935 Ford V-8 poster, shows the Ford V-8 engine, original	215	360	550
1935 Ford V-8 poster, shows the Ford V-8 engine, reproduction by Banner King	30	50	75

Automobile Poster Art

Description	Good	Very Good	Excellent
1934/1935 Fiat, "Balilla" poster	200	325	500

	Good	Very Good	Excellent
1935 Fiat, "Manifesto Fiat" poster for Fiat 1500 by C. Riccobaldi	155	260	400
1936 Fiat, "Dipinato Fiat 500" poster, by M. Sironi	175	290	450
Fiat 509, "Centaur" poster, 30 x 25 inches, color	175	290	450
1899 Fiat, "Victoria" poster, 30 x 25 inches	315	525	800
1930 Renault, "Renault 1930," poster. Reinastella model depicted	175	290	450
1925 Renault, "Aviation/Automobile" poster	200	325	500
1962 Chevrolet Golden Anniversary showroom poster, 32 x 18 inches	10	20	30

Automobile Trading Card Sets

Description	Good	Very Good	Excellent
Bilderdienst (German), automotive cigarette card set, circa 1930s	80	120	200
Bowman, antique automobile card set, 48 cards, 1953	230	300	400
Donruss, Odd Rods trading cards, 44 cards, 1969	80	120	200
Fleer, Kustom Cars I trading cards, 30 cards, 1974	30	50	75
Full-Speed, (Dutch) automotive cigarette cards, by Piet Olyslager, 1971	30	50	75
Goudey, auto license plate card set, 66 cards, 1938	75	150	250
John Player & Sons, (Great Britain) automotive cigarette card set with English and American cars, circa 1935	115	200	300
Lambert & Butler, Third Series, automotive cigarette card set, 1926	115	200	300
Milton Bradley, American Heritage card set, 40 cards, 1961	60	100	150
Mobil Oil Company, "Great Days of Motoring" trading cards, 1966	30	50	75
Signal Oil, antique automobile card set, 63 cards, 1953	115	200	300
Tip Top Bread, sports cars card set, 28 cards, circa 1950s	300	425	600
Topps, "Autos of 1977" trading cards, 99 cards, 1976	30	50	75

	Good	Very Good	Excellent
Topps, sports cars card set, 66 cards, 1961	115	200	300
Turkey Red, automotive cigarette card set, 50 cards, circa 1910	200	325	500

Automobile Photographs

Description	Good	Very Good	Excellent
1866 Dudgeon steam wagon, photograph	4	7	10
1901 Panhard, photo of car in New York to Buffalo Race, by J.A. Sietz, Syracuse, N.Y., framed, 8 x 10	4	7	10
1904-1906 and 1908-1912 Vanderbilt Cup race photos, by Spooner & Wells (each)	5	8	12
1951 publicity shot of young ladies fixing tire of 1946 Ford	2	4	8
1963 publicity shot of cast in 1933 Ford from "The Three Stooges Go Around the World in a Daze"	5	8	12

Automobile Factory Photographs

Description	Good	Very Good	Excellent
1902 Studebaker Electric, press kit with seven photos (9 x 12 inches for newspapers; 8 x 10 inches for period magazines)	40	65	100
(2) Model T Ford, factory publicity photos (original)	25	40	60
1925 Wills Sainte Claire factory photo (copied from Manning Brothers original negative)	4	6	10
1930 Marmon factory photo, Model 78 sedan, car with actress Lupe Velez	2	3	7
1932 Studebaker Commander Regal sedan photo with Laurel and Hardy at Hal Roach Studios	2	3	7
1932 Packard factory photo, phaeton with actress Jean Harlow	4	6	10
1937 Nash Ambassador, factory photo with car and baseball player Babe Ruth	4	6	10
1935-1941 Ford/Lincoln/Mercury photos by N.W. Ayer Advertising Agency (each photo)	235	390	600
1941 Pontiac factory photo, Torpedo sedan with adventurer Lowell Thomas	2	3	7

Description	Good	Very Good	Excellent
1942 Studebaker "Commander" 8 Deluxe Cruising Sedan retouched factory photo (car depicted is actually a Studebaker President model)	2	3	7
1948 Austin (English) factory photo	2	3	7
1948 Tucker photo (Preston Tucker with car by factory)	6	8	12
1949 Kaiser, factory photo, "camera car"	4	6	10
1952 Kaiser and Henry J, press kit with six 8 x 10-inch b&w photos, 8-1/2 x 11 inches	60	100	150
1959 Studebaker factory photo, Lark at Miami Beach hotel	2	3	7
1957 Chevrolet press packet with mislabeled 1956 Corvette photo	14	25	37
1957 Pontiac Bonneville, factory publicity photo	6	8	12
1963 Studebaker Avanti photo, with designer Raymond Loewy	6	8	12
1980 Chevrolet Corvette, factory photo, original print	4	6	10

Automotive Postcards

Description	Good	Very Good	Excellent
1923 Chevrolet, truck, postcard	6	10	15
1923 Chevrolet, car, postcard	4	6	10
1927 Chevrolet, car, postcard	4	6	10
1928 Chevrolet, car, postcard	4	6	10
1933 Chevrolet, car, postcard, full-color	4	6	10
1937 Chevrolet, cars, postcards, set of 12, full-color	60	100	150
1940 Chevrolet, postcard	3	5	7
1941 Chevrolet, postcard	3	5	7
1942 Chevrolet, postcard	3	5	7
1946 Chevrolet postcard, Dealers Supply Company, brown-toned	3	5	8
1952 Hudson Hornet four-door sedan, postcard	2	3	5
1952 Chevrolet, postcard	3	5	7
1954 Chevrolet, postcard	3	5	7
1955 Chevrolet, postcard	4	6	10

1956 Chevrolet, postcard	4	6	10
1957 Chevrolet, postcard	4	6	10
1958 Chevrolet postcard, Dealers Supply Company, brown-toned	2	3	5
1958 Pontiac Bonneville Sport Coupe postcard	2	5	8
1958 Chevrolet, postcard	4	6	10
1959 Chevrolet, postcard	4	6	10
1960 Chevrolet, postcard	3	5	7
1960 Ford Starliner postcard	3	5	7
1961 Chevrolet, postcard	2	3	5
1962 Chevrolet, postcard	2	3	5
1963 Chevrolet, postcard	2	3	5
1963 Rambler American 440-H, postcard	2	3	5
1964 Chevrolet, postcard	2	3	5
1965 Chevrolet, postcard	2	3	5
1966 Chevrolet, postcard	2	3	5
1967 Chevrolet, postcard	2	3	5
1967 Chevrolet Camaro, Indianapolis 500 Pace Car, postcard	4	6	10
1967 Chevrolet Camaro, Indianapolis 500 Pace Car, postcard, large	5	8	12
1968 Chevrolet, postcard	2	3	5
1969 Chevrolet, postcard	2	3	5
1970 Chevrolet, postcard	2	3	5
1971 Chevrolet, postcard	2	3	5
1972 Chevrolet, postcard	.50	1	2
1973 Chevrolet, postcard	.50	1	2
1974 Chevrolet, postcard	.50	1	2
1975 Chevrolet, postcard	.50	1	2
1976 Chevrolet, postcard	.50	1	2
1977 Chevrolet, postcard	.50	1	2
1978 Chevrolet, postcard	.50	1	2
1979 Chevrolet, postcard	.50	1	2

1980 Chevrolet, postcard	.50	1	2
1981 Chevrolet, postcard	.30	.50	1
1982 Chevrolet, postcard	.30	.50	1
1983 Chevrolet, postcard	.30	.50	1
1984 Chevrolet, postcard	.30	.50	1
1985 Chevrolet, postcard	.30	.50	1
1986 Chevrolet, postcard	.30	.50	1
1987 Chevrolet postcard	.30	.50	1
1988 Chevrolet, postcard	.30	.50	1
1989 Chevrolet, postcard	.30	.50	1
1990 Chevrolet, postcard	.30	.50	1
1991 Chevrolet, postcard	.30	.50	1
1992 Chevrolet, postcard	.30	.50	1
1993 Chevrolet, postcard	.30	.50	1
1994 Chevrolet, postcard	.30	.50	1
1954 Chevrolet, Corvette, postcard, red-toned	10	16	25
1954 Chevrolet, Corvette, postcard, green-toned	10	16	25
1958 Chevrolet, Corvette, postcard	10	16	25
1959 Chevrolet, Corvette, postcard	10	16	25
1960 Chevrolet, Corvette, postcard	10	16	25
1961 Chevrolet, Corvette, postcard	10	16	25
1962 Chevrolet, Corvette, postcard	10	16	25
1963 Chevrolet, Corvette, postcard	10	16	25
1964 Chevrolet, Corvette, postcard	10	16	25
1965 Chevrolet, Corvette, postcard	10	16	25
1966 Chevrolet, Corvette, postcard	10	16	25
1968 Chevrolet, Corvette, postcard	4	6	10
1969 Chevrolet, Corvette, postcard	4	6	10
1970 Chevrolet, Corvette, postcard	4	6	10
1971 Chevrolet, Corvette, postcard	4	6	10
1972 Chevrolet, Corvette, postcard	3	4	7
1973 Chevrolet, Corvette, postcard	3	4	7

1974 Chevrolet, Corvette, postcard	3	4	7
1975 Chevrolet, Corvette, postcard	3	4	7
1976 Chevrolet, Corvette, postcard	2	3	5
1977 Chevrolet, Corvette, postcard	2	3	5
1978 Chevrolet, Corvette, postcard	2	3	5
1978 Chevrolet Corvette, Indianapolis 500 Pace Car, postcard (issued by West Coast collector, not by Chevrolet)	1	2	3
1979 Chevrolet, Corvette, postcard	2	3	5
1980 Chevrolet, Corvette, postcard	2	3	5
1981 Chevrolet, Corvette, postcard	2	3	5
1982 Chevrolet, Corvette, postcard	2	3	5
1984 Chevrolet, Corvette, postcard	2	3	5

(**NOTE**: The 1970 and 1971 Corvette postcards are the same. Two-card sets showing the coupe and the convertible were issued in 1963 and 1964)

Chevrolet, dealership, postcard, Florida dealer, Roger Dean Chevrolet	4	6	10
Chevrolet, dealer postcard, Kansas City, Missouri dealer, Lane-Goddard Chevrolet	4	6	10
1954 Chevrolet dealer postcard, Baltimore, Maryland dealer, Park Circle Chevrolet, (shows 150 model)	9	15	22
1957 Chevrolet dealer postcard, Wheaton, Maryland dealer, Tom's Chevrolet (shows Bel Airs)	12	19	30

Car Christmas Cards

Description	Good	Very Good	Excellent
1927 Ford, Model A, "Merry Christmas" greeting card (shows 1928 Ford)	5	8	12
1939 Chevrolet greeting card, "Happy and Prosperous New Year," (shows 1940 Chevrolet Special Deluxe Sport Coupe)	6	10	15
1955 Ford, Christmas card and phonograph record (1956 Ford Victoria hardtop depicted)	6	10	15

Automotive "Comparison" Advertisements

Description	Good	Very Good	Excellent
1969 Lincoln Continental, advertisement, (promotes Wisconsin dealers), shows a 1931 SEP Lincoln advertisement)	1	2	5
1970 Ford Pinto, advertisement, "Put a Pinto in your portfolio"	1	2	5
1975 Cadillac, advertisement, (shows a 1930 Cadillac Series 452-A Roadster)	1	2	5
1975 Cadillac, advertisement, (shows a 1931 Cadillac Phaeton)	1	2	5
1975 Cadillac, advertisement, (shows a 1933 Cadillac Model 355 dual-cowl Phaeton)	1	2	5
1975 Cadillac, advertisement, (shows a 1932 Cadillac Model 355 Convertible)	1	2	5
1976 Buick Regal, advertisement, (shows a 1953 Buick Roadmaster)	1	2	5
1977 Buick Riviera, advertisement, (shows a 1963 Buick Riviera)	1	2	5

(**NOTE**: The following advertisements all feature cars of two or more eras in the same advertisement)

Description	Good	Very Good	Excellent
1929 Pierce-Arrow advertisement, from 2/29 issue of *House Beautiful* "Reproduced from a painting by Adolph Treidler," (shows older advertising art of 1912 model)	4	6	10
1929 Pierce-Arrow advertisement, from 2/29 issue of *Country Life* "Twenty years ago," (shows older advertising art of 1919 model)	4	6	10
1930 Pierce-Arrow advertisement, from 3/30 issue of *Fortune*, "The Tyranny of Tradition," (shows the advertising artwork for 1919 car)	4	6	10
1931 Pierce-Arrow advertisement, (with Adolphus Busch)	4	6	10
1931 Pierce-Arrow advertisement, from the 4/31 issue of *Sportsman* magazine (with Stephen Baker)	4	6	10
1931 Pierce-Arrow advertisement, from 4/31 issue of *House Beautiful* (with New York Governor Horace White)	4	6	10
1932 Pierce-Arrow advertisement, (shows 12-cylinder Club Sedan with reproduction of 1908 ad artwork)	4	6	10

1933 Packard advertisement, from 5/33 issue of *Fortune*, "Buy your car in '33 the way they did in 1903," (has Albert Dorne drawing of 1903 Packard showroom)	4	6	10
1934 Packard advertisement, from 5/34 issue of *Fortune* "Maybe you were that boy"	4	6	10
1937 Packard, advertisement, from 2/13/37 issue of *Saturday Evening Post*	4	6	10
1946 Packard advertisement, from 11/14/46 issue of *Saturday Evening Post*, Clipper Deluxe four-door sedan (shows 1902, 1923 and 1946 Packards)	2	3	7
1953 Nash Ambassador, advertisement, from 8/1/53 issue of *Saturday Evening Post*, "To the boy who wanted a Stutz Bearcat."	2	3	7
1973 Chrysler advertisement, from 10/1/72 issue of *Fortune*, (showing a 1924 Chrysler sedan)	1	2	5
1973 Chrysler advertisement, from 2/73 issue of *Smithsonian*, (showing a 1941 Chrysler Town & Country "barrelback")	1	2	5
1973 Chrysler advertisement, from 4/73 issue of *Fortune*, (showing a 1946 Chrysler Town & Country Convertible)	1	2	5
1973 Chrysler advertisement, from 3/5/73 issue of *Sports Illustrated*, (showing a 1946 Chrysler Town & Country Convertible)	1	2	5
1975 Corvette advertisement, from 11/14/74 issue of *Sports Illustrated*	1	2	5
1975 Cadillac advertisement, from 12/74 issue of *Fortune*	1	2	5
1975 Cadillac advertisement, from 1/20/75 issue of *Newsweek*	1	2	5
1975 Buick advertisement, from 1/1/75 issue of *Psychology Today*	1	2	5
1976 Buick advertisement, from 10/27/75 issue of *Newsweek*	1	2	5
1976 Buick advertisement, from 10/1/76 issue of *Classic* magazine	1	2	5
1977 Buick advertisement, from 10/76 issue of *Esquire*	1	2	5

(**NOTE:** Pierce-Arrow advertisements showing cars from two different eras also appeared in the following issues of leading magazines: 2/2/29 *Literary Digest*; 3/29 *House Beautiful*; 3/16/29 *Literary Digest*; 4/13/29 *Literary Digest*; 5/11/29 *Literary Digest*; 6/8/29 *Literary Digest*; 8/31/29 *Literary Digest*; 9/14/29 *Literary Digest*; 10/19/29 *Literary Digest*; 11/2/29 *Literary Digest*; 11/29 *House Beautiful*; 3/30 *House Beautiful*; 4/30 *House & Garden*; 5/3/30 *Literary Digest*; 6/7/30 *Literary Digest*; 9/30 *Sportsman*; 9/30 *House Beautiful*; 9/6/30 *Literary Digest*; 10/30 *House Beautiful*; 10/11/30 *Literary Digest*).

Automotive Advertisements, Full-Line

Description	Good	Very Good	Excellent
1928 Chevrolet, full-line advertisement	4	6	10
1931 Chevrolet, full-line advertisement	4	6	10
1932 Chevrolet, full-line advertisement	6	10	15
1934 Chevrolet, full-line advertisement	4	6	10
1935 Chevrolet, full-line advertisement	4	6	10
1936 Chevrolet, full-line advertisement	3	5	8
1939 Chevrolet, full-line advertisement	3	5	8
1940 Chevrolet, full-line advertisement	3	5	8
1949 Chevrolet, full-line advertisement	2	3	5
1952 Chevrolet, full-line advertisement	2	3	5
1954 Chevrolet, full-line advertisement	2	3	5
1955 Chevrolet, full-line advertisement	4	6	10
1955 Chevrolet, full-line (station wagons only) ad	3	5	8
1956 Chevrolet, full-line advertisement	4	6	10
1956 Chevrolet, full-line (station wagons only) ad	3	5	8
1957 Chevrolet, full-line advertisement	4	6	10
1957 Chevrolet, full-line (station wagons only) ad	3	5	8
1958 Chevrolet, full-line advertisement	3	5	8
1938 Pontiac, full-line advertisement	3	5	8
1939 Pontiac, full-line advertisement	3	5	8
1940 Pontiac, full-line advertisement	3	5	8
1941 Pontiac, full-line advertisement	3	5	8
1942 Pontiac, full-line advertisement	3	5	8
1948 Pontiac, full-line advertisement	2	3	5
1946 Buick, full-line advertisement	2	3	5
1947 Buick, full-line advertisement	2	3	5
1948 Buick, full-line advertisement	2	3	5
1942 Plymouth full-line advertisement	2	3	5
1953 Plymouth full-line advertisement	2	3	5
1955 Ford full-line (cars) advertisement	2	3	5

Description	Good	Very Good	Excellent
1956 Ford, full-line (station wagons only) ad	2	3	5
1955 Mercury, full-line advertisement	2	3	5
1957 Mercury, full-line advertisement	2	3	5
1949 Oldsmobile, full-line advertisement, "Here they come, the new Futurmatics"	2	3	5

Automotive Advertisements, General

Description	Good	Very Good	Excellent
1934 Plymouth advertisement, (*Cosmopolitan*)	2	4	8
1934 Plymouth advertisement, "New Series," Walter P. Chrysler posed near car	3	6	9
1936 Lincoln-Zephyr, small format advertisement, from 2/36 issue of *Fortune*	3	5	8
1936 Lincoln-Zephyr, small format advertisement, from 3/21/36 *Saturday Evening Post*	3	5	8
1936 Lincoln-Zephyr, small format advertisement, from 4/36 issue of *Fortune*	3	5	8
1936 Lincoln-Zephyr, small format advertisement, from 7/36 issue of *Fortune*	3	5	8
1937 Lincoln-Zephyr, small format advertisement, from 10/12/36 issue of *Time*	3	5	8
1937 Lincoln-Zephyr, small format advertisement, from 11/36 issue of *Fortune*	3	5	8
1937 Lincoln-Zephyr, small format advertisement, from the 12/36 issue of *National Geographic*	3	5	8
1937 Lincoln-Zephyr, small format advertisement, from 12/36 issue of *Fortune*	3	5	8
1937 Lincoln-Zephyr, small format advertisement, from the 2/37 issue of *National Geographic*	3	5	8
1937 Lincoln-Zephyr, small format advertisement, from the 3/37 issue of *National Geographic*	3	5	8
1937 Lincoln-Zephyr, small format advertisement, from 4/37 issue of *Esquire*	3	5	8
1937 Lincoln-Zephyr, small format advertisement, from 7/3/37 issue of *The Saturday Evening Post*	3	5	8
1937 Lincoln-Zephyr, small format advertisement, from the 8/37 issue of *National Geographic*	3	5	8
1938 Lincoln-Zephyr, small format advertisement, from the 11/20/37 issue of *The Saturday Evening Post*	3	5	8

1938 Lincoln-Zephyr, small format advertisement, from 12/18/37 issue of *Collier's*	3	5	8
1938 Lincoln-Zephyr, small format advertisement, from the 1/38 issue of *National Geographic*	3	5	8
1938 Lincoln-Zephyr, small format advertisement, from the 3/38 issue of *National Geographic*	3	5	8
1938 Lincoln-Zephyr, small format advertisement, from 3/38 issue of *Esquire*	3	5	8
1938 Lincoln-Zephyr, small format advertisement, from 3/4/38 issue of *The Saturday Evening Post*	3	5	8
1938 Lincoln-Zephyr, small format advertisement, from the 5/38 issue of *National Geographic*	3	5	8
1939 Lincoln-Zephyr, small format advertisement, from 12/10/38 issue of *The Saturday Evening Post*	3	5	8
1939 Lincoln-Zephyr, small format advertisement, from 2/39 *National Geographic*	3	5	8
1939 Lincoln-Zephyr, small format advertisement, from 2/18/39 *The Saturday Evening Post*	3	5	8
1939 Lincoln-Zephyr, small format advertisement, from 3/39 *Fortune*	3	5	8
1939 Lincoln-Zephyr, small format advertisement, from 3/4/39 issue of *The Saturday Evening Post*	3	5	8
1939 Lincoln-Zephyr, small format advertisement, from 4/1/39 issue of *The Saturday Evening Post*	3	5	8
1939 Lincoln-Zephyr, small format advertisement, from 5/39 issue of *Fortune*	3	5	8
1939 Lincoln-Zephyr, small format advertisement, from 6/12/39 issue of *Time*	3	5	8
1939 Lincoln-Zephyr, small format advertisement, from 7/15/39 issue of *The Saturday Evening Post*	3	5	8
1939 Lincoln-Zephyr, small format advertisement, from 7/15/39 issue of *Time*	3	5	8
1939 Lincoln-Zephyr, small format advertisement, from 8/12/39 issue of *The Saturday Evening Post*	3	5	8
1940 Lincoln-Zephyr, small format advertisement, from 10/14/39 issue of *The Saturday Evening Post*	3	5	8
1940 Lincoln-Zephyr, small format advertisement, from 11/27/39 issue of *Time*	3	5	8
1940 Lincoln-Zephyr, small format advertisement, from 3/4/40 issue of *Time*	3	5	8
1940 Lincoln-Zephyr, small format advertisement, from 3/30/40 issue of *The Saturday Evening Post*	3	5	8

1940 Lincoln-Zephyr, small format advertisement, from 4/27/40 issue of *The Saturday Evening Post*	3	5	8
1940 Lincoln-Zephyr, small format advertisement, from 6/10/40 issue of *Time*	3	5	8
1941 Lincoln-Zephyr, small format advertisement, from 9/28/40 issue of *The Saturday Evening Post*	3	5	8
1941 Lincoln-Zephyr, small format advertisement, from 10/12/40 issue of *New Yorker*	3	5	8
1941 Lincoln-Zephyr, small format advertisement, from 10/12/40 issue of *The Saturday Evening Post*	3	5	8
1941 Lincoln-Zephyr, small format advertisement, from the 11/40 issue of *National Geographic*	3	5	8
1941 Lincoln-Zephyr, small format advertisement, from 11/11/40 issue of *Life*	3	5	8
1941 Lincoln-Zephyr, small format advertisement, from 12/2/40 issue of *Life*	3	5	8
1941 Lincoln-Zephyr, small format advertisement, from 12/2/40 issue of *Time*	3	5	8
1941 Lincoln-Zephyr, small format advertisement, from 12/40 issue of *Fortune*	3	5	8
1941 Lincoln-Zephyr, small format advertisement, from 12/14/40 issue of *The Saturday Evening Post*	3	5	8
1941 Lincoln-Zephyr, small format advertisement, from 12/16/40 issue of *Life*	3	5	8
1941 Lincoln-Zephyr, small format advertisement, from the 1/41 issue of *National Geographic*	3	5	8
1941 Lincoln-Zephyr, small format advertisement, from 1/13/41 issue of *Life*	3	5	8
1941 Lincoln-Zephyr, small format advertisement, from 2/3/41 issue of *Life*	3	5	8
1941 Lincoln-Zephyr, small format advertisement, from 2/22/41 issue of *The Saturday Evening Post*	3	5	8
1941 Lincoln-Zephyr, small format advertisement, from 2/24/41 issue of *Life*	3	5	8
1941 Lincoln-Zephyr, small format advertisement, from the 3/41 issue of *National Geographic*	3	5	8
1941 Lincoln-Zephyr, small format advertisement, from the 3/8/41 issue of *The Saturday Evening Post*	3	5	8
1941 Lincoln-Zephyr, small format advertisement, from 3/17/41 issue of *Life*	3	5	8
1941 Lincoln-Zephyr, small format advertisement, from 3/22/41 issue of *The Saturday Evening Post*	3	5	8

1941 Lincoln-Zephyr, small format advertisement, from 4/7/41 issue of *Life*	3	5	8
1941 Lincoln-Zephyr, small format advertisement, from 4/28/41 issue of *Life*	3	5	8
1941 Lincoln-Zephyr, small format advertisement, from the 5/41 issue of *National Geographic*	3	5	8
1941 Lincoln-Zephyr, small format advertisement, from 5/5/41 issue of *Life*	3	5	8
1941 Lincoln-Zephyr, small format advertisement, from 5/17/41 issue of *The Saturday Evening Post*	3	5	8
1941 Lincoln-Zephyr, small format advertisement, from 5/19/41 issue of *Life*	3	5	8
1941 Lincoln-Zephyr, small format advertisement, from 6/16/41 issue of *Life*	3	5	8
1942 Lincoln-Zephyr, small format advertisement, from 9/29/41 *Life*	3	5	8
1942 Lincoln-Zephyr, small format advertisement, from 10/20/41 issue of *Life*	3	5	8
1942 Lincoln-Zephyr, small format advertisement, from 10/25/41 issue of *The Saturday Evening Post*	3	5	8
1942 Lincoln-Zephyr, small format advertisement, from 11/10/41 issue of *Life*	3	5	8
1942 Lincoln-Zephyr, small format advertisement, from 11/15/41 issue of *The Saturday Evening Post*	3	5	8
1942 Lincoln-Zephyr, small format advertisement, from the 1/42 issue of *National Geographic*	3	5	8
1958 Edsel, advertisement, from 7/22/57 issue of *Life*	1	2	3
1958 Edsel, advertisement, from 8/5/57 issue of *Life*	1	2	3
1958 Edsel, advertisement, from 8/19/57 issue of *Life*	1	2	3
1958 Edsel, advertisement, from 9/2/57 issue of *Life*	1	2	3
1958 Edsel, advertisement, from 9/9/57 issue of *Life*	1	2	3
1958 Edsel, advertisement, from 9/14/57 issue of *The Saturday Evening Post*	1	2	3
1958 Edsel, advertisement, from 9/30/57 issue of *Life*	1	2	3
1958 Edsel, advertisement, from 10/5/57 issue of *The Saturday Evening Post*	1	2	3

1958 Edsel, advertisement, from the 10/14/57 issue of *Life*	1	2	3
1958 Edsel, advertisement, from 10/19/57 issue of *The Saturday Evening Post*	1	2	3
1958 Edsel, advertisement, from 10/28/57 issue of *Life*	1	2	3
1958 Edsel, advertisement, from 11/2/57 issue of *The Saturday Evening Post*	1	2	3
1958 Edsel, advertisement, from 11/11/57 issue of *Life*	1	2	3
1958 Edsel, advertisement, from 11/16/57 of *The Saturday Evening Post*	1	2	3
1958 Edsel, advertisement, from 11/25/57 issue of *Life*	1	2	3
1958 Edsel, advertisement, from 11/30/57 issue of *The Saturday Evening Post*	1	2	3
1958 Edsel, advertisement, from 4/14/58 issue of *Life*	1	2	3
1958 Edsel, advertisement, from 6/16/58 issue of *Life*	1	2	3
1959 Edsel, advertisement, from 11/29/58 issue of *The Saturday Evening Post*	1	2	3
1959 Edsel, advertisement, from 12/22/58 issue of *Life*	1	2	3
1959 Edsel, advertisement, from 1/19/59 issue of *Life*	1	2	3
1959 Edsel, advertisement, from 4/1/59 issue of *Holiday*	1	2	3

(**NOTE**: Edsels in other advertisements of other companies)

1957 Edsel, advertisement, from 10/12/57 issue of *The Saturday Evening Post* (Champion Spark Plug Company ad)	1	2	3
1957 Edsel, advertisement, from 12/7/57 issue of *The Saturday Evening Post* (Gulf Oil Company ad)	1	2	3
1958 Edsel, advertisement, from 2/10/58 issue of *Life* (ad of Simonize Wax)	1	2	3
1953 Cadillac, Eldorado, advertisement from 2/24/53 issue of *Look* (AC Spark Plug Company ad)	1	2	3
1953 Cadillac, Eldorado, advertisement from 8/29/53 issue of *The Saturday Evening Post* (AC Spark Plug Company ad)	2	3	5

1953 Cadillac, Eldorado, advertisement from 9/7/53 issue of *Life* (AC Spark Plug Company ad)	1	2	3
1954 Cadillac, Eldorado, advertisement from 8/23/54 issue of *Life*	2	3	5
1955 Cadillac, Eldorado, advertisement from 3/55 issue of *Holiday*	2	3	5
1955 Cadillac, Eldorado, advertisement from 4/55 issue of *Fortune*	2	3	5
1955 Cadillac, Eldorado, advertisement from 5/55 issue of *Holiday*	2	3	5
1955 Cadillac, Eldorado, advertisement from 6/55 issue of *Fortune*	2	3	5
1955 Cadillac, Eldorado, advertisement from 7/55 issue of *Holiday*	2	3	5
1955 Cadillac, Eldorado, advertisement from 8/55 issue of *Fortune*	2	3	5
1956 Cadillac, Eldorado, advertisement from 3/56 issue of *Fortune*	2	3	5
1956 Cadillac, Eldorado, advertisement from 3/56 issue of *Holiday*	2	3	5
1957 Cadillac, Eldorado, advertisement from 11/12/56 issue of *Life*	2	3	5
1958 Cadillac, Eldorado, advertisement from 12/16/57 issue of *Life*	2	3	5
1958 Cadillac, Eldorado, advertisement from 3/58 issue of *Fortune*	2	3	5
1959 Cadillac, Eldorado, advertisement from 10/11/58 issue of *The Saturday Evening Post*	2	3	5
1960 Cadillac, Eldorado, advertisement from 2/60 issue of *Holiday*	1	2	3
1963 Cadillac, Eldorado, advertisement from 3/22/63 issue of *Life*	1	2	3
1963 Cadillac, Eldorado, advertisement from 4/63 issue of *Holiday*	1	2	3
1967 Cadillac, Eldorado, advertisement from 11/66 issue of *Holiday*	1	2	3

(**NOTE**: A beginner's collection of early color auto advertisements.)

1925 Cadillac, advertisement from 3/25 issues of *Harper's*, *Review Of Reviews* and *Century*	3	5	8
1925 Cadillac, advertisement from 4/25 issues of *Harper's*, *Review Of Reviews*, *Atlantic*	3	5	8

1925 Cadillac, advertisement from 4/25 and 5/25 issues of *Harper's*, *Review Of Reviews*	3	5	8
1925 Cadillac, advertisement from 4/25 and 11/25 issues of *Harper's*	3	5	8
1933 Cadillac, advertisement from 4/33 and 2/33 issues of *National Geographic*	3	4	7
1933 Cadillac, advertisement from 3/33 issue of *National Geographic*	3	4	7
1933 Cadillac, advertisement from 4/33 issue of *National Geographic*	3	4	7
1933 Cadillac, advertisement from 5/33 issue of *National Geographic*	3	4	7

(**NOTE**: These are the first color car advertisements to appear in *National Geographic*. Buick followed shortly thereafter, as did Dodge.)

1920 Chalmers, advertisement, from the 6/20 issue of *Century*	2	3	5
1925 Diana, advertisement, from the 9/25 issue of *Harper's*	2	3	5
1925 Diana, advertisement, from the 10/25 issue of *Century*	2	3	5
1925 Diana, advertisement, from the 11/25 issue of *Harper's*	2	3	5
1918 Franklin, advertisement	2	3	5
1919 Franklin, advertisement	2	3	5
1920 Franklin, advertisement	2	3	5

(**NOTE**: Franklin color advertisements appeared in various magazines).

1922 Haynes, advertisement from 12/22 issue of *Schribners*	2	3	5
1923 Haynes, advertisement, from 3/23 issue of *Century*	2	3	5
1924 Haynes, advertisement, from 3/24 issue of *Harper's*	2	3	5
1924 Haynes, advertisement, from 4/24 issue of *Harper's*	2	3	5
1918 Jordan, advertisement, from the 2/18 issue of *The World's Work*	3	4	7
1920 Jordan, advertisement, from 4/20 issue of *Century*	3	4	7
1920 Jordan, advertisement, from 6/20 issue of *Century*	3	4	7

1924 Lincoln, advertisement, from 1/24 issue of *Harper's*	2	3	5
1924 Lincoln, advertisement, from 3/24 issue of *Harper's*	2	3	5
1924 Lincoln, advertisement, from 5/24 issue of *Harper's*	2	3	5
1924 Lincoln, advertisement, from 7/24 issue of *Harper's*	2	3	5
1924 Lincoln, advertisement, from 9/24 issue of *Harper's*	2	3	5
1924 Lincoln, advertisement, from 10/24 issue of *Harper's*	2	3	5
1924 Lincoln, advertisement, from 11/24 issue of *Harper's*	2	3	5
1924 Lincoln, advertisement, from 12/24 issue of *Harper's*	2	3	5
1926 Lincoln, advertisement, from 1/26 issue of *Harper's*	2	3	5
1926 Lincoln, advertisement, from 2/26 issue of *Harper's*	2	3	5
1926 Lincoln, advertisement, from 3/26 issue of *Harper's*	2	3	5
1926 Lincoln, advertisement, from 4/26 issue of *Harper's*	2	3	5
1926 Lincoln, advertisement, from 5/26 issue of *Harper's*	2	3	5
1926 Lincoln, advertisement, from 6/26 issue of *Harper's*	2	3	5
1926 Lincoln, advertisement, from 7/26 issue of *Harper's*	2	3	5
1926 Lincoln, advertisement, from 8/26 issue of *Harper's*	2	3	5
1926 Lincoln, advertisement, from 12/26 issue of *Harper's*	2	3	5
1922 Maxwell, advertisement, from 11/22 issue of *Review Of Reviews*	2	3	4
1922 Maxwell, advertisement, from 12/22 issue of *Review Of Reviews*	2	3	4
1925 Moon, advertisement, from 6/25 issue of *Review Of Reviews*	2	3	4
1925 Moon, advertisement, from 4/25 issue of *Harper's*	2	3	4

1925 Moon, advertisement, from 5/25 issue of *Review Of Reviews*	2	3	4
1925 Moon, advertisement, from 7/25 issue of *Atlantic*	2	3	4
1925 Moon, advertisement, from 7/25 issue of *Review Of Reviews*	2	3	4
1925 Moon, advertisement, from 8/1/25 issue of *Harper's*	2	3	4
1911 Oldsmobile, advertisement, from 6/17/11 issue of *The Outlook*	3	4	7
1911 Pierce-Arrow, advertisement, from 9/11 issue of *Everybody's Magazine*	3	4	7
1913 Pierce-Arrow, advertisement, from 10/13 issue of *Century*	4	6	10
1914 Pierce-Arrow, advertisement, from 1/14 issue of *Century*	4	6	10
1915 Pierce-Arrow, advertisement, from 7/14/15 issue of *The Outlook*	4	6	10
1915 Pierce-Arrow, advertisement, from 10/20/15 issue of *The Outlook*	4	6	10
1915 Pierce-Arrow, advertisement, from 1/15 issue of *Century*	4	6	10
1921 Pierce-Arrow, advertisement, from 11/21 issue of *Century*	3	4	7
1927 Pierce-Arrow, advertisement, from 10/27 issue of *Atlantic*	3	4	7
1919 Rauch & Lang Electric, advertisement, from 3/19 issue of *Review Of Reviews*	3	4	7
1920 Standard, advertisement, from 2/20 issue of *Century*	2	3	5
1921 Standard, advertisement, from 2/21 issue of *Harper's*	2	3	5
1921 Standard, advertisement, from 11/21 issue of *Century*	2	3	5
1919 Studebaker, advertisement, from 6/19 issue of *Review Of Reviews*	2	3	5
1913 Stevens-Duryea, advertisement, from 11/13 issue of *Harper's*	1	2	3
1910 Woods Electric, advertisement from 6/18/10 issue of *The Outlook*	2	3	5

Car Magazines

Description	Good	Very Good	Excellent
American Automobile Digest magazine, July 1921	15	30	55
Auto Age magazine, April 1956 (with preview of GM Motorama	10	20	45
Automobile Dealer and Repairer magazine, October 1912	15	30	55
Automobile Topics magazine, April 26, 1924	12	25	50
Car Craft magazine, September 1958	4	8	11
Car Life magazine, August 1956	8	18	40
Cycle and Automobile Trade Journal magazine, March 1, 1905	15	30	55
Goodyear News magazine, April 1961	2	5	8
Hot Rod magazine, April 1951 (size increased 16 pages)	20	35	65
Motor magazine, September 1937	12	25	50
Motor Age magazine, May 5, 1927	15	30	55
Motor Age magazine, July 1940	2	5	8
Motor Trend magazine, September 1949 (Vol. 1, No. 1)	35	75	125
Motor World magazine, May 2, 1923	15	30	55
Popular Hot Rodding magazine, January 1964	4	8	11
Popular Mechanics magazine, January 1952 (50th Anniversary issue w/ 500 pages)	8	18	40
Popular Mechanics magazine, February 1954 (w/ 344 pages including Special 1954 Auto Section)	4	8	11
Rod & Custom magazine, May 1953 (Vol. 1, No. 1)	10	20	45
Speed Mechanics magazine, November 1964	3	7	10
Sports Cars Illustrated magazine, January 1958	4	8	11

Truck Magazines

Description	Good	Very Good	Excellent
Cummins *the dependable diesel,* Vol. 10, No. 1	2	5	8
Fleet Owner magazine, July 1955	3	7	10

	Good	Very Good	Excellent
Fleet Owner magazine, September 1955	3	7	10
Overdrive magazine, June 1972	1	2	4
Overdrive magazine, November 1973	1	2	4

Auto Racing Magazines

Description	Good	Very Good	Excellent
Auto Speed and Sport magazine, January 1952 (Vol. 1, No. 1)	15	20	25
Auto Speed and Sport magazine, all other issues	7	12	15
Motorsport magazine, October 1950 (Vol. 1, No. 1)	15	20	25
Motorsport magazine, all other issues	7	12	15
Motorsport magazine, all annuals	10	15	20
on the Grid magazine, June 1960 (Vol. 1, No. 1)	15	20	25
on the Grid magazine, all other issues	7	12	15
Speed Age magazine, May 1947 (Vol. 1, No. 1)	25	60	100
Speed Age magazine, all other issues from 1940s	15	25	35
Speed Age magazine, all issues from 1950s (black-and-white cover)	6	11	14
Speed Age magazine, all issues from 1950s (color covers)	7	12	15
Speed Age magazine, all annuals	15	20	25
Stock Car Racing magazine, May 1966 (Vol. 1, No. 1)	20	35	50
Stock Car Racing magazine, all other issues from 1960s	5	7	10
Stock Car Racing magazine, all issues from 1970s to present	3	5	8
Auto Sport Review magazine, April 1952	5	9	13
Motorsport magazine, August/September 1956	4	8	12
Racing Pictorial magazine, 1959-1969 Annuals	15	30	40
Racing Pictorial magazine, 1970s and later	8	20	30
Today's Motor Sports magazine, September 1961	5	9	13
USAS Autosports magazine, March/April 1964	5	9	13

Auto Racing Programs

Description	Good	Very Good	Excellent
Alcyon Speedway (Pitman, New Jersey) Stock Car Races program, 1958	8	22	30
Daytona 500 Official Program, Daytona International Speedway, 1959 (first event)	100	150	250
Daytona 500 Official Program, Daytona International Speedway, 1964	125	175	275
Daytona 500 Official Program, Daytona International Speedway, 1969	8	22	30
Daytona 500 Official Program, Daytona International Speedway, 1974	20	35	45
Indianapolis 500 Official Program, Indianapolis Motor Speedway, 1911 (first event)	850	1300	1500
Indianapolis 500 Official Program, Indianapolis Motor Speedway, 1920	525	625	800
Indianapolis 500 Official Program, Indianapolis Motor Speedway, 1930	225	325	500
Indianapolis 500 Official Program, Indianapolis Motor Speedway, 1941 (last prewar race)	50	75	150
Indianapolis 500 Official Program, Indianapolis Motor Speedway, 1950	30	45	60
Indianapolis 500 Official Program, Indianapolis Motor Speedway, 1960	15	30	40
Indianapolis 500 Official Program, Indianapolis Motor Speedway, 1966 (50th running)	8	22	30
International Speed Trials Official Program, Daytona Beach, Florida, 1935	200	250	350
Lucky Irish Horan Hell Drivers thrill show program, 1954	8	22	30
Mustang Auto Daredevils Tournament of Thrills Official Year Book, 1967	8	22	30
Pleasantville (New Jersey) Speedway Souvenir Auto Racing Program, 1956	8	22	30
Spirit of America brochure detailing Craig Breedlove's 1963 World Land Speed Record run, distributed by Shell Oil, 1964	7	10	15

1942 Chrysler/Mopar "Distinctive Custom-built" accessories catalog. EXC-$37

1941 Oldsmobile accessories booklet; "Styled To Lead, Built To Last." EXC-$40

1939 Nash accessories catalog "To Make a Great Car Greater." EXC-$35

1939 Graham accessories booklet; "It Looks Like a Million...It's Priced For The Millions." EXC-$35

Wynn's Bonneville streamliner, 1957 decal, 11 inches wide by 7 inches deep. EXC-$30 (see separate story on collectible racing decals). (Phil Hall photo)

Daytona International Speedway Firecracker 250 race, early-1960s decal, 7 inches wide by 4 inches deep. EXC-$15. (Phil Hall photo)

These four Champion cast iron motorcycles date from the 1920s-1930s. Prices vary greatly depending upon condition and size $175-$450 each (see separate story on motorcycle collectibles).
(Roger Pribbenow photo)

A pair of motorized collectibles, a Cushman scooter (yellow, left) and Allstate scooter (red, marketed by Sears), both restored to number one condition. The Cushman is valued at $6,500 in excellent condition while the Allstate is valued at $3,000.

Harley-Davidson woolen long sleeve shirt from the 1930s. $200-$300.
(Roger Pribbenow photo)

Matchbook collecting is a large part of the ephemera hobby. The collector vehicle hobby has many colorful examples to choose from including these gold-finished matchbooks promoting Brockway trucks. EXC-$4.00 (see separate story on big rig collectibles). (Andy Hill, Jr. photo)

Factory postcard, this one depicting a new 1963 Rambler American 440-H two-door hardtop, sent from dealerships to prospective customers. The "H" designation and the car's gold on white colors might lead some to believe this is a Hurst edition 440, but it's not. Postcards are 5-1/2 inches wide by 3-1/2 inches deep. EXC-$5.

1963 RAMBLER AMERICAN **440-H** HARDTOP

Limited-edition glazed ceramic Willys banks, molded to represent Pro Street drag race cars. Currently valued at $50 (see separate story on collectible ceramic cars).

Buddy L open cab Wrecking Truck (this example restored), 1928-1929, 26-1/2 inches long by 13-1/2 inches high with 7-1/2-inch boom, brass handrails and disc wheels with aluminum "tires". EXC-$3,800.

Hot Wheels "Mutt Mobile", #5185, issued in 1971, blue with white top. EXC-$150. (Hot Wheels is a trademark of Mattel)

Hot Wheels "Ice T", #6184, issued in 1971, yellow. EXC-$125. (Hot Wheels is a trademark of Mattel)

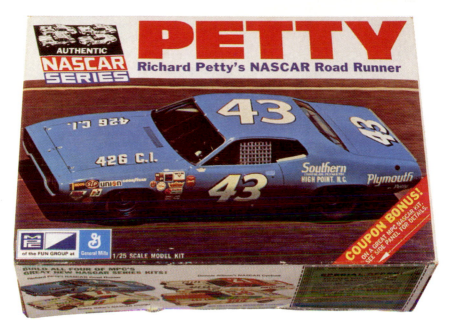

Richard Petty's NASCAR Road Runner, part of MPC's
Authentic NASCAR Series of model kits, #1701, 1/25th scale.
EXC-$225.

AMT's three-in-one model kit of 1957 Chevrolet
"Pepper Shaker", T-280-225, 1/25th scale. EXC-$40.

A trio of popular petroliana collectibles: 1) a two-gallon Around The World motor oil can, 2) a two-quart Cross Country motor oil pouring can and 3) one-quart glass bottle of Standard Iso-Vis 30-weight oil with capped pouring spout. 1) EXC-$70. 2) EXC-$100. 3) EXC-$90.

A pair of round five-gallon containers from Iowa Motor Oil, circa 1930, and Sinclair Opaline Motor Oil, circa 1925. EXC-$100 to $225.

Metalcraft Shell Motor Oil stake bed truck (comes with eight oil drums, not shown). EXC-$800.

Known by several names, including utility/penetrating/handy/household oil, a "six-pack" of hand-held lubricating oil cans representing (l to r): Cities Service, Archer, RPM, Sinclair, Mopar and Skelly. Prices in excellent condition vary from $15-$50.

Texaco Fire-Chief Gasoline tin sign, 1947, 15 inches wide by 24 inches deep. EXC-$145.

Coin banks were a common premium item used by service stations and car dealerships. Left to right: 1) Blue Sunoco gas pump, 2) Veedol motor oil can, 3) Buick Fireball Eight globe-type promotional, 4) Johnson motor oil can, 5) En-Ar-Co motor oil container, and 6) Skelly Tagolene motor oil can. Prices in excellent condition vary from $30 to $150.

Pinback buttons were another popular giveaway/premium item for service stations and car dealerships. Represented here (top left, clockwise): Cities Service, Skelly, Buick and Studebaker. Prices in excellent condition vary from $15-$75.

A Marx City Sanitation Dept. truck, circa 1948, 12-3/4 inches long, with "Help Keep Your City Clean" graphics. EXC-$335.

Smith-Miller "L" Mack Mobilgas tanker, 1952. EXC-$1,200.

A "six-pack" of glass one-quart oil bottles with cork, cap or screw-on tops. Oil brands represented are (l to r): Linco Marathon, Standard Polarine, Sunoco, Castrol, Penn Bee and Long Life. Prices in excellent condition vary from $30-$120.

A variety of tire company ashtray/pen holder/clock premiums. Brands represented include Armstrong, Kelly-Springfield and B.F. Goodrich. Prices in excellent condition vary from $25-$150.

Automotive replacement items, in original containers/packaging, are sought-after collectibles. Left is a five-pound can of Acme transmission grease from the Purity Oil Co. EXC-$20. Right is a set of AC spark plugs in a tin box. EXC-$65.

Bell Ethyl gasoline globe, 13.5-inch inserts on Gill ripple body, circa 1935-1941, from Bell Oil and Gas of Tulsa, Okla. EXC-$750.

A trio of children pose with a "junior" 1958 DeSoto at a DeSoto/Plymouth dealership while mom and dad (at right) and a salesman look on. These "kiddie" cars were either electric powered or housed a small gas-operated engine (usually five hp or less) in the rear. Price when new was in the $350-$500 range. EXC-$15,000.

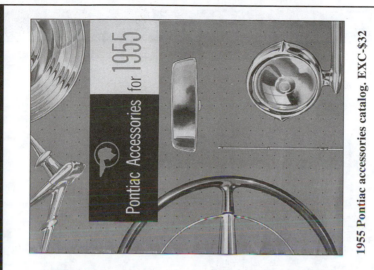

1955 Pontiac accessories catalog. EXC-$32

1954 Ford accessories booklet. EXC-$32

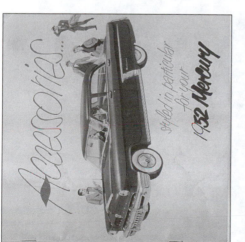

1952 Mercury accessories catalog. EXC-$32

(Note: The excellent (EXC) condition value of each item pictured is provided in the photo captions. Each item pictured may or may not be in excellent condition, but is shown to give visual representation of that item)

1955 Chevrolet accessories catalog. EXC-$37

1956 Dodge accessories booklet "...to accent your success." EXC-$25

1958 Chevrolet accessories catalog. EXC-$37

(Note: The excellent (EXC) condition value of each item pictured is provided in the photo captions. Each item pictured may or may not be in excellent condition, but is shown to give visual representation of that item)

1956 DeSoto accessories catalog featuring "optional equipment for your modern driving pleasure." EXC-$26

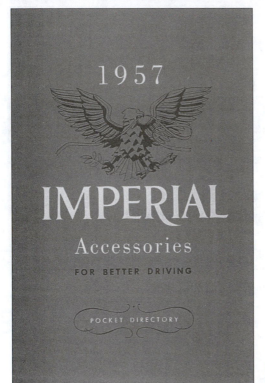

1957 Imperial accessories pocket directory "For Better Driving." EXC-$32

1958 Rambler accessories booklet. EXC-$22

1960 Buick "engineer approved" accessories booklet for the Turbine Drive Buick. EXC-$11

1960 Corvair custom features catalog. EXC-$22

**1961 Rambler American accessories that are "American Motors Approved."
EXC-$22**

1961 Buick "engineer
approved" accessories
catalogue. EXC-$26

1961 Oldsmobile accessories booklet. EXC-$32

1963 Mercury Comet accessories booklet. EXC-$22

1963 Dodge Options & Accessories booklet "To Give You The Most Fun With Your 1963 Dodge." EXC-$22

(Note: The excellent (EXC) condition value of each item pictured is provided in the photo captions. Each item pictured may or may not be in excellent condition, but is shown to give visual representation of that item)

1963 Mopar accessories booklet (spiral bound vertical format). EXC-$22

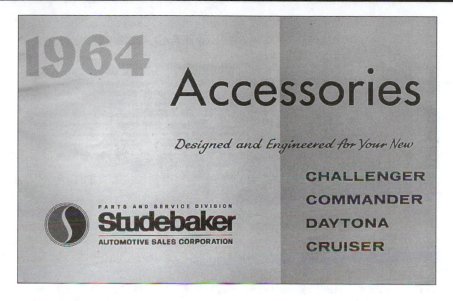

1964 Studebaker accessories catalog. EXC-$25

1966 American Motors Approved Accessories booklet. EXC-$22

Camaro

custom feature accessories for '67

1967 Camaro Custom Feature Accessories catalog. EXC-$32

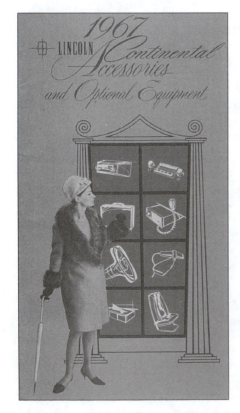

1967 Lincoln Continental Accessories and Optional Equipment booklet. EXC-$26

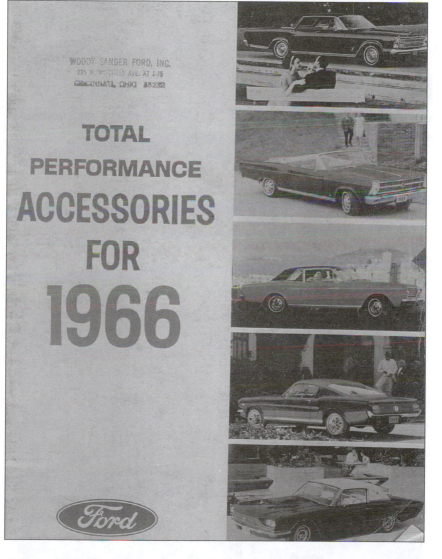

1966 Ford Total Performance Accessories catalog. EXC-$26

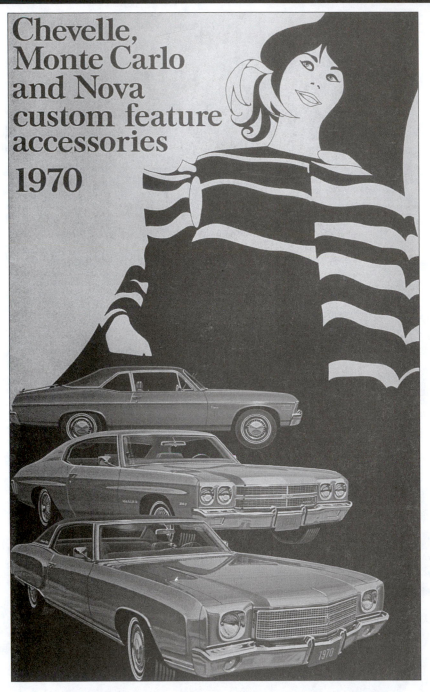

Chevelle, Monte Carlo and Nova custom feature accessories 1970

1970 Chevelle, Monte Carlo, and Nova custom feature accessories catalog.
EXC-$32

ARE YOU SURE YOU DIDN'T FORGET SOMETHING?

1971 Buick "Are You Sure You Didn't Forget Something?" accessories brochure. EXC- $18

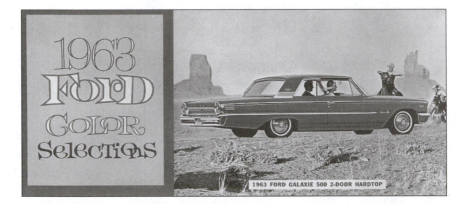

1963 FORD GALAXIE 500 2-DOOR HARDTOP

1963 Ford single and two-tone color selection booklet detailing "Diamond Lustre" finishes. EXC-$14

1961 Oldsmobile single color selection booklet detailing "Magic Mirror" finishes. EXC-$22

A pair of photographs from a Kaiser-Frazer press kit showcasing the 1952 Kaiser Virginian and Henry J Corsair deLuxe models. The press kit contains photographs of each of the new models as well as feature articles introducing each model and its specifications, all contained in a folder. EXC-$150

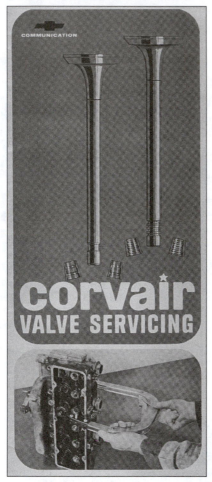

1964 Corvair valve servicing booklet.
EXC-$22

(Note: The excellent (EXC) condition value of each item pictured is provided in the photo captions. Each item pictured may or may not be in excellent condition, but is shown to give visual representation of that item)

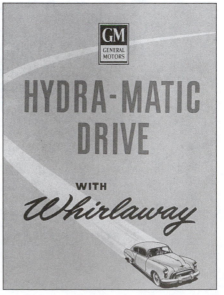

1949 Oldsmobile Hydra-Matic Drive history manual from General Motors. EXC-$40

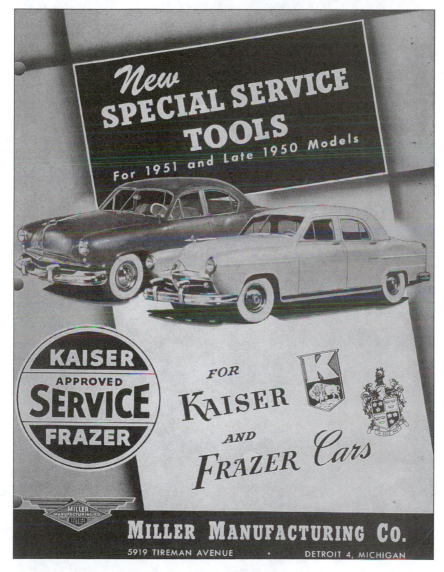

1951 Kaiser-Frazer special service tool update from Miller Mfg. Co. EXC-$32

1916-1928 Chevrolet Four-Cylinder Model Parts catalog issued July 1, 1940. EXC-$30

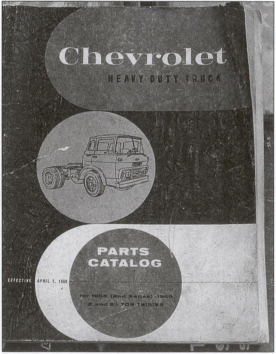

1955-1960 Chevrolet heavy-duty truck parts catalog for 2nd Series and 2 and 2-1/2-ton trucks. EXC-$37

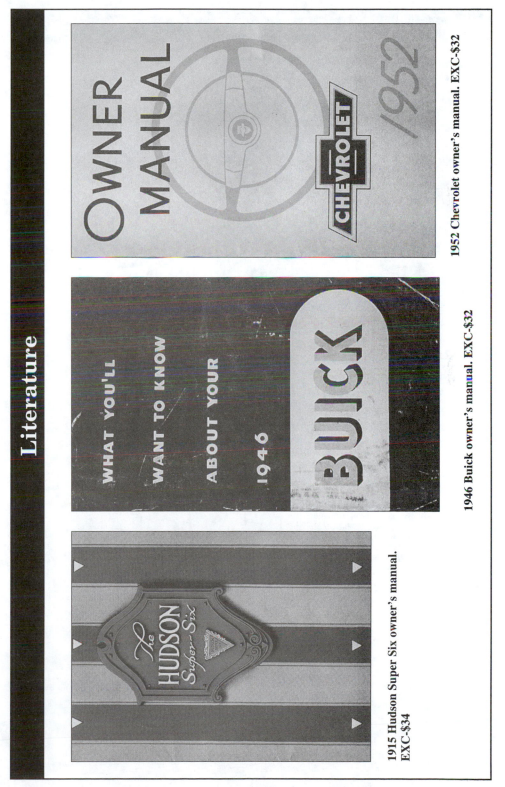

1952 Chevrolet owner's manual. EXC-$32

1946 Buick owner's manual. EXC-$32

1915 Hudson Super Six owner's manual. EXC-$34

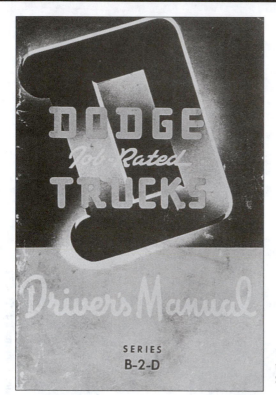

1952 Dodge "Job Rated" truck driver's manual. EXC-$16

(Note: The excellent (EXC) condition value of each item pictured is provided in the photo captions. Each item pictured may or may not be in excellent condition, but is shown to give visual representation of that item)

1953 FORD TRUCK OPERATOR'S MANUAL

FORD DIVISION
FORD MOTOR COMPANY

FORM 3651-53-F

1953 Ford truck operator's manual. EXC-$16

Literature

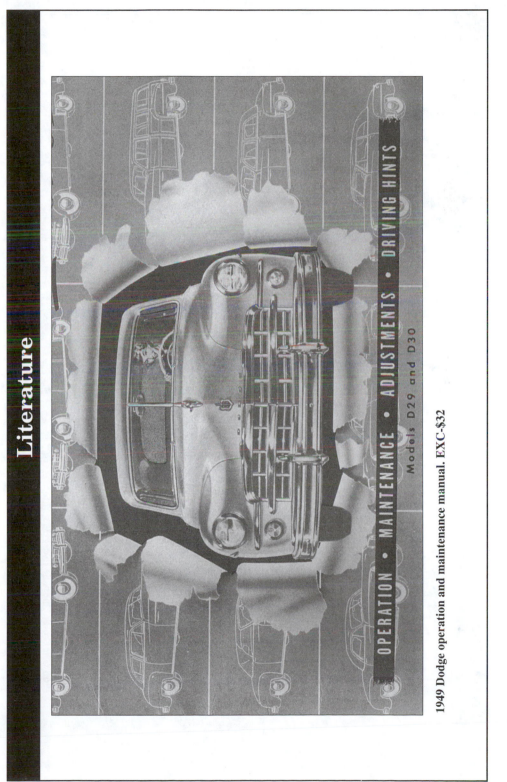

OPERATION • MAINTENANCE • ADJUSTMENTS • DRIVING HINTS

Models D29 and D30

1949 Dodge operation and maintenance manual. EXC-$32

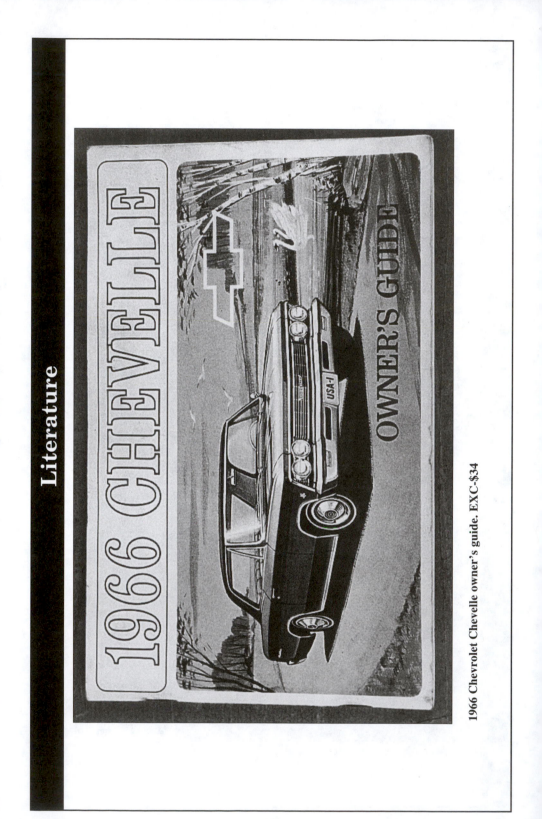

1966 Chevrolet Chevelle owner's guide. EXC-$34

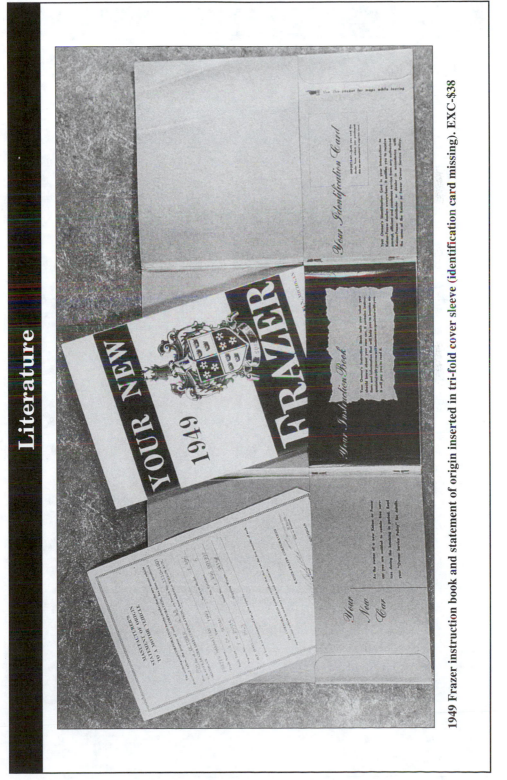

1949 Frazer instruction book and statement of origin inserted in tri-fold cover sleeve (identification card missing). EXC-$38

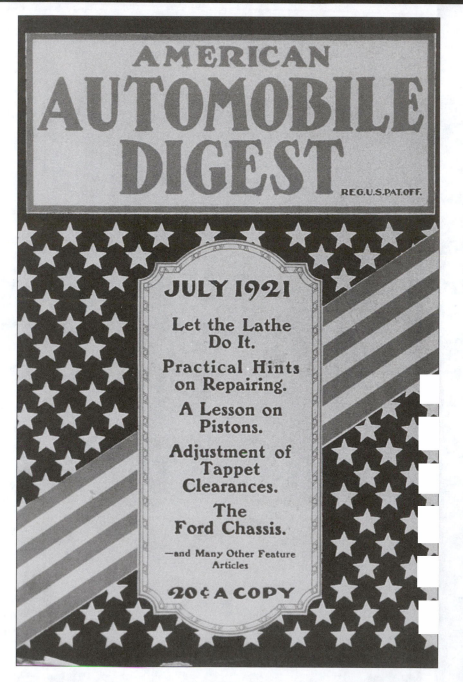

July 1921 issue of *American Automobile Digest* magazine featuring "A Lesson on Pistons." EXC-$55

Literature

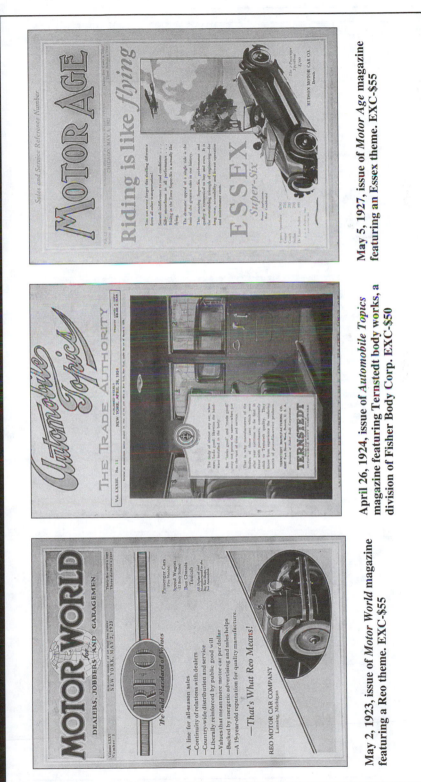

May 5, 1927, issue of *Motor Age* magazine featuring an Essex theme. EXC-$55

April 26, 1924, issue of *Automobile Topics* magazine featuring Ternstedt body works, a division of Fisher Body Corp. EXC-$50

May 2, 1923, issue of *Motor World* magazine featuring a Reo theme. EXC-$55

Literature

August 1956 issue of *Car Life* magazine with feature on how to "soup up" the family sedan. EXC-$40

April 1951 issue of *Hot Rod* magazine with a drag strip theme. EXC-$65

September 1937 issue of *Motor* magazine featuring news of 1938 model introductions. EXC-$50

May 1947 (Vol. 1, No. 1) issue of *Speed Age* magazine with feature on the 1947 Indianapolis 500. EXC-$100

(Note: The excellent (EXC) condition value of each item pictured is provided in the photo captions. Each item pictured may or may not be in excellent condition, but is shown to give visual representation of that item)

Literature

All information and photos courtesy
of the Phil Hall collection.

October 1950 (Vol. 1, No. 1) issue of *Motorsport* magazine featuring coverage of most classes of racing as well as antique cars. EXC-$25

September 1958 issue of *Speed Age* magazine featuring racing's wildest weekend. EXC-$15

November 1951 issue of *Speed Age* magazine with biography of driver Cliff Bergere. EXC-$15

Literature

June 1960 (Vol. 1, No. 1) issue of *on the Grid* magazine featuring coverage of Sebring 12 hour race. EXC-$25

April 1952 issue of *Auto Sport Review* with coverage of Pan-American Road Race. EXC-$13

August/September 1956 issue of *Motorsport* magazine with coverage of Daytona Speed Week action. EXC-$15

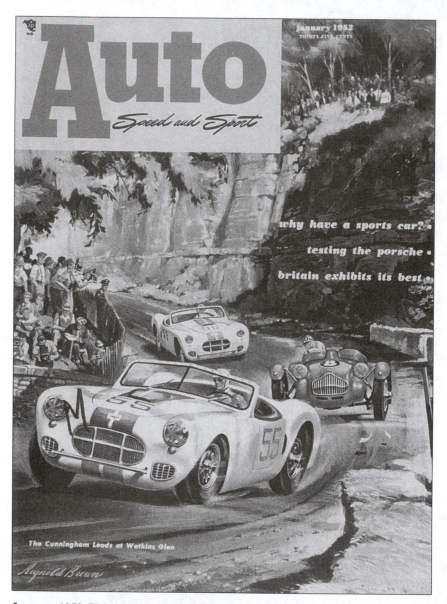

January 1952 (Vol. 1, No. 1) issue of *Auto Speed and Sport* magazine with Watkins Glen artwork on cover. EXC-$25

Literature

The 1961-62 Annual *Racing Pictorial*
magazine featuring coverage of A.J. Foyt,
Ned Jarrett, and Bill Muncey. EXC-$40

September 1961 issue of *Today's Motor
Sports* featuring coverage of the Golden
Anniversary Indianapolis 500. EXC-$13

March/April 1964 issue of *USAS Autosports*
magazine featuring Gary Bettenhausen
biography. EXC-$13

1967 official year book for the Mustang Auto Daredevils Tournament of Thrills. EXC-$30

1956 souvenir program from the Pleasantville (New Jersey) Speedway. EXC-$30

1958 stock car race program from the Alcyon Speedway in Pitman, New Jersey. EXC-$30

1935 official program for the International Speed Trials from Daytona Beach, Florida. EXC-$350

Literature

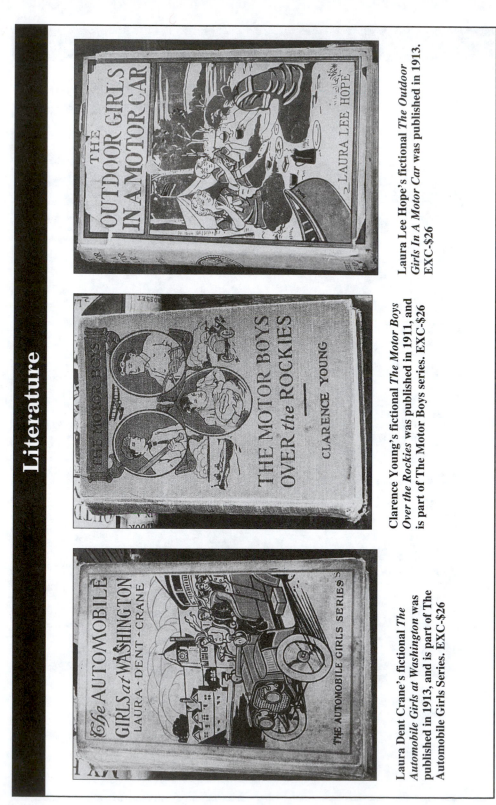

Laura Dent Crane's fictional *The Automobile Girls at Washington* was published in 1913, and is part of The Automobile Girls Series. EXC-$26

Clarence Young's fictional *The Motor Boys Over the Rockies* was published in 1911, and is part of The Motor Boys series. EXC-$26

Laura Lee Hope's fictional *The Outdoor Girls In A Motor Car* was published in 1913. EXC-$26

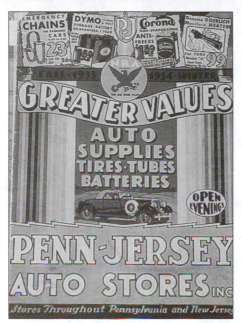

1933-1934 Penn-Jersey Auto Stores parts catalog. EXC-$40

(Note: The excellent (EXC) condition value of each item pictured is provided in the photo captions. Each item pictured may or may not be in excellent condition, but is shown to give visual representation of that item)

1939 Chicago Automobile Show souvenir booklet *An Age of Wheelprints*. EXC-$75

Literature

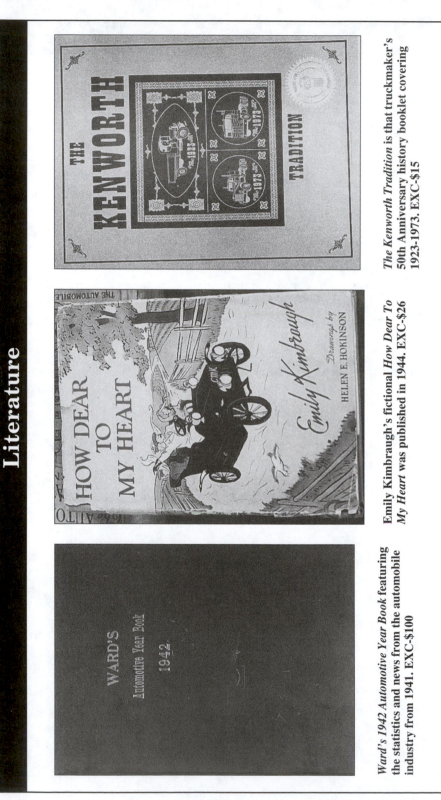

The Kenworth Tradition is that truckmaker's 50th Anniversary history booklet covering 1923-1973. EXC-$15

Emily Kimbraugh's fictional *How Dear To My Heart* was published in 1944. EXC-$26

Ward's 1942 Automotive Year Book featuring the statistics and news from the automobile industry from 1941. EXC-$100

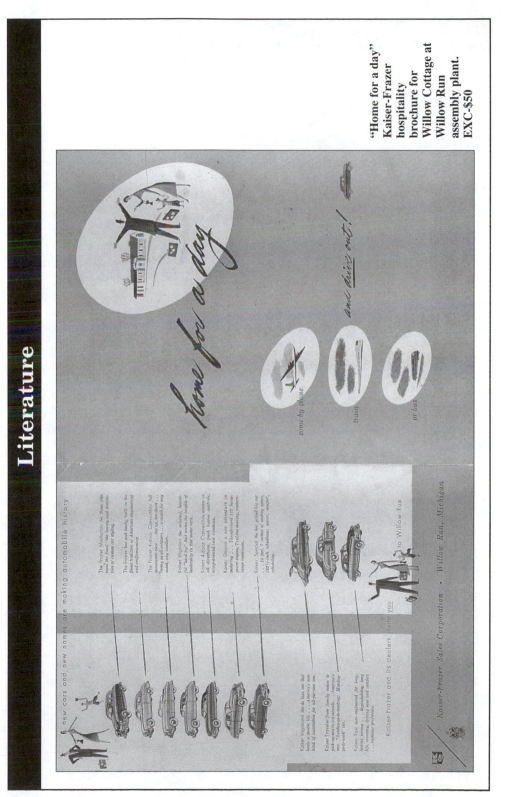

**"Home for a day"
Kaiser-Frazer
hospitality
brochure for
Willow Cottage at
Willow Run
assembly plant.
EXC-$50**

"From Pencil to Proving Ground" booklet detailing Ford's Rogue assembly plant.
EXC-$22

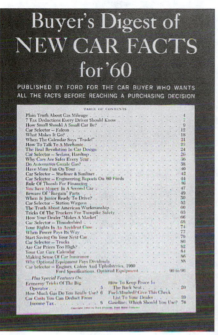

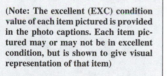

Buyer's Digest of NEW CAR FACTS for '60

PUBLISHED BY FORD FOR THE CAR BUYER WHO WANTS
ALL THE FACTS BEFORE REACHING A PURCHASING DECISION

Buyer's Digest of New Car Facts for 1960, published by FoMoCo for car buyers to get to know the products and services available to them when purchasing an automobile. EXC-$25

HOW A MODERN COMPACT CAR IS BUILT...

A picture story of the manufacture of the RAMBLER...... the car that sparked the new automobile revolution

(Note: The excellent (EXC) condition value of each item pictured is provided in the photo captions. Each item pictured may or may not be in excellent condition, but is shown to give visual representation of that item)

"How A Modern Compact Car Is Built" booklet, published in 1960 by American Motors explaining the construction of the Rambler. EXC-$15

1948 Gatso Type 4000 (produced in Holland) sales brochure. EXC-$15

1954 Anglia (English Ford) De Luxe sales catalog shaped like a tailfin. EXC-$15

Literature

1958 Plymouth all-line sales catalog that might have inspired Stephen King to write his bestseller *Christine*. EXC-$30

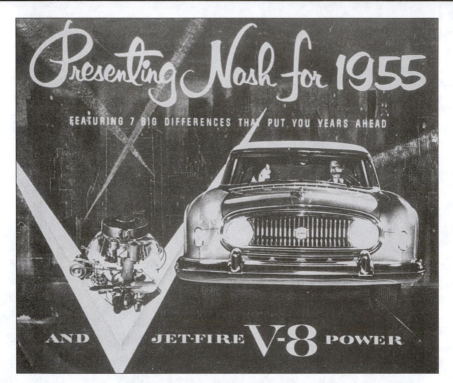

1955 Nash all-line sales brochure highlighting Jet-Fire V-8 power. EXC-$17

1959 Checker Model A-9 taxicab sales catalog. EXC-$22

The 1965 Corvair Sprint catalog, published in 1965 by John Fitch and Co., Inc., detailing its conversion of the Corvair into a high-performance machine for sale to the public. EXC-$22

1971 Trabant 601 (produced in East Germany) sales brochure. EXC-$18

1963 Checker 40th Anniversary all-line sales brochure. EXC-$17

A 1958 postcard promoting the new Pontiac Bonneville Sport Coupe in a futuristic setting. EXC-$8

1960 Ford Starliner postcard titled "A Wonderful New World of Performance." EXC-$7

1938 The Phantom Corsair sales catalog. EXC-$100

(Note: The excellent (EXC) condition value of each item pictured is provided in the photo captions. Each item pictured may or may not be in excellent condition, but is shown to give visual representation of that item)

Buick Wildcat promotional brochure "Trial flight in Fiberglas and steel", circa 1953. EXC-$65

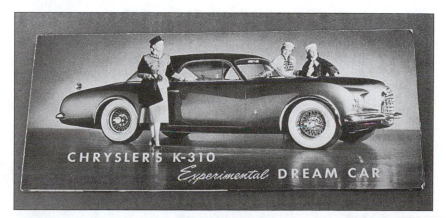

Chrysler K-310 promotional brochure "Experimental Dream Car", circa 1951. EXC-$65

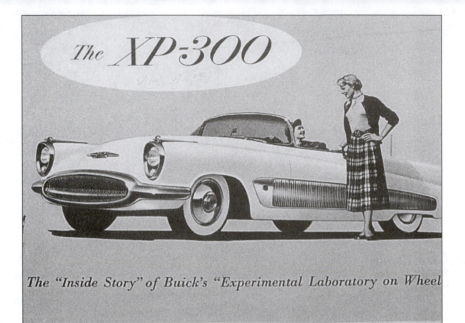

Buick XP-300 promotional brochure "The 'Inside Story' of Buick's 'Experimental Laboratory on Wheels'", circa 1951. EXC-$55

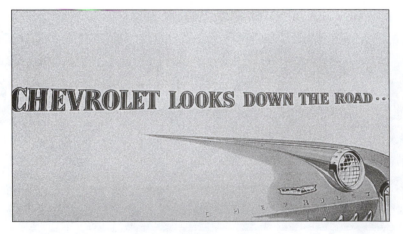

Chevrolet Biscayne promotional brochure "Chevrolet Looks Down the Road", circa 1955. EXC-$55

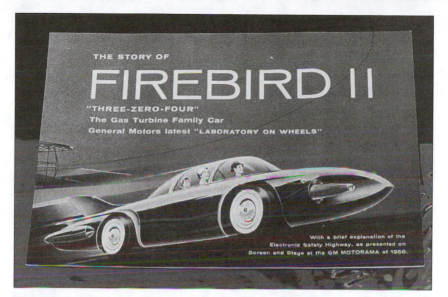

General Motors Firebird II promotional brochure "The Story of Firebird II Three-Zero-Four - The Gas Turbine Family Car - General Motors latest 'Laboratory on Wheels'", circa 1953. EXC-$55

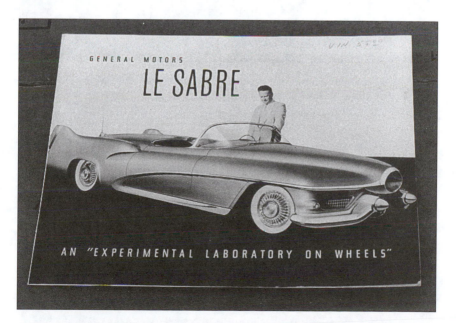

General Motors LaSabre promotional brochure "An Experimental Laboratory on Wheels", circa 1951. EXC-$65

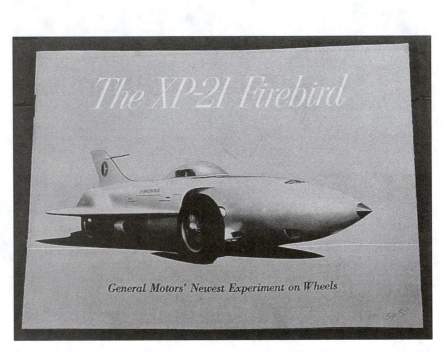

The XP-21 Firebird promotional brochure "General Motors' Newest Experiment on Wheels", circa 1954. EXC-$65

(Note: The excellent (EXC) condition value of each item pictured is provided in the photo captions. Each item pictured may or may not be in excellent condition, but is shown to give visual representation of that item)

Mack Truck all-line sales brochure, full color, circa 1956. EXC-$150

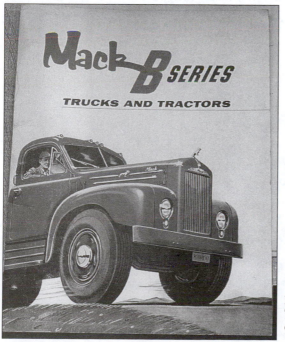

Mack B-Series Trucks and Tractors sales brochure, circa 1954. EXC-$125

1963 publicity photo of movie cast with 1933 Ford taxicab from "The Three Stooges Go Around The World In A Daze". EXC-$12

1951 publicity photo of young ladies changing a tire on a 1946 Ford. EXC-$8

Literature

April 1961 issue of *Goodyear News* magazine with a feature on tire testing at 100 mph. EXC-$8

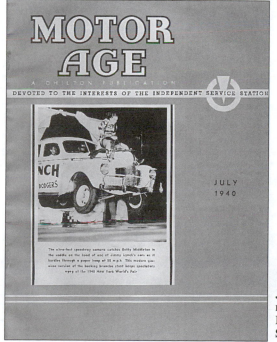

July 1940 issue of *Motor Age* magazine "Devoted to the Interests of the Independent Service Station". EXC-$8

Literature

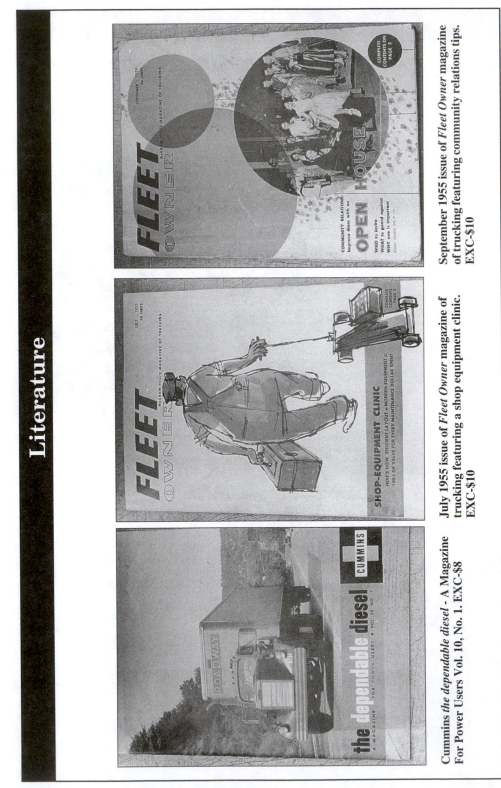

Cummins *the dependable diesel* - A Magazine For Power Users Vol. 10, No. 1. EXC-$8

July 1955 issue of *Fleet Owner* magazine of trucking featuring a shop equipment clinic. EXC-$10

September 1955 issue of *Fleet Owner* magazine of trucking featuring community relations tips. EXC-$10

Spirit of America brochure detailing Craig Breedlove's 1963 World Land Speed Record run, distributed by Shell Oil, 1964. EXC-$15

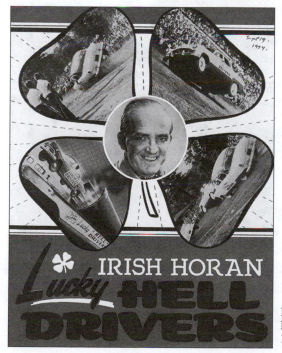

Lucky Irish Horan Hell Drivers thrill show program, 1954. EXC-$30

LICENSE PLATES

California License Plates

Description	Good	Very Good	Excellent
1908 California license plate, issued by Automobile Club of Southern California	115	195	300

(**NOTE**: There were several different designs of these, most of them porcelain with black or white numbers and the abbreviation CAL on them. The first state-issued plates were provided by the auto-owner to a registration number assigned from Sacramento. This was supposed to be black on white and carry either CAL or STATE OF CALIFORNIA on it. Most carried the CAL although some did not and many were white on black. The numbers increased well into the six digits by the end of 1913 when the first dated porcelain plates--the 1914 white on bright red versions--were issued. There was a local registration in San Francisco by the Golden Gate Park Commission to allow cars to travel through the park. These may have been issued as early as 1902 and a snapshot I recently discovered shows one on a 1904 Rambler. Probably all of those plates were destroyed by the earthquake in San Francisco in 1906 and this one depicted in the photograph is the first I've ever seen anywhere! - **Keith Marvin**)

Description	Good	Very Good	Excellent
1914 California license plate, porcelain, red with white numbers	110	180	225
1915 California license plate, porcelain, yellow with black numbers	80	130	200
1916 California license plate, porcelain, white with blue numbers	110	180	225

(**NOTE**: This plate, first issued in 1916, was used for four years, with a revalidating symbol, e.g.: a lead bear in 1916, a yellow poppy in 1917, a green mission bell in 1918, and a red star in 1920. Registrations for those years were, respectively: 219,440; 289,800; 363,462; and 414,097. - **Keith Marvin**)

Description	Good	Very Good	Excellent
1924 California license plate, bright green with white numbers	80	130	200

(**NOTE**: I've been told that there were no seven digit plates in California in 1923, one was made that year with #1-000-000! [See "California Hits the Big 1 Million Combination", *Tags 'N' Stuff*, Concord, N.C., December 1994.] The article carried a photo of such a plate. - **Keith Marvin**)

Description	Good	Very Good	Excellent
1927 California license plate, red with white numbers	60	100	150
1939 California license plate, "California World's Fair" (only use), blue with yellow/orange numbers	20	33	50
1939 California license plate, "California World's Fair" wording with art showing bridge and skyline	20	33	50
1939 California license plate, "Cal '39," (non-World's Fair; rarest plate issued in California in 1939)	27	45	70
1940 California license plate, first round-cornered design, yellow with black numbers	17	28	45
1942 California license plate, with date strip as part of plate, black with yellow numbers	20	33	50

(**NOTE**: The 1941 plates were revalidated for 1942 with a black on yellow embossed metal strip covering the yellow on black 19 CALIFORNIA 41. New registration plates had the strip made integrally with the plate. In 1943, the plates were revalidated by an embossed red on white tab with a 'V' [for Victory] on it and in 1944, as noted below, a windshield sticker was used. - **Keith Marvin**)

Description	Good	Very Good	Excellent
1944 California registration sticker for windshield (rare)	11	23	35
1951 California license plate, black with yellow numbers	12	28	42

Description	Good	Very Good	Excellent
1955 California license plate, black with yellow numbers	12	28	42
1956 California license plate, (smaller), yellow with black numbers	12	28	42
1963 California license plate, black with yellow/orange numbers	12	28	42
1970 California license plate, blue with yellow numbers	11	23	35

U.S./Canadian License Plates

Description	Good	Very Good	Excellent
1903 Commonwealth of Massachusetts, license plates; number, plus "Mass. Automobile Register," first year, steel-coated plates with dark blue porcelain	140	230	350

(**NOTE**: This series continued in use until Dec. 31, 1907, but with the increasing numbers, the plates became larger and the dies were consequently slightly changed as the sizes increased. - **Keith Marvin**)

1903 Ontario, Canada license plate; black-and-silver metal numbers and Provincial coat-of-arms	500	750	1000

(**NOTE**: This was Ontario's first plate and was used into 1905 when it was supplanted with a flat rubber type. The plates were few as only 178 motor vehicles were registered in 1904 and 535 in 1905. Since those 1903 assignments carried into 1904, they were retained, and in 1905 the rubber ones replaced them. I've also seen counterfeits—good ones—of this marker. - **Keith Marvin**)

1905 Vermont license plate, "Vermont Automobile Register", first issue, porcelain, dark blue with with numbers	140	230	350
1905 Wisconsin license plate, first issue, black with silver numbers	140	230	350

(**NOTE**: This first issue ran from 1905 through 1911. Any cars registered before 1911 carried them. For 1911, a silver on green set was supplied. This was dated and is rare. But these were only supplied to new registrations, which answers the question as otherwise the original issue was retained until 1912. - **Keith Marvin**)

1914 New York license plate, white with black numbers	140	230	350
1909-15 New Jersey license plate, steel with porcelain enameled surface, 6 x 14-1/2 inches, gray with bright red numbers	140	230	350
1917 Arizona license plate, with steer head (first use of graphics on a U.S. plate), black with white numbers	160	200	275
1923 Florida license plate, state outline graphic (first use), black with orange numbers	40	65	100
1926 New Hampshire license plate, rock formation graphic (only use), dark with white numbers	75	125	200
1928 Massachusetts license plate, fish graphic (only use), green with white numbers	75	125	200
1930 New Hampshire license plate, 5-7/8 x 12-1/2 inches, dark green with white numbers	13	25	40

1931 South Carolina license plate, "The Iodine State" (first use), white with dark numbers	20	35	55
1932 Arkansas license plate, all characters in italics, black with orange numbers	20	35	55
1932 Louisiana license plate, pelican graphic and front and rear labeled plates, red with white numbers	30	45	70
1932 New Mexico license plate, "Sunshine State" (only use, predated Florida by 17 years), forest green with white numbers	20	35	55
1934 Arizona license plate, 5-1/2 x 10-1/4 inches, copper plate with copper numbers recessed in blue field	30	45	70
1936 Maine license plate, (smaller) "Vacationland" (first use), blue with white numbers	20	35	55
1936 Rhode Island license plate, "300th Year" (only use), longer plate, black with white numbers	160	200	275
1936 Wyoming license plate, cowboy on bucking horse graphic (first use), white with black numbers	20	35	55
1938 Montana license plate, steer head graphic (only use until 1970s) and state outline graphic, orange with black numbers	20	35	55
1939 North Carolina license plate, first of three consecutive years of using gothic-type characters, red with white numbers	30	45	70
1940 Arizona license plate, "Grand Canyon State" (first use), white with dark numbers	12	22	35
1940 Nebraska license plate, state capitol graphic (first use), blue with red/orange numbers	20	35	55
1941 Georgia license plate, "Peach State", blue with light-yellow/orange peach graphic and numbers (first use of reflectorized plates in U.S.)	30	45	70
1941 Idaho license plate, "Scenic Idaho" (first use), goldenrod with black numbers	12	22	35
1941 Mississippi license plate, county names added (first use), black with white numbers	13	25	40
1942 Maryland license plate, "Drive Carefully" (first use), silver with black numbers	12	22	35
1942 New Mexico license plate, "The Land Of Enchantment", white with black numbers	15	30	45
1944 Virginia license plate, plate is embossed fiberboard (only use), yellow/orange with dark numbers	20	35	55
1947 Connecticut license plate, unpainted aluminum with green numbers	15	30	45
1947 Idaho license plate, "Vacation Wonderland" (only use), dark blue with white numbers	15	30	45

1947 Utah license plate, "This Is The Place" (only use), black with orange numbers	20	35	55
1948 Alaska license plate, first appearance of state flag, goldenrod with blue numbers	12	22	35
1948 Arkansas license plate, "Opportunity Land", silver with black numbers	10	20	30
1948 Illinois license plate, made of compressed paper, 5-1/2 x 11-3/8 inches, orange with black numbers	20	35	55
1948 Utah license plate, "The Friendly State" (only use), black with white numbers	20	35	55
1948 Vermont license plate, "Green Mountains" (first use), smaller plate, black with orange numbers	20	35	55
1949 Kansas license plate, "The Wheat State" (first use), silver with black numbers	10	20	30
1950 Hawaii license plate, light yellow with large dark numbers	35	50	75
1950 Minnesota license plate, "10,000 Lakes" (first use), black with white numbers	12	22	35
1950 Montana license plate, "The Treasure State" (first use) with state outline graphic, black with white numbers	12	22	35
1951 Florida license plate, "Keep Florida Green" (only use), goldenrod with dark numbers	15	30	45
1951 Kansas license plate, plate shaped like state (first use), dark blue with white numbers	13	25	40
1951 Kentucky license plate, "Tour Kentucky" (first use), silver with black numbers	15	30	45
1951 New York, "The Empire State" (first use), yellow with black numbers	10	20	30
1952 South Dakota license plate, illustration of Mount Rushmore (first use), white with red numbers	13	25	40
1953 Iowa license plate, "The Corn State" (first use), white with black numbers	10	20	30
1954 Illinois license plate, "Land of Lincoln" (first use), black with white numbers	12	22	35
1954 Louisiana license plate, "Louisiana Yams" (only use) with embossed pelican graphic, white with blue numbers	12	22	35
1954 Michigan license plate, "Water Wonderland" (first use), blue with yellow/orange numbers	12	22	35
1955 Alabama license plate, "Heart of Dixie" (first use), green with white numbers	12	22	35
1955 Oklahoma license plate, "Visit Oklahoma" (first use), black with white numbers	12	22	35
1955 Tennessee license plate, shaped like state, white with red numbers	30	45	70

1956 Florida license plate, "Sunshine State", dark blue with white numbers	10	20	35
1956 Indiana license plate, "Drive Safely" (first use), black with orange numbers	10	20	30
1956 Nebraska license plate, "The Beef State" (first use), black with white numbers	10	20	30
1956 North Dakota license plate, "Peace Garden State" (first use), white with light blue numbers	10	20	30
1957 Wisconsin license plate, farm, black with white numbers	12	22	35
1958 Colorado license plate, skier graphic (only use), white with green numbers	13	25	40
1961 Hawaii license plate, "Aloha State" (first use), dark green with white numbers	12	22	35
1961 Nevada license plate, dark blue with silver numbers	10	20	30
1964 Wisconsin license plate, dealer, butter yellow with black numbers	10	20	30
1964-65 Louisiana license plate prototype (made at Angola State Prison, but not adopted for use), 6 x 12 inches	25	50	75
1965 Washington, D.C. Presidential Inauguration license plate (valid to use Jan. 1 to March 31, 1965), red-white-blue combination with U.S. Flag, 6 x 12 inches	35	70	120
1965 West Virginia license plate, "Mountain State" (first use), dark blue with orange numbers	10	20	30
1965 Wisconsin license plate, "America's Dairyland", burgundy with white numbers	10	20	30
1966 Arizona license plate, "Grand Canyon State", white with black numbers	10	20	30
1967 Montana license plate, "Big Sky Country" (first use), blue with yellow numbers	10	20	30
1967 Wyoming license plate, dark red with white numbers	10	20	30
1968 Idaho license plate, "Famous Potatoes", white with green numbers	10	20	30
1968 Louisiana license plate, "Sportsman's Paradise", white with green numbers	10	20	30
1968 Michigan license plate, "Great Lake State" (first use), forest green with yellow/orange numbers	10	20	30
1969 Arizona license plate, "Grand Canyon State", bright yellow with dark blue numbers	10	20	30
1969 Nevada license plate, truck, dark blue with white numbers	10	20	30
1970 Northwest Territories of Canada Centennial license plate, 6 x 12 inches (shaped like a polar bear), blue with white numbers	35	45	55

Description			
Early 1970s Vermont Gubernatorial license plate, silk-screened and reflectorized, 6 x 12 inches, white with apple green numbers	35	45	55
1971 New Hampshire license plate, "Live Free Or Die" (first use), white with dark numbers	6	10	20
1971 Pennsylvania license plate, Liberty Bell graphic (first use), black with orange numbers	6	10	20
1973 Arizona license plate, non-commercial, yellow with green numbers	6	10	20
1973 Wyoming license plate, truck, white with black numbers	6	10	20
1976 Alaska license plate, first appearance of bear standing in front of mountains, white with red numbers	13	25	40
1985 District of Columbia special "50th American President Inaugural" license plates	12	20	30

(**NOTE**: These plates were initially used in 1933 with FDR's first Inauguration. They are scarce. In the beginning, they were only issued to cars participating in the event but later were allowed for those who were representatives of their committees to the event and were legally used in place of one's regular state plate, the thing being that they were issued with a temporary D.C. registration and carried exclusively from January through March 31st. Such a carrier simply kept the plates of his own state in the car if questioned. - **Keith Marvin**)

1986 Iowa license plate, dark blue with white numbers	5	10	20

License Plate Tag Toppers

Description	Good	Very Good	Excellent
License plate tag topper, Farm Bureau Mutual Insurance	8	13	20
License plate tag topper, Silvertown Safety League	12	20	30
License plate tag topper, cat	16	26	40
License plate tag topper, Chevrolet dealer	30	50	75
License plate tag topper, State Farm Insurance	8	13	20
License plate tag topper, American Automobile Association (AAA)	6	10	15
License plate tag topper, Griffith Motor Car Company, Carthage, Missouri	16	26	40
License plate tag topper, Brewer Motor Car Company, Manhattan, Kansas	16	26	40
License plate tag topper, Livingood Lincoln-Chrysler-Plymouth	16	26	40
License plate tag topper, auto parts store	8	13	20

(**NOTE**: Plain, tin car dealer tag toppers sell for approximately $30 in top condition and proportionately less in lesser conditions).

Allied Forces In Southern Europe (1950s And 1960s). These plates were among the most attractively designed--if not the most attractive--of a vast variety of military issues used by Allied and other specific forces in the years following World War II. Measuring 6 x 12 inches, the design carries obvious European overtones such as the high, thin-stroked numbers (including broken '4's), but good copies of these plates are scarce due to a notably thin and possibly inferior coating of white paint that constitutes the background. Thus, most of the surviving plates exhibit patches of bare metal on them.

The color combination includes a black numeric combination against the white background, abbreviation "AFSE" and outer border with the coat-of-arms of Venice depicting a golden lion, horizontal dash and inner border against a shield of scarlet.

Headquarters of the Allied Forces in Southern Europe's location was at Naples. The numeric system as shown, upon reaching 9999, switched to a prefix letter, hyphen and three numbers, later proceeding to three numbers and a suffix letter but without the hyphen.

The series was supplanted during 1969 with the current type that also measures 6 x 12 inches, is black on white and with the abbreviation "AFI" top center. EXC-$45 (Plate source: James K. Fox, Mentor, Ohio)

(Note: The excellent (EXC) condition value of each item pictured is provided in the photo captions. Each item pictured may or may not be in excellent condition, but is shown to give visual representation of that item)

License Plates

ARIZONA 1934- Copper has never been popular among colors, shades and metallic combinations on license plates, although it has been used in Arizona on plates as early as 1916 and on and off ever since and occasionally in other constituencies such as the taxicab series used by Mexico in 1947.

What sets the series above apart from the rank and file is that the plates were made of pure copper in Arizona starting with the white on copper tags used in 1932 and culminating with the 1934 type.

This is the only license plate to have been issued a patent by the U.S. Patent Office (see lower left on outer border). The 1933 series, natural copper on black and identically designed except for the placement of the state name and date under the numbers was not similarly patented.

This plate, which measures 5-1/2 x 10-1/4 inches, is natural inner border, section around "ARIZONA-1934" and letter-number combination are recessed. The inner section surrounding the letters and numbers, state name and date as well as outer painted border are embossed. The curious four-digit numeric-letter system was used by Arizona from 1932 through 1936. EXC-$70

1955 Tennessee license plate shaped like the state and numbered for radio operator, 5 x 12 inches, black with white numbers. EXC-$70

This is an "essay", a design made for consideration by the state. These plates were made at the Angola State Prison in Louisiana for the 1964-65 biennial issue. When a plate's design has been chosen, and copies are made, these are known as "prototypes" and color schemes are tried until a decision is made and that result will be the final plate. The plate is embossed including the oblong center and the letter therein is recessed, in this case B, which indicates the State Police Prefecture in which it is issued. Size is 6 x 12 inches. EXC-$75

This is my own idea of what a perfect license plate should be, visually and readily identifiable. The New Hampshire plate was white on dark-green, carried its state abbreviation and date clearly and utilized the entire plate surface with large, wide-stroked and clear numbers. Size: 5-7/8 x 12-1/2 inches. EXC-$40

Since the First Inauguration of FDR in 1933, the Inaugural plates have existed (except in 1945 when we were still at war and it was eliminated). The first plates were pretty well restricted to officials and those with clout although at the time of LBJ's Inauguration (this plate), anyone attending the event in an official capacity could order the plates and use them legally (with a temporary D.C. registration) and keep one's home state plates and registration in the car. Today, they may be ordered by anyone for a fee from the Inauguration Committee and only carried in addition to one's home state plates. In 1965 they could be substituted from January to March 31st for one's home plates.

The above were my plates (as a Representative to the Inauguration from the Town of Brunswick, New York) Democratic Committee and I used them through March 31, 1965. They are reflectorized with blue numbers on white. Top strip is white on red and bottom strip is white on blue. U.S. Flag is in true colors and D.C. flag in red and white. Plate was flat-surfaced. Measured 6 x 12 inches. EXC-$120

Many of the early plates were made of heavy steel and heavily coated with a flat porcelain enameled surface (prone to chip if hit with a sharp object). Plate measured 6 x 14-1/2 inches and was manufactured by the Horace E. Fine Co. of Trenton, New Jersey. Colors: Bright-red on gray. To the right is the "Manufacturer's seal" that had to be on the plate to make it legal. New Jersey used these porcelain plates from 1909 through 1915. EXC-$350

Many western, Midwestern states (plus Florida) issue special plates for members of Indian tribes. This is the current plate in use by the Turtle Mountain Band of the Chippewa Tribe in North Dakota. The plate is silk-screened except for the numbers that are embossed. Top and bottom are red and "Turtle Mountain Chippewa" numbers letters around seal are black, the seal being in lemon-yellow. The plate measures 6 x 12 inches. Note the expiration stickers in the upper left corners. EXC-$10

Illinois 1948 - With the advent of World War II when metal became scarce several states (Alaska, then still a territory; Arkansas, Illinois, Louisiana, some Missouri, Montana, Virginia, and Wyoming), issued plates made of compressed paper and held together with a glue-like material that used soybean oil. During this period, the plates were popular as food with farm animals who could smell it and get close enough to eat the plates. Illinois kept on issuing these plates through 1938. This plate is black on orange and measures 5-1/2 x 11-3/8 inches. EXC-$55

Northwest Territories, Canada, 1970— The "Polar Bear" plate design was first used in the Northwest Territories in 1970, and have been used ever since. The plate shown was white on blue, these colors having been used exclusively as alternating combinations (some with revalidating stickers) ever since with the exceptions of 1974 and 1977 when red on white was employed. The current issue is blue on white, carries CANADA'S ARCTIC and NORTHWEST TERRITORIES above and below the numbers that go well into the five digits. The hyphen has been eliminated and the plates are revalidated annually by a sticker that is placed within the frame of the bear's front left leg.

The measurements of 6 x 12 inches (standard for North America) have been maintained. Only the design has been changed but does conform to those measurements. The majority of registrations may currently be found in the communities of Fort Smith, Hay River, Inuvit (above the Arctic Circle) and the capital city of Yellowknife. Northwest Territory's first license plates did not appear until 1941.

Early in 1992, the Northwest Territories were split into two sections, the Eastern part populated by some 17,000 Intuits (Eskimos) in an icebound land more than three times the size of Texas and named Nunavut. The western half retains the polar bear design.

The above plate was used on a car owned by a physician in Yellowknife. EXC-$55 (Plate source: Robert N. Tuthill, Springfield, Massachusetts)

(Note: The excellent (EXC) condition value of each item pictured is provided in the photo captions. Each item pictured may or may not be in excellent condition, but is shown to give visual representation of that item)

Connecticut 1947 - Although date inserts, tabs, windshield stickers had been used before 1937, that was the year that the state decided to cut costs by issuing a "permanent" plate such as L/M 530. The first number of years the plates were made of aluminum. Later steel was used. The 1937 insert was yellow; 1938 silver, 1939 green, etc., the plates being of black characters on a natural aluminum silver background. This design was used through 1947 such as this one with a green insert. The plates of 1948 through 1954 varied in design carrying CT to the right of the insert and in 1955 and 1956, CONN. EXC-$45

Wyoming 1967 - The cowboy astride the bucking bronco has been a part of the Wyoming plate design consistently since 1936. White on Red. 6 x 12 inches. The prefix number 8 denotes the county in which the plate was issued. EXC-$30

1941 Georgia license plate with peach logo, 6 x 12 inches, blue with peach-colored logo. EXC-$70

1950 Hawaii license plate, 6 x 12 inches, white with oversized numbers. EXC-$75

MASCOTS & BADGES

An Old Dog, A New Trick

Years ago I purchased a 1929 Lincoln Opera Coupe. It was a good old unrestored automobile, but unfortunately a barn beam had fallen on the front of the car. It bent the sun visor without breaking the glass and slightly damaged the hood. It also bent the greyhound mascot down. Well, who can drive a Lincoln with the dog going downhill?

I decided to try and straighten the mascot using a small torch. Applying a moderate amount of heat I simultaneously slowly pulled up on the mascot. The greyhound regained its former proud stance and the Lincoln provided me with many miles of motoring pleasure.

- Ken Buttolph

Antique Auto Turn Signals

Description	Good	Very Good	Excellent
Circa mid-1930s "wig-wag" taillight (accessory type)	60	125	175
1918 British "aluminum-hand" signaling device	900	1600	2000
1920s Outlook combination stop/taillight (beehive shape; prismatic)	50	100	125

Mascots And Hood Ornaments

Description	Good	Very Good	Excellent
Boyce Moto Meter on dog bone base	40	80	125
Boyce Moto Meter with internal marque identification and winged base	30	60	100
Boyce Moto Meter with internal marque and car company identification	20	40	80
1912 Boyce Moto Meter	16	26	40
Early 1920s Boyce Moto Meter on a flip-top cap with wings, used on Packards	50	100	190
Late teens Pierce-Arrow hood mascot (archer on knees)	90	160	250
1920 Minerva hood mascot (Athena)	40	80	125
1929-1937 Duesenberg hood mascot ("Duesenbird")	310	440	650
1930s Bugatti Royale hood mascot, designed by Rembrandt Bugatti (Rampant Elephant)	250	360	500
1933 Buick hood mascot (Goddess)	80	120	200
1932 Chevrolet hood mascot (Eagle)	65	110	175
1928 Pontiac hood mascot (Indian)	60	95	150
1929 Pontiac hood mascot (Indian)	60	95	150
1930 Pontiac hood mascot (Indian)	40	80	125
1931 Pontiac hood mascot (Indian)	40	80	125
1932 Pontiac hood mascot (Indian)	40	80	125
1927-1928 Oakland hood mascot (Eagle)	80	120	200
1928-1931 Ford hood mascot (Quail)	85	150	225
1934 Ford hood mascot (Greyhound)	100	175	275
1935 Ford hood mascot (Greyhound)	60	95	150
1936 Ford hood mascot (Greyhound)	60	95	150

1936 Ford hood mascot (Lazy 8)	40	80	125
1932 Chrysler hood mascot (first use of Gazelle mascot)	85	150	225
1949 DeSoto hood mascot (head of Spanish explorer Hernando DeSoto)	30	60	100
1950 DeSoto hood mascot (head of Spanish explorer Hernando DeSoto)	30	60	100
1933 Plymouth hood mascot (Goddess)	60	95	150
1924 Franklin hood mascot (first use of Lion mascot)	80	120	200
1928 Franklin Airman hood mascot ("Spirit of St. Louis")	130	220	350
1929 Gardner hood mascot (Griffin)	85	150	225
1934-1935 Hudson hood mascot (stylized bird in flight)	60	95	150
1928 Kissel hood mascot (Eagle)	110	190	300
1928-1929 Pierce-Arrow hood mascot (Archer with foot down)	100	175	275
1912-1928 Moon hood ornament (Crescent Moon)	30	60	100
1929 Packard hood mascot ("Goddess of Speed")	100	175	275
1930 Packard hood mascot (often called Adonis, but correctly titled Dauphin)	250	360	500
1938-1940 Packard hood ornament (Pelican)	65	110	175
1926-1935 Stutz hood ornament (Egyptian Sun God Ra)	110	190	300
1931-1934 Studebaker hood mascot (Goose)	60	95	150
1927-1933 Lincoln hood mascot (Greyhound with radiator cap)	130	220	350

(**NOTE**: A variation of the Greyhound mascot was used until 1939 on Model K Lincolns.)

1956 Lincoln hood ornament (Knight)	40	80	125
1925-1928 Diana hood ornament ("Diana")	175	325	550
1927-1930 LaSalle hood ornament ("Sieur de LaSalle")	175	325	550
1926-1930 Cadillac hood mascot (Herald)	260	375	550
1930-1932 Cadillac LaSalle hood ornament (Heron)	250	360	500
1933-1936 Cadillac hood ornament, V-12 and V-16 cars, special order (Goddess)	110	190	300
1932 Dodge hood ornament (first use of Ram mascot by Dodge)	85	150	225
1946 Dodge hood ornament (Ram mascot refined)	30	60	100
1951 Dodge hood ornament (Ram mascot refined)	30	60	100
1953 Dodge hood ornament (Ram mascot refined)	30	60	100

Description	Good	Very Good	Excellent
1954 Dodge hood ornament (Ram mascot refined)	30	60	100
1909 Goobo, God of Good Luck, hood mascot, aftermarket novelty type created by L.V. Aronson	14	23	35
1911 Rolls-Royce, hood mascot "Spirit of Ecstasy," by Charles Sykes	60	95	150
1926 Liberty Bell hood mascot, aftermarket fraternal type done for "Odd Fellows"	10	16	25
1920s hood ornament, aftermarket novelty type (Pan)	30	50	75
Rolls-Royce hood mascot (Spirit of Ecstacy)	175	325	550
Hood ornament, aftermarket novelty type (aero engine)	30	50	75
Hood ornament, aftermarket novelty type (aero engine) with Boyce Moto Meter	35	65	110
Hood ornament, aftermarket novelty type (god Mercury running)	31	55	80
Hood ornament, aftermarket novelty type (Minute Man)	30	50	75
Wall plaque, shaped like 1950s style DeSoto hood ornament; this is probably a dealer promotional item	40	80	125

Lalique Glass Mascots

Description	Good	Very Good	Excellent
1915 Lalique crystal glass, dragonfly hood ornament. First mascot by Rene Lalique	470	780	1200

(**NOTE**: All the following Lalique glass mascots were produced in the 1920s and 1930s. Only the values for mascots in excellent condition are listed due to the unique nature of this collectible.)

Description	Good	Very Good	Excellent
Cinq Chevaux (five horses)	-	-	15,000
Coq (cockerel)	-	-	4,000
Etoile Filante (shooting star)	-	-	25,000
Faucon (falcon)	-	-	4,000
Grande Libellule (large dragonfly - 8-1/4 inches tall)	-	-	8,000
Grenouille (frog)	-	-	25,000
Hibou (owl)	-	-	40,000
Hirondelle (swallow)	-	-	4,500
Houden Coq (crowing cockerel)	-	-	6,000
Levrier (greyhound)	-	-	5,500
Paon (peacock)	-	-	20,000
Petite Libellule (small dragonfly - 6-1/4 inches tall)	-	-	7,500

Poisson (fish)	-	-	4,000
Renard (fox)	-	-	200,000
Sanglier (boar)	-	-	3,000
Tete d' Aigle (eagle's head)	-	-	5,500
Tete de Belier (ram's head)	-	-	9,000
Tete de Coq (cockerel's head)	-	-	7,000
Tete de Faucon (falcon's head)	-	-	3,500
Tireur d' Arc (archer)	-	-	4,000
Victoire ("The Spirit of the Wind")	-	-	10,000
Vitesse (speed)	-	-	13,000

Auto and Truck Radiator Scripts & Nameplates

Description	Good	Very Good	Excellent
Freightliner radiator emblem	7	12	19
Interstate nickled namescript	8	13	20
Duesenberg nameplate	26	42	65
Empire nameplate	6	10	15
Texan nameplate	8	13	20
Wolverine nameplate (with red insert)	8	13	20
Beggs Six nameplate (porcelain with red glass background)	8	13	20
Diana badge (oval, black background)	8	13	20
Kaiser badge (postwar, chrome buffalo)	12	19	30
Frazer badge (postwar, coat-of arms)	12	19	30
Bentley "wings" (B with black label)	18	29	45
Bentley "wings" (B with green label)	16	26	40
Bentley "wings" (B with red label)	16	26	40
Bentley "wings" (B with blue label)	16	26	40
Bugatti nameplate	26	42	65
Cadillac radiator script	16	26	40
Klondike radiator script	150	200	250
Willys-Knight "WK" radiator script	10	16	25

Freightliner truck radiator shell script. EXC-$19

(Note: The excellent (EXC) condition value of each item pictured is provided in the photo captions. Each item pictured may or may not be in excellent condition, but is shown to give visual representation of that item)

Klondike automobile radiator script. EXC-$250

Archer mascot used on Pierce-Arrow automobiles in the 1920s. EXC-$250

(Note: The excellent (EXC) condition value of each item pictured is provided in the photo captions. Each item pictured may or may not be in excellent condition, but is shown to give visual representation of that item)

Spirit of Ecstacy mascot used on Rolls-Royce automobiles in the 1920s. EXC-$150

A rare Goddess mascot used on 1933 Buicks. EXC-$200

Boyce Moto Meter on a flip-top cap with wings used on early Packards. EXC-$190

The Rene Lalique "Tete de Coq" glass hood mascot, here adding elegance to a Duesenberg. EXC-$7,000

Hood Ornaments

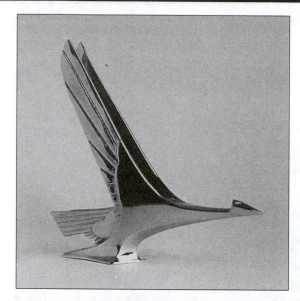

Left: Goose mascot used on 1931-1934 Studebakers. EXC-$150

Below: Stylized bird mascot used on 1934 Hudsons. EXC-$150

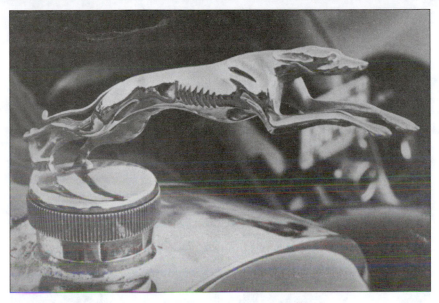

Greyhound mascot used on 1927-1933 Lincolns. EXC-$350

Boyce Moto Meter with a dog bone decorative base, here used on a Marmon. EXC-$125

Hood Ornaments

Rampant Elephant mascot used on 1930s Bugatti Royale automobiles. EXC-$500

"Diana" mascot used on 1925-1928 Diana automobiles. EXC-$550

Boyce Moto Meter with internal marque identification--Oldsmobile, in this case--and winged base. EXC-$100

Boyce Moto Meter with internal marque identification--Moon--as well as car company identification and location. EXC-$80

Hood Ornaments

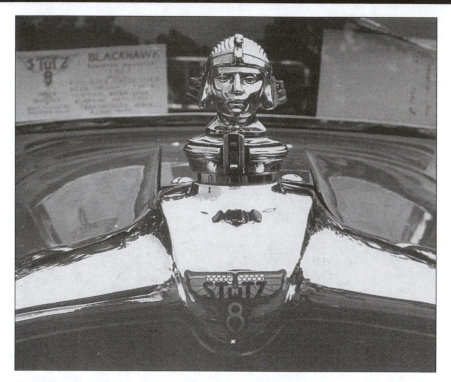

Egyptian Sun God Ra mascot used on 1926-1935 Stutz automobiles. EXC-$300

Crescent Moon radiator cap ornament used on 1912-1928 Moon automobiles. EXC-$100

Hood Ornaments

Goddess mascot used on 1933-1936 Cadillac V-12 and V-16 engined automobiles. EXC-$300

(Note: The excellent (EXC) condition value of each item pictured is provided in the photo captions. Each item pictured may or may not be in excellent condition, but is shown to give visual representation of that item)

"Herald" mascot used on 1926-1930 Cadillac automobiles. EXC-$550

Hood Ornaments

Goddess of Speed mascot on flip-top cap used on late 1920s Packards. EXC-$275

"Adonis"/Dauphin mascot used on 1930 Packard automobiles. EXC-$500

MODEL KITS

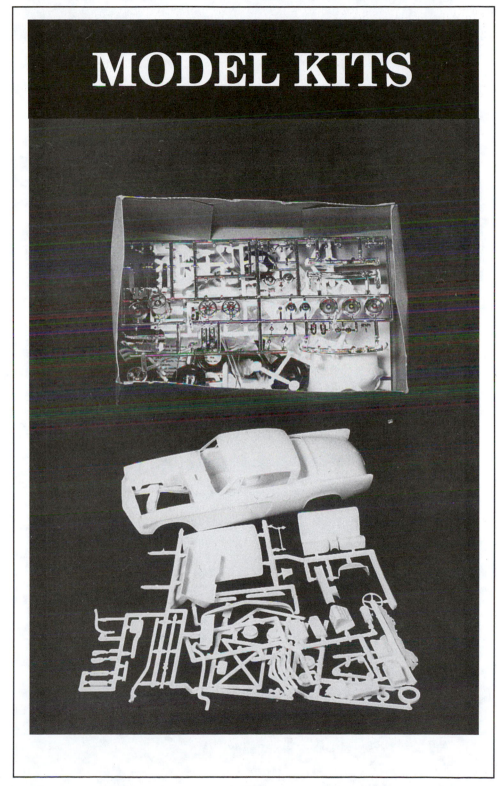

Model Kits

Co.	Name	Year	No.	Good	V.G.	Excellent	Scale
AMT	1925 Model T Roadster/Pickup	1987	6512	6	18	20	1/25
AMT	"Cop Out" 1925 Ford Model T Paddy Wagon	1969	T319	15	45	50	1/25
AMT	1927 Model T Ford	1983	6582	6	18	20	1/25
AMT	1927 Street Rod T	1973	T143	15	22	40	1/25
AMT	1929 Ford Woodie/Pickup	1987	6518	5	13	15	1/25
AMT	1929 Ford Model A Roadster Trophy Series	1967	2829	25	65	75	1/25
AMT	1932 Chrysler Imperial Convertible	1987	6514	5	13	15	1/25
AMT	1932 Ford Roadster	1983	6585	5	13	15	1/25
AMT	1932 Ford V-8 (3-in-1 kit)	1960	232	25	65	75	1/25
AMT	1932 Ford Vickie	1983	6573	5	13	15	1/25
AMT	1932 Ford Victoria Fire Chief	1972	T177	6	21	35	1/25
AMT	1933 Willys Coupe	1983	6570	5	13	15	1/25
AMT	1936 Ford Convertible	1983	6591	5	18	25	1/25
AMT	1941 Plymouth Coupe	1983	6583	10	25	35	1/25
AMT	1949 Ford Coupe	1967	2249	15	45	50	1/25
AMT	1949 Ford (Crusin' USA by Barris)	1980	2255	6	18	20	1/25
AMT	1949 Ford (Street Rods)	1975	T290	10	25	35	1/25
AMT	1949 Ford Coupe (Tournament of Thrills)	1973	T444	30	85	100	1/25
AMT	1949 Mercury (3-in-1 kit)	1963	2349	25	65	75	1/25
AMT	1950 Ford Convertible Customizing Series	1987	6831	5	13	15	1/25
AMT	1950 Ford Convertible (Tournament of Thrills)	1973	T445	30	85	100	1/25
AMT	1951 Chevy Convertible (Crusin' USA by Barris)	1980	2253	10	25	35	1/25
AMT	1953 Corvette	1986	6519	5	13	15	1/25
AMT	1953 Corvette	1976	T310	10	20	25	1/25
AMT	1953 Studebaker "Double Whammy" (3-in-1 kit)	1971	T262	15	45	50	1/25
AMT	1955 Mercedes gullwing	1989	6871	5	13	15	1/25
AMT	1956 Ford Hardtop Show n Go Series (3-in-1 kit)	1969	T271	12	35	40	1/25
AMT	1956 Ford "Haulin Vicky" Hardtop	1967	2356	15	45	50	1/25

AMT	1957 Chevrolet Bel Air "Pepper Shaker" (3-in-1 kit)	1968	T280	15	45	50	1/25
AMT	1957 Ford Thunderbird "Here Comes The Judge" drag car	1968	T235	25	65	75	1/25
AMT	1957 Ford Two Door Hardtop	1968	T285	12	35	40	1/25
AMT	1958 Chevrolet Impala (3-in-1 kit)	1964	2758	30	85	100	1/25
AMT	1959 Chevrolet El Camino	1989	6897	5	13	15	1/25
AMT	1959 Corvette convertible "Reggie Jackson" series (really a 1960 model)	1981	PK4183	12	35	40	1/25
AMT	1960 Ford Sunliner Convertible	1960	11160	60	175	200	1/25
AMT	1960 Edsel Ranger Convertible (3-in-1 kit)	1960	22260	60	175	200	1/25
AMT	1960 Mercury Parklane Convertible	1960	33360	30	85	100	1/25
AMT	1961 Pontiac Bonneville Hardtop (3-in-1 kit)	1961	K621	45	125	150	1/25
AMT	1962 Chevrolet Corvette (3-in-1 kit)	1962	S922	100	250	300	1/25
AMT	1962 Ford Galaxie 500	1969	T134	30	85	100	1/25
AMT	1962 Mercury Monterey (3-in-1 kit)	1962	K322	40	110	130	1/25
AMT	1962 Pontiac Bonneville Hardtop (3-in-1 kit)	1962	S622	80	140	175	1/25
AMT	1962 Pontiac Bonneville Convertible (3-in-1 kit)	1962	K612	45	125	150	1/25
AMT	1963 Chevrolet Impala (3-in-1 kit)	1963	6723	45	125	150	1/25
AMT	1963 Buick Electra Hardtop (3-in-1 kit)	1963	6523	40	100	125	1/25
AMT	1963 Chevrolet Impala SS Convertible (3-in-1 kit)	1963	06-713	30	85	100	1/25
AMT	1963 Mercury Meteor Hardtop (3-in-1 kit)	1963	05-363	45	125	150	1/25
AMT	1963 Studebaker Avanti Prestige Series	1989	6872	5	15	25	1/25
AMT	1964 Ford Fairlane 500 Hardtop (3-in-1 kit)	1964	5164	40	100	125	1/25
AMT	1964 Ford Galaxie modified stock car	1970	T193	40	100	125	1/25
AMT	1964 Mercury Marauder (3-in-1 kit)	1964	6324	40	100	125	1/25
AMT	1965 Chevy El Camino	1987	6507	6	18	20	1/25
AMT	1965 Chrysler Imperial (3-in-1 kit)	1965	6815	25	65	90	1/25
AMT	1965 Ford Galaxie Crusin' USA Series (3-in-1 kit)	1980	2263	5	15	25	1/25
AMT	1965 Ford Fairlane modified stock car	1970	T191	40	100	125	1/25

AMT	1965 Lincoln Continental Prestige Series	1987	6504	5	15	25	1/25
AMT	1965 Lincoln Continental (3-in-1 kit)	1965	6415	25	65	75	1/25
AMT	1965 Oldsmobile 88 modified stock car	1971	T190	40	100	125	1/25
AMT	1965 Pontiac Bonneville Prestige Series	1987	6503	5	15	25	1/25
AMT	1965 Pontiac Tempest GTO Hardtop Elegance Trophy Series	1967	3205	20	60	75	1/25
AMT	1966 Buick Skylark modified stock car	1970	T189	40	100	125	1/25
AMT	1966 Chevy modified stock car	1971	T192	40	100	125	1/25
AMT	1966 Ford Fairlane 500 (3-in-1 kit)	1965	5166	20	60	75	1/25
AMT	1966 Ford Galaxie 500 XL (3-in-1 kit)	1977	2204	10	25	30	1/25
AMT	1966 Ford Galaxie 500 XL (3-in-1 kit)	1965	6126	25	65	90	1/25
AMT	1966 Ford Galaxie 500 XL (3-in-1 kit)	1987	6517	10	25	30	1/25
AMT	1966 Mercury Park Lane Hardtop (3-in-1 kit)	1965	6326	20	60	75	1/25
AMT	1966 T-Bird Hardtop/Convertible (3-in-1 kit)	1977	2208	10	25	30	1/25
AMT	1966 Thunderbird Convertible "Cus-tomizing Series"	1987	6833	5	13	15	1/25
AMT	1968 Fairlane Torino GT (3-in-1 kit)	1968	5168	35	100	120	1/25
AMT	1969 Chevrolet Camaro Official Pace Car (53rd Annual Indian-apolis 500) (3-in-1 kit)	1969	T333	60	175	200	1/25
AMT	1969 Chevrolet Chevelle SS-396 convertible (2-in-1 kit)	1977	2211	30	85	100	1/25
AMT	1969 Chevrolet Corvair Monza (2-in-1 kit)	1972	T374	20	60	75	1/25
AMT	1969 Ford Torino Cobra (3-in-1 kit)	1969	Y904	35	100	120	1/25
AMT	1969 Lincoln Continental	1969	Y907	30	85	100	1/25
AMT	1970 Chevrolet Impala "Fire Chief Car"	1970	T223	15	45	50	1/25
AMT	1970 Chevrolet Monte Carlo "Coco Carlo" (3-in-1 kit)	1970	T326	60	175	200	1/25
AMT	1971 Monte Carlo	1971	T119	35	100	120	1/25
AMT	1972 Ford Torino National Stock Racer Series	1973	T391	20	60	75	1/25
AMT	1972 Pontiac Ventura II Super Sport Sprint	1972	T379	20	60	75	1/25
AMT	1973 Mustang Mach I Street Machine Series	1981	PK4167	15	45	50	1/25

AMT	1976 Chevy Nova SS Street Machine Series	1981	PK4168	8	22	25	1/25
AMT	1977 AMC Matador X	1977	T480	10	25	35	1/25
AMT	1977 Chevrolet Corvette Sting Ray	1977	T483	15	45	50	1/25
AMT	1977 Ford F-350 "Boonie Boss" pickup	1977	T412	25	65	75	1/25
AMT	1923 Ford Model T Depot Hack	1976	T142	10	25	35	1/25
AMT	1964 289 Cobra "Reggie Jackson Series"	1981	PK4182	8	22	25	1/25
AMT	1929 Ford Model A "Ala Kart" Roadster (double kit)	1968	T254	30	85	100	1/25
AMT	1966 Sunbeam Tiger	1979	2003	20	55	65	1/25
AMT	American LaFrance Aero Chief		T6634	30	55	65	
AMT	American LaFrance Ladder Truck		T598	50	85	100	
AMT	American LaFrance Pumper		T599	35	60	70	
AMT	"Mighty Max" 1975 AMC Gremlin X	1975	T451	10	25	35	1/25
AMT	B. Baker #21 Valvoline NASCAR Ford T-Bird	1983	8042	12	35	40	1/25
AMT	B. Parsons #72 Kings Row NASCAR Chevrolet Laguna	1974	T429	25	65	75	1/25
AMT	Plymouth Barracuda "Fireball 500" customized movie car	1967	911	45	125	150	1/25
AMT	B. Allison #12 Coca Cola NASCAR Chevrolet Malibu	1973	T373	35	100	120	1/25
AMT	B. Allison #12 Coca Cola NASCAR Chevrolet Monte Carlo	1972	T421	45	125	150	1/25
AMT	B. Allison #12 Matador Sportsman Stock Car		3030	25	65	75	1/25
AMT	Bobby Unser Indy Olsonite Eagle		T273	15	45	50	1/25
AMT	Budweiser 1923 Ford Model T Delivery Van	1978	2401	10	25	30	1/25
AMT	C. Yarborough #28 Hardee's NASCAR Chevrolet Monte Carlo	1983	8045	15	40	45	1/25
AMT	"Right On" 1970 Ford Maverick Pro Stock	1973	T348	15	45	50	1/25
AMT	Car Craft Dream Rod	1965	2165	40	100	125	1/25
AMT	"Boondocker" 1972 Chevrolet Blazer	1976	T200	20	55	65	1/25
AMT	Chevelle Drag Racing Team "Time Machine"(3-kits-in-1)	1967	6750	30	85	100	1/25
AMT	Craig Carter #56 IMSA Chevrolet Camaro	1982	6540	10	25	30	1/25
AMT	D. Allison #88 Diehard NASCAR Chevrolet Laguna	1974	T380	20	55	65	1/25

AMT	D. Waltrip #11 Pepsi NASCAR Chevrolet Monte Carlo	1983	8043	15	45	50	1/25
AMT	Dan Gurney Indy 500 Lotus	1976	T154	18	50	60	1/25
AMT	Don Garlits Wynn's Jammer top fuel dragster "Checkered Flag Series	1965	2167	65	85	100	1/25
AMT	TV Tommy Ivo rear engine top fuel dragster	1972	T174	40	100	125	1/25
AMT	"Macho Machine" Ford Ranger XLT pickup	1978	2707	15	45	50	1/25
AMT	1940 Willys Coupe Gasser Series	1968	T242	25	65	75	1/25
AMT	Ford Leva Car Mach 1	1959	160	25	70	80	1/16
AMT	1964 Ford Cobra (3-in-1 kit) Roadster Trophy Series	1965	2170	40	100	125	1/25
AMT	"Novacaine" 1972 Chevrolet Funny Car	1972	T382	15	45	50	1/25
AMT	G. Johncock #28 Pylon NASCAR Chevrolet Chevelle	1974	T395	25	65	75	1/25
AMT	A. Kulwicki #7 Zerex NASCAR Ford T-Bird	1990	6739	25	65	75	1/25
AMT	Grant King Sprint Car	1975	T168	15	40	45	1/25
AMT	1958 Edsel Pacer Funny Car	1968	F158	40	100	125	1/25
AMT	J. Rutherford McLaren 1974 Indy 500 winner	1974	T260	15	45	50	1/25
AMT	1963 Indy 500 Lotus/offy (2-kits-in-1)	1969	T362	50	75	90	1/25
AMT	Jim Cushman Plymouth Duster Sportsman Stock Car	1976	T230	40	100	125	1/25
AMT	J. Rutherford McLaren 1975 Gatorade Indy Car	1975	T256	15	45	50	1/25
AMT	K. Petty #7 Seven-Eleven NASCAR Ford Thunderbird	1983	8047	10	20	30	1/25
AMT	KISS Custom 1973 Chevrolet Van	1978	2501	18	40	60	1/25
AMT	"Streaker" 1965 Oldsmobile F-85 convertible Funny Car	1968	F162	25	65	75	1/25
AMT	"Jolly Green Gasser" 1965 Ford Galaxie 500 XL drag car	1969	T334	30	85	100	1/25
AMT	L. Pond #54 Masters NASCAR Chevrolet Chevelle	1975	T443	30	85	100	1/25
AMT	"Nitro Charger" 1972 Dodge Funny Car	1972	T179	25	65	75	1/25
AMT	1925 Porter "My Mother The Car" TV series car	1966	904	25	65	75	1/25
AMT	N. Bonnett #21 Citgo NASCAR Ford T-Bird	1990	6733	25	65	75	1/25
AMT	Mercedes-Benz 300SL Gullwing Coupe	1978	2304	8	20	25	1/25

AMT	Mercedes-Benz 300SL Gullwing Coupe (Trophy Series)	1965	2065	15	45	50	1/25
AMT	Graveyard Ghoul Duo coach and Drag-U-La from "The Munsters" TV series (double kit)	1969	T309	45	125	150	1/25
AMT	Parnelli Jones Watson Roadster 63 Indy 500 Winner	1976	T162	20	70	85	1/25
AMT	Peanut 1 Chevrolet Monza Funny Car "The Quarter Mile Smile" (Jimmy Carter caricature)	1977	2801	25	65	75	1/25
AMT	"Wild Hoss" 1978 Ford Bronco 4x4	1979	2708	15	45	50	1/25
AMT	Penske PC-6 '79 Indy 500 Winner	1979	3007	10	30	35	1/25
AMT	Penske McLaren Indy Special	1974	T264	15	45	50	1/25
AMT	Penske PC-6 Indy CAM2 Special	1979	3000	10	30	35	1/25
AMT	Penske PC-6 Indy Gould Charge	1979	3001	10	30	35	1/25
AMT	Penske PC-6 Indy Norton Spirit	1979	3002	10	30	35	1/25
AMT	Piranha AA/fuel dragster	1967	910	30	85	100	1/25
AMT	R. Petty #43 Dart Kit Car	1976	T229	45	125	150	1/25
AMT	R. Petty #43 STP NASCAR Pontiac Grand Prix	1983	8044	15	40	45	1/25
AMT	D. Earnhardt #15 Wrangler NASCAR Ford T-Bird	1983	8046	15	45	50	1/25
AMT	"High Stepper" 1953 Ford F-100 pickup	1978	2704	15	45	50	1/25
AMT	1962 Silhouette w/ trailer Prestige Series	1964	2162	30	85	100	1/25
AMT	Sonny and Cher Mustangs-Barris customs (2-in-1)	1967	907	35	50	75	1/25
AMT	"Sun Chaser" 1973 Chevrolet Custom Van	1977	T402	10	30	35	1/25
AMT	1961 Chevrolet Apache pickup	1961	K731	45	125	150	1/25
AMT	Thomas Flyer (New York to Paris race winner)	1976	T232	15	35	45	1/25
AMT	"Tuff Truk" 1977 Ford F-350 Ranger pickup	1977	T413	35	50	75	1/25
AMT	National Winners King T by Don Tognotti and Wild Dream by Joe Wilhelm (double kit)	1965	2164	45	125	150	1/25
AMT	"Vantasy" 1965 Dodge Custom Camper	1976	T201	35	50	75	1/25
AMT	"Vantom" 1976 Ford Econoline custom van	1976	T418	10	35	45	1/25
AMT/Ertl	1923 Bell System Ford Model T Van	1984	3264	8	22	25	1/25
AMT/Ertl	1949 Mercury (3-in-1 kit) Customizing Series	1987	6830	5	15	20	1/25

AMT/Ertl	1950 Ford Convertible (2-in-1 kit) Customizing Series	1987	6831	5	15	20	1/25
AMT/Ertl	1955 Chevrolet Nomad (3-in-1 kit)	1984	6592	8	22	25	1/25
AMT/Ertl	1963 Ford Galaxie 500 XL Prestige Series	1987	6501	5	15	20	1/25
AMT/Ertl	"Back To The Future" DeLorean movie car	1990	6122	8	22	25	1/25
AMT/Ertl	Customized Pontiac "Monkee Mobile" TV show convertible	1990	6058	5	15	20	1/25
AMT/Ertl	1983 GMC "The A Team" TV show van	1986	6616	5	15	20	1/25
Airfix	1910 B Type Bus (Old Bill)		471	5	15	20	1/32
Airfix	1933 Alfa Romeo with Figures		0201	5	13	15	1/32
Aurora	1903 Rambler		151	5	13	15	
Aurora	1909 Stanley Streamer		154	10	25	30	1/16
Aurora	1912 T Truck		629	5	13	15	1/32
Aurora	1922 T Sedan		622	5	13	15	1/32
Aurora	1922 Ford "Double Deuce" (2-in-1 kit)	1963	568	45	65	75	1/25
Aurora	1924 Buick		556	10	30	35	
Aurora	1927 Model T Sad Sack		507	8	22	25	
Aurora	1932 Ford Ramrod		509	10	25	30	
Aurora	1932 Skid-Do		554	12	35	40	
Aurora	1934 Ford (stock and street)	1963		12	25	40	1/25
Aurora	1940 Maserati Special		525	12	35	40	
Aurora	1965 Ford GT racer		595	12	35	40	1/25
Aurora	40 Ton Flat Bed Trailer Trucker with Power Shovel		683	50	150	175	1/64
Aurora	5000 Gal. Gas Trailer Truck		682	50	150	175	1/64
Aurora	5000 Gal. Milk Trailer Truck		681	50	150	175	1/64
Aurora	1964 Aston Martin DB4	1965	562	45	65	75	1/25
Aurora	Austin Healey		550	11	30	35	
Aurora	Austin Healey		516	10	25	30	
Aurora	Baja Boot		681	12	35	40	1/32
Aurora	Chevy Custom Pickup		555	12	35	40	
Aurora	Chrysler 392 Fuel Injected Engine		844	10	20	30	
Aurora	Corvette		519	8	22	25	
Aurora	Cunningham (Famous Sports Cars)		515	12	35	40	1/32

Aurora	Customized Corvette		545	10	30	35	
Aurora	Customized T		548	12	35	40	
Aurora	Customized T-Bird		547	8	22	25	
Aurora	Drop Out Bus		591	10	30	35	1/32
Aurora	Ferrari		514	6	18	20	
Aurora	1962 Ferrari Berlinetta GTO	1964	563	45	65	75	1/25
Aurora	Ford Mustang 2+2		665	11	30	35	
Aurora	Ford T Dragster Speedster		535	8	22	25	
Aurora	1961 Jaguar XKE	1962	566	45	65	75	1/25
Aurora	Jaguar XK120		512	10	25	30	
Aurora	MG Sports Car		511	8	22	25	
Aurora	1963 Maserati 350 GT	1964	564	45	65	75	1/25
Aurora	Show Trailer		530	8	22	25	
Aurora	Stanley Streamer (original issue, Old Timers Series)		573	10	30	35	1/16
Aurora	Studebaker Avanti		560	12	35	40	1/25
Aurora	Stutz Bearcat		571	8	22	25	
Aurora	Tepee "T"		597	10	25	30	1/32
Aurora	Thunderbird		520	6	18	20	
Aurora	Triumph Spitfire		538	9	26	30	
Aurora	XKE Jaguar Convertible (Famous Sports Car Series)		567	18	50	60	1/25
Entex	1914 Dennis Motor Fire Engine		8473	25	65	75	1/19
Entex	1928 Lincoln L Sedan by Dietrich, Convertible (50th Anniversary Edition)		2205	20	55	65	1/16
Entex	Martini Porsche Transporter C-900 Tractor with 27-foot trailer		9103	15	45	50	1/32
Ertl	International Off Road Scout II		8024	10	25	30	1/25
Ertl	International Transtar Co. 4070A		8000	25	65	75	1/25
Ertl	International Transtar II Eagle		8017	10	25	30	1/25
Ertl	Smokey & the Bandit II Trailer		8036	10	30	35	1/25
Ertl	Volvo N-10		8037	10	25	30	1/25
Hawk	Alky Saltzer		600	5	13	15	
Hawk	Bobcat Sports Roadster		633	8	22	25	1/48
Hawk	Chaparral II		03	6	18	20	1/32

Hawk	1909 Hupmobile (reissue of Keepsake K-11/Strombecker T-2)	1964	635	10	15	25	1/24
Hawk	1909 Hupmobile (reissue of Keepsake K-11/Strombecker T-2), gold plated, includes display case	1969	301	15	25	40	1/24
Hawk	Indy Racer		210	45	125	150	1/24
Hawk	Lancia Ferrari		01	6	18	20	1/32
Hawk	Lotus 30 Ford Powered		02	6	18	20	1/32
Hawk	Maserati 5000 GT		04	6	18	20	1/32
Hawk	Monte Carlo Sport Roadster		528	6	18	20	
Hawk	Peeler IV		201	8	22	25	
Hawk	Powered Bonneville Racer Bonnie Buggy		602	8	22	25	1/48
Hawk	1902 Rambler (reissue of Keepsake K-10/Strombecker T-1)	1964	634	10	15	25	1/24
Hawk	1902 Rambler (reissue of Keepsake K-10/Strombecker T-1), gold plated, includes display case	1969	300	15	25	40	1/24
Hawk	San Francisco Cable Car		517	6	18	20	1/48
Heller	Brabham BT 33		80748	10	25	30	1/24
Heller	Ferrari 512S		80747	10	25	30	1/24
Heller	Lotus 49B		80749	10	25	30	1/24
Heller	Porsche 917K		80746	10	25	30	1/24
Hubley	1954 Mercedes-Benz 300SL roadster	1960	152K	20	65	75	1/24
Hubley	1954 Mercedes-Benz 300SL hardtop	1960	153K	20	65	75	1/24
Hubley	1956 Renault Dauphine	1960	159K	15	45	50	1/24
Hubley	1956 Triumph TR3 roadster	1960	150K	15	45	50	1/24
Hubley	1959 Nash Metropolitan convertible (4-in-1 kit)	1960	158K	30	85	100	1/24
Hubley	1960 Ford Country Squire station wagon (4-in-1 kit)	1960	154K	45	125	150	1/24
Hubley	1960 Ford Fairlane	1960	156K	45	125	150	1/24
Hubley	1960 Rolls-Royce Phantom V Silver Cloud	1960	157K	15	45	50	1/24
I.M.C.	1948 Ford Convertible	1966	105	20	55	65	1/25
I.M.C.	1948 Ford Coupe	1967	115	20	55	65	1/25
I.M.C.	1963 Ford Cougar II	1966	103	30	85	100	1/25
I.M.C.	1964 Ford GT	1966	104	15	45	50	1/25
I.M.C.	1965 Dodge A-100 "Little Red Wagon" wheelstanding pickup	1966	107	30	85	100	1/25

I.M.C.	1966 Lotus/Ford Indy 500 winner	1966	111	20	55	65	1/25
I.M.C.	1966 Mark II Ford GT	1977	112	15	45	50	1/25
Imai	1907 Itala 120 HP		1000	20	60	70	1/16
Imai	Bianchi		783	20	60	70	1/16
Imai	Ferrari 275 GTB (James Bond)		625	15	45	50	1/32
Imai	Volkswagen Super Beetle Cabriolet		2416	15	45	50	1/24
Imai	Volkswagen Super Beetle Hardtop		2417	15	45	50	1/24
Jo-Han	1960 DeSoto Adventurer Hardtop (3-in-1 kit)	1960	2760	10	25	45	1/25
Jo-Han	1961 Chrysler New Yorker (3-in-1 kit)	1961	2661	15	45	50	1/25
Jo-Han	1961 Rambler American	1961	2961	15	45	50	1/25
Jo-Han	1962 Cadillac Fleetwood	1962	C-4862	45	125	150	1/25
Jo-Han	1962 Dodge Dart Convertible	1962	5462	15	45	50	1/25
Jo-Han	1962 Oldsmobile Cutlass F-85 Hardtop	1962	4162	10	25	45	1/25
Jo-Han	1962 Plymouth Fury Convertible	1962	5362	15	45	50	1/25
Jo-Han	1962 Studebaker Lark Convertible	1962	5062	10	25	45	1/25
Jo-Han	1963 Oldsmobile Starfire Hardtop (3-in-1 kit)	1963	2163	35	55	75	1/25
Jo-Han	1963 Plymouth Fury Convertible (3-in-1 kit)	1963	3263	35	55	75	1/25
Jo-Han	1964 Cadillac Coupe DeVille (3-in-1 kit)	1964	C-364	15	45	50	1/25
Jo-Han	1964 Chrysler Turbine Gold Cup Series	1964		35	100	125	1/25
Jo-Han	1964 Dodge "Ramcharger" Funny Car	1964	GC-1064	35	100	125	1/25
Jo-Han	1966 AMC Marlin Fastback (3-in-1 kit)	1966	C-1900	35	55	75	1/25
Jo-Han	1966 Plymouth Fury III Hardtop	1966	C-1266	35	55	75	1/25
Jo-Han	1967 AMC Ambassador Hardtop	1967	C-1367	15	45	50	1/25
Jo-Han	1967 Chrysler 300 Hardtop	1967	C-1167	35	55	75	1/25
Jo-Han	1969 Oldsmobile Toronado (3-in-1 kit)	1969	C-1869	35	55	75	1/25
Jo-Han	1969 Plymouth Roadrunner	1969	C-1669	35	55	75	1/25
Jo-Han	1970 AMC Rebel "The Machine"	1984	C-2670	10	25	45	1/25
Jo-Han	1970 Oldsmobile Cutlass 4-4-2	1970	C-115	10	25	45	1/25
Jo-Han	1971 Oldsmobile Toronado Pikes Peak Hill Climb Racer	1971	C-111	30	85	100	1/25

Jo-Han	1972 AMC Hornet Funny Car	1972	C-209	15	45	50	1/25
Jo-Han	1966 Cadillac Ambulance Gold Cup Series	1966	GC-500	15	45	50	1/25
Jo-Han	1966 Cadillac "Heavenly Hearse"		GC-600	10	25	45	1/25
Jo-Han	Mark Donohue 1969 AMC Javelin Trans Am Racer		C-105	10	25	45	1/25
Jo-Han	"Rambunctious" Gene Snow 1970 Dodge Challenger Funny Car	1970	C-201	15	45	50	1/25
Jo-Han	1960 Plymouth Police Emergency Wagon		C-5100	8	10	15	1/25
Jo-Han	"Golden Commando" 1964 Plymouth Fury Super Stock	1964	GC-964	35	55	75	1/25
Jo-Han	"Dyno" Don Nicholson 1972 Ford Maverick Pro Stock	1972	C-204	15	45	50	1/25
Jo-Han	Richard Petty #43 1970 Plymouth Superbird		GC1470	10	25	45	1/25
Jo-Han	Sox & Martin 1970 Plymouth Superbird Super Stock	1970	C-1970	35	55	75	1/25
Jo-Han	"Tinker's Toy" 1970 Oldsmobile Cutlass 4-4-2 Funny Car	1970	C-104	35	55	75	1/25
Keepsake	1902 Rambler	1954	K-10	13	22	35	1/24
Keepsake	1909 Hupmobile	1954	K-11	13	22	35	1/24
Lindberg	1929 SSK Mercedes Benz by Paul Lindberg		668	8	22	25	1/24
Lindberg	50s Beach Bum		3153	6	18	20	
Lindberg	American La France 900 Pumper Fire Engine (motorized, 8" long)		610M	10	25	30	
Lindberg	Big Red Rod (motorized)		651M	15	45	50	1/8
Lindberg	Bobtail "T" (motorized)			25	65	75	1/8
Lindberg	Kustom Koffin		6031	8	22	25	
Lindberg	Orange Crate (motorized)		651M	12	35	40	1/8
Lindberg	Red Devil Bob Tail "T" Roadster		674	40	100	125	1/8
Lindberg	Search & Rescue CB Patrol Vehicle		691	15	45	50	1/12
Lindberg	Triumph TR3 by Paul Lindberg		605	6	18	20	1/32
Lindberg	White Lightning Supermodified		6030	20	55	65	1/24
MPC	1926 Ford Model T "Street Beast"		0771	10	45	50	1/25
MPC	1928 Ford Model T pickup		304	12	35	40	1/25
MPC	1928 Lincoln "Gangbusters"		200	12	35	40	1/25
MPC	1932 Ford Coupe "American Graffiti" movie car		1-0671	25	65	75	1/25

MPC	1953 Ford F-100 "Hot Tub" pickup	1981	0851	12	35	40	1/25
MPC	1956/57 Corvette	1966	301	40	100	125	1/25
MPC	1957 Corvette "Super Zinger"	1972	2600	10	45	50	1/25
MPC	1957 Chevrolet "Rockin' Roller"		0809	10	25	30	1/25
MPC	1964 Corvette Stingray	1964	1-149	80	225	275	1/25
MPC	1965 Dodge Custom 880 Convertible	1965		25	65	75	1/25
MPC	1965 Dodge Monaco 2+2 Hardtop	1965		30	85	100	1/25
MPC	1966 Pontiac Tempest GTO Hardtop	1966		75	150	175	1/25
MPC	1967 Chevrolet Corvette	1967	1-567	45	125	150	1/25
MPC	1967 Dodge "Thunder Charger"	1967	0608	25	65	75	1/25
MPC	1967 Ford Mustang 2+2 Fastback	1967	1367	75	150	175	1/25
MPC	1967 Oldsmobile Toronado	1967	1467	10	45	50	1/25
MPC	1967 Pontiac Bonneville Convertible	1967	1067	45	125	150	1/25
MPC	1967-1/2 Pontiac Firebird Hardtop (3-in-1 kit)	1967	1567	75	150	175	1/25
MPC	1967 Pontiac Tempest GTO Funny Car	1967	1167	45	125	150	1/25
MPC	1968 Chevrolet Camaro SS396 Hardtop	1968	1-968	75	150	175	1/25
MPC	1968 Dodge Charger R/T	1968	768	45	125	150	1/25
MPC	1968 Plymouth Barracuda Fastback	1968	268	40	100	125	1/25
MPC	1969 Chevrolet Impala Hardtop	1969	369	30	85	100	1/25
MPC	1969 Ford Mustang Mach 1 2+2 Fastback	1969	1369	40	100	125	1/25
MPC	1969 Oldsmobile Cutlass 4-4-2 W-30 (2-in-1 kit)	1988	6228	6	18	20	1/25
MPC	1969 Pontiac Grand Prix	1969	2169	30	85	100	1/25
MPC	1970 Dodge Challenger	1970	1470	25	65	75	1/25
MPC	1970 Ford Mustang 2+2 Fastback	1970	1370	40	100	125	1/25
MPC	1970 Mercury Cyclone GT "Spoiler"	1970	2470	40	100	125	1/25
MPC	1970 Pontiac Tempest GTO (2-in-1 kit)	1987	6281	6	18	20	1/25
MPC	1971 Chevrolet Corvette Convertible	1971	7106	75	150	175	1/25
MPC	1971 Mercury Cougar XR-7 Hardtop	1971	7122	30	85	100	1/25
MPC	1971 Pontiac Firebird Trans Am	1971	0451	25	65	75	1/25

MPC	1972 Chevrolet Chevelle SS454 Hardtop	1984	0736	10	45	50	1/25
MPC	1972 Plymouth Roadrunner	1972	7225	25	65	75	1/25
MPC	1973 Chevrolet Caprice Hardtop w/ trailer	1973	7304	25	65	75	1/25
MPC	1973 Mercury Cougar	1973	7322	30	85	100	1/25
MPC	1974 Chevrolet Vega (3-in-1 kit)	1974	7427	15	45	50	1/25
MPC	1974 Ford Pinto	1974	7412	10	25	45	1/25
MPC	1974 Plymouth Duster	1974	7426	15	45	50	1/25
MPC	1975 Corvette Convertible (3-in-1 kit)	1975	7505	25	65	75	1/25
MPC	1975 Pontiac Firebird	1975	7515	15	45	50	1/25
MPC	1976 AMC Pacer X	1976	7601	8	22	25	1/25
MPC	1976 Chevrolet Monza 2+2	1976	7616	8	22	25	1/25
MPC	1976 Dodge Dart	1976	7610	15	45	50	1/25
MPC	1976 Plymouth Volare	1976	7625	10	25	45	1/25
MPC	1977 Chevrolet Nova	1977	7707	10	25	45	1/25
MPC	1977 Dodge Monaco "Force 440" Police Car	1978	0723	15	45	50	1/25
MPC	1977 Pontiac Ventura	1977	7703	8	22	25	1/25
MPC	1978 Chevrolet Camaro Z-28 (2-in-1 kit)	1978	7819	10	40	45	1/25
MPC	1978 Chevrolet Corvette Indy 500 Pace Car	1978	3710	10	25	45	1/25
MPC	1978 Pontiac Firebird	1978	7815	15	45	50	1/25
MPC	1979 Ford Mustang Cobra Indy Pace Car	1980	0785	10	25	45	1/25
MPC	1982 Chevrolet Camaro Z-28 IMSA Race Car	1982	0814	10	25	45	1/25
MPC	1982 Ford EXP	1982	0818	8	22	25	1/25
MPC	1983 Dodge Omni Charger Turbo 2.2	1983	0836	8	22	25	1/25
MPC	1983 Ford Mustang GT	1983	0837	9	24	35	1/25
MPC	1984 Chevrolet Camaro Z-28 T-top	1984	0875	9	24	35	1/25
MPC	1984 Dodge Shelby Charger	1984	0876	5	13	15	1/25
MPC	1984 Pontiac Fiero	1984	0877	8	22	25	1/25
MPC	1985 Chevrolet Corvette	1985	3727	5	13	15	1/25
MPC	1985 Dodge Daytona Turbo	1985	0714	5	13	15	1/25
MPC	1985 Ford Mustang SVO	1985	0771	8	22	25	1/25

MPC	1985 Pontiac Fiero GT	1985	0715	5	13	15	1/25
MPC	1985 Pontiac Firebird Trans Am	1985	0733	5	13	15	1/25
MPC	1986 Chevrolet Camaro Z-28 IROC	1986	0775	5	13	15	1/25
MPC	1988 Chevrolet Beretta GT (2-in-1 kit)	1988	6261	5	13	15	1/25
MPC	"The Avenger" 1969 Plymouth Barracuda		1-0860	10	25	45	1/25
MPC	#39 Pepsi NASCAR 1975 Chevrolet Laguna		1712	25	65	75	1/25
MPC	B. Isaac #15 STA Power NASCAR 1973 Ford Torino		1710	50	150	175	1/25
MPC	B. Parson #55 Copenhagen NASCAR Chevrolet Monte Carlo		1302	15	45	50	1/25
MPC	Barris Bed Buggy	1969	0621	25	65	75	1/25
MPC	Barris Ice Cream Truck	1969	0614	25	65	75	1/25
MPC	Barris Mail Truck		0618	30	85	100	1/25
MPC	Bentley		1-2003	15	45	50	1/12
MPC	"Beverly Hillbillies" TV show Oldsmobile truck (Barris custom)	1968	612	30	85	100	1/25
MPC	Bill Shrewsberry 1973 Dodge "L.A. Dart" wheelstander	1973	0761	45	125	150	1/25
MPC	"Black Belt" 1981 Pontiac Firebird Funny Car	1981	0801	10	25	45	1/25
MPC	D. Allison #21 Purolator NASCAR 1971 Mercury Cyclone		1704	50	150	175	1/25
MPC	"Bushwacker" Military 1978 Jeep with Recoilless Rifle or Machine Gun	1983	0873	8	22	25	1/25
MPC	B. Baker #11 NASCAR 1971 Dodge Charger	1972	1702	40	100	125	1/25
MPC	Cale Yarborough #11 Kar Kare NASCAR 1973 Chevy Chevelle		1709	40	100	125	1/25
MPC	"Cannonball Run" Grand National Malibu movie car		0681	15	40	45	1/25
MPC	"The Cat" 1973 Mercury Cougar	1982	0830	5	13	15	1/25
MPC	Christie Fire Engine		2002	15	40	45	1/12
MPC	"Color Me Gone" 1967 Dodge Charger Funny Car	1967	700	40	100	125	1/25
MPC	Dan Gurney's Rislone Special Eagle Indy Car		802	45	125	150	1/25
MPC	Datsun Mini Pickup "California Sunshine"		729	10	25	30	1/25
MPC	D. Pearson #21 Chattanooga Chew NASCAR Chevrolet Monte Carlo		1301	15	45	50	1/25

MPC	D. Pearson NASCAR #33 Pontiac Tempest GTO (clear body)		1706	60	175	200	1/25
MPC	Dick Jesse 1967 Pontiac Tempest "Mr. Unswitchable" Funny Car	1967	701	45	125	150	1/25
MPC	Don Garlits "Swamp Rat 1" Top Fuel Dragster	1972	0753	45	125	150	1/25
MPC	"Dukes of Hazzard" TV show "General Lee" 1969 Dodge Charger	1980	0661	15	45	50	1/25
MPC	"Dyno Don" Nicholson 1975 Ford Pinto Pro Stock	1975	1760	25	65	75	1/25
MPC	Fiat Rail Rod Slingshot dragster	1976	0715	15	40	45	1/25
MPC	"Burnout Bird" 1981 Pontiac Firebird Funny Car	1981	0802	15	40	45	1/25
MPC	1982 Toyota Supra	1982	0841	8	22	25	1/25
MPC	Gapp & Roush Ford Pinto Pro Stock	1974	1762	15	45	50	1/25
MPC	"The Good Guys" TV show custom 1928 Lincoln Taxi	1968	616	25	65	75	1/25
MPC	Bill Jenkins "Grumpy's Vega" 1973 Chevrolet Pro Stock	1972	1757	25	65	75	1/25
MPC	"Hardcastle & McCormick" TV show Coyote Roadster		0684	8	22	25	1/25
MPC	"Hot Streak" 1980 Chevrolet Monza 2+2	1980	0784	5	13	15	1/25
MPC	"Hurst Hemi Under Glass" 1968 Plymouth Barracuda Funny Car	1968	0717	45	125	150	1/25
MPC	Icy Cycle Wild Custom Bike		415	12	35	40	1/12
MPC	Indy 500 Hall of Fame (3-kits-in-1)	1988	6246	8	22	25	1/25
MPC	Jim Hurtubise #56 Miller NASCAR 1971 Chevrolet Chevelle		1703	45	125	150	1/25
MPC	Tank Truck "Lil Gasser" Show Car Series	1987	6222	5	13	15	1/25
MPC	Mako Shark Mark IV 427 w/ trailer	1966	500	25	65	75	1/25
MPC	McLaren MK 8A		0571	30	85	100	1/20
MPC	"Wheeler Dealer" 1979 Chevrolet Monte Carlo	1979	0731	12	35	40	1/25
MPC	#3 1971 Chevrolet Monte Carlo Modified Stocker		2754	25	65	75	1/25
MPC	"Outcast" Custom C-Cab Van Show Car	1987	6223	5	13	15	1/25
MPC	P. Parsons #66 Skoal NASCAR Chevrolet Monte Carlo		1304	15	45	50	1/25
MPC	Pro Street 1967 Ford Mustang	1985	0764	5	13	15	1/25
MPC	D. Brooks #22 Golden Products NASCAR 1970 Dodge Daytona		1705	70	200	255	1/25

MPC	R. Wallace #2 Alugard Pontiac Grand Prix 2+2		1303	15	40	45	1/25
MPC	"Ramchargers" Top Fuel Dragster	1968	0749	30	85	100	1/25
MPC	"Brute Force" Top Fuel Dragster	1980	0703	10	30	35	1/25
MPC	R. Petty #43 NASCAR 1971 Plymouth Roadrunner	1971	1701	70	200	225	1/25
MPC	R. Petty #43 STP NASCAR 1974 Dodge Charger		1713	70	200	225	1/25
MPC	Richard Petty #43 STP NASCAR 1973 Dodge Charger		1708	60	175	200	1/25
MPC	"Ridge Runner" 1975 Ford Pinto Modified	1975	0710	15	45	50	1/25
MPC	"Scat City" 1970 Dodge Super Bee Funny Car	1970	0730	25	65	75	1/25
MPC	"Slammer" 1977 Ford Van (police van)	1977	3064	10	25	30	1/20
MPC	"Sorcerer" 1978 Ford Van		415	25	65	75	1/25
MPC	1982 Pontiac Grand Prix Southern Stocker Series	1982	0846	10	25	30	1/25
MPC	1982 Chevy Monte Carlo Southern Stocker Series	1982	0738	10	25	30	1/25
MPC	1982 Buick Regal Southern Stocker Series	1982	0845	10	25	30	1/25
MPC	R. Leong "Hawaiian" 1971 Dodge Charger Funny Car	1971	0748	25	65	75	1/25
MPC	D. Trickle #99 1969 Ford Mustang Stock Car	1974	2753	60	175	200	1/25
MPC	"The Visible Van" 1977 Ford Van		3062	10	30	35	1/20
MPC	"Bearcats" TV show 1914 Stutz Bearcat		0630	20	55	65	1/25
MPC	"Color Me Gone" 1971 Dodge Challenger Funny Car	1971	0756	30	85	100	1/25
Monogram	1929 Ford Roadster Pickup Early Iron Series	1987	7555	8	22	25	1/24
Monogram	1930 Ford Model A Cabriolet		7552	10	30	35	1/24
Monogram	1930 Ford Model A Coupe Special Interest Series		7551	8	22	25	1/24
Monogram	1930 Ford Model A Phaeton (3-in-1 kit)	1961	PC64	15	40	45	
Monogram	1931 Rolls-Royce Phantom II		PC109	20	55	65	1/24
Monogram	1932 Cadillac V-16 Town Car		2305	20	55	65	1/24
Monogram	1932 Ford Big Deuce		2602	25	75	85	
Monogram	1934 Ford Cabriolet (4 Star Issue)		PC119	20	55	65	1/24
Monogram	1940 Ford Pickup (4-in-1 kit)	1964	PC91	20	50	65	1/24

Monogram	1940 Ford Pickup "Lemon Crate"	1980	2265	10	25	30	1/24
Monogram	1955 Chevrolet Bel Air (4 Star Issue)	1963	PC83	45	125	150	1/24
Monogram	1955 Ford F-100 Panel Truck "Bootlegger"	1988	2772	5	13	15	1/24
Monogram	1956 Ford T-Bird Convertible	1982	2289	5	13	15	1/24
Monogram	1957 Chevrolet Bel Air	1977	2225	5	13	15	1/24
Monogram	1958 Ford Thunderbird (4 Star Issue)	1964	PC89	45	125	150	1/24
Monogram	1965 Ford Mustang 2+2	1985	2713	5	13	15	1/24
Monogram	1965 Ford Mustang Shelby GT-350	1985	2700	10	25	30	1/24
Monogram	1965 Chevrolet Corvette (4 Star Issue)		PC126	60	175	200	1/8
Monogram	1966 Chevrolet Chevelle Malibu SS "Street Rat"	1978	2229	5	13	15	1/24
Monogram	1966 Ford Mustang Shelby GT-350H	1986	2736	6	18	20	1/24
Monogram	1968 Pontiac Tempest GTO Street Machine	1984	2208	8	22	25	1/24
Monogram	1969 Chevrolet Camaro	1978	2230	6	18	20	1/24
Monogram	1970 Chevrolet Chevelle Malibu SS 454	1980	2268	6	18	20	1/24
Monogram	1970 Plymouth GTX	1982	2293	6	18	20	1/24
Monogram	1978 Chevrolet Corvette Indy Pace Car	1978	2253	15	45	50	1/24
Monogram	1982 Pontiac Firebird Trans Am	1983	2281	6	18	20	1/24
Monogram	1983 Ford Mustang LX Convertible	1983	2222	8	22	25	1/24
Monogram	B. Allison #22 Miller NASCAR 1984 Buick Regal	1983	2298	15	45	50	1/24
Monogram	B. Baker #1 UNO NASCAR 1982 Buick Regal	1983	2205	15	45	50	1/24
Monogram	B. Elliott #9 Coors NASCAR 1985 Ford T-Bird	1985	2244	12	35	40	1/24
Monogram	B. Elliott #9 Melling NASCAR 1983 Ford T-Bird	1983	2207	15	45	50	1/24
Monogram	"Bad Medicine" Dragster Show Rod	1986	2744	6	18	20	1/24
Monogram	"Beer Wagon" Ford Truck Show Rod		PC189	10	25	30	1/24
Monogram	Big Red Baron Show Car with Fokker Triplane & Helmeted Skull		2506	20	55	65	1/12
Monogram	Big T		PL78	40	100	125	1/8
Monogram	Big T Ford (4 Star Issue)		PC78	60	175	200	1/8

Monogram	Bob Glidden Chief Auto Parts 1984 Ford T-Bird Pro Stock	1984	2210	10	25	30	1/24
Monogram	Bobby Davis Jr. Sprint Car (World of Outlaws)	1988	2777	10	25	30	1/24
Monogram	Boot Hill Express Funeral Wagon Show Rod	1967	PC188	25	65	75	1/24
Monogram	Brad Doty Sprint Car (World of Outlaws)	1987	2752	10	25	30	1/24
Monogram	Kenny Bernstein Budweiser King 1985Ford Tempo Funny Car	1986	2726	10	25	30	1/24
Monogram	Frank Iaconio Motorcraft 1985 Ford T-Bird Pro Stock	1986	2727	10	25	30	1/24
Monogram	Bugatti 35B Grand Prix Racer	1966	PC133	15	45	50	1/24
Monogram	C. Yarborough #29 Hardee's NASCAR 1987 Olds Cutlass	1987	2754	15	30	35	1/24
Monogram	Casey Luna Ford Sprint Car (World of Outlaws)	1988	2775	10	25	30	1/24
Monogram	Joe Schubeck "Hurst Hairy Olds" Twin Engine Funny Car	1968	PC175	60	175	200	1/24
Monogram	D. Earnhardt #15 Wrangler NASCAR 1983 Ford T-Bird	1983	2206	15	45	50	1/24
Monogram	D. Waltrip #11 Mountain Dew NASCAR 1982 Buick Regal	1983	2204	15	45	50	1/24
Monogram	D. Waltrip #11/N. Bonnett #12 Budweiser NASCAR 1984 Chevrolet Monte Carlos (2-kits-in-1)	1986	2245	30	85	100	1/24
Monogram	D. Waltrip #17 Tide NASCAR 1987 Chevrolet Monte Carlo	1987	2755	15	40	45	1/24
Monogram	Dale Pulde "Miller Warrior" 1985 Pontiac Trans Am Funny Car	1985	2712	15	40	45	1/24
Monogram	Don Prudhomme Pepsi 1985 Pontiac Trans Am Funny Car	1985	2711	15	40	45	1/24
Monogram	"Elvira" TV star 1958 Ford T-Bird	1988	2783	6	18	20	1/24
Monogram	Firecracker Custom Fire Engine		5985	20	55	65	1/24
Monogram	Ford Mustang IMSA Race Car	1982	2297	12	35	40	1/24
Monogram	1986 Ford Mustang GTP		2708	12	35	40	1/24
Monogram	1927 Ford Model T Street Roadster w/ trailer	1975	2200	15	40	45	1/24
Monogram	Frank Iaconio 1984 Chevrolet Camaro Pro Stock	1984	2217	12	35	40	1/24
Monogram	"Futurista" Custom 3-wheeler (4 Star Issue)	1967	PC108	70	200	225	1/24
Monogram	Golden "T" Street Rod		2609	12	35	40	1/8
Monogram	H. Gant #33 Skoal Bandit NASCAR 1985 Chevrolet Monte Carlo	1985	2706	25	65	75	1/24
Monogram	Hemi Fiat		6704	10	30	35	1/32

Monogram	"Firebolt" Jet Powered Salt Flats Racing Car, (4 Star Issue)		PC51	75	200	250	1/24
Monogram	1941 Lincoln Continental Cabriolet		PC174	25	65	75	1/24
Monogram	"Long John" front engine rail dragster	1960	PC59	30	85	100	
Monogram	Mack Bulldog Stake Truck		7537	10	30	35	1/32
Monogram	Midget Racer #7 (Monogram's first plastic kit), with cardboard display	1954	P1	200	275	350	
Monogram	Ford Mustang Miller IMSA Race Car	1982	2296	12	35	40	1/24
Monogram	N. Bonnett #75 Valvoline NASCAR 1989 PontiacGrand Prix	1989	2787	25	65	75	1/24
Monogram	"Paddy Wagon" 1912 Ford Show Rod	1985	2733	5	13	15	1/24
Monogram	"Pie Wagon" Ford Show Rod	1986	2745	5	13	15	1/24
Monogram	R. Bouchard #47 Valvoline NASCAR 1984 Buick Regal	1985	2707	15	40	45	1/24
Monogram	R. Petty #43 STP NASCAR 1985 Pontiac Grand Prix	1985	2722	20	50	55	1/24
Monogram	R. Rudd #15 Motorcraft NASCAR 1986 Ford T-Bird	1986	2723	15	40	45	1/24
Monogram	Rear-Engined Scarab (4 Star Issue)		PC124	30	80	90	1/24
Monogram	Red Barron Show Rod	1985	2704	6	18	20	1/24
Monogram	Reher & Morrison 1984 Chevrolet Camaro Pro Stock	1984	2216	15	40	45	1/24
Monogram	Rickie Smith Motorcraft 1984 Ford T-Bird Pro Stock	1984	2218	15	40	45	1/24
Monogram	Sammy Swindell Sprint Car (World of Outlaws)	1987	2751	10	25	30	1/24
Monogram	"Sand Shark" Show Rod		2207	15	40	45	1/24
Monogram	Billy Meyer 7-Eleven 1985 Ford Mustang Funny Car	1985	2710	10	25	30	1/24
Monogram	"Slingshot" Front Engine Dragster w/ driver	1959	PC49	25	65	75	1/32
Monogram	Steve Kinser Sprint Car (World of Outlaws)	1987	2753	10	25	30	1/24
Monogram	T'Rantula Dragster Show Rod	1986	2746	5	13	15	1/24
Monogram	T. Labonte #44 Piedmont NASCAR 1984 Chevrolet Monte Carlo	1986	2299	20	50	55	1/24
Monogram	T. Richmond #25 Folgers NASCAR 1986 Chevrolet Monte Carlo	1986	2734	20	65	75	1/24
Monogram	"The Untouchables" TV show 1931 Rolls-Royce and 1930 Ford Coupe (2-kits-in-1)		6047	10	30	35	1/25
Monogram	"White Lightin'" 1985 Pontiac Firebird Pro Street	1987	2748	5	13	15	1/24

Monogram	"Yellow Jacket" 1930 Ford Model A	1962	PC76	25	65	75	
Palmer	1959 Mark IV Continental		205	25	65	75	1/24
Palmer	1960 Alfa Romeo (3-in-1 customizing kit)		6011	20	40	50	1/24
Palmer	1960 Karmann Ghia (3-in-1 customizing kit)		6012	25	65	75	1/24
Palmer	1961 Chevrolet Corvair (3-in-1 customizing kit)		6153	25	65	75	1/24
Palmer	1964 Chevrolet Impala (3-in-1 customizing kit)		6414	12	35	40	1/32
Palmer	1965 Ford Galaxie 500XL Convertible (3-in-1 customizing kit)		6503	12	35	40	1/32
Palmer	1970 Corvette Stingray Convertible (motorized, 3-in-1 kit)		M701	6	18	20	1/25
Pyro	Auburn Speedster 851		228	10	20	25	
Pyro	1935 Auburn Speedster		331	8	22	25	1/25
Pyro	1948 Lincoln Continental		330	8	22	25	1/25
Pyro	Alfa Romeo		C320	5	13	15	1/32
Pyro	Serpent Custom Show Rod		C83	10	30	35	1/16
Pyro	VW Beach Buggy		C333	10	20	25	1/32
Renwal	1903 Rambler		133	8	22	25	1/48
Renwal	1910 Stanley Streamer		132	6	18	20	1/48
Renwal	1916 Stutz Bearcat		139	6	18	20	1/48
Renwal	1925 Ford Model T		135	6	18	20	1/48
Renwal	1929 Ford Model A		145	6	18	20	1/48
Renwal	1932 Ford Model B		146	6	18	20	1/48
Renwal	1966 Packard		104	20	55	65	1/25
Revell	1904 Olds Delivery Van (Highway Pioneers-Series 3)		H44	8	20	25	1/32
Revell	1910 Bentley 4.5-liter (Highway Pioneers)		H63	5	13	15	
Revell	1913 Maxwell (Highway Pioneers)		H24	40	100	125	1/16
Revell	1913 Mercedes Torpedo (Highway Pioneers-Series 4)		H54	6	18	20	1/32
Revell	1914 Stutz Bearcat (Highway Pioneers-Series 2)		H38	6	18	20	1/32
Revell	1926 Ford Model T "Canned Heat" Roadster	1973	H1448	20	55	65	1/25
Revell	1927 Ford Model T Phaeton Street Rod	1982	7238	8	20	25	1/25
Revell	1932 Ford V-8 Jalopy (Highway Pioneers)		H80	10	25	30	1/32

Revell	1941 Willys Show Car		H1283	15	45	50	1/25
Revell	1941 Willys "Swindler II" Coupe		H1287	25	65	75	1/25
Revell	1950 Austin Healey 100-Six ("S") Roadster	1959	H1217	40	115	135	1/25
Revell	1953 Chevrolet Panel Delivery	1973	H1376	10	20	25	1/25
Revell	1954 Volkswagen Micro Bus	1964	H1228	60	175	200	1/25
Revell	1953 Jaguar XK120 (Highway Pioneers-Series 4)		H56	5	13	15	1/32
Revell	1955 Chevrolet Bel Air Hardtop (2-in-1 kit)	1965	H1276	25	65	75	1/25
Revell	1956 Lincoln "Futura" Experimental Car		H1210	60	175	200	1/25
Revell	1957 Cadillac Eldorado Brougham	1957	H1214	125	200	250	1/25
Revell	1957 Chevrolet Bel Air Sport Coupe	1963	H1284	25	65	75	1/25
Revell	1957 Chevrolet Nomad	1964	H1260	25	65	75	1/25
Revell	1957 Ford Country Squire Station Wagon	1957	H1220	45	125	150	1/25
Revell	1957 Ford Ranchero	1960	H1240	30	85	100	1/25
Revell	1959 Chevrolet Corvette	1959	H1232	25	65	75	1/25
Revell	1959 Ford Fairlane 500 Skyliner w/ Retractable Top ("S")	1959	H1227	45	125	150	1/25
Revell	1962 Chrysler Imperial Crown Hardtop Metalflake Series	1962	H1265	30	85	100	1/25
Revell	1962 Dodge Dart 440	1962	H1252	25	65	75	1/25
Revell	1965 Dodge Lancer Custom	1965	H1263	15	45	50	1/25
Revell	1969 Ford Mustang Convertible	1969	H1261	45	125	150	1/25
Revell	1970 Ford Mustang Hardtop	1970	H1212	30	85	100	1/25
Revell	1972 Datsun 240Z		H1401	15	45	50	1/25
Revell	1979 McLaren Mustang		7315	8	20	25	1/25
Revell	1980 Mercury Capri Turbo	1980	7206	8	20	25	1/25
Revell	Austin Healey 3000		H1256	10	25	30	1/32
Revell	Baja Humbug		H1361	8	22	25	
Revell	Bekin's Moving Van		H1403	25	65	75	
Revell	Big Bad Van Custom Chevy Van		H1290	10	25	30	1/16
Revell	Billy Carter's "Redneck Power Pickup"	1978	H1385	15	40	45	1/25
Revell	Bob Glidden Motorcraft 1987 Ford T-Bird Pro Stock	1987	7167	8	20	25	1/25

Revell	"Brute Force" Custom 1977 Chevrolet Van	1977	H1394	10	30	35	1/25
Revell	Camaro Pro Street Machine and Modified Custom T Roadster (2-kits-in-1)		8907	10	25	30	1/25
Revell	Chevy Two Ton Truck		H1401	15	45	50	
Revell	"Chopped Deuce" 1932 Ford	1976	H1335	12	40	45	1/25
Revell	Chopped Hog		H1237	12	40	45	1/8
Revell	Competition Austin-Healey		H1244	30	85	100	1/25
Revell	Dallas Cowboy Cheerleader's 1979 Ford Van	1979	6405	10	25	30	1/20
Revell	Deluxe Volkswagen Station Wagon		H1267	30	85	100	1/25
Revell	Don "The Snake" Prudhomme Army Rear Engine Dragster and Chevrolet Vega Funny Car (2-kits-in-1)		7464	40	100	125	1/16
Revell	Don Garlits "Swamp Rat" Top Fuel Dragster	1974	H1460	25	45	50	1/25
Revell	Folgers 1987 Ford Mustang GTO IMSA Race Car	1987	7154	6	18	20	1/25
Revell	Ford Auto Transport Truck		T6021	12	40	45	1/87
Revell	#98 Ken Miles 1966 Ford GT-40	1989	7131	6	18	20	1/25
Revell	Ford V-8 Hot Rod		H60	10	30	35	1/32
Revell	Global Van Lines Tractor & Trailer		T6018	12	40	45	1/87
Revell	Harley-Davidson Electra Glide (original issue)		H1224	25	75	85	1/8
Revell	Honda Racing Bike (original 1960s issue)		H1234	20	60	70	1/8
Revell	Jeep Golden Hawk		7841	5	13	15	1/16
Revell	Karmann Ghia ("S") Cadet Series)		H901	18	50	60	1/41
Revell	Herbie "The Love Bug" 1963 Volkswagen Movie Car		H950	15	45	50	1/25
Revell	Mercedes-Benz		H1285	25	65	75	
Revell	Mercury Montclair Customizing Kit ("S")		H1233	70	200	225	1/32
Revell	Mickey Thompson 1960 Attempt 1 Salts Flats Racer w/ trailer	1963	H1288	25	65	75	1/25
Revell	Mickey Thompson Funny Car Hot Rod Series		7444	18	50	55	1/16
Revell	Mickey Thompson "Revellaser" 1972 Ford Pinto Funny Car	1972	H1442	20	55	65	1/25
Revell	1931 Model A Sedan Delivery, 1926 Model T Sedan and 1934 Roadster Ford Classics Series (3-kits-in-1)	1986	7446	10	30	35	1/25

Company	Name	Year	No.	Good	V.G.	Excellent	Scale
Revell	Mickey Thompson Four Engine "Challenger" Salt Flats Racer and TV Tommy Ivo Four Engine "Showboat" Dragster Monster Machines Series (2-kits-in-1)	1987	7501	10	25	30	1/25
Revell	Motorcraft 1987 Ford Mustang GTO IMSA Race Car	1987	7155	5	13	15	1/25
Revell	Nash		H47	8	22	25	
Revell	1956 Pontiac Club De Mer (Pre "S")		H1213	100	275	325	1/25
Revell	1960 Porsche Carrera		H1238	12	35	40	1/25
Revell	Porsche Speedster		H1204	12	35	40	1/25
Revell	"Road Agent" Ed Roth Show Rod		H1274	45	125	150	1/25
Revell	7-Eleven 1987 Ford Mustang GTO IMSA Race Car	1987	7153	5	13	15	1/25
Revell	"Chi-Town Hustler" Funny Car (Hot Rod Series)		7478	18	50	55	1/16
Revell	Tony Nancy Hall of Fame Dragsters (3-kits-in-1)	1987	7502	18	50	55	1/25
Revell	Whipple & McCulloch "Revellution" 1972 Plymouth Duster Funny Car	1972	H1465	25	65	75	1/25
Revell	Wild Willie Borsch "Wild Man Charger" 1972 Dodge Funny Car	1973	H1450	30	80	90	1/25
Revell	"Woodstock" 1930 Ford Model A Woodie	1974	H1324	15	45	50	1/25
Ringo	1911 Rolls-Royce (Silver Ghost)		206	8	22	25	1/32
Ringo	Alfa Romeo Type 158-159 "Alfetta"		207	8	22	25	1/24
Ringo	Ferrari		C-542	18	25	35	1/24
Strom-becker	1902 Rambler (reissue of Keepsake K-10)	1960	T-2	10	30	35	1/24
Strom-becker	1909 Hupmobile 16 hp Roadster (reissue of Keepsake K-11)	1960	T-1	10	30	35	1/24
Strom-becker	1932 Ford		D71	6	18	20	
Strom-becker	BRM Formula 1		8135	8	22	25	
Strom-becker	Lotus Ford Racer (motorized)		9465	25	65	75	1/24
Strom-becker	MG-A Twin-Cam		D55	45	125	150	1/24
Strom-becker	Scarab (motorized)		D62	15	45	50	

Other Kits

Company	Name	Year	No.	Good	V.G.	Excellent	Scale
Handi-craft	fire engine (molding kit)		803	65	105	125	
Hubley	Indy 500 racer (metal kit)		852K	30	50	90	

Hudson	miniatures, balsa wood			13	22	35	
ITC (Ideal Toy Corp.)	1940 Mercury (remote control)	1961		45	60	75	1/25
ITC (Ideal Toy Corp.)	1951 Ford (remote control)	1961		45	60	75	1/25
Miley's	Model T Ford Parcel Post Van, seven inches long, cast aluminum (reproduction of 1930s cast iron toy), black with red wheels, parcel post graphics			25	40	50	
Miley's	Model T Ford Telephone Line Maintenance Truck, seven inches long, cast aluminum (reproduction of 1930s cast iron toy),			25	40	50	
Revell	1957 Ford Ranchero (motorized)	1960	H1241	15	30	45	
Ungar Jalopy	(battery-operated kit)	1966	1041	20	40	75	

Dealer Promotional Models

Description	Good	Very Good	Excellent
AMT 3-in-1 model car kit, 1958 Buick (first year; most common)	50	95	175
AMT 3-in-1 model car kit, 1958 Ford (first year; hardest to locate)	115	195	300
AMT 3-in-1 model car kit, 1958 Chevrolet (first year; second hardest to locate)	115	195	300
AMT 1949 Plymouth Special Deluxe dealer promotional model, wind-up	35	80	120
AMT 1950 Plymouth Special Deluxe dealer promotional model, wind-up	35	80	120
AMT 1949 Ford Custom dealer promotional model, wind-up	40	90	150
AMT 1950 Ford Custom dealer promotional model, wind-up	35	85	130
AMT 1951 Ford Custom dealer promotional model, wind-up	35	85	130
AMT 1950 Studebaker Commander Starlight dealer promotional model, wind-up	50	95	175
AMT (labeled as Aluminum Model Toys) 1951 Pontiac Chieftain Deluxe dealer promotional model	30	75	110
AMT 1953 Ford Crestline convertible dealer promotional model	50	95	175
AMT 1953 Studebaker Commander Regal Starliner dealer promotional model	35	80	120
AMT 1954 Pontiac Chieftain two-door hardtop dealer promotional model	35	80	120

AMT 1954 Buick Skylark convertible dealer promotional model	125	220	325
AMT 1955 Buick Century convertible dealer promotional model	50	95	175
AMT 1955 Ford Fairlane Victoria two-door hardtop dealer promotional model	40	95	150
AMT 1956 Ford Fairlane Sunliner dealer promotional model	80	170	250
AMT 1956 Lincoln Continental dealer promotional model	70	100	200
AMT 1956 Studebaker Golden Hawk dealer promotional model	70	100	200
AMT 1957 Buick Roadmaster two-door hardtop dealer promotional model	70	100	200
AMT 1957 Ford Custom 300 dealer promotional model	150	260	400
AMT 1957 Ford Thunderbird convertible dealer promotional model	80	170	250
AMT 1958 Edsel Pacer convertible dealer promotional model	80	170	250
AMT 1959 Edsel Corsair convertible dealer promotional model	70	105	225
AMT 1960 Edsel Ranger convertible dealer promotional model	70	105	225
AMT 1960 Buick dealer promotional model (with portholes)	40	95	150
AMT 1960 Buick dealer promotional model (without portholes)	40	95	150
AMT 1960 Buick chassis, dealer promotional model (dealer only edition)	125	220	325
AMT 1960 Lincoln Continental convertible dealer promotional model	30	75	110
AMT 1960 Pontiac Bonneville convertible dealer promotional model	40	95	150
AMT 1960 Rambler dealer promotional model (see-through body)	40	95	150
AMT 1961 Ford F-100 pickup dealer promotional model	70	100	200
AMT 1961 Ford Galaxie Starliner dealer promotional model	50	95	175
AMT 1961 Pontiac Bonneville convertible dealer promotional model	70	100	200
AMT 1961 Pontiac Tempest four-door sedan dealer promotional model	35	85	125
AMT 1962 Buick Electra 225 hardtop dealer promotional model	125	220	325
AMT 1962 Chevrolet Impala SS dealer promotional model (metallic gold)	160	280	475
AMT 1962 Chevrolet dealer promotional model (in bubble with 1911 Chevrolet model)	275	455	700
AMT 1962 Imperial Crown convertible dealer promotional model	160	280	475

AMT 1963 Chevrolet Chevy II station wagon dealer promotional model	40	95	150
AMT 1963 Chevrolet Corvair Monza convertible dealer promotional model	125	220	325
AMT 1963 Chevrolet Impala SS convertible dealer promotional model	145	220	375
AMT 1963 Ford Thunderbird Sports Roadster dealer promotional model	150	260	400
AMT 1963 Mercury Comet S-22 convertible dealer promotional model	150	260	400
AMT 1963 Mercury Meteor S-33 dealer promotional model	125	220	325
AMT 1964 Chevrolet El Camino pickup dealer promotional model	50	95	175
AMT 1964 Mercury Park Lane dealer promotional model (w/ Breezeway window)	150	260	400
AMT 1964 Pontiac Grand Prix dealer promotional model	50	95	175
AMT 1965 Buick Wildcat convertible dealer promotional model	145	220	375
AMT 1965 Chevrolet Corvette convertible dealer promotional model	225	400	650
AMT 1965 Chevrolet Malibu station wagon dealer promotional model	50	95	175
AMT 1965 Oldsmobile 88 convertible dealer promotional model	50	95	175
AMT 1965 Pontiac GTO convertible dealer promotional model	145	220	375
AMT 1966 Buick Skylark two-door hardtop dealer promotional model	145	220	375
AMT 1966 Chevrolet Corvair Corsa two-door hardtop dealer promotional model	90	175	275
AMT 1966 Ford Falcon Futura dealer promotional model	40	95	150
AMT 1966 Mercury Comet Cyclone GT dealer promotional model (Indy 500 Pace Car)	90	175	275
AMT 1967 Chevrolet Camaro SS convertible dealer promotional model (Indy 500 Pace Car)	160	280	475
AMT 1967 Chevrolet Fleetside pickup dealer promotional model	50	95	175
AMT 1967 Plymouth Barracuda dealer promotional model	90	175	275
AMT 1969 Buick Riviera dealer promotional model	40	95	150
AMT 1969 Ford Galaxie 500XL dealer promotional model	45	75	100
AMT 1970 Chevrolet Impala SS convertible dealer promotional model	40	95	150
AMT 1970 Chevrolet Monte Carlo dealer promotional model	50	95	175

AMT 1971 Ford Mustang Mach 1 dealer promotional model	115	195	300
AMT 1971 Ford Torino Cobra dealer promotional model	115	195	300
Banthrico Inc., dealer promotional model metal bank, 1950 Chevrolet Deluxe two-door sedan	50	95	175
Banthrico Inc., dealer promotional model metal bank, 1951 Lincoln four-door sedan	40	95	150
Banthrico Inc., dealer promotional model metal bank, 1953 Dodge Coronet four-door sedan	40	95	150
Banthrico Inc., dealer promotional model metal bank, 1953 Kaiser Manhattan four-door sedan	150	260	400
Banthrico Inc., dealer promotional model metal bank, 1953 Nash Rambler Country Club two-door hardtop	50	95	175
Hubley dealer promotional model, 1957 Renault Dauphine four-door sedan	25	50	75
Hubley dealer promotional model, 1958 Mercedes-Benz convertible	40	95	150
Hubley dealer promotional model, 1958 Triumph TR3 convertible	70	100	200
Hubley dealer promotional model, 1959 Metropolitan convertible	160	280	475
Hubley dealer promotional model, 1959 Metropolitan hardtop	120	200	350
Hubley dealer promotional model, 1959 Opel Rekord two-door sedan	15	40	65
Hubley dealer promotional model, 1960 Ford Country Sedan station wagon	40	95	150
Hubley dealer promotional model, 1960 Ford Fairlane four-door sedan	40	95	150
Hubley dealer promotional model, 1960 Rolls-Royce Silver Cloud	40	95	150
Hubley dealer promotional model, 1961 Metropolitan convertible	175	350	550
Hubley dealer promotional model, 1962 Ford Country Sedan station wagon	40	95	150
Jo-Han model car kit, 1956 Oldsmobile 98 Holiday four-door hardtop	45	75	100
Jo-Han model car kit, 1959 Plymouth (first Jo-Han models)	75	130	200
Jo-Han model car kit, 1959 Dodge Custom Royal (first Jo-Han models)	75	130	200
Jo-Han model car kit, 1959 Cadillac (first Jo-Han models)	75	130	200
Jo-Han model car kit, 1959 Oldsmobile (first Jo-Han models)	75	130	200
Jo-Han model car kit, 1959 Plymouth Police Car	90	145	225

Jo-Han model car kit, 1961 Studebaker Lark two-door hardtop	45	75	100
Jo-Han model car kit, 1962 Dodge Police Car	75	130	200
1961-1962 model car kit, Jo-Han, Plymouth Police Car "Car 54 Where Are You?"	15	25	40
Jo-Han model car kit, 1964 Cadillac Coupe deVille convertible	50	95	150
Jo-Han model car kit, 1966 Cadillac Coupe deVille two-door hardtop	35	80	120
Jo-Han model car kit, 1967 Cadillac Coupe deVille convertible	35	85	125
Jo-Han model car kit, 1967 Cadillac Coupe deVille two-door hardtop	35	75	100
Jo-Han model car kit, 1968 Cadillac Eldorado two-door hardtop	35	75	100
Jo-Han model car kit, 1969 Oldsmobile Toronado	20	40	65
Jo-Han model car kit, 1970 Ford Maverick	15	25	40
Jo-Han model car kit, 1975 Oldsmobile Cutlass	15	25	40
1978 Jo-Han, Cadillac Coupe de Ville (Basil Green Metallic)	15	25	40
1978 Jo-Han, Cadillac Coupe de Ville (Mediterranean Blue Metallic)	15	25	40
1978 Jo-Han, Cadillac Coupe de Ville (Western Saddle Metallic)	15	25	40
1978 Jo-Han, Cadillac Coupe de Ville (Carmine Red)	20	30	45
MPC model kit, 1964 Corvette (first MPC model)	80	120	250
MPC model kit, 1975 AMC Pacer X	15	25	40
MPC model kit, 1977 Chevrolet Chevette	5	15	30
1978 MPC model kit, Chevrolet Monza	5	15	30
1978 MPC model kit, Chevrolet Chevette	5	15	30
1978 MPC model kit, Chevrolet Monte Carlo	10	20	35

(**NOTE**: The Chevrolet Monza, Chevette and Monte Carlo all came in three different colors, Dark Camel, Light Blue and Medium Green)

1978 MPC, Corvette (all-Silver without "lip" on paint parting line)	45	75	100
1978 MPC, Corvette (all-Silver with "lip" on paint parting line) (Rare)	50	100	150
1978 MPC, Corvette Silver Anniversary (Charcoal and Silver)	20	40	65
1978 MPC Pontiac Firebird Trans Am (Starlight Black)	15	25	40
1978 MPC Pontiac Firebird Trans Am (Platinum Metallic)	15	30	45
1978 MPC Plymouth Volare without Road Runner decal option (Starlight Blue Metallic)	5	15	30

1978 MPC Plymouth Volare without Road Runner decal option (Spitfire Orange)	5	15	30
1978 MPC Plymouth Volare with Road Runner decal option (Starlight Blue Metallic)	15	20	35
1978 MPC Plymouth Volare with Road Runner decal option (Spitfire Orange)	15	20	35
1978 MPC Dodge Monaco (Augusta Green Metallic)	5	15	30
1978 MPC Dodge Monaco (Starlight Blue Metallic)	5	15	30
Monogram dealer promotional model, 1955 Cadillac Coupe de Ville	110	190	300
Monogram dealer promotional model, 1955 Cadillac Convertible	110	190	300
Monogram dealer promotional model, 1956 Cadillac Coupe de Ville	40	85	125
National Products, 1938 Studebaker Commander sedan, metal dealer promotional model	250	600	950
National Products, 1940 Buick Super sedan, metal dealer promotional model	375	750	1,200
National Products, 1948 Chevrolet Fleetline Aero Sedan, metal dealer promotional model	145	220	375
National Products, 1948 Dodge B Series pickup, metal dealer promotional model	145	220	375
National Products, 1948 GMC FC Series pickup, metal dealer promotional model	75	130	200
National Products, 1949 Chrysler New Yorker sedan, metal dealer promotional model	145	220	375
National Products, 1949 DeSoto Custom sedan, metal dealer promotional model	110	190	300
National Products, 1949 Nash 600 sedan, metal dealer promotional model	70	125	175
National Products, 1949 Pontiac Chieftain sedan, metal dealer promotional model	110	190	300
National Products, 1949 Studebaker Commander sedan, metal dealer promotional model	85	150	240
National Products, 1950 Lincoln Cosmopolitan sedan, metal dealer promotional model	200	380	500
National Products, 1952 Ford F-1 pickup, metal dealer promotional model	145	220	375
Product Miniature Co., 1949 International Metro delivery van dealer promotional model (U.S. Mail truck)	200	380	500
Product Miniature Co., 1951 Chevrolet Deluxe Coupe dealer promotional model	75	130	200

Product Miniature Co., 1951 Chevrolet Deluxe four-door sedan dealer promotional model	75	130	200
Product Miniature Co., 1952 Chevrolet Deluxe two-door sedan dealer promotional model	70	125	175
Product Miniature Co., 1953 Chevrolet Bel Air two-door hardtop dealer promotional model	70	125	175
Product Miniature Co., 1953 Chevrolet Corvette dealer promotional model	260	425	650
Product Miniature Co., 1953 Chevrolet Handyman station wagon dealer promotional model (1/20th scale)	145	220	375
Product Miniature Co., 1953 International R-110 pickup dealer promotional model	145	220	375
Product Miniature Co., 1954 Chevrolet 150 four-door sedan dealer promotional model	65	120	165
Product Miniature Co., 1955 Chevrolet 210 four-door sedan dealer promotional model	85	150	240
Product Miniature Co., 1956 Chevrolet Bel Air four-door station wagon dealer promotional model	35	75	115
Product Miniature Co., 1956 Chevrolet Bel Air four-door hardtop dealer promotional model	85	150	240
Product Miniature Co., 1956 Chevrolet Cameo pickup dealer promotional model	50	95	175
Product Miniature Co., 1956 Ford Country Sedan station wagon dealer promotional model	85	150	240
Product Miniature Co., 1957 Chevrolet Bel Air four-door station wagon dealer promotional model	45	75	100
Product Miniature Co., 1958 International A-100 pickup dealer promotional model	55	90	135
Product Miniature Co., 1959 Opel Rekord dealer promotional model	45	75	100
Product Miniature Co., 1959 Volkswagen Karmann Ghia dealer promotional model	40	95	150
Product Miniature Co., 1963 Chevrolet Corvette dealer promotional model	85	145	225
Product Miniature Co., Tru Miniature series of dealer promotional models, 1954 Nash Ambassador four-door sedan	55	90	135
Revell model car kit, 1957 Ford Country Squire Station Wagon (1/25th scale)	90	150	235
Revell model car kit, 1957 Ford Ranchero Sedan-Pickup (1/25th scale)	30	50	75
Revell model car kit, 1959 Ford Skyliner Retractable Convertible (1/25th scale)	30	50	75
SMP model truck kit, 1958 Chevrolet Apache Fleetside Series 3200 pickup	80	120	250

Dealer promotional model, 1951 Packard. Henney ambulance, AMT (1/20th scale hot-stamped acetate)	400	550	800
Dealer promotional model, 1956 AMC Rambler. Clear plastic	110	190	300
Dealer promotional model, 1957 AMC Rambler. Clear plastic	110	190	300
Dealer promotional model, 1948-1953 Jo-Han Chevrolet (B.F. Goodrich service truck)	50	95	175
Dealer promotional model, 1957 Pontiac, Bonneville convertible, designed by Jack K. Stuart as PMD General Manager Award	95	165	250
Dealer promotional model, 1958 Pontiac, Bonneville Sport Coupe, designed by Jack K. Stuart as PMD General Manager Award	95	165	250
Dealer promotional model, 1963 experimental turbine car, made for Chrysler Corp.	40	95	150
Dealer promotional model, Mills Bakery 1/25th scale delivery van/Wilson Dairy 1/25th scale delivery van	20	50	75

Model Kits

Monogram's first plastic model kit issue in 1954 was this #7 Midget Racer with cardboard display. EXC-$350

Ringo Toy Corp. 1/24th scale model of a Ferrari racer. EXC-$35

Revell motorized model of 1957 Ford Ranchero from 1960. EXC-$45

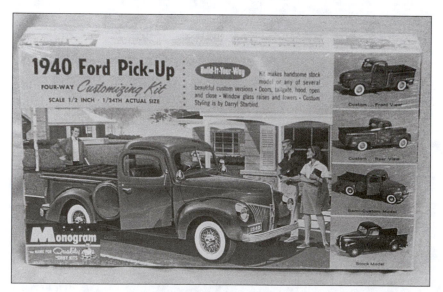

Monogram 1/24th scale model of four-in-one 1940 Ford pickup from 1964. EXC-
$65

MPC 1/25th scale model of 1967 Pontiac GTO funny car version. EXC-$150

MPC 1/25th scale model of Dick Jesse's "Mr. Unswitchable" funny car. EXC-$150

AMT 1/25th scale model of Sonny & Cher Ford Mustangs customized by George Barris. EXC-$75

MPC 1/25th scale model of two-in-one Beverly Hillbillies television truck from 1968. EXC-$100

MPC 1/25th scale model of "Scat City" Dodge funny car. EXC-$75

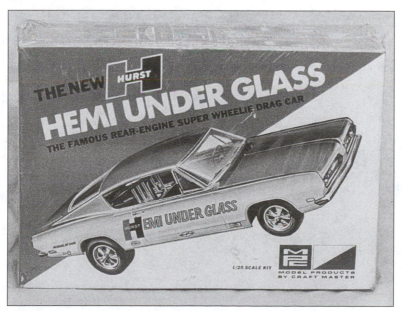

MPC 1/25th scale model of Hurst "Hemi Under Glass" Plymouth drag car. EXC-$150

Aurora 1/25th scale model of Ford GT racer from 1965. EXC-$40

AMT 1/25th scale model of three-in-one Chevelle Drag Team. EXC-$100

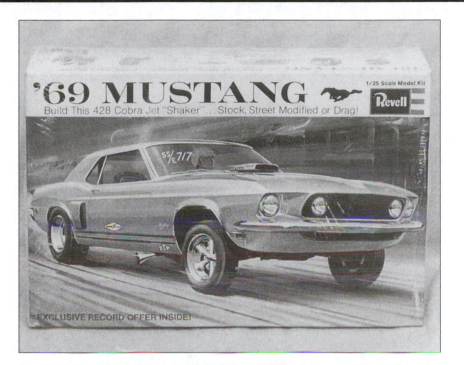

Revell 1/25th scale model of 1969 Ford Mustang 428 Cobra Jet "Shaker" from 1969. EXC-$100

MPC 1/25th scale model of Fiat Rail Rod "Slingshot" dragster from 1976. EXC-$45

Revell 1/25th scale model of Mickey Thompson's Attempt I racer from 1963. EXC-$75

Hubley metal kit of Indianapolis 500 Racer. EXC-$90

Model Kits

AMT 1/32nd scale model of Ford Leva car. EXC-$80

Pyro 1/32nd scale model of VW Beach Buggy from Deluxe Classics series. EXC-$25

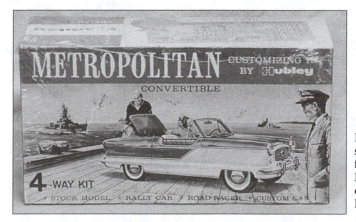

Hubley 1/24th scale model of four-in-one Metropolitan convertible. EXC-$100

AMT 1/25th scale model of two-in-one Indy 500 combo featuring Ford Lotus and Offy Roadster. EXC-$90

Monogram 1/32nd scale model of "slingshot" dragster. EXC-$75

Revell model of Pontiac Club de Mer. EXC-$325

AMT 1/25th scale model of 1966 Chevy from Modified Stocker series. EXC-$125

AMT 1/25th scale model of 1965 Ford Fairlane from Modified Stocker series. EXC-$125

Pyro All American Classic Auburn Speedster 851. EXC-$25

Aurora 1/25th scale model of two-in-one Double Deuce 1922 Ford from 1963. EXC-$75

Handi-craft Auto Casting Set #803 fire engine. EXC-$125

Ideal Toy Corp. 1/25th scale model of remote controlled customized 1940 Mercury from 1961. EXC-$75

Ungar battery operated Jalopy Kit from 1966. EXC-$75

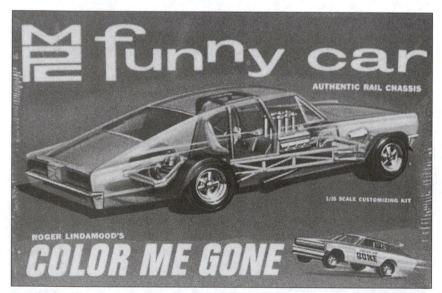

MPC 1/25th scale model of Roger Lindamood's "Color Me Gone" Dodge funny car. EXC-$125

AMT 1/25th scale model of two-in-one 1969 Chevrolet Chevelle SS-396 convertible. EXC-$100

AMT 1/25th scale model of three-in-one 1970 Chevrolet Monte Carlo "Coco Carlo". EXC-$200

Jo-Han 1/25th scale model of two-in-one 1971 Oldsmobile Toronado Pikes Peak Hill Climb Racer. EXC-$100

Models

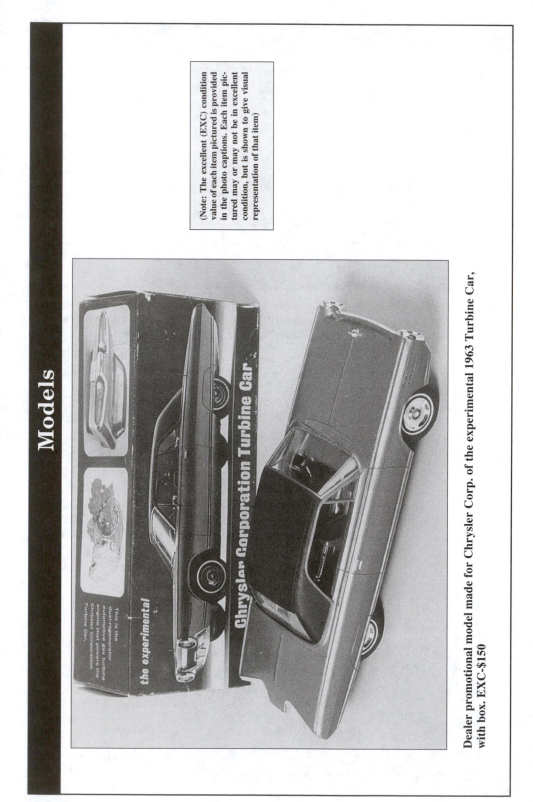

Dealer promotional model made for Chrysler Corp. of the experimental 1963 Turbine Car, with box. EXC-$150

Banthrico Inc. metal bank promotional model of 1950 Chevrolet Deluxe two-door sedan. EXC-$175

Banthrico Inc. metal bank promotional model of 1951 Lincoln four-door sedan. EXC-$150

Banthrico Inc. metal bank promotional model of 1953 Nash Rambler Country Club two-door hardtop. EXC-$175

A pair of AMT Plymouth Special Deluxe four-door sedan wind-up promotional models, the 1950 version (left) and 1949 version (right). Respectively, EXC-$120 and EXC-$120.

Models

A trio of AMT Ford Custom four-door sedan wind-up promotional models, (l to r) the 1949, 1950, and 1951 versions. Respectively, EXC-$150, EXC-$130, and EXC-$130

AMT 1950 Studebaker Commander Starlight two-door wind-up promotional model. EXC-$175

AMT (labeled as Aluminum Model Toys) 1951 Pontiac Chieftain Deluxe four-door sedan promotional model. EXC-$110

AMT 1953 Studebaker Commander Regal Starliner promotional model. EXC-$120

AMT 1954 Pontiac Chieftain two-door hardtop promotional model. EXC-$120

AMT 1955 Buick Century convertible promotional model. EXC-$175

AMT 1955 Ford Fairlane Victoria two-door hardtop promotional model. EXC-$150

AMT 1956 Ford Fairlane Sunliner promotional model. EXC-$250

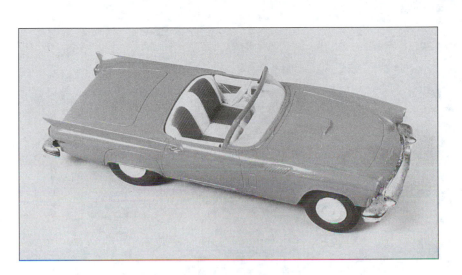

AMT 1957 Ford Thunderbird convertible promotional model. EXC-$250

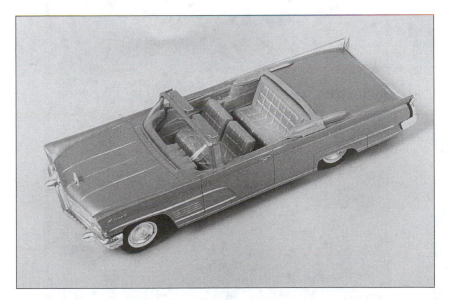

AMT 1960 Lincoln Continental convertible promotional model. EXC-$110

Models

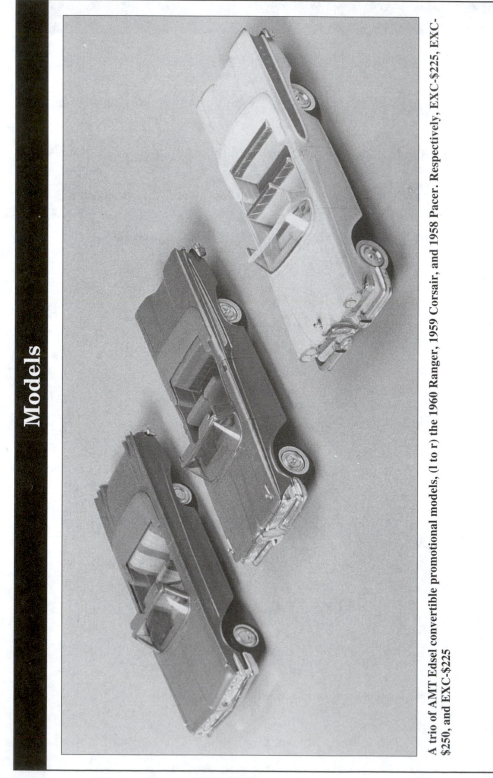

A trio of AMT Edsel convertible promotional models, (l to r) the 1960 Ranger, 1959 Corsair, and 1958 Pacer. Respectively, EXC-$225, EXC-$250, and EXC-$225

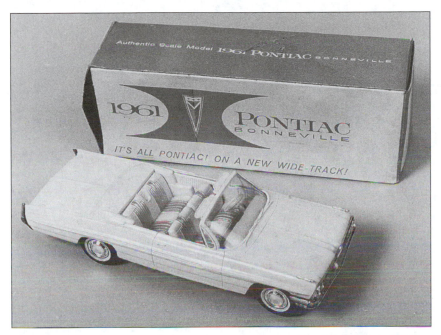

AMT 1961 Pontiac Bonneville convertible promotional model with box. EXC-$200

AMT 1966 Chevrolet Corvair Corsa two-door hardtop promotional model. EXC-$275

Hubley 1959 Metropolitan promotional model. EXC-$350

Hubley 1961 Metropolitan convertible promotional model. EXC-$550

Jo-Han Models 1961 Studebaker Lark two-door hardtop promotional model. EXC-$100

Jo-Han Models 1964 Cadillac Coupe deVille convertible promotional model. EXC-$150

Jo-Han Models 1967 Cadillac Coupe deVille promotional model. EXC-$100

Jo-Han Models 1968 Cadillac Eldorado promotional model. EXC-$100

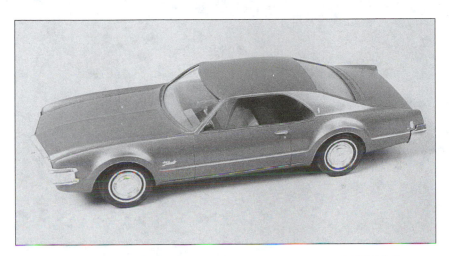

Jo-Han Models 1969 Oldsmobile Toronado promotional model. EXC-$65

Jo-Han Models 1970 Ford Maverick promotional model. EXC-$40

Jo-Han Models 1975 Oldsmobile Cutlass promotional model. EXC-$40

MPC 1975 AMC Pacer X promotional model. EXC-$40

MPC 1977 Chevrolet Chevette promotional model. EXC-$30

Product Miniature Co. 1954 Nash Ambassador four-door sedan, part of the Tru-Miniature Series of promotional models. EXC-$135

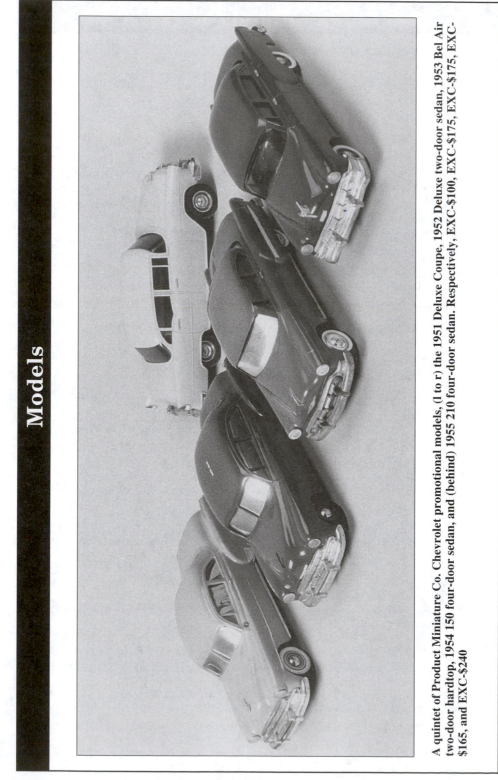

A quintet of Product Miniature Co. Chevrolet promotional models, (l to r) the 1951 Deluxe Coupe, 1952 Deluxe two-door sedan, 1953 Bel Air two-door hardtop, 1954 150 four-door sedan, and (behind) 1955 210 four-door sedan. Respectively, EXC-$100, EXC-$175, EXC-$175, EXC-$165, and EXC-$240

Product Miniature Co. 1951 Chevrolet Deluxe four-door sedan promotional model. EXC-$200

Product Miniature Co. 1956 Chevrolet Bel Air four-door station wagon promotional model. EXC-$130

TOY VEHICLES

Arcade

Cars

Name	Description	Good	Ex	Mint
Andy Gump and Old 348	bright red car, green trim, green disc wheels with red hubcaps, cast iron, 7-1/4" long, 1923	1500	2500	3800
Auto Racer	cast iron, 7-3/4" long, 1922	425	560	775
Boattail Racer	nickel plated wheels, cast iron, 5" long	75	115	150
Buick Coupe	green body, cast iron, 8-1/2" long, 1927	3000	5000	7500
Buick Sedan	green body, cast iron, 8-1/2" long, 1927	1500	2500	3800
Checker Cab	deep green, cast iron, 9" long	1500	1750	2200
Checker Cab	plain two row checker, cast iron, 8" long	1750	2000	2500
Checker Cab	yellow body with black roof, cast iron, 9-1/4" long, 1932	15000	20000	25000
Chevrolet Cab	metal tires, cast iron, 8" long, 1920s	500	850	1200
Chevrolet Coupe	Arizona gray body, spare wheel and tire on rear of car, with or without rubber balloon tires, cast iron, 8-1/4" long, 1929	1300	1550	2000
Chevrolet Sedan	Algerian blue body, spare wheel and tire on rear of car, with or without rubber balloon tires, cast iron, 8-1/4" long, 1929	1500	1750	2200
Chevrolet Superior Roadster	cast iron, 7" long, 1924	1500	1750	2200
Chevrolet Superior Sedan	cast iron, 7" long, 1924	400	750	1000
Chevrolet Superior Touring Car	cast iron, 7" long, 1923	1300	1550	2000
Chevrolet Utility Coupe	cast iron, 7" long, 1924	850	1275	1700
Coupe	with or without rubber tires, removable driver, cast iron, 9" long, 1922	1375	2575	3750
DeSoto Sedan	white rubber wheels, cast iron, 4" long, 1936	175	250	350
Ford Coupe	nickel-plated wheels, no driver, cast iron, 6" long, 1923	150	225	325
Ford Coupe	with or without rubber tires, cast iron, 6-1/2" long, 1924	325	450	550
Ford Rumble Seat Coupe	cast iron, 6-3/4" long, 1934	150	225	325
Ford Fordor Sedan	with or without rubber tires, removable driver, 6-1/2" long, 1924	325	450	550

		Good	Ex	Mint
Ford Sedan and Covered Wagon Trailer	cast iron, sedan 12" long, trailer 5-1/2" long, 1937	850	1200	1800
Ford Touring Car	with or without rubber tires, removable driver, cast iron,6-1/2" long, 1923	450	650	900
Ford Tudor Sedan	with or without rubber tires, removable driver, cast iron, 6-1/2" long, 1920s	400	600	850
Ford Tudor Sedan	visor over front windshield, with or without rubber tires, driver, cast iron, 6-1/2" long, 1926	450	600	865
Ford Yellow Cab	special edition for Chicago World's Fair, cast iron, 6-7/8" long, 1933	700	1000	1500
Limousine Yellow Cab	yellow with black body stripe, nickel-plated driver, spare tire at rear, cast iron, 8-1/2" long, 1930	650	850	1300
Model A Coupe	cast iron, 4-1/8" long	100	185	275
Model A Coupe	rumble seat, cast iron, 6-3/4" long, 1928	650	850	1300
Model A Coupe	rumble seat, cast iron, 5" long, 1928	225	325	450
Model A Tudor	cast iron, 6-3/4" long 1928	500	750	1000
Model A Fordor	orange, cast iron, 6-3/4" long, 1928	350	525	700
Model T	rubber tires, 6" long	125	185	250
Model T Sedan, center door	cast iron, 6-1/2" long, 1923	100	150	200
Pierce Arrow Coupe	"Silver Arrow" on sides, cast iron, 7-1/4" long, 1934	250	325	525
Plymouth Sedan	cast iron, 4-3/4" long, 1934	350	525	700
Pontiac Sedan	white rubber wheels, cast iron, 4-1/4" long, 1936	125	185	250
Red Top Cab	cast iron, 8" long, 1924	700	1200	2500
Reo Coupe	cast iron, 9-3/8" long, 1931	1000	2500	5000
Sedan with Red Cap Trailer	cast iron, sedan 5-7/8" long, trailer 2-1/2" long, 1939	250	400	650
Yellow Cab	rubber tires, cast iron, 8" long, 1923	500	750	1000
Yellow Cab	rubber tires, cast iron, 9" long, 1927	600	825	1200
Yellow Cab	rubber tires, cast iron, 5-1/4" long, 1927	500	750	1000
Yellow Cab	bright yellow body, black top, white rubber wheels with black centers, cast iron, 8-1/4" long, 1936	950	2000	4000
Yellow Cab	yellow with "Yellow Cab" in black on top, cast iron, 4-1/4" long, 1936, "Darmalee" Cab	5000	7500	10000

Emergency Vehicles

Name	Description	Good	Ex	Mint
Ambulance	cast iron, 6" long, 1932	250	400	650
Chevrolet Wrecker	cast iron, 4-1/4" long, 1936	175	265	350
Fire Engine	red enamel with gold striping, cast iron, 7-1/2" long, 1923	275	415	550

Name	Description	Good	Ex	Mint
Fire Engine	red, white rubber tires with green centers, cast iron, 4-1/2" long, 1936	125	175	250
Fire Engine	red trimmed in gold bronze, white rubber wheels with blue centers, cast iron, 6-1/4" long, 1936	150	225	300
Fire Engine	red trimmed in gold bronze, white rubber wheels with blue centers, cast iron, 9" long, 1936	500	775	1000
Fire Ladder Truck	red trimmed in gold bronze, white rubber wheels with blue centers, cast iron, 7" long, 1936	175	265	350
Fire Ladder Truck	red trimmed in gold bronze, ladders yellow, white rubber wheels blue centers, cast iron, 12-1/2" long with ladders, 1936	475	750	950
Fire Pumper	with six firemen, cast iron, 13-1/4" long, 1938	500	775	1000
Fire Trailer Truck	red trimmed in gold bronze, two-piece fire engine, cast iron, truck 16-1/4" long, with ladders 20" long, 1936	500	775	1000
Ford Wrecker	cast iron, 8-1/4" long, 1929	475	750	950
International Wrecker	steel and cast iron, 13" long, 1940	550	850	1200
Mack Fire Apparatus Truck	bright red truck, hose reel, removable extention ladders, bell that rings, cast iron, 21" long, 1929	550	850	1200
Mack Fire Apparatus Truck	red trimmed in gold, yellow extension ladders, imitation hose, nickeled driver, nickeled bell that rings, 21" long, 1936	1000	1500	3000
Mack Wrecker	cast iron, 12-1/2" long, 1930	1000	2500	5000
Plymouth Wrecker	cast iron, 4-3/4" long, 1934	150	225	300

Trucks

Name	Description	Good	Ex	Mint
"Yellow Baby" Dump Truck	cast iron, 10-1/2" long, 1923	800	1200	1500
Auto Express 548 Truck	flatbed, cast iron, 9" long	225	350	450
Borden's Milk Bottle Truck	"Borden's" cast on side, cast iron, 6-1/4" long, 1936	800	1600	3000
Carry-Car Truck and Trailer Set	red truck, green trailer, with three 3-3/4" Austin vehicles, cast iron, 14-1/4" long, 1934	650	1150	1700
Carry-Car Truck and Trailer Set	red truck, green trailer, with four vehicles, cast iron, 28" long, 1936	1500	3000	4500
Chevrolet Panel Delivery Van	white rubber tires with colored centers, cast iron, 4" long, 1936	125	200	300
Chevrolet Utility Express Truck	cast iron, 9-1/4" long, 1923	450	675	1200
Chevrolet Stake Truck	cast iron, 9" long, 1925	1500	1750	2200
Dump Truck	cast iron, 6-1/2" long, 1941	175	350	500
Dump Truck	red chassis, green dump body, white rubber tires with green centers, cast iron, 4-1/2" long, 1936	75	100	150

Ford Anthony Dump Truck	nickel-plated spoked wheels, black enamel finish with gray dump body, cast iron, 8-1/2" long, 1926	1250	2000	2500
Ford Weaver Wrecker	cast iron, 8-1/4" long, 1928	700	950	1400
Ford Weaver Wrecker, Model T	cast iron, 11" long, 1926	600	875	1300
Ford Weaver Wrecker, Model A	cast iron, 11" long, 1926	550	800	1200
Gasoline Truck	cast iron, 13" long, 1920s	600	900	1200
Ice Truck	red, cast iron, 7" long, 1940	175	350	500
International Delivery Truck	cast iron, 9-1/2" long, 1936	1500	3000	4500
International Dump Truck	cast iron, 10-3/4" long, 1931	1200	1500	2000
International Dump Truck	white rubber wheels with red centers, cast iron, 10-1/2" long, 1936	1200	1500	2000
International Dump Truck	red cab, green dump, cast iron, 9-1/2" long, 1937	450	650	850
International Dump Truck	cast iron, 11-1/8" long, 1941	600	750	1250
International Pickup	cast iron, 9-1/2" long, 1941	550	750	950
International Stake Truck	white rubber wheels with red centers, cast iron, 12" long, 1935	1200	1500	2000
International Stake Truck	yellow, cast iron, 9-1/2" long, 1937	750	1500	2200
Mack Dump Truck	assorted colors trimmed in gold bronze, "Mack" decals on doors, dual rear wheels, cast iron, 12-1/4" long, 1936	750	1125	1500
Mack Dump Truck	cast iron, 13" long	375	565	750
Mack Dump Truck	light grey or blue, gold trim, white tires, cast iron, 12" long, 1925	700	1050	1400
Mack Gasoline Truck	cast iron, 13-1/4" long, 1925	750	1500	2200
Mack High Dump	nickel-plated levers mechanically raise the dump bed, cast iron, 8-1/2" long, 1931	750	1125	1500
Mack High Dump	cast iron, 12-3/8" long, 1931	750	1500	2200
Mack Ice Truck	ice blocks and tongs, cast iron, 8-1/2" long, 1931	475	775	1000
Mack Ice Truck	ice blocks and tongs, cast iron, 10-5/8" long, 1930	375	565	750
Mack Lubrite Tank Truck	cast iron, 13-1/4" long, 1925	1100	1800	2500
Mack Tank Truck	cast iron with tin tank, 12-3/4" long, 1929	1200	1800	2900
Mack Tank Truck	assorted colors with gold trim, nickeled driver, dual rear wheels, tank holds water, cast iron, 13" long, 1936	1100	1800	2500
Mack Tank Truck	nickel-plated driver, cast iron, 13-1/4" long, 1925	1100	1800	2500
Model-A Stakebody Truck	iron wheels, cast iron, 7-1/2" long, 1920s	150	225	300
Pontiac Stake Truck	white rubber tires, cast iron, 6-1/4" long, 1935	225	350	500

Name	Description	Good	Ex	Mint
Pontiac Stake Truck	white rubber tires, cast iron, 4-1/4" long, 1936	65	95	165
Red Baby Dump Truck	bright red truck, white enameled tires, crank dump, cast iron, 10-3/8" long, 1923	475	775	1000
Red Baby Truck	bright red truck, white enameled tires, cast iron, 10-3/4" long, 1923	475	775	1000
White Delivery Truck	cast iron, 8-1/4" long, 1929	3550	4200	5500
White Dump Truck	cast iron, 11-1/2" long, 1929	10000	15000	20000
White Moving Van	cast iron, 13-1/2" long, 1929	6000	8500	13000

Vehicle Banks

Name	Description	Good	Ex	Mint
Ford Touring Car Bank	removable driver, cast iron, 6-1/2" long, 1925	650	975	1300
Mack Dump Truck Bank	cast iron, 13" long	375	565	750
Yellow Cab Bank	cast iron, 8" long, 1924	475	775	1000
Yellow Cab Bank	with or without rubber tires, cast iron, 9" long, 1926	600	900	1200
Yellow Cab Bank	cast iron, 8-1/2" long, 1930	650	1400	2000

Auburn

Cars

Name	Description	Good	Ex	Mint
1948 Buick sedanet	rubber, 7-1/4" long	50	75	100
Airport Limousine	rubber, 7-1/2" long	10	20	25
1950 Cadillac sedan	rubber, 7-1/4" long	40	65	85
1935 Ford coupe	rubber, 4" long, 1930s	30	45	60
Race Car	red, rubber, 6" long	40	65	85
Race Car With Goggled Driver	rubber, 10-1/2" long, high fin	50	75	100
Open Racer	white plastic tires, boattail, 4-3/4" long	25	40	50
Sedan	green rubber, license #500R	15	25	30

Emergency Vehicles

Name	Description	Good	Ex	Mint
Fire Engine	red, rubber, 8" long	15	25	30
Fire Truck No. 614	black rubber wheels	10	20	25
Krazy Tow Set, Hot Rod and Tow Truck	vinyl	50	75	100

Trucks

Name	Description	Good	Ex	Mint
2-1/2 Ton Truck		20	30	40
Army Jeep	olive drab	5	7	10
Army Recon Half Truck	bright green	10	15	20
Stake Truck	rubber	15	25	30
Telephone Truck	6-1/2" long	35	55	75

Buddy L

Cars

Name	Description	Good	Ex	Mint
Army Staff Car	olive drab body, 15-3/4" long, 1964	100	150	200
Bloomin' Bus	chartreuse body, white roof and supports, similar to VW minibus, 10-3/4" long, 1969	90	135	180
Buddywagon	red body with white roof, 10-3/4" long, 1966	100	150	200
Buddywagon	red body with white roof, no chrome on front, 10-3/4" long, 1967	95	145	190
Colt Sportsliner	red open body, white hardtop, off-white seats and interior, 10-1/4" long, 1967	35	50	70
Colt Sportsliner	light blue-green open body, white hardtop, pale tan seats and interior, 10-1/4" long, 1968	30	45	65
Colt Utility Car	red open body, white plstic seats, floor and luggage space, 10-1/4" long, 1967	35	50	70
Colt Utility Car	light orange body, tan interior, 10-1/4" long, 1968	30	45	65
Country Squire Wagon	off-white hood fenders, end gate and roof, brown woodgrain side panels, 15-1/2" long, 1963	85	130	175

Name	Description	Good	Ex	Mint
Country Squire Wagon	red hood fenders, end gate and roof, brown woodgrain side panels, 15" long, 1965	75	115	150
Deluxe Convertible Coupe	metallic blue enamel front, sides and deck, cream top retracts into rumble seat, 19" long, 1949	300	450	600
Desert Rats Command Car	light tan open body, light beige interior, black .50-caliber machine gun swivels on post between seats, 10-1/4" long, 1967	50	75	100
Desert Rats Command Car	light tan open body, light beige interior, black .50-caliber machine gun swivels on post between seats, 10-1/4" long, blackwall tires, 1968	45	65	90
Flivver Coupe	black with red eight-spoke wheels, black hubs, aluminum tires, flat, hardtop roof on enclosed glass-window-style body, 11" long, 1924	775	1100	1550
Flivver Roadster	black with red eight-spoke wheels, black hubs, aluminum tires, simulated soft, folding top, 11" long, 1924	750	1000	1500
Jr. Camaro	metallic blue body, white racing stripes across hood nose, 9" long, 1968	50	75	100
Jr. Flower Power Sportster	purple hood, fenders and body, white roof and supports, white plastic seats, lavender and orange five-petal blossom decals on hood top, roof, and sides, 6" long, 1969	35	55	75
Jr. Sportster	blue hood and open body, white hardtop and upper sides, 6" long, 1968	35	55	75
Mechanical Scarab Automobile	red radically streamlined body, bright metal front and rear bumpers, 10-1/2" long, 1936	200	300	500
Police Colt	deep blue open body, white hardtop, "POLICE" across top of hood, "POLICE 1" on sides, 10-1/4" long, 1968	50	75	100
Ski Bus	white body and roof, similar to VW minibus, 10-3/4" long, 1967	75	115	150
Station Wagon	light blue/green body and roof, 15-1/2" long, 1963	75	115	150
Streamline Scarab	red, radically streamlined body, non-mechanical, 10-1/2" long, 1941	145	225	290
Suburban Wagon	powder blue or white body and roof, 15-1/2" long, 1963	75	115	150
Suburban Wagon	gray/green body and roof, 15-3/4" long, 1964	70	100	140
Town and Country Convertible	maroon front, hood, rear deck and fenders, gray top retracts into rumble seat, 19" long, 1947	300	450	600
Travel Trailer and Station Wagon	red station wagon, two-wheel trailer with red lower body and white steel camper-style upper body, 27-1/4" long, 1965	150	225	300
Yellow Taxi with Skyview	yellow hood, roof and body, red radiator front and fenders, 18-1/2" long, 1948	300	450	600

Emergency Vehicles

Name	Description	Good	Ex	Mint
Aerial Ladder and Emergency Truck	red with white ladders, bumper and steel disc wheels, three 8-rung steel ladders, 22-1/4" long, 1952	200	300	400

Aerial Ladder and Emergency Truck	red with white ladders, bumper and steel disc wheels, three 8-rung steel ladders, no rear step, no siren or SIREN decal, 22-1/4" long, 1953	225	345	450
Aerial Ladder Fire Engine	red tractor, wraparound bumper and semi-trailer, two aluminum 13-rung extension ladders on sides, swivel-base aluminum central ladder, 26-1/2" long, 1960	125	185	250
Aerial Ladder Fire Engine	red tractor and semi-trailer, white plastic bumper with integral grille guard, two aluminum 13-rung extension ladders on sides, swivel-base aluminum central ladder, 26-1/2" long, 1961	125	185	250
Aerial Ladder Fire Engine	red tractor and semi-trailer, chrome one-piece wraparound bumper, slotted grille, two aluminum 13-rung extension ladders on sides, swivel-base aluminum central ladder, 26-1/2" long, 1966	125	185	250
Aerial Ladder Fire Engine	red cab-over-engine tractor and semi-trailer units, two 13-rung white sectional ladders and swivel-mounted aerial ladder with side rails, 25-1/2" long, 1968	100	150	200
Aerial Ladder Fire Engine	snub-nose red tractor and semi-trailer, white swivel-mounted aerial ladder with side rails, two white 13-rung sectional ladders, 27-1/2" long, 1970	100	150	200
Aerial Truck	red with nickel ladders, black hand wheel, brass bell, and black hubs, 39" long with ladder down, 1925	850	1300	1700
American LaFrance Aero-Chief Pumper	red cab-over-engine and body, white underbody, rear step and simulated hose reels, black extension ladders on right side, 25-1/2" long, 1972	100	150	200
Brute Fire Pumper	red cab-over-engine body and frame,two yellow 5-rung sectional ladders on sides of open body, 5-1/4" long, 1969	35	50	75
Brute Hook-N-Ladder	red cab-over-engine tractor and detachable semi-trailer, white elevating, swveling aerial ladder with side rails, 10" long, 1969	30	40	55
Extension Ladder Fire Truck	red with silver ladders and yellow removable rider seat, enclosed cab, 35" long, 1945	200	300	400
Extension Ladder Rider Fire Truck	duo-tone slant design, tractor has white front, lower hood sides and lower doors, red hood top, cab and frame, red semi-trailer, white 10-rung and 8-rung ladders, 32-1/2" long, 1949	150	225	300
Extension Ladder Trailer Fire Truck	red tractor with enclosed cab, boxy fenders, red semi-trailer with fenders, two white 8-rung side ladders, 10-rung central extension ladder, 29-1/2" long, 1955	200	300	400
Extension Ladder Trailer Fire Truck	red tractor unit and semi-trailer, enclosed cab, two white 13-rung side extension ladders on sides, white central ladder on swivel base, 29-1/2" long, 1956	125	185	250
Fire and Chemical Truck	duo-tone slant design, white front, lower hood sides and lower doors, rest is red, bright-metal or white eight-rung ladder on sides, 25" long, 1949	125	185	250
Fire Department Emergency Truck	red streamlined body, enclosed cab, chrome one-piece grille, bumper, and headlights, 12-3/4" long, 1953	100	150	200
Fire Engine	red with nickel-plated upright broiler, nickel rims and flywheels on dummy water pump, brass bell, 23-1/4" long, 1925-29	500	800	1600
Fire Engine	red with nickel rim flywheels on dummy pump, brass bell, dim-or-bright electric headlights, 25-1/2" long, 1933	450	750	1500

Fire Hose and Water Pumper	red with two white five-rung ladders, two removable fire extinguishers, enclosed cab, 12-1/2" long, 1950	100	150	200
Fire Hose and Water Pumper	red with two white five-rung ladders, one red/white removable fire extinguisher, enclosed cab, 12-1/2" long, 1952	100	150	200
Fire Pumper with Action Hydrant	red wraparound bumper, hood cab and cargo section, aluminum nine-rung ladders, white hose reel, 15" long, 1960	75	115	150
Fire Pumper	red cab-over-engine and open body, 11-rung white 10" ladder on each side, 16-1/4" long, 1968	100	150	200
Fire Truck	red with white ladders, black rubber wheels, enclosed cab, 12" long, 1945	75	115	150
Fire Truck	duo-tone slant design, tractor has white front, lower hood sides and lower doors, red hood top, cab and frame, red semi-trailer, rubber wheels with black tires, 32-1/2" long, 1953	200	300	400
Fire Truck	bright red with black inverted L-shaped crane mounted in socket on seat back, open driver's seat, 26" long, 1924	500	900	1850
Fire Truck	bright red with black inverted L-shaped crane mounted in socket on seat back, red floor, open driver's seat, 26" long, 1925	450	800	1600
Fire Truck	bright red, red floor, open driver's seat, 26" long, 1928	350	700	1200
Fire Truck	red with black solid-rubber Firestone tires on red seven-spoke embossed metal wheels, two 18-1/2" red steel sectional ladders, 26" long, 1930	500	900	1850
Fire Truck	red with nickel or white ladders, bright-metal radiator grille and black removable rider saddle, 25-1/2" long, 1935	250	375	500
Fire Truck	duo-tone slant design, yellow front, single-bar bumper, hood sides and removable rider seat, rest is red, 25-1/2" long, 1936	500	750	1000
Fire Truck	duo-tone slant design, yellow front, bumper, hood sides and skirted fenders, rest is red, nickel ladders, 28-1/2" long, 1939	550	850	1100
Fire Truck	red with two white ladders, enclosed cab, bright metal grille and headlights, 25" long, 1948	125	200	250
GMC Deluxe Aerial Ladder Fire Engine	white tractor and semi-trailer units, golden 13-rung extension ladder on sides, golden central aerial ladder, black and white DANGER battery case with two flashing lights, 28" long, 1959	225	345	450
GMC Extension Ladder Trailer Fire Engine	red tractor with chrome GMC bar grille, red semi-trailer, white 13-rung extension ladders on sides, white swiveling central ladder with side rails, 27-1/4" long, 1957	100	250	400
GMC Fire Pumper with Horn	red with aluminum-finish 11-rung side ladders and white reel of black plastic hose in open cargo section, chrome GMC bar grille, 15" long, 1958	150	200	300
GMC Hydraulic Aerial Ladder Fire Engine	red tractor unit with chrome GMC bar grille, red semi-trailer, white 13-rung extension ladders on sides, white swiveling central ladder, 26-1/2" long, 1958	125	185	250

GMC Red Cross Ambulance	all white, removable fabric canopy with a red cross and "Ambulance" in red, 14-1/2" long, 1960	150	250	400
Hook & Ladder Fire Truck	medium-dark red, with black inverted L-shaped crane mounted in socket on seat back, open driver's seat, 26" long, 1923	1200	1800	2400
Hose Truck	red with two white hose pipes, white cord hose on reeland brass nozzle, electric headlights with red bulbs, 21 3/4" long, 1933	500	750	1000
Hydraulic Aerial Truck	duo-tone slant design, yellow bumper, radiator front, fenders, lower hood sides and removable rider saddle, rest is red, nickel extension ladders, 41" long with ladders, 1939	1500	2500	4500
Hydraulic Aerial Truck	red with black removable rider saddle and twisted-wire removvble pull-n-ride handle, nickel extension ladders, 40" long, 1933	1000	2000	3000
Hydraulic Aerial Truck	duo-tone slant design, yellow front, single-bar bumper, chassis, radiator, front fender, lower sides and removable rider saddle, rest is red, 40" long with ladders down, 1936	550	825	1100
Hydraulic Aerial Truck	red with brass bell on cowl, nickel ladders mounted on 5-1/2" turntable rotated by black hand wheel, 39" long, 1927	850	1300	1700
Hydraulic Aerial Truck	red with brass bell on cowl, nickel ladders mounted on 5-1/2" turntable rotated by black hand wheel, two-bar nickel front bumper, 39" long, 1930	1000	1500	2500
Hydraulic Aerial Truck	red with brass bell on cowl, nickel ladders mounted on 5-1/2" turntable rotated by black hand wheel, two-bar nickel front bumper, nickel-rim headlights in red shells, 39" long, 1931	1200	1750	2500
Hydraulic Aerial Truck	duo-tone slant design, red hood and body, yellow rider seat, nickel extension ladders, 41" long with ladders, 1941	650	975	1300
Hydraulic Water Tower Truck	red with nickel water tower, dim/bright electric head-lights, brass bell, 44-7/8" long with tower down, 1933	1200	2000	3000
Hydraulic Water Tower Truck	red with nickel water tower, dim/bright electric headlights, brass bell, added-on bright-metal grille, 44-7/8" long with tower down, 1935	2000	4000	6000
Hydraulic Water Tower Truck	duo-tone slant design, yellow bumper, hood sides, front fenders, rest is red, electric headlights, added-on bright-metal grille, 44-7/8" long with tower down, 1936	1200	2000	3000
Hydraulic Water Tower Truck	duo-tone slant design, yellow front, single-bar bumper and hood sides, red hood top, enclosed cab and water tank, brass bell, nickel water tower, 46" long with tower down, 1939	1200	2000	4500
Hydraulic Snorkel Fire Pumper	red cab-over-engine and open rear body, white 11-rung 10" ladder on each side, snorkel pod with solid sides, 21" long, 1969	100	150	200
Jr. Fire Emergency Truck	red cab-over-engine and body, one-piece chrome wraparound narrow bumper and 24-hole grille with plastic vertical-pair headlights, 6-3/4" long, 1968	50	75	100
Jr. Fire Emergency Truck	red cab-over-engine and body, wider one-piece chrome wraparound narrow bumper and four-slot grille with two square plastic headlights, 6-3/4" long, 1969	50	75	100

Jr. Fire Snorkel Truck	red cab-over-engine and body, chrome one-piece narrow wraparound bumper and 24-hole grille with plastic vertical-pair headlights, 11-1/2" long, 1968	100	150	200
Jr. Fire Snorkel Truck	red cab-over-engine and body, full-width chrome one-piece bumper and four-slot grille with two square plastic headlights, 11" long, 1969	60	150	200
Jr. Hook-n-Ladder Aerial Truck	red cab-over-engine tractor and semi-trailer, white high-sides ladder, chrome one-piece wraparound bumper and 24-hole grille, plastic veritcal-pair headlights, 17" long, 1967	100	150	200
Jr. Hook-n-Ladder Aerial Truck	red cab-over-engine tractor with one-piece four-slot grille and two square plastic headlights, red semi-trailer, white high-sides ladder, plastic vertical-pair headlights, 17" long, 1969	75	115	150
Jr. Hook-n-Ladder Aerial Truck	red cab-over-engine tractor and semi-trailer, white high-sides ladder, one-piece chrome four-slot grille, two square plastic headlights, 17" long, 1969	75	115	150
Ladder Fire Truck	red with bright-metal V-nose radiator, headlights and ladder, black wooden wheels, 12" long, 1941	125	200	250
Ladder Truck	red with two yellow sectional ladders, enclosed square cab, 22-3/4" long, 1933	250	375	500
Ladder Truck	red with two yellow ladders, enclosed square cab with sharply protruding visor, 22-3/4" long, 1934	200	300	400
Ladder Truck	red with two yellow ladders, enclosed square cab with sharply protruding visor, bright-metal radiator front, 22-3/4" long, 1935	250	375	500
Ladder Truck	duo-tone slant design, white front, hood sides, fenders and two ladders, rest is red, square enclosed cab with sharply protruding visor, 22-3/4" long, 1936	150	225	300
Ladder Truck	duo-tone slant design, white front, hood sides, fenders and two ladders, rest is red, square enclosed cab with sharply protruding visor, no headlights, 22-3/4" long, 1937	135	200	275
Ladder Truck	duo-tone slant design, white front, fenders, hood sides and two ladders, rest is red, enclosed cab, 24" long, 1939	1500	2500	4500
Ladder Truck	red with bright-metal grille and headlights, two white ladders, 24" long, 1939	100	200	300
Ladder Truck	red with yellow severely streamlined, skirted fenders and lower doors, white ladders, bright-metal grille, no bumper, 17-1/2" long, 1940	200	300	400
Ladder Truck	modified duo-tone slant design, white front, front fenders and lower doors, white ladders, bright-metal grille, no bumper, 17-1/2" long, 1941	200	300	400
Ladder Truck	red with two white ladders, bright-metal radiator grille and headlights, 24" long, 1941	125	200	250
Police Squad Truck	yellow front and front fenders, dark blue-green body, yellow fire extinguisher, 21-1/2" long over ladders, 1947	150	300	550
Pumping Fire Engine	red with nickel stack on boiler, nickel rims on pump flywheels, nickel-rim headlights and searchlight, 23-1/2" long, 1929	3000	3500	4000
Rear Steer Trailer Fire Truck	red with two white 10-rung ladders, chrome one-piece grille, headlights and bumper, 20" long, 1952	75	100	200

Name	Description	Good	Ex	Mint
Red Cross Ambulance	all white, removable fabric canopy with a red cross and "Ambulance" in red, 14-1/2" long, 1958	60	95	125
Suburban Pumper	red station wagon body, white plastic wraparound bumpers, one-piece grille and double headlights, 15" long, 1964	100	150	200
Texaco Fire Chief American LaFrance Pumper	promotional piece, red rounded-front enclosed cab and body, white one-pice underbody, running boards and rear step, 25" long, 1962	200	300	400
Trailer Ladder Truck	duo-tone slant design, tractor unit has yellow front, lower hood sides and lower doors, red hood top, enclosed cab and semi-trailer, nickel 10-rung ladders, 30" long with ladders, 1940	200	300	400
Trailer Ladder Truck	all red with cream removable rider saddle, three bright metal 10-rung ladders, 20" long over ladders, 1941	150	225	300
Water Tower Truck	red with nickel two-bar front bumper, red nickel-rim headlights plus searchllight on cowl, nickel latticework water tower, 45-1/2" long with tower down, 1929	3000	4500	6000

Trucks

Name	Description	Good	Ex	Mint
Air Force Supply Transport	blue with blue removable fabric canopy, rubber wheels, decals on cab doors, 14-1/2" long, 1957	125	250	350
Air Mail Truck	black front, hood fenders, enclosed cab and opening doors, red enclosed body and chassis, 24" long, 1930	675	1000	1400
Allied Moving Van	tractor and semi-trailer van, duo-tone slant design, black front and lower sides, orange hood top, cab and van body, 29-1/2" long, 1941	600	900	1200
Army Electric Searchlight Unit	shiny olive drab flatbed truck, battery operated searchlight, 14-3/4" long, 1957	125	225	325
Army Half-Track and Howitzer	olive drab with olive drab carriage, 12-1/2" truck, 9-3/4" gun, overall 22-1/2" long, 1953	100	150	200
Army Half-Track with Howitzer	olive drab steel, red firing knob on gun, 17" truck, 9-3/4" gun, overall 27" long, 1955	100	150	200
Army Medical Corps Truck	white, black rubber tires on white steel disc wheels, 29-1/2" long, 1941	125	185	250
Army Searchlight Repair-It Truck	shiny olive drab truck and flatbed cargo section, 15" long, 1956	125	175	225
Army Supply Truck	shiny olive drab truck and removable fabric cover, 14-1/2" long, 1956	100	150	175
Army Transport Truck and Trailer	olive drab truck, 20-1/2" long, trailer 34-1/2" long, 1940	250	350	450
Army Transport with Howitzer	olive drab, 12" truck, 9-3/4" gun, overall 28" long, 1953	100	150	200
Army Transport with Howitzer	olive drab steel, 17" truck, 9-3/4" gun, overall 27" long, 1955	150	250	350

Army Transport with Howitzer	olive drab steel, re-firing knob on gun, 17" truck, 9-3/4" gun, overall 27" long, 1954	115	175	230
Army Transport with Tank	olive drab, 15-1/2" long truck, 11-1/2" long detachable two-wheel trailer, overall 26-1/2" long, 7-1/2" long tank, 1959	100	150	200
Army Troop Transport with Howitzer	dark forest green truck and gun, canopy mixture of greens, 14" long truck, 12" long, gun, overall 25-3/4" long, 1965	100	150	200
Army Truck	olive drab, 20-1/2" long, 1939	110	175	225
Army Truck	olive drab, 17" long, 1940	150	200	250
Atlas Van Lines	green tractor unit, chrome one-piece toothed grille and headlights, green lower half of semi-trailer van body, cream upper half, silvery roof, 29" long, 1956	200	300	400
Auto Hauler	yellow cab-over-engine tractor unit and double-deck semi-trailer, three 8" long vehicles, 25-1/2" long, 1968	75	115	150
Auto Hauler	snub-nose medium blue tractor unit and double-deck semi-truck trailer, three plstic coupes, overall 27-1/2" long, 1970	65	95	130
Baggage Rider	duo-tone horizontal design, green bumper, fenders and lower half of truck, white upper half, 28" long, 1950	250	175	500
Baggage Truck	black front, hood, and fenders, doorless cab, yellow four-post stake sides, two chains across back, 26-1/2" long, 1927	800	1000	2000
Baggage Truck	black front, hood, and fenders, open door cab, yellow four-post stake sides, two chains across back, 26-1/2" long, 1930	1500	1750	2500
Baggage Truck	green front, hood, and fenders, non-open doors, yellow cargo section slat sides, 26-1/2" long, 1933-34	1000	2000	3000
Baggage Truck	green front, hood, and fenders, non-open doors, yellow cargo section solid sides, 26-1/2" long, 1933	1000	2000	3000
Baggage Truck	green front, hood, and fenders, non-open doors, yellow cargo section slat or solid sides, metal grille, 26-1/2" long, 1935	1000	2000	3000
Baggage Truck	duo-tone slant design, yellow fenders, green hood top, cab, and removable rider seat, 26-1/2" long, 1936	1200	2400	3600
Baggage Truck	duo-tone slant design, yellow skirted fenders and cargo section, green hood top, enclosed cab, 27-3/4" long, 1938	300	600	1000
Baggage Truck	green hood, fenders, and cab, yellow cargo section, no bumper, 17-1/2" long, 1945	175	265	350
Baggage Truck	black front, hood, and fenders, enclosed cab with opening doors, nickel-rim, red-shell headlights, yellow stake body, 26-1/2" long, 1930-32	3000	5000	7000
Big Brute Dumper	yellow cab-over-engine, frame and tiltback dump section with cab shield, striped black and yellow bumper, black grille, 8" long, 1971	50	75	100
Big Brute Mixer Truck	yellow cab-over-engine, body and frame, white plastic mixing drum, white plastic seats, 7" long, 1971	25	50	75
Big Fella Hydraulic Rider Dumper	duo-tone slant design, yellow front and lower hood, red upper cab, dump body and upper hood, rider seat has large yellow sunburst-style decal, 26-1/2" long, 1950	110	175	225

Big Mack Dumper	off-white front, hood cab and chassis, blue-green tiltback dump section, white plastic bumper, 20-1/2" long, 1964	75	115	150
Big Mack Dumper	yellow front, hood cab, chassis and tiltback dump section, black plastic bumper, 20-1/2" long, 1967	75	115	150
Big Mack Dumper	yellow front, hood cab, chassis and tiltback dump section, black plastic bumper, single rear wheels, 20-1/2" long, 1968	60	95	125
Big Mack Dumper	yellow front, hood cab, chassis and tiltback dump section, black plastic bumper, heavy-duty black balloon tires on yellow plastic five-spoke wheels, 20-1/2" long, 1971	60	95	125
Big Mack Hydraulic Dumper	red hood, cab and tiltback dump section with cab shield, white plastic bumper, short step ladder on each side, 20-1/2" long, 1968	50	75	100
Big Mack Hydraulic Dumper	white hood, cab and tiltback dump section with cab shield, white plastic bumper, short step ladder on each side, 20-1/2" long, 1969	50	75	100
Big Mack Hydraulic Dumper	red hood, cab and tiltback dump section with cab shield, dump body sides have a large circular back, white plastic bumper, short step ladder on each side, 20-1/2" long, 1970	50	75	100
Boat Transport	blue flatbed truck carrying 8" litho metal boat, boat deck white, hull red, truck 15" long, 1959	300	550	750
Borden's Milk Delivery Van	white upper cab-over-engine van body and sliding side doors, yellow lower body, metal-handle yellow plastic tray and six white milk bottle with yellow caps, 11-1/2" long, 1965	125	200	275
Brute Car Carrier	bright blue cab-over-engine tractor unit and detachable double-deck semi-trailer, 2 plastic cars, 10" long, 1969	60	95	125
Brute Cement Mixer Truck	sand-beige cab-over-engine body and frame, white plastic mixing drum, white plastic seats, 5-1/4" long, 1968	35	55	75
Brute Cement Mixer Truck	blue cab-over-engine body and frame, white plastic mixing drum, white plastic seats, white-handled crank rotates drum, 5-1/4" long, 1969	35	55	75
Brute Dumper	red cab-over-engine body and cab shield on tiltback dump section, wide chrome wraparound bumper, 5" long, 1968	35	55	75
Brute Monkey House	yellow cab-over-engine body, striped orange and white awning roof, cage on back, two plastic monkeys, 5" long, 1968	50	75	100
Brute Monkey House	yellow cab-over-engine body, red and white awning roof, cage on back, two plastic monkeys, 5" long, 1969	35	55	75
Brute Sanitation Truck	lime green cab-over-engine and frame, white open-top body, wide chrome wraparound bumper, 5-1/4" long, 1969	50	75	100
Camper	bright medium blue steel truck and camper body, 14-1/2" long, 1964	60	95	125
Camper	medium blue truck and back door, white camper body, 14-1/2" long, 1965	50	75	100
Camper-N-Cruiser	powder blue pickup truck and trailer, pale blue camper body, 24-1/2" long, 1963	60	95	125

Camper-N-Cruiser	bright medium blue camper with matching boat trailer and 8-1/2" long plastic sport cruiser, overall 27" long, 1964	50	75	100
Campers Truck	turquoise pickup truck, pale turquoise plastic camper, 14-1/2" long, 1961	50	75	100
Campers Truck with Boat	green/turquoise pickup truck, lime green camper body, red plastic runabout boat on camper roof, 14-1/2" long, 1962	50	100	150
Campers Truck with Boat	green/turquoise pickup, no side mirror, lime green camper body with red plastic runabout boat on top, 14-1/2" long, 1963	50	100	150
Camping Trailer and Wagon	bright medium blue suburban wagon, matching teepee trailer, overall 24-1/2" long, 1964	60	95	125
Cattle Transport Truck	red with yellow stake sides, 15" long, 1956	75	115	150
Cattle Transport Truck	green and white with white stake sides, 15" long, 1957	75	115	150
Cement Mixer Truck	turquoise body, tank ends, and chute, white side ladder, water tank, mixing drum and loading hopper, 16-1/2" long, 1964	60	95	125
Cement Mixer Truck	red body, tank ends, and chute, white side ladder, water tank, mixing drum and loading hopper, 15-1/2" long, 1965	75	115	150
Cement Mixer Truck	red body, tank ends, and chute, white water tank, mixing drum and loading hopper, black wall tires, 15-1/2" long, 1967	60	95	125
Cement Mixer Truck	red body, tank ends, and chute, white water tank, mixing drum and loading hopper, whitewall tires, 15-1/2" long, 1968	50	75	100
Cement Mixer Truck	snub-nosed yellow body, cab, frame and chute, white plastic mixing drum, loading hopper and water tank with yellow ends,16" long, 1970	35	55	75
Charles Chip Delivery Truck Van	tan/beige body, decal on sides has brown irregular center resembling a large potato chip, 1966	125	200	275
City Baggage Dray	green front, hood, and fenders, non-open doors, yellow stake-side cargo section, 19" long, 1934	150	300	400
City Baggage Dray	green front, hood, and fenders, non-open doors, yellow stake-side cargo section, bright metal grille, 19" long, 1935	150	300	400
City Baggage Dray	duo-tone slant design, green front and fenders, yellow hood top and cargo section, 19" long, 1936	150	300	400
City Baggage Dray	duo-tone slant design, green front and fenders, yellow hood top and cargo section, dummy headlights, 19" long, 1937	150	300	400
City Baggage Dray	duo-tone slant design, green front and skirted fenders, yellow hood top, enclosed cab and cargo section, 20-3/4" long, 1938	125	275	350
City Baggage Dray	light green with aluminum-finish grille, no bumper, black rubber wheels, 20-3/4" long, 1939	100	250	300
City Baggage Dray	cream with aluminum-finish grille, no bumper, black rubber wheels, 20-3/4" long, 1940	100	250	300
Coal Truck	black hopper body and fully enclosed cab with opening doors, red wheels, 25" long, 1930	900	1500	2000

Coal Truck	black front, hood, fenders, doorless cab, red chassis and disc wheels, 25" long, 1926	900	1500	2000
Coal Truck	black front, hood, fenders, sliding discharge door on each side of hopper body, red chassis and disc wheels, 25" long, 1927	900	1500	2000
Coca-Cola Bottling Route Truck	bright yellow, with small metal hand truck, six or eight yellow cases of miniature green Coke bottles, 14-3/4" long, 1955	125	175	250
Coca-Cola Bottling Route Truck	bright yellow, with two small metal hand trucks and eight yellow cases of miniature green Coke bottles, 14-3/4" long, 1957	110	175	225
Coca-Cola Delivery Truck	orange/yellow cab and double-deck, open-side cargo, two small hand trucks, four red and four green cases of bottles, 15" long, 1960	100	150	200
Coca-Cola Delivery Truck	orange/yellow cab and double-deck, open-side cargo, two small hand trucks, four red and four green cases of bottles, 15" long, 1963	75	100	150
Coca-Cola Delivery Truck	orange/yellow cab and double-deck, open-side cargo, two small hand trucks, four red and four green cases of bottles, 15" long, 1964	60	95	125
Coca-Cola Delivery Truck	red lowercab-over-engine and van body, white upper cab, left side of van lifts to reveal 10 miniature bottle cases, 9-1/2" long, 1971	25	50	75
Coke Coffee Co. Delivery Truck Van	black lower half of body, orange upper half, roof and sliding side doors, 1966	85	130	175
Colt Vacationer	blue/white Colt sportsliner with trailer carrying 8-1/2" long red/white plastic sport cruiser, overall 22-1/2" long, 1967	60	95	125
Curtiss Candy Trailer Van	blue tractor and bumper, white semi-trailer van, blue roof, chrome one-piece toothed grille and headlights, white drop-down rear door, 32-3/4" long with tailgate/ramp lowered, 1955	250	400	500
Dairy Transport Truck	duo-tone slant design, red front and lower hood sides, white hood top, cab and semi-trailer tank body, tank opens in back, 26" long, 1939	150	225	300
Deluxe Auto Carrier	turquoise tractor unit, aluminum loading ramps, three plastic cars, overall 34" long including, 1962	100	175	250
Deluxe Camping Outfit	turquoise pickup truck and camper, and 8-1/2" long plastic boat on pale turquoise boat trailer, overall 24" long, 1961	60	95	125
Deluxe Hydraulic Rider Dump Truck	duo-tone slant design, red front and lower hood sides, white upper cab, dump body and chassis, red or black removable rider saddle, 26" long, 1948	175	265	350
Deluxe Motor Market	duo-tone slant design, red front, curved bumper, lower hood and cab sides, white hood top, body and cab, 22-1/4" long, 1950	250	350	500
Deluxe Rider Delivery Truck	duo-tone horizontal design, deep blue lower half, gray upper half, red rubber disc wheels, black barrel skid, 22-3/4" long, 1945	125	200	275
Deluxe Rider Delivery Truck	duo-tone horizontal design, gray lower half, blue upper half, red rubber disc wheels, black barrel skid, 22-3/4" long, 1945	125	200	275

Name	Description			
Deluxe Rider Dump Truck	various colors, dual rear wheels, no bumper, 25-1/2" long, 1945	75	115	150
Double Hydraulic Self-Loader-N-Dump	green front loading scoop with yellow arms attached to cab sides, yellow hood and enclosed cab, orange frame and wide dump body, 29" long with scoop lowered, 1956	85	130	175
Double Tandem Hydraulic Dump and Trailer	truck has red bumper, hood, cab and frame, four-wheel trailer with red tow and frame, both with white tiltback dump bodies, 38" long, 1957	85	130	175
Double-Deck Boat Transport	light blue steel flatbed truck carrying three 8" white plastic boats with red decks, truck 15" long, 1960	150	250	400
Dr. Pepper Delivery Truck Van	red, white, and blue, 1966	85	130	175
Dump Body Truck	black front, hood, open driver's seat and dump section, red chassis, crank windlass with ratchet raises dump bed, 25" long, 1921	800	1400	2000
Dump Body Truck	black front, hood, open driver's seat and dump section, red chassis, chain drive dump mechanism, 25" long, 1923	1200	1800	2500
Dump Truck	black enclosed cab and opening doors, front and hood, red dump body and chassis, crank handle lifts dump bed, 24" long, 1931	750	1125	1500
Dump Truck	yellow upper hood and enclosed cab, red wide-skirt fenders and open-frame chassis, blue dump body, no bumper, 17-1/4" long, 1940	85	130	175
Dump Truck	black enclosed cab and opening doors, front and hood, red dump body and chassis, simple lever arrangement lifts dump bed, 24" long, 1930	650	975	1300
Dump Truck	yellow enclosed cab, front and hood, red dump section, no bumper, 20" long, 1934	275	415	550
Dump Truck	yellow enclosed cab, front and hood, red dump section, no bumper, bright-metal radiator, 20" long, 1935	325	485	650
Dump Truck	duo-tone slant design, yellow enclosed cab and hood, red front and dump body, no bumper, bright-metal headlights, 20" long, 1936	250	375	500
Dump Truck	duo-tone slant design, yellow enclosed cab and hood, red front and dump body, no bumper, dummy headlights, 20" long, 1937	250	375	500
Dump Truck	duo-tone slant design, red lower cab, lower hood, front and dump body, yellow upper hood, upper cab and chassis, no bumper, 22-1/4" long, 1939	250	375	500
Dump Truck	duo-tone slant design, red front, fenders and lower doors, white upper, bright radiator grille and headlights, no bumper, 22-1/4" long, 1939	250	375	500
Dump Truck	green with cream hood top and upper enclosed cab, no bumper, bright-metal headlights and grille, 22-1/4" long, 1941	85	130	175
Dump Truck	white upper hood, enclosed cab, wide-skirt fenders and open-frame chassis, orange dump body, bright-metal grille, no bumper, 17-3/8" long, 1941	85	130	175
Dump Truck	red hood top and cab, white or cream dump body and frame, no bumper, 17-1/2" long, 1945	75	115	150

Dump Truck	various colors, black rubber wheels, 12" long, 1945	50	75	100
Dump Truck	duo-tone slant design, red front, fenders and dump body, yellow hood top, upper sides, upper cab and chassis, no bumper, 22-1/2" long, 1948	125	185	250
Dump Truck-Economy Line	dark blue dump body, remainder is yellow, bright-metal grille and headlights, no bumper or running boards, 12" long, 1941	75	115	150
Dump-n-Dozer	orange husky dumper truck and orange flatbed four-wheel trailer carrying orange bulldozer, 23" long including trailer, 1962	75	115	150
Dumper with Shovel	turquoise body, frame and dump section, white one-piece bumper and grille guard, large white steel scoop shovel, 15" long, 1962	75	115	150
Dumper with Shovel	medium green body, frame and dump section, white one-piece bumper and grille guard, no side mirror, large white steel scoop shovel, 15" long, 1963	75	115	150
Dumper with Shovel	medium green body, frame and dump section, white one-piece bumper and grille guard, no side mirror, large white steel scoop shovel, spring suspension on front axle only, 15" long, 1964	75	115	150
Dumper with Shovel	orange body, frame and dump section, chrome one-piece grille, no bumper guard, no side mirror, large white steel scoop shovel, no spring suspension, 15-3/4" long, 1965	75	115	150
Express Trailer Truck	red tractor unit, hood, fenders and enclosed cab, green semi-trailer van with removable roof and drop-down rear door, 23-3/4" long, 1933	350	525	700
Express Trailer Truck	red tractor unit, hood, fenders and enclosed cab, green semi-trailer van with removable roof and drop-down rear door, bright-metal dummy headlights, 23-3/4" long, 1934	350	525	700
Express Truck	all black except red frame, enclosed cab with opening doors, nickel-rim, red-shell headlights, six rubber tires, double bar front bumper, 24-1/2" long, 1930-32	3000	4500	6000
Farm Machinery Hauler Trailer Truck	blue tractor unit, yellow flatbed semi-trailer, 31-1/2" long, 1956	125	185	250
Farm Supplies Automatic Dump	duo-tone slant design, blue curved bumper, front, lower hood sides and cab, yellow upper hood, cab and rest of body, 22-1/2" long, 1950	125	185	250
Farm Supplies Dump Truck	duo-tone slant design, red front, fenders and lower hood sides, yellow upper hood, cab and body, 22-3/4" long, 1949	125	185	250
Farm Supplies Hydraulic Dump Trailer	green tractor unit, long cream body on semi-trailer, 14 rubber wheels, 26-1/2" long, 1956	100	150	200
Fast Delivery Pickup	yellow hood and cab, red open cargo body, removable chain across open back, 13-1/2" long, 1949	100	150	200
Fast Freight Truck	white tractor unit, removable open top cargo trailer, 20" long, 1948	100	150	200
Finger-Tip Steering Hydraulic Dumper	powder blue bumper, fenders, hood, cab and frame, white tiltback dump body, 22" long, 1959	75	115	150

Fisherman	light tan pickup truck with tan steel trailer carrying plastic 8-1/2" long sport crusier, overall 24-1/4" long, 1962	75	115	150
Fisherman	pale blue/green station wagon with four-wheel boat trailer carrying plastic 8-1/2" long boat, overall 27-1/2" long, 1963	75	115	150
Fisherman	metallic sage green pickup truck with boat trailer carrying plastic 8-1/2" long sport cruiser, overall 25" long, 1964	75	115	150
Fisherman	sage gray/green and white pickup truck with steel trailer carrying plastic 8-1/2" long sport cruiser, overall 25" long, 1965	60	95	125
Flivver Dump Truck	black with red eight-spoke wheels, black hubs, aluminum tires, flat, open dump section with squared-off back with latching, drop-down endgate, 11" long, 1926	750	1000	1500
Flivver Huckster Truck	black with red eight-spoke wheels, black hubs, aluminum tires, flat, continous hard top canopy extending from enclosed cab over cargo section, 14" long, 1927	2500	4000	5500
Flivver One-Ton Express Truck	black with red eight-spoke wheels, black hubs, aluminum tires, flat, enclosed cab, operating steering wheel, open cargo section, 14-1/4" long, 1927	3500	5000	6500
Flivver Scoop Dump Truck	black with red eight-spoke wheels, 12-1/2" long, 1926-27, 1929-30	1500	2500	3500
Flivver Truck	black with red eight-spoke wheels with aluminum tires, black hubs, 12" long, 1924	800	1000	1500
Ford Flivver Dump Cart	black with red eight-spoke wheels, black hubs, aluminum tires, flat, short open dump section tapers to point on each side, 12-1/2" long, 1926	1500	2500	3500
Frederick & Nelson Delivery Truck Van	medium green body, roof and sliding side doors, 1966	125	200	275
Freight Delivery Stake Truck	red hood, bumper, cab and frame, white cargo section, yellow three-post, three-slat removable stake sides, 14-3/4" long, 1955	75	125	150
Front Loader Hi-Lift Dump Truck	red scoop and arms attached to white truck at rear fenders, green dump body, 17-3/4" long with scoop down and dump body raised, 1955	85	130	175
Giant Hydraulic Dumper	red bumper, frame, hood and cab, light tan tiltback dump body and cab shield 23-3/4" long, 1960	125	185	250
Giant Hydraulic Dumper	overall color turquoise, dump lever has a red plastic tip, 22-3/4" long, 1961	135	200	275
Giraffe Truck	powder blue hood, white cab roof, high-sided open-top cargo section, two orange/yellow plastic giraffes, 13-1/4" long,1968	60	95	125
GMC Air Force Electric Searchlight Unit	all blue flatbed, off white battery operated searchlight swivel mount, decals on cab doors, 14-3/4" long, 1958	200	300	400
GMC Airway Express Van	green hood, cab and van body, latching double rear doors, shiny metal drum coin bank and metal hand truck, 17-1/2" long with rear doors open, 1957	250	350	450
GMC Anti-Aircraft Unit with Searchlight	15" truck with four-wheel trailer, battery operated, over 25-1/4" long, 1957	250	350	450

Item	Description			
GMC Army Hauler with Jeep	shiny olive drab tractor unit and flatbed trailer, 10" long jeep, overall 31-1/2" long, 1958	200	300	400
GMC Army Transport with Howitzer	shiny olive drab, 14-1/2" long, truck, overall with gun 22-1/2" long, 1957	200	300	400
GMC Brinks Armored Truck Van	silver gray, barred windows on sides and in double doors, coin slot and hole in roof, brass padlock with two keys, pouch, play money, three gray plastic guard figures, 16" long, 1958	300	350	450
GMC Coca-Cola Route Truck	lime/yellow, with small metal hand truck and eight cases of miniature green Coke bottles, 14-1/8" long, 1957	200	300	400
GMC Coca-Cola Route Truck	orange/yellow, with two small metal hand trucks and eight cases of miniature green Coke bottles, 14-1/8" long, 1958	200	300	400
GMC Construction Company Dumper	pastel blue including control lever on left and dump section with cab shield, hinged tailgate, chrome GMC bar grille, six wheels, 16" long, 1958	200	300	400
GMC Construction Company Dumper	pastel blue including control lever on left and dump section with cab shield, hinged tailgate, chrome GMC bar grille, four wheels, 16" long, 1959	150	250	350
GMC Deluxe Hydraulic Dumper	pastel blue, chrome GMC bar grille, attached headlights, yellow steel scoop shovel on left side, 19" long over scraper blade, 1959	200	300	400
GMC Highway Giant Trailer	blue tractor, blue and white van, chrome GMC bar grille and headlights, blue roof on semi-trailer, white tailgate doubles as loading ramp, 18-wheeler, 31-1/4" long, 1957	250	350	450
GMC Highway Giant Trailer Truck	blue tractor, blue and white van, chrome GMC bar grille and headlights, blue roof on semi-trailer, white tailgate doubles as loading ramp, 14-wheeler, 30-3/4" long, 1958	200	300	400
GMC Husky Dumper	red hood, bumper, cab and chassis, chrome GMC bar grille and nose emblem, white oversize dump body, red control lever on right side, 17-1/2" long, 1957	150	250	350
GMC Self-Loading Auto Carrier	yellow tractor and double-deck semi trailer, three plastic cars, overall 33-1/4" long, 1959	200	300	400
GMC Signal Corps Unit	both olive drab, 14-1/4" long truck with removable fabric canopy, 8" long four-wheel trailer, 1957	150	200	250
Grocery Motor Market Truck	duo-tone slant design, yellow front, lower hood sides, fenders and lower doors, white hood top, enclosed cab and body, no bumper, 20-1/2" long, 1937	275	415	550
Grocery Motor Market Truck	duo-tone slant design, yellow front, lower hood sides, skirted fenders and lower doors, white hood top, cab and body, no bumper, 21-1/2" long, 1938	275	415	550
Heavy Hauling Dumper	red hood, bumper, cab and frame, cream tiltback dump body, 20-1/2" long, 1955	75	125	150
Heavy Hauling Dumper	red hood, bumper, cab and frame, cream oversize dump body, hinged tailgate, 21-1/2" long, 1956	75	125	150
Heavy Hauling Hydraulic Dumper	green hood, cab and frame, cream tiltback dump body, and cab shield, raising dump body almost to vertical, 23" long, 1956	75	125	150
Hertz Auto Hauler	bright yellow tractor and double-deck semi-trailer, three plastic vehicles, 27" long, 1965	100	150	200

Hi-Lift Farm Supplies Dump	red plastic front end including hood and enclosed cab, yellow dump body, cab shield and hinged tailgate, 21-1/2" long, 1953	100	175	225
Hi-Lift Farm Supplies Dump	all steel, red front end including hood and enclosed cab, yellow dump body, cab shield and hinged tailgate, 23-1/2" long, 1954	100	175	225
Hi-Lift Scoop-n-Dump Truck	orange truck with deeply fluted sides, dark green scoop on front rises to empty load into hi-lift cream/yellow dump body, 16" long, 1952	85	130	175
Hi-Lift Scoop-n-Dump Truck	orange truck with deeply fluted sides, dark green scoop on front rises to empty load into hi-lift light cream dump body, 16" long, 1953	85	130	175
Hi-Lift Scoop-n-Dump Truck	orange truck with deeply fluted sides, dark green scoop on front rises to empty load into deep hi-lift slightly orange dump body, 16" long, 1955	75	115	150
Hi-Lift Scoop-n-Dump Truck	orange hood, fenders and cab, yellow front loading scoop and arms attached to fenders, white frame, dump body and cab shield, 17-3/4" long, 1956	75	115	150
Hi-Lift Scoop-n-Dump Truck	blue hood, fenders and cab, yellow front loading scoop and arms attached to fenders, white frame, dump body, cab shield, and running boards, 17-3/4" long, 1957	60	95	125
Hi-Tip Hydraulic Dumper	orange hood, cab and frame, cream tiltback dump body, and cab shield, raising dump body almost to vertical, 23" long, 1957	75	115	150
Highway Hawk Trailer Van	bronze cab tractor, chrome metallized plastic bumper, grille, air cleaner and exhaust, 19-3/4" long, 1985	50	75	100
Highway Maintenance Truck with Trailer	orange with black rack of four simulated floodlights behind cab, 19-1/2" long including small two-wheel trailer, 1957	100	150	200
Husky Dumper	orange wraparound bumper, body, frame and dump section, hinged tailgate, plated dump lever on left side, 15-1/4" long, 1960	75	115	150
Husky Dumper	white plastic wraparound bumper, tan body, frame and dump section, hinged tailgate, plated dump lever on left side, 15-1/4" long, 1961	75	115	150
Husky Dumper	bright yellow, chrome one-piece bumper, slotted rectangular grille and double headlights, 14-1/2" long, 1966,	75	115	150
Husky Dumper	red hood, cab, chassis and dump section, chrome one-piece bumper and slotted grille with double headlights, 14-1/2" long, 1968	60	95	125
Husky Dumper	yellow hood, cab, fram and tiltback dump section with cab shield, crome one-piece wraparound bumper, 14-1/2" long, 1969	50	75	100
Husky Dumper	snub-nose red body, tiltback dump section, cab shield, full-width chrome bumperless grille, deep-tread whitewall tires, 14-1/2" long, 1970	50	75	100
Husky Dumper	snub-nose red body, tiltback dump section snda cab shield, full-width chrome bumperless grille, white-tipped dump-control lever on left, deep-tread whitewall tires, 14-1/2" long, 1971	50	75	100
Hydraulic Auto Hauler with Four GMC Cars	powder blue GMC tractor, 7" long plastic cars, overall 33-1/2" long including loading ramp, 1958	250	350	450

Hydraulic Construction Dumper	red front, cab and chassis, large green dump section with cab shield, 15-1/4" long, 1962	60	95	125
Hydraulic Construction Dumper	tan/beige front, cab and chassis, large green dump section with cab shield, 15-1/4" long, 1963	60	95	125
Hydraulic Construction Dumper	bright blue front, cab and chassis, large green dump section with cab shield, 15-1/2" long, 1964	50	75	100
Hydraulic Construction Dumper	bright green front, cab and chassis, large green dump section with cab shield, 14" long, 1965	50	75	100
Hydraulic Construction Dumper	medium blue front, cab and chassis, large green dump section with cab shield, 15-1/4" long, 1967	50	75	100
Hydraulic Dump Truck	black front, hood, fenders, open seat, and dump body, red chassis and disc wheels with aluminum tires, 25" long, 1926	500	800	1000
Hydraulic Dump Truck	black front, hood, fenders, dark reddish maroon dump body, red chassis and disc wheels with seven embossed spokes, black hubs, 25" long, 1931	750	900	1300
Hydraulic Dump Truck	black front, hood, fenders and enclosed cab, red dump body, chassis and wheels with six embossed spokes, bright hubs, 24-3/4" long, 1933	325	485	650
Hydraulic Dump Truck	duo-tone slant design, red hood sides, dump body and chassis, white upper hood, cab and removable rider seat, electric headlights, 24-3/4" long, 1936	300	500	700
Hydraulic Dump Truck	duo-tone slant design, red front, lower hood sides, dump body and chassis, white upper hood and cab, 26-1/2" long, 1939	250	475	650
Hydraulic Dumper	green, plated dump lever on left side, large hooks on left side hold yellow or off-white steel scoop shovel, white plastic side mirro and grille guard, 17" long, 1961	125	185	250
Hydraulic Dumper with Shovel	green, plated dump lever on left side, large hooks on left side hold yellow or off-white steel scoop shovel, 17" long, 1960	125	185	250
Hydraulic Hi-Lift Dumper	duo-tone slant design, green hood nose and lower cab sides, remainder white with chrome grille, enclosed cab, 24" long, 1953	75	115	150
Hydraulic Hi-Lift Dumper	green hood, fenders, cab, and dump-body supports, white dump body with cab shield, 22-1/2" long, 1954	85	130	175
Hydraulic Hi-Lift Dumper	blue hood, fenders, cab, and dump-body supports, white dump body with cab shield, 22-1/2" long, 1955	75	115	150
Hydraulic Husky Dumper	red body, frame, dump section and cab shield, 15-1/4" long, 1962	75	115	150
Hydraulic Husky Dumper	red body, white one-piece bumper and grille guard, heavy side braces on dump section, 14" long, 1963	50	75	100
Hydraulic Rider Dumper	duo-tone slant design, yellow front and lower hood, red upper cab, dump body and upper hood, 26-1/2" long, 1949	175	265	350
Hydraulic Sturdy Dumper	lime green hood, cab, frame and tiltback dump section, green lever on left side controls hydraulic dumping, 14-1/2" long, 1969	50	75	100

Hydraulic Sturdy Dumper	yellow hood, cab, fram and tiltback dump section, green lever on left side controls hydraulic dumping, 14-1/2" long, 1969	50	75	100
Hydraulic Sturdy Dumper	snub-nose green/yellow body, cab and tiltback dump section, white plastic seats, 14-1/2" long, 1970	50	75	100
Hydraulic Highway Dumper with Scraper Blade	orange with row of black square across scraper edges, one-piece chrome eight-hole grille and double headlights, 17-3/4" long over blade and raised dump body, 1958	75	115	150
Hydraulic Highway Dumper	orange with row of black square across scraper edges, one-piece chrome eight-hole grille and double headlights, no scraper blade, 17-3/4" long over blade and raised dump body, 1959	50	75	100
Ice Truck	black front, hood, fenders and doorless cab, yellow open cargo section, canvas sliding cover, 26-1/2" long, 1926	800	1000	1750
Ice Truck	black front, hood, fenders and enclosed cab, yellow open cargo section, canvas, ice cakes, miniature tongs, 26-1/2" long, 1930	750	900	1500
Ice Truck	black front, hood, fenders and enclosed cab, yellow ice compartment, canvas, ice cakes, tongs, 26-1/2" long, 1933-34	550	700	1300
Ice Truck	black front, hood, fenders and enclosed cab, yellow ice compartment, 26-1/2" long, 1933	750	900	1500
IHC "Red Baby" Express Truck	red doorless roofed cab, open pickup body, chassis and fenders, 24-1/4" long, 1928	1000	1250	2000
IHC "Red Baby" Express Truck	red with black hubs and aluminum tires, 24-1/4" long, 1929	1000	1250	2000
Insurance Patrol	red with open driver's seat and body, brass bell on cowl and full-length handrails, 27" long, 1925	650	1000	1300
Insurance Patrol	red with open driver's seat and body, brass bell on cowl and full-length handrails, no CFD decal, 27" long, 1928	625	950	1250
International Delivery Truck	red with removable black rider saddle, black-edged yellow horizontal strip on cargo body, 24-1/2" long, 1935	225	350	450
International Delivery Truck	duo-tone slant design, red front, bumper and lower hood sides, yellow hood top, upper sides, cab and open cargo body, 24-1/2" long, 1936	200	300	400
International Delivery Truck	duo-tone slant design, red front, bumper and lower hood sides, yellow hood top, upper sides, cab and open cargo body, bright metal dummy headlights, 24-1/2" long, 1938	150	225	300
International Dump Truck	red with bright-metal radiator grille, and black removable rider saddle, 25-3/4" long, 1935	325	485	650
International Dump Truck	duo-tone slant design, yellow radiator, fenders, lower hood and detachable rider seat, rest of truck is red, 25-3/4" long, 1936	325	485	650
International Dump Truck	red, with red headlights on radiator, black removable rider saddle, 25-3/4" long, 1938	125	185	250
International Railway Express Truck	duo-tone slant design, yellow front, lower hood sides and removable top, green hood top, enclosed cab and van body, electric headlights, 25" long, 1937	350	525	700

International Railway Express Truck	duo-tone slant design, yellow front, lower hood sides and removable top, green hood top, enclosed cab and van body, dummy headlights, 25" long, 1938	350	525	700
International Wrecker Truck	duo-tone slant design, yellow upper cab, hood, and boom, red lower cab, fenders, grille and body, rubber tires, removable rider seat, 32" long, 1938	600	900	1800
Jewel Home Service Truck Van	dark brown body and sliding side doors, 1967	125	200	275
Jewel Home Shopping Truck Van	pale mint green upper body and roof, darker mint green lower half, no sliding doors, 1968	125	200	275
Jolly Joe Ice Cream Truck	white with black roof, black tires and wooden wheels, 17-1/2" long, 1947	225	350	450
Jolly Joe Popsicle Truck	white with black roof, black tires and wooden wheels, 17-1/2" long, 1948	275	425	550
Jr. Animal Ark	fuschia lapstrake hull, four black tires, 10 pairs of plastic animals, 5" long, 1970	35	55	75
Jr. Auto Carrier	yellow cab-over-engine tractor unit and double-deck semi-trailer, two red plastic cars, 15-1/2" long, 1967	50	75	100
Jr. Auto Carrier	bright blue cab-over-engine tractor unit and double-deck semi-trailer, two plastic cars, 17-1/4" long, 1969	60	95	125
Jr. Beach Buggy	yellow hood, fenders and topless jeep body, red plastic seats, white plastic surfboard that clips to roll bar and windshield, truck 6" long, 1969	50	75	100
Jr. Beach Buggy	lime green hood, fenders and topless jeep body, red plastic seats, lime green plastic surfboard that clips to roll bar and windshield, truck 6" long, 1971	35	55	75
Jr. Buggy Hauler	fuschia jeep body with orange seats, orange two-wheel trailer tilts to unload sandpiper beach buggy, 12" long including jeep and trailer, 1970	35	55	75
Jr. Camper	red cab and pickup body wih yellow camper body, 7" long, 1971	50	75	100
Jr. Canada Dry Delivery Truck	green/lime cab-over-engine body, hand truck, 10 cases of green bottles, 9-1/2" long, 1968	100	150	200
Jr. Canada Dry Delivery Truck	green/lime cab-over-engine body, hand truck, 10 cases of green bottles, 9-1/2" long, 1969	85	130	175
Jr. Cement Mixer Truck	blue cab-over-engine body, frame and hopper, white plastic mixing drum, white plastic seats, 7-1/2" long, 1968	50	75	100
Jr. Cement Mixer Truck	blue cab-over-engine body, frame and hopper, white plastic mixing drum, white plastic seats, wide one-piece chrome bumper, 7-1/2" long, 1969	35	55	75
Jr. Dump Truck	red cab-over-engine, frame and tiltback dump section, plastic vertical headlights, 7-1/2" long, 1967	50	75	100
Jr. Dumper	avocado cab-over-engine, frame and tiltback dump section with cab shield, one-piece chrome bumper and four-slot grille, 7-1/2" long, 1969	35	55	75
Jr. Giraffe Truck	turquoise cab-over-engine body, white cab roof, plastic giraffe, 6-1/2" long, 1968	50	75	100
Jr. Giraffe Truck	turquoise cab-over-engine body, white cab roof, plastic giraffe, 6-1/4" long, 1969	35	55	75

Jr. Kitty Kennel	pink cab-over-engine body, white cab roof, four white plastic cats, 6-1/4" long, 1969	55	85	115
Jr. Kitty Kennel	pink cab-over-engine body, white cab roof, four colored plastic cats, 6-1/4" long, 1968	60	95	125
Jr. Sanitation Truck	blue cab-over-engine, white frame, refuse body and loading hopper, 10" long, 1968	75	115	150
Jr. Sanitation Truck	yellow cab-over-engine and underframe, refuse body and loading hopper, full width bumper and grille, 10" long, 1969	75	115	150
Junior Line City Dray	black, front, hood and fenders, license plate, 24" long, 1930	1500	2500	4000
Junior Line Dairy Truck	stake-bed style truck, black front, hood, and enclosed cab with opening doors, blue/green stake body, red chassis, six miniature milk cans with removable lids, 24" long, 1930	1500	2500	4000
Junior Line Dump Truck	black enclosed cab, front, hood and chassis, red dump body front and back are higher than sides, 21" long, 1933	1500	2500	4000
Junior Line Air Mail Truck	black enclosed cab, red chassis and body, headlights and double bar bumper, six rubber tires, 24" long, 1930-32	400	650	1200
Kennel Truck	medium blue pickup body and cab, clear plastic 12 section kennel with 12 plastic dogs fits in cargo box, 13-1/2" long, 1964	60	95	125
Kennel Truck	turquoise pickup body and cab, clear plastic 12 section kennel with 12 plastic dogs fits in cargo box, 13-1/2" long, 1965	60	95	125
Kennel Truck	bright blue pickup body and cab, clear plastic 12 section kennel with 12 plastic dogs fits in cargo box, 13-1/4" long, 1966	100	150	200
Kennel Truck	bright blue pickup body and cab, clear plastic 12 section kennel with 12 plastic dogs fits in cargo box, 13-1/4" long, 1967	85	130	175
Kennel Truck	cream/yellow pickup body and cab, clear plastic 12 section kennel with 12 plastic dogs fits in cargo box, 13-1/4" long, 1968	75	115	150
Kennel Truck	red/orange pickup body and cab, yellow roof, six section kennel with six plastic dogs fits in cargo box, 13-1/4" long, 1969	60	95	125
Kennel Truck	snub-nosed red/orange body and cab, plastic kennel section in back, six kennels with six plastic dogs, 13-1/4" long, 1970	60	95	125
Lumber Truck	black front, hood, fenders, cabless open seat and low-sides cargo bed, red bumper, chassis and a pair of removable solid stake sides, load of lumber pieces, 24" long, 1924	750	1000	1500
Lumber Truck	black front, hood, fenders, doorless cab and low-sides cargo bed, red bumper, chassis and a pair of remov-able solid stake sides, load of lumber, 25-1/2" long, 1926	1000	1300	2700
Mack Hydraulic Dumper	red front, hood, cab, chassis and tiltback dump section with cab shield, white plastic bumper, 20-1/2" long, 1965	60	95	125

Mack Hydraulic Dumper	red front, hood, cab, chassis and tiltback dump section with cab shield, white plastic bumper, short step ladder on each side, 20-1/2" long, 1967	50	75	100
Mack Quarry Dumper	orange front, hood cab and chassis, blue-green tiltback dump section, white plastic bumper, 20-1/2" long, 1965	75	115	150
Mammoth Hydraulic Quarry Dumper	deep green hood, cab and chassis, red tiltback dump section, black plastic bumper, 23" long, 1962	75	115	150
Mammoth Hydraulic Quarry Dumper	deep green hood, red cab, chassis and tiltback dump section, black plastic bumper, 22-1/2" long, 1963	60	90	125
Marshall Field's Delivery Truck Van	hunter green body, sliding doors and roof, 1966	125	200	275
Milk Farms Truck	white body, black roof, short hood with black wooden headlights, 13-1/2" long, 1945	175	350	525
Milk Farms Truck	light cream body, red roof, nickel glide headlights, sliding doors, 13" long, 1949	125	200	275
Milkman Truck	medium blue hood, cab and flatbed body, white side rails, eight 3" white plastic milk bottles, 14-1/4" long, 1961	110	175	225
Milkman Truck	deep cream hood, cab and flatbed body, white side rails, fourteen 3" white plastic milk bottles with red caps, 14-1/4" long, 1962	100	150	200
Milkman Truck	light blue hood, cab and flatbed body, white side rails, 14 3" white plastic milk bottles, 14-1/4" long, 1963	85	130	175
Milkman Truck	light yellow hood, cab and flatbed body, white side rails, 14 3" white plastic milk bottles, 14-1/4" long, 1964	75	115	150
Milkman Truck	medium blue hood, cab and flatbed body, white side rails, eight 3" white plastic milk bottles, 14-1/4" long, 1961	110	175	225
Milkman Truck	deep cream hood, cab and flatbed body, white side rails, 14 3" white plastic milk bottles with red caps, 14-1/4" long, 1962	100	150	200
Milkman Truck	light blue hood, cab and flatbed body, white side rails, 14 3" white plastic milk bottles, 14-1/4" long, 1963	85	130	175
Milkman Truck	lime yellow hood, cab and flatbed body, white side rails, 14 3" white plastic milk bottles, 14-1/4" long, 1964	75	115	150
Mister Buddy Ice Cream Truck	white cab-over-engine van body, pale blue or off-white plastic underbody and floor, 11-1/2" long, 1964	75	115	150
Mister Buddy Ice Cream Truck	white cab-over-engine van body, red plastic underbody and floor, 11-1/2" long, 1966	60	95	125
Mister Buddy Ice Cream Truck	white cab-over-engine van body, red plastic underbody and floor, red bell knob, 11-1/2" long, 1967	60	95	125
Model T Flivver Truck	black with red eight-spoke wheels with aluminum tires, black hubs, 12" long, 1924	1000	1500	2000
Motor Market Truck	duo-tone horizontal design, white hood top, upper cab and high partition in cargo section, yellow-orange grille, fenders, lower hood and cab sides, 21-1/2" long, 1941	200	350	550
Moving Van	black front, hood and seat, red chassis and disc wheels with black hubs, green van body, roof extends forward above open driver's seat, 25" long, 1924	1200	2000	3000

Name	Description			
Overland Trailer Truck	yellow tractor, enclosed cab, red semi-trailer and four-wheel full trailer with removable roofs, 39-3/4" long, 1935	350	525	700
Overland Trailer Truck	duo-tone slant design, green and yellow tractor unit with yellow cab, red semi-trailer and four-wheel full trailer with yellow removable roofs, 39-3/4" long, 1936	325	485	650
Overland Trailer Truck	duo-tone slant design, green and yellow semi-streamlined tractor and green hood sides, yellow hood, chassis, enclosed cab, 40", 1939	350	550	700
Overland Trailer Truck	duo-tone horizontal design, red and white tractor has red front, lower half chassis, chassis, enclosed cab, 40", 1939	350	550	700
Pepsi Delivery Truck	powder blue hood and lower cab, white upper cab and double-deck cargo section, two hand trucks, four blue cases of red bottles, four red cases of blue bottles, 15" long, 1970	60	95	125
Polysteel Boat Transport	medium blue soft plastic body, steel flatbed carrying 8" white plastic runabout boat with red deck, truck 12-1/2" long, 1960	75	115	150
Polysteel Coca-Cola Delivery Truck	yellow plastic truck, slanted bottle racks, eight red Coke cases with green bottles, small metal hand truck, 12-1/2" long, 1961	50	75	100
Polysteel Coca-Cola Delivery Truck	yellow plastic truck, slanted bottle racks, eight green Coke cases with red bottles, small metal hand truck, 12-1/4" long, 1962	60	95	125
Polysteel Dumper	green soft molded plastic front, cab and frame, yellow steel dump body with sides rounded at back, hinged tailgate, 13" long, 1959	100	150	200
Polysteel Dumper	medium blue soft molded plastic front, cab and frame, off-white steel dump body with sides rounded at back, hinged tailgate, 13" long, 1960	85	130	175
Polysteel Dumper	orange plastic body and tiltback dump section with cab shield, "Come-Back Motor", 13" long, 1961	75	115	150
Polysteel Dumper	orange plastic body and tiltback dump section with cab shield, no "Come-Back Motor", no door decals, 13-1/2" long, 1962	60	95	125
Polysteel Hydraulic Dumper	beige soft molded-plastic front, cab and frame, off-white steel dump section with sides rounded at rear, 13" long, 1959	60	95	125
Polysteel Hydraulic Dumper	red soft molded-plastic front, cab and frame, light green steel dump section with sides rounded at rear, 13" long, 1960	75	115	150
Polysteel Hydraulic Dumper	yellow soft plastic body, frame and tiltback ribbed dump section with cab shield, 13" long, 1961	75	115	150
Polysteel Hydraulic Dumper	red soft plastic body, frame and tiltback ribbed dump section with cab shield, 13" long, 1962	60	95	125
Polysteel Milk Tanker	red soft plastic tractor unit, light blue/gray semi-trailer tank with red ladders and five dooms, 22" long, 1961	60	95	125
Polysteel Milk Tanker	turquoise soft plastic tractor unit, light blue/gray semi-trailer tank with red ladders and five dooms, 22" long, 1961	60	95	125

Polysteel Milkman Truck	light blue soft plastic front, cab and frame, light yellow steel open cargo section with nine oversized white plastic milk bottles, 11-3/4" long, 1960	75	115	150
Polysteel Milkman Truck	light blue soft plastic front, cab and frame, light blue steel open cargo section with nine oversized white plastic milk bottles, 11-3/4" long, 1961	60	95	125
Polysteel Milkman Truck	turquoise soft plastic front, cab and frame, light blue steel open cargo section with nine oversized white plastic milk bottles with red caps, 11-3/4" long, 1962	35	55	75
Polysteel Highway Transport	red soft plastic tractor, cab roof lights, double horn, radio antenna and side fuel tanks, white steel semi-trailer van, 20-1/2" long, 1960	100	150	200
Polysteel Supermarket Delivery	medium blue soft molded-plastic front, hood, cab and frame, steel off-white open cargo section, 13" long, 1959	75	115	150
Pull-N-Ride Baggage Truck	duo-tone horizontal design, light cream upper half, off-white lower half and bumper, 24-1/4" long, 1953	150	225	300
R E A Express Truck	dark green cab-over-engine van body, sliding side doors, double rear doors, white plastic one-piece bumper, 11-1/2" long, 1964	200	300	400
R E A Express Truck	dark green cab-over-engine van body, sliding side doors, double rear doors, white plastic one-piece bumper, no spring suspension, 11-1/2" long, 1965	130	195	260
R E A Express Truck	dark green cab-over-engine van body, sliding side doors, double rear doors, white plastic one-piece bumper, no spring suspension, side doors are embossed "BUDDY L", 11-1/2" long, 1966	125	185	250
Railroad Transfer Rider Delivery Truck	duo-tone horizontal design, yellow upper half, hood top, cab and slatted caro sides, green lower half, small hand truck, two milk cans with removable lids, 23-1/4" long, 1949	95	115	150
Railroad Transfer Store Door Delivery	duo-tone horizontal design, yellow hood top, cab and upper body, red lower half of hood and body, small hand truck, two metal drums with coin slots, 23-1/4" long, 1950	85	130	175
Railway Express Truck	red tractor unit, enclosed square cab, green 12-1/4" long two-wheel semi-trailer van with removable roof, "Wrigley's Spearmint Gum" poster on trailer sides, 23" long, 1935	375	565	750
Railway Express Truck	duo-tone slant design, tractor unit has white skirted fendersand hood sides, green hood top, enclosed cab and chassis, green semi-trailer with white removable roof, 25" long, 1939	350	475	700
Railway Express Truck	duo-tone slant design, tractor has silvery and hood sides, green hood top, enclosed cab, green semi-trailer, "Wrigley's Spearmint Gum" poster on trailer sides, 23" long, 1935	400	600	800
Railway Express Truck	black front hood, fenders, seat and low body sides, dark green van body, red chassis, 25" long, 1926	500	800	1600
Railway Express Truck	dark green or light green screen body, double-bar nickel front bumper, brass radiator knob, red wheels, 25" long, 1930	500	1000	2000

Railway Express Truck	yellow and green tractor unit has white skirted fendersand hood sides, green hood top, enclosed cab and chassis, green semi-trailer with yellow removable roof, 25" long, 1940	325	485	650
Railway Express Truck	duo-tone horizontal design, tractor unit has yellow front, lower door and chassis, green hood top and enclosed upper cab, semi-trailer has yellow lower sides, 25" long, 1941	325	485	650
Railway Express Truck	deep green plastic "Diamond T" hood and cab, deep green steel frame and van body with removable silvery roof, small two-wheel hand truck, steel four-rung barrel skid, 21" long, 1952	200	300	400
Railway Express Truck	green plastic hood and cab, green steel high-sides open body, frame and bumper, small two-wheel hand truck, steel four-rung barrel skid, 20-3/4" long, 1953	125	185	250
Railway Express Truck	green all-steel hood, cab, frame and high-sides open bady, sides have three horizontal slots in upper back corners, 22" long, 1954	75	115	150
Ranchero Stake Truck	medium green, white plastic one-piece bumper and grille guard, four-post, four-slat fixed stake sides and cargo section, 14" long, 1963	50	75	100
Rider Dump Truck	duo-tone horizontal design, yellow hood top, upper cab and upper dump body, red front, hood sides, lower doors and lower dump body, no bumper, 21-1/2" long, 1945	160	245	325
Rider Dump Truck	duo-tone horizontal design, yellow hood top, upper cab and upper dump body, red front, hood sides, lower doors and lower dump body, no bumper, 23" long, 1947	75	115	150
Rival Dog Food Delivery Van	cream front, cab and boxy van body, metal drum coin bank with "RIVAL DOG FOOD" label in blue, red, white and yellow, 16-1/2" long, 1956	160	245	325
Robotoy	black fenders and chassis, red hood and enclosed cab with small visor, green dump body's front and back are higher than sides, 21-5/8" long, 1932	650	900	1200
Rockin' Giraffe Truck	powder blue hood, cab, and high-sided open-top cargo section, two orange and yellow plastic giraffes, 13-1/4" long, 1967	75	115	150
Ruff-n-Tuff Cement Mixer Truck	yellow snub-nosed cab-over-engine body, frame and water-tank ends, white plastic water tank and mixing drum, white seats, 16" long, 1971	35	55	75
Ruff-n-Tuff Log Truck	yellow snub-nose cab-over-engine, frame and shallow truck bed, black full-width grille, 16" long, 1971	50	75	100
Ryder City Special Delivery Truck Van	duo-tone horizontal design, yellow upper half including hood top and cab, brown removable van roof, warm brown front and lower half of van body, 24-1/2" long, 1949	150	225	300
Ryder Van Lines Trailer	duo-tone slant design, black front and lower hood sides and doors, deep red hood top, enclosed cab and chassis, 35-1/2" long, 1949	350	525	700
Saddle Dump Truck	duo-tone slant design, yellow front, fenders and removable rider seat, red enclosed square cab and dump body, no bumper, 19-1/2" long, 1937	200	300	400

Name	Description			
Saddle Dump Truck	duo-tone slant design, yellow front, fenders, lower hood and cab, and removable rider seat, rest of body red, no bumper, 21-1/2" long, 1939	125	185	250
Saddle Dump Truck	duo-tone horizontal design, deep blue hood top, upper cab and upper dump body, orange fenders radiator front lower two-thirds of cab and lower half of dump body, 21-1/2" long, 1941	85	130	175
Sand and Gravel Truck	black body, doorless roofed cab and steering wheel, red chassis and disc wheels with black hubs, 25-1/2" long, 1926	650	1000	1200
Sand and Gravel Truck	dark or medium green hood, cab, roof lights and skirted body, white or cream dump section, 13-1/2" long, 1949	100	150	200
Sand and Gravel Truck	duo-tone horizontal design, red front, bumper, lower hood, cab sides, chassis and lower dump body sides, white hood top, enclosed cab and upper dump body, 23-3/4" long, 1949	350	525	700
Sand and Gravel Truck	black with red chassis and wheels, nickel-rim, red-shell headlights, enclosed cab with opening doors, 25-1/2" long, 1930-32	2000	3000	5000
Sand and Gravel Rider Dump Truck	duo-tone horizontal design, blue lower half, yellow upper half including hoop top and enclosed cab, 24" long, 1950	350	525	700
Sand Loader and Dump Truck	duo-tone horizontal design, yellow hood top and upper dump blue cab sides, frame and lower dump body, red loader on dump with black rubber conveyor belt, 24-1/2" long, 1950	175	265	350
Sand Loader and Dump Truck	duo-tone horizontal design, yellow hood top and upper dump blue cab sides, frame and lower dump body, red loader on dump with black rubber conveyor belt, 24-1/2" long, 1952	60	95	125
Sanitation Service Truck	blue front fenders, hood, cab and chassis, white encllosed dump section and hinged loading hopper, one-piece chrome bumper, plastic windows in garbage section, 16-1/2" long, 1967	100	150	200
Sanitation Service Truck	blue front fenders, hood, cab and chassis, white encllosed dump section and hinged loading hopper, one-piece chrome bumper, no plastic windows in garbage section, 16-1/2" long, 1968	75	115	150
Sanitation Service Truck	blue snub-nose hood, cab and frame, white cargo dump body and rear loading unit, two round plastic headlights, 17" long, 1972	75	115	150
Sears Roebuck Delivery Truck Van	gray/green and off-white, no side doors, 1967	125	200	275
Self-Loading Auto Carrier	medium tan tractor unit, three plastic cars, overall 34" long including loading ramp, 1960	85	130	175
Self-Loading Boat Hauler	pastel blue tractor and semi-trailer with three 8-1/2" long boats, overall 26-1/2" long, 1962	150	225	350
Self-Loading Boat Hauler	pastel blue tractor and semi-trailer with three 8-1/2" long boats, no side mirror on truck, overall 26-1/2" long, 1963	150	225	350
Self-Loading Car Carrier	lime green tractor unit, three plastic cars, overall 33-1/2" long including, 1963	75	115	150

Self-Loading Car Carrier	beige/yellow tractor unit, three plastic cars, overall 33-1/2" long including, 1964	60	95	125
Shell Pickup and Delivery	reddish orange hood and body, open cargo sectionwith solid sides, chain across back, red coin-slot oil drum with Shell emblem and lettering, 13-1/4" long, 1950	135	200	275
Shell Pickup and Delivery	yellow/orange hood and body, open cargo section, three curved slots toward rear in sides, chains across back, red coin-slot oil drum with Shell emblem and lettering, 13-1/4" long, 1952	125	185	250
Shell Pickup and Delivery	yellow/orange hood and body, open cargo section with three curved slots toward rear in sides, red coin-slot oil drum with Shell emblem and lettering, 13-1/4" long, 1953	110	175	225
Smoke Patrol	lemon yellow body, six wheels, garden hose attaches and water squirts through large chrome swivel-mount water cannon on rear deck, 7" long, 1970	50	75	100
Sprinkler Truck	black front, hood, fenders and cabless open driver's seat, red bumper and chassis, bluish/gray/green water tank, 25" long, 1929	1000	1500	2000
Stake Body Truck	black cabless open driver's seat, hood, front fenders and flatbed body, red chassis and five removable stake sections, 25" long, 1921	1000	1500	2000
Stake Body Truck	black cabless open driver's seat, hood, front fenders and flatbed body, red chassis and five removable stake sections, cargo bed with low sidesboards, drop-down tailgate, 25" long, 1924	1000	1500	2000
Standard Coffee Co. Delivery Truck Van	1966	125	200	275
Standard Oil Tank Truck	duo-tone slant design, white upper cab and hood, red lower cab, grille, fenders and tank, rubber wheels, electric headlights, 26" long, 1936-37	1000	1500	2000
Stor-Dor Delivery	red hood and body, open cargo body with four horizontal slots in sides, plated chains across open back, 14-1/2" long, 1955	85	130	175
Street Sprinkler Truck	black front, hood, front fenders and cabless open driver's seat, red bumper and chassis, bluish/gray/green water tank, 25" long, 1929	750	900	1800
Street Sprinkler Truck	black front, hood, and fenders, open cab, nickel-rim, red-shell headlights, double bar front bumper, bluish/gray-/green water tank, six rubber tires, 25" long, 1930-32	1000	1500	2000
Sunshine Delivery Truck Van	bright, yellow cab-over-engine van body and opening double rear doors, off-white plastic bumper and under body, 11-1/2" long, 1967	125	200	275
Super Motor Market	duo-tone horizontal design, white hood top, upper cab and high partition in cargo section, yellow/orange lower hood and cab sides, semi-trailer carrying supplies, 21-1/2" long, 1942	300	500	700
Supermarket Delivery	all white with rubber wheels, enclosed cab, pointed nose, bright metal one-piece grille, 13-3/4" long, 1950	125	185	250
Supermarket Delivery	blue bumper, front, hood, cab and frame, one-piece chrome four-hole grille and headlights, 14-1/2" long, 1956	75	115	150
Tank and Sprinkler Truck	black front, hood, fenders, doorless cab and seat, dark green tank and side racks, black or dark green sprinkler attachment, 26-1/4" long with sprinkler attachment, 1924	1000	1500	2000

319

Teepee Camping Trailer and Wagon	maroon suburban wagon, two-wheel teepee trailer and its beige plastic folding tent, overall 24-1/2" long, 1963	150	225	300
Texaco Tank Truck	red steel GMC 550-series blunt-nose tractor and semi-trailer tank, 25" long, 1959	175	250	400
Tom's Toasted Peanuts Delivery Truck Van	light tan/beige body, no seat or sliding doors, blue bumpers, floor and underbody, 11-1/2" long, 1973	125	200	275
Trail Boss	red, square-corner body with sloping sides, open cockpit, white plastic seat, 7" long, 1970	35	55	75
Trail Boss	lime green, square-corner body with sloping sides, open cockpit, yellow plastic seat, 7" long, 1971	35	55	75
Trailer Dump Truck	cream tractor unit with enclosed cab, dark blue semi-trailer dump body with high sides and top-hinged opening endgate, no bumper, 20-3/4" long, 1941	75	115	150
Trailer Van with Tailgate Loader	green high-impacted styrene plastic tractor on steel frame, cream steel detachable semi-trailer van with green roof and crank operated tailgate, 33" long with tailgate lowered, 1953	125	185	250
Trailer Van with Tailgate Loader	green steel tractor, bumper, chrome one-piece toothed grille and headlights, cream van with green roof and tailgate loader, 31 3/4" long, with tailgate down, 1954lgate lowered, 1953	125	185	250
Trailer Van Truck	red tractor and van roof, blue bumper, white semi-trailer van, chrome one-piece toothed grille and headlights, white drop-down rear door, 29" long with tailgate/ramp lowered, 1956	150	225	300
Traveling Zoo	red high side pickup with yellow plastic triple-cage unit, six compartments with plastic animals, 13-1/4" long, 1965	85	130	175
Traveling Zoo	red high side pickup with yellow plastic triple-cage unit, six compartments with plastic animals, 13-1/4" long, 1967	75	115	150
Traveling Zoo	yellow high side pickup with red plastic triple-cage unit, six compartments with plastic animals, 13-1/4" long, 1969	75	115	150
Traveling Zoo	snub-nosed yellow body and cab, six red plastic cages with six plastic zoo animals, 13-1/4" long, 1970	60	95	125
U.S. Army Half-Track and Howitzer	olive drab, 12-1/2" truck, 9-3/4" gun, overall 22-1/2" long, 1952	125	200	275
U.S. Mail Truck	shiny olive green body and bumper, yellow-cream removable van roof, enclosed cab, 22-1/2" long, 1953	225	400	575
U.S. Mail Delivery Truck	blue cab, hood, bumper, frame and removable roof on white van body, 23-1/4" long, 1956	200	350	500
U.S. Mail Delivery Truck	white upper cab-over-engine, sliding side doors and double rear doors, red belt-line stripe on sides and front, blue lower body, 11-1/2" long, 1964	100	150	200
United Parcel Delivery Van	duo-tone horizontal design, deep cream upper half with brown removable roof, chocolate brown front and lower half, 25" long, 1941	250	450	650
Utility Delivery Truck	duo-tone slant design, blue front and lower hood sides, gray hood top, cab and open body with red and yellow horizontal stripe, 22-3/4" long, 1940	250	450	650

Utility Delivery Truck	duo-tone horizontal design, green upper half including hood top, dark cream lower half, green wheels, red and yellow horizontal stripe, 22-3/4" long, 1941	125	185	250
Utility Dump Truck	duo-tone slant design, red front, lower doord and fenders, gray chassis and enclosed upper cab, royal blue dump body, yellow removable rider seat, 25-1/2" long, 1940	125	185	250
Utility Dump Truck	duo-tone slant design, red front, lower door and fenders, gray chassis, red upper hood, upper enclosed cab and removable rider seat, yellow body, 25-1/2" long, 1941	85	130	175
Van Freight Carriers Trailer	bright blue streanlined tractor and enclosed cab, cream/yellow semi-trailer van, removable silvery roof, 22" long, 1949	75	115	150
Van Freight Carriers Trailer	red streamlined tractor, bright blue enclosed cab, cream/yellow semi-trailer van, white removable van roof, 22" long, 1952	60	95	125
Van Freight Carriers Trailer	red streamlined tractor, bright blue enclosed cab, light cream/white semi-trailer van with removable white roof, 22" long, 1953	125	185	250
Wild Animal Circus	red tractor unit and semi-trailer, three cages with plastic elephant, lion, tiger, 26" long, 1966	150	225	300
Wild Animal Circus	red tractor unit and semi-trailer, three cages with six plastic animals, 26" long, 1967	110	175	225
Wild Animal Circus	red tractor unit and semi-trailer, trailer cage doors lighter than body, 26" long, 1970	100	150	200
Wrecker Truck	black front, hood, and fenders, open cab, four rubber tires, red wrecker body, 26-1/2" long, 1930	1000	1500	2500
Wrecker Truck	duo-tone slant design, red upper cab, hood, and boom, white lower cab, grille, fenders, body, rubber wheels, electric headlights, removable rider seat, 31" long, 1936	500	1000	2000
Wrecker Truck	black open cab, red chassis and bed, disc wheels, 26-1/2" long, 1928-29	1400	2500	3800
Wrigley Express Truck	forest green with chrome one-piece, three-bar grille and headlights, "Wrigley's Spearmint Gum" poster on sides, 16-1/2" long, 1955	135	200	275
Zoo-A-Rama	lime green Colt Sportsliner with four-wheel trailer cage, cage contains plastic tree, monkeys and bears, 20-3/4" long, 1967	100	150	200
Zoo-A-Rama	sand yellow four-wheel trailer cage, matching Colt Sportsliner with white top, three plastic animals, 20-3/4" long, 1968	100	150	200
Zoo-A-Rama	greenish yellow four-wheel trailer cage, matching Colt Sportsliner with white top, three plastic animals, 20-3/4" long, 1969	85	130	175

Corgi

Name	Description	Good	Ex	Mint
Adams Drag-Star	4-3/8" long, orange body, red nose, gold engines, chrome pipes and hood panels, amber windshield, driver, black catwalk	18	27	45
Adams Probe 16	3-5/8" long, one-piece body, blue sliding canopy, in three colors; metallic burgundy, or metallic lime/gold with and without racing stripes	16	24	40
Agricultural Set	#69 Massey Ferguson tractor, #62 trailer, #438 Land Rover, #484 Farm Truck, #71 harrow, #1490 skip, and accessories	120	180	350
Agricultural Set	vehicle and accessory set in two versions, with #55 tractor and yellow trailer, 1962-64; with #60 tractor and red trailer, 1965-66	280	420	750
Agricultural Set	with mustard yellow conveyor	60	90	150
Alfa Romeo P33 Pininfarina	3-5/8" long, in two versions, with either gold or black spoiler	16	24	40
All Winners Set	five vehicle set in three versions: white Mustang and Marcos, red Ferrari, silver Corvette and gold Jaguar, 1966 only; prior vehicles in other colors; or Toronado, Ferrari, MGB, Corvette and Jaguar	160	240	450
Allis-Chalmers AFC 60 Fork Lift	4-3/8" long, yellow body with white engine hood, with driver	14	21	35
AMC Pacer	4-3/4" metallic dark red body, white Pacer X decals, working hatch, clear windows, light yellow interior, chrome bumpers, grille & headlights, black plastic grille & tow hook, suspension, chrome wheels	14	21	35
AMC Pacer Rescue Car	4-7/8" long, with chrome roll bars and red roof lights, in white with black engine hood, in two versions: with or without Secours decal	16	24	40
American La France Ladder Truck	11-1/8" long, red working cab, trailer and ladder rack, in either red/chrome body with red wheels or red/white body with unpainted wheels	60	90	150
AMX 30D Recovery Tank	6-7/8" long, olive drab body with black plastic turret and gun, with accessories and three figures	32	48	80
Army Equipment Transporter	9-1/2" long, olive drab cab and trailer with white U.S. Army decals	70	105	175
Army Troop Transporter	5-1/2" long, olive drab, with white U.S. Army decals	70	105	175
Aston Martin DB4	3-3/4" long, red or yellow body with working hood, detailed engine, clear windows, plastic interior, silver lights, grille, license plate & bumpers, red taillights, rubber tires, working scoop on early models	44	66	110
Aston Martin DB4	3-3/4" white top & aqua green sides, yellow plastic interior, racing #1, 3 or 7	50	75	125

Austin A40	3-1/8" long, one-piece light blue or red body with clear windows, silver lights, grille and bumpers, smooth wheels, rubber tires	34	51	85
Austin A40-Mechanical	3-1/8" long, same as 216-A but with friction motor and red body, black roof	52	78	130
Austin A60 Driving School	3-3/4" medium blue body with silver trim, left hand drive steering wheel, one-piece body, clear windows, shaped wheels, rubber tires	44	66	110
Austin A60 Motor School	3-3/4" long, light blue body with silver trim, red interior, single body casting, right hand drive steering wheel, two figures, silver bumpers, grille, headlights & trim, red taillights, L plate decals, suspension, shaped wheels rubber tires	44	66	110
Austin Cambridge	3-1/2" long, one-piece body in several colors, clear windows, silver lights, grille and bumpers, smooth wheels, rubber tires; colors include gray, green/gray, silver/green, aqua	40	60	100
Austin Cambridge-Mechanical	3-1/2" long, same as model 201-A but with fly wheel motor, available in orange, cream, light or dark gray body colors	50	75	125
Austin London Taxi	3-7/8" long, one-piece body, clear windows, black body with yellow plastic interior, with or without driver, smooth or rubber wheels	36	54	90
Austin London Taxi	4-5/8" long, black body with two working doors, light brown interior	14	21	35
Austin London Taxi/Reissue	3-7/8" long, updated version with Whizz Wheels, black or maroon body	14	21	35
Austin Mini Countryman	3-1/8" long, turquoise body with two working doors, in three versions, one with shaped wheels, the others with cast wheels and with or without aluminum parts	52	78	150
Austin Mini Van	3-1/8" long, with two working doors, clear windows, metallic deep green body	40	60	100
Austin Mini-Metro	3-1/2", three versions with plastic interior, working rear hatch and doors, clear windows, folding seats, chrome headlights, or ange taillights, black plastic base, grille, bumpers, Whizz Wheels	18	27	45
Austin Mini-Metro Datapost	3-1/2", white body, blue roof, hood & trim, red plastic interior, hepolite & #77 decals, working hatch & doors, clear windows, folding seats, chrome headlights, orange taillights, Whizz Wheels	12	18	30
Austin Police Mini Van	3-1/8" long, dark blue body with policeman and dog figures, white police decals	70	105	175
Austin Seven Mini	2-3/4" red or yellow body, yellow interior, silver bumpers, grille & headlights, orange taillights, suspension, shaped wheels, rubber tires	50	75	125
Austin-Healey	3-1/4" cream body, red seats or red body cream seats, clear windshield, one-piece body, sheet metal base, silver grille, bumpers, headlights, smooth wheels, rubber tires	50	75	125
Avengers Set	two vehicles and two figures with umbrellas; green or red Bentley	275	425	800
Basil Brush's Car	3-5/8" long, red body, dark yellow chassis, gold lamps and dash, Basil Brush figure, red plastic wheels, plastic tires	70	105	175

Batbike	4-1/4" black body, one-piece body, black & red plastic parts, gold engine & exhaust pipes, clear windshield, chrome stand, black plastic five spoked wheels, Batman and decals	40	60	125
Batboat	5-1/8" long, black plastic boat, red seats, fin and jet, blue windshield, Batman and Robin figures, gold cast trailer, large black/yellow decals on fin, cast wheels, plastic tires	60	90	175
Batboat	5-1/8" long, black plastic boat with Batman and Robin figures, small decals on fin, Whizz Wheels on trailer	30	45	100
Batcopter	5-1/2" long, black body with yellow/red/black decals, red rotors, Batman figure	26	39	95
Batman Set	three-vehicle set: Batmobile, Batboat with trailer and Batcopter, Whizz Wheels on trailer	110	175	300
Batmobile	5" long, gold hubs, bat logos on door, maroon interior, black body, plastic rockets, gold headlights & rocket control, tinted canopy, working front chain cutter, no tow hook	200	300	500
Batmobile	5" long, chrome hubs with red bat logos on door, maroon interior, red plastic tires, gold tow hook, plastic rockets, gold headlight & rocket control, tinted canopy with chrome support, chain cutter	140	210	350
Batmobile	5" long, chrome hubs with red bat logos on door, light red interior, regular wheels, gold tow hook, plastic rockets, gold headlights and rocket control, tinted canopy with chrome support	80	120	200
Batmobile	5" long, gold hubs, bat logos on door, maroon interior, black body, plastic rockets, gold headlights & rocket control, tinted canopy, working front chain cutter, with two hooks	180	270	450
Batmobile, Batboat & Trailer	four versions: red bat hubs on wheels, 1967-72; red tires and chrome wheels, 1973; black tires, big decals on boat, 1974-76; chrome wheels, sm. boat decals, Whizz Wheels on trailer, 1977-81 each set	240	360	650
Beach Buggy & Sailboat	purple buggy, yellow trailer and red/white boat	20	30	50
Beast Carrier Trailer	4-1/2" long, red chassis, yellow body and tailgate, four plastic calves, red plastic wheels, black rubber tires	24	36	60
Beatles' Yellow Submarine	5" long, yellow and white body, working hatches with two Beatles in each	180	270	450
Bedford AA Road Service Van	3-5/8" long, dark yellow body in two versions, divided windshield, 1957-59, single windshield, 1960-62	50	75	125
Bedford Army Tanker	7-3/8" long, olive drab cab and tanker, with white U.S. Army decals	140	210	350
Bedford Articulated Horse Box	10" long, cast cab, lower body and three working ramps, yellow interior, plastic upper body, with horse and Newmarket Racing Stables decals, dark metallic green or light green or light green body with either orange or yellow upper	32	48	80
Bedford Car Transporter	10-1/4" black die cast cab base with blue cab, yellow semi trailer, blue lettering decals and/or red cab, pale green upper & blue lower semi-trailer, white decals, lower tailgate, clear windshield, silver bumper, grille, headlights & wheels	70	105	175

Bedford Car Transporter	10-5/8" long, red cab with blue lower and light green upper trailer, working ramp, yellow interior, clear windows, white wording and Corgi dog decals	60	90	150
Bedford Carrimore Low Loader	8-1/2" red or yellow cab, metallic blue semi trailer & tailgate, available with smooth and/or shaped wheels	60	90	150
Bedford Carrimore Low Loader	9-1/2" long, yellow cab and working tailgate, red trailer, clear windows, red interior, suspension, shaped wheels, rubber tires	56	84	140
Bedford Corgi Toys Van	3-1/4" long, both with Corgi Toys decals, with either yellow body/blue roof or yellow upper/blue lower body	70	105	175
Bedford Daily Express Van	3-1/4" long, dark blue body with white Daily Express decals, divided windshield, smooth wheels, rubber tires	60	90	150
Bedford Dormobile	3-1/4" long, in two versions and several colors: divided windshield with either cream, green or metallic maroon body; or single windshield with yellow body/blue roof in either shaped or smooth wheels	50	75	125
Bedford Dormobile-Mechanical	3-1/4" long, with friction motor, dark metallic red or turquoise body	60	90	150
Bedford Evening Standard Van	3-1/4" long, clear windows, smooth wheels, rubber tires, in two colors: black body/silver roof or black lower body/silver upper body and roof, both with same Evening Standard decals	52	78	130
Bedford Fire Tender	3-1/4" long, divided windshield, red or green body, each with different decals	60	90	150
Bedford Fire Tender	3-1/4" long, single windshield version, red body with either black ladders and smooth wheels or unpainted ladders and shaped wheels	60	90	150
Bedford Fire Tender-Mechanical	3-1/4" long, with friction motor, red body with Fire Dept. decals	70	105	175
Bedford Giraffe Transporter	red Bedford truck with blue giraffe box with Chipperfield decal, three giraffes	70	105	175
Bedford KLG Van-Mechanical	3-1/4" long, with friction motor, in either red body with K.L.G. Spark Plugs decals, or dark blue body with Daily Express decals	70	105	175
Bedford Machinery Carrier	9-1/4" long, red or blue cab, both with silver trailer with working ramps, removable fenders, working winch with line, smooth wheels, rubber tires	80	120	200
Bedford Military Ambulance	3-1/4" long, with clear front and white rear windows, olive drab body with Red Cross decals, with or without suspension	56	84	140
Bedford Milk Tanker	7-3/4" long, light blue cab and lower semi, white upper tank with blue/white Milk decals	110	165	275
Bedford Milk Tanker	7-1/2" long, light blue cab and lower semi, white upper tank, with blue/white Milk decals, shaped wheels, rubber tires	100	150	250
Bedford Mobilgas Tanker	7-3/4" long, red cab and tanker with red/white/blue Mobilgas decals, shaped wheels, rubber tires	100	150	250
Bedford Mobilgas Tanker	7-5/8" long, either red or blue cab with Mobilgas decals, shaped wheels, rubber tires	100	150	250
Bedford Tanker	7-1/2" long, red cab with black chassis, plastic tank with chrome catwalk, Corgi Chemco decals	14	21	35

Name	Description			
Bedford TK Tipper Truck	4-1/8" long, four color variations	26	39	65
Bedford Utilecon Ambulance	3-1/4" long, divided windshield, cream body with red/white/blue decals, smooth wheels	50	75	125
Beep Beep London Bus	4-3/4" long, battery operated working horn, red body, black windows, BTA decals	26	39	65
Belgian Police Range Rover	4" long, white body, working doors, red interior, with Belgian Police decals	22	33	55
Bell Army Helicopter	5-1/4" long, two-piece olive/tan camo body, clear canopy, olive green rotors, U.S. Army decals	24	36	60
Bell Rescue Helicopter	5-3/4" long, two-piece blue body with working doors, red interior, yellow plastic floats, black rotors, white N428 decals	20	30	50
Bentley Continental	4-1/4" four different versions, red interior, clear windows, chrome grille & bumpers, jewel headlights, red jeweled taillights luggage & spare wheel in trunk, suspension, shaped wheels, gray rubber tires	44	66	110
Bentley T Series	4-1/2" red rose body, cream interior, working hood, trunk & doors, clear windows, folding seats, chrome bumper/grille, jewel headlights, orange taillights, detailed engine, suspension	36	54	90
Berliet Articulated Horse Box	10-7/8" long, bronze cab and lower semi body, cream chassis, white upper body, black interior, three working ramps, National Racing Stables decals, horse figures	30	45	75
Berliet Fruehauf Dumper	11-1/4" yellow cab, fenders & dumper, black cab & semi chassis, plastic orange dumper body or dark orange, black interior, stack, dump knob & semi hitch, two black plastic trailer rest wheels, chrome headlights with amber lenses, black grille	30	45	75
Berliet Holmes Wrecker	5" red cab & bed, blue rear body, white chassis, black interior, two gold booms & hooks, yellow dome light, driver, amber lenses & red/white/blue stripes	30	45	75
Bertone Barchetta Runabout	3-1/4" long, black interior, amber windows, die cast air foil, suspension, red/yellow Runabout decals, Whizz Wheels	12	18	30
Bertone Shake Buggy	3-3/8" long, clear windows, green interior, gold engine, in four versions: yellow upper/white lower body with either spoked or solid chromed wheels; or metallic mauve upper/white lower body with either	12	18	30
BMC Mini-Cooper	3" white body, black working hood, trunk, two doors, red interior, clear windows, folding seats, chrome bumpers, grille, jewel headlights, red taillights, orange/black stripes & #177 decals, suspension, detailed enginer, Whizz Wheels	34	51	85
BMC Mini-Cooper Magnifique	2-7/8" long, metallic blue or olive green body versions with working doors, hood and trunk, clear windows and sunroof, cream interior with folding seats, jewel headlights, cast wheels, plastic tires	34	51	85
BMC Mini-Cooper S	3" bright yellow body, red plastic interior, chrome plastic roof rack with two spare wheels, clear windshield, one-piece body silver grille, bumpers, headlights, red taillights, suspenison, Whizz Wheel	44	66	110

Name	Description			
BMC Mini-Cooper S Rally	2-7/8" long, red body, white roof, chrome roof rack with two spare tires, Monte Carlo Rally and #177 decals, in two versions: shaped wheels/rubber tires, or cast wheels/plastic tires	40	60	100
BMC Mini-Cooper S Rally Car	2-7/8" long, red body, white roof, five jewel headlights, Monte Carlo Rally decals with either number 52 (1965) or two (1966) with drivers' autographs on roof	60	90	150
BMC Mini-Cooper S Rally Car	2-7/8" long, red body, white roof with six jewel headlights, RAC Rally and #21 decals	60	90	150
BMW M1	5" yellow body, black plastic base, rear panel & interior, white seats, clear windshield, multicolored stripes, lettering & #25 decal, black grille & headlights, red taillights, four spoked wheels	14	21	35
BMW M1 BASF	4-7/8" long, red body, white trim with black/white BASF and #80 decals	12	18	30
Breakdown Truck	3-7/8" long, red body, black plastic boom with gold hook, yellow interior, amber windows, black/yellow decals, Whizz Wheels	12	18	30
British Leyland Mini 1000	3-3/8" long, metallic blue body, working doors, black base, clear windows, white interior, silver lights, grille and bumper, Union Jack decal on roof, Whiz Wheels	18	27	45
British Leyland Mini 1000	3-1/4" long, red interior, chrome lights, grille and bumper, #8 decal, in three colors: silver body with decals, 1978-82; silver body, no decals; orange body with extra hood stripes, 1983 on	16	24	40
British Racing Cars	set of three cars, three versions: blue Lotus, green BRM, green Vanwall, all with smooth wheels, 1959; same cars with shaped wheels, 1960-61; red Vanwall, green BRM and blue Lotus, 1963, each set	150	225	375
BRM Racing Car	3-1/2" long, silver seat, dash and pipes, smooth wheels, rubber tires, in three versions: dark green body, 1958-60; light green body with driver and various number decals 1961-65; light green body, no driver	50	75	125
Buck Rogers Starfighter	6-1/2" long, white body with yellow plastic wings, amber windows, blue jets, color decal, Buck and Wilma figures	36	54	90
Buick & Cabin Cruiser	three versions: light blue, dark metallic blue or gold metallic Buick	80	120	200
Buick Police Car	4-1/8" long, metallic blue body with white stripes and Police decals, chrome light bar with red lights, orange taillights, chrome spoke wheels	18	27	45
Buick Riviera	4-1/4" long, metallic gold or dark blue, pale blue or bronze body, red interior, gray steering wheel, & tow hook, clear windshield, chrome grille & bumpers, suspension, Tan-o-lite tail & headlights, spoked wheels & rubber tires	30	45	75
Cadillac Superior Ambulance	4-1/2" long, battery operated, in two versions; red lower/cream upper body, or white lower/blue upper body	60	90	150
Cafe Racer Motorcycle		12	18	30
Campbell Bluebird	5-1/8" long, blue body, red exhaust, clear windshield, driver, in two versions: with black plastic wheels, 1960;with metal wheels and rubber tires	70	105	175

Canadian Mounted Police Set	blue Land Rover with Police sign on roof and RCMP decals, plus mounted Policeman	30	45	75
Captain America Jetmobile	6" white body, metallic blue chassis, black nose cone, red shield & jet, red-white-blue Captain America decals, light blue seats & driver, chrome wheels, red tires	24	36	60
Captain Marvel Porsche	4-3/4" white body, gold parts, red seat, driver, red-yellow-blue Captain Marvel decals, black plastic base, gold wheels	20	30	50
Car Transporter & Cars	Scammell transporter with five cars; Ford Capri, the Saint's Volvo, Pontiac Firebird, Lancia Fulvia, MGC GT, Marcos 3 Litre, set	200	300	600
Car Transporter & Four Cars	two versions: with Fiat 1800, Renault Floride, Mercedes 230SE and Ford Consul, 1963-65; with Chevy Corvair, VW Ghia, Volvo P-1800 and Rover 2000, 1966 only, each set	200	300	600
Carrimore & Six Cars	sold by mail order only	240	360	700
Carrimore Car Transporter	three versions: transporter with Riley, Jaguar, Austin Healey and Triumph, 1957-60; with four American cars, 1959; with Triumph, Mini, Citroen and Plymouth, 1961-62, each set	300	450	800
Caterpillar Tractor	4-1/4", Tc-12 lime green body with black or white rubber treads, gray plastic seat, driver figure, controls, stacks	70	105	175
Centurion Mark III Tank		30	45	75
Centurion Tank & Transporter	olive colored tank and transport	52	78	130
Chevrolet Astro I	4-1/8" long, dark metallic green/blue body with working rear door, cream interior with two passengers, in two versions: with either gold wheels with red plastic hubs or Whizz wheels	18	27	45
Chevrolet Camaro SS	4" long, blue or turquoise body with white stripe, cream interior, working doors, white plastic top, clear windshield, folding seats, silver air intakes, red taillights, black grille & headllights, suspension, Whizz Wheels	30	45	95
Chevrolet Camaro SS	4" long, metallic lime-gold body with two working doors, black roof and stripes, red interior, cast wheels, plastic tires	30	45	75
Chevrolet Caprice Classic	5-7/8" long, working doors and trunk, whitewall tires, in two versions: light metallic green body with green interior or silver on blue body with brown interior	24	36	60
Chevrolet Caprice Classic	6" long, white upper body, red sides with red/white/blue stripes and #43 decals, tan interior	24	36	60
Chevrolet Caprice Fire Chief Car	5-3/4" red body, red-white-orange decals, chrome roof bar, opaque black windows, red dome light, chrome bumpers, grille & headlights, orange taillights, Fire Dept. & Fire Chief decals, chrome wheels	28	42	70
Chevrolet Caprice Police Car	5-7/8" long, black body with white roof, doors and trunk, red interior, silver light bar, Police decals	20	30	50
Chevrolet Caprice Taxi	5-7/8" long, orange body with red interior, white roof sign, Taxi and TWA decals	20	30	50

Chevrolet Charlie's Angels Van	4-5/8" long, light rose-mauve body with Charlie's Angels decals, in two versions: either solid or spoked chrome wheels	10	15	40
Chevrolet Coca-Cola Van	4-5/8" long, red body, white trim, with Coca Cola logos	14	21	35
Chevrolet Corvair	3-3/4" three body versions with yellow interior & working hood, detailed engine, clear windows, silver bumpers, headlights & trim, red taillights, rear window blind, shaped wheels, rubber tires	36	54	90
Chevrolet Impala	4-1/4" long, pink body, yellow plastic interior, clear windows, silver headlights, bumpers, grille and trim, suspension, die cast base with rubber tires	50	75	125
Chevrolet Impala	4-1/4" tan body, cream interior, gray steering wheel, clear windshields, chrome bumpers, grille, headlights, suspension, red taillights shaped wheels & rubber tires	50	75	125
Chevrolet Impala Fire Chief	4-1/8" long, red body, yellow interior, in three versions: with four white doors, with round shield decals on two doors, or with white decals on doors	52	78	130
Chevrolet Impala Fire Chief	4" long, with Fire Chief decal on hood, yellow interior with driver, in two versions: either all red body or red on white body	52	78	130
Chevrolet Impala Police Car	4" long, black lower body and roof, white upper body, yellow interior with driver, Police and Police Patrol decals on doors and hood	52	78	130
Chevrolet Impala Taxi	4-1/4" light orange body, base with hexagonal panel under rear axle & smooth wheels, or two raised lines & shaped wheels, one-piece body, clear windows, plastic interior, silver grille, headlights & bumpers, rubber tires	50	75	125
Chevrolet Impala Yellow Cab	4" long, red lower body, yellow upper, red interior with driver, white roof sign, red decals	80	120	200
Chevrolet Kennel Club Van	4" long, white upper, red lower body, working tailgate and rear windows, green interior, dog figures, kennel club decals, cast wheels, rubber tires	56	84	140
Chevrolet Performing Poodles Van	4" blue upper body & tailgate, red lower body & base, clear windshield, pale blue interior with poodles in back & ring of poodles & trainer, plastic tires	160	240	450
Chevrolet Rough Rider Van	4-5/8" long, yellow body with working rear doors, cream interior, amber windows, Rough Rider decals	12	18	30
Chevrolet Spider-Van	4-5/8" long, dark blue body with Spider-Man decals, in two versions: with either spoke or solid wheels	26	39	65
Chevrolet State Patrol Car	4" black body, State Patrol decals, smooth wheels with hexagonal panel or raised lines & shaped wheels, yellow plastic interior, gray antenna, clear windows, silver bumpers, grille, headlights & trim, rubber tires	50	75	125
Chevrolet Superior Ambulance	4-3/4" long, white body, orange roof and stripes, two working doors, clear windows, red interior with patient on stretcher and attendant, Red Cross decals	30	45	75
Chevrolet Vanatic Van	4-5/8" long, off white body with Vanatic decals	10	15	25
Chevrolet Vantastic Van	4-5/8" long, black body with Vantastic decals	10	15	25
Chieftain Medium Tank		30	45	75

Chitty Chitty Bang Bang	6-1/4" metallic copper body, dark red interior & spoked wheels, figures, black chassis with silver running boards, silver hood, horn, brake, dash, tail & headlights, gold radiator, red & orange wings, handbrake operates	160	250	425
Chopper Squad Helicopter		20	30	50
Chopper Squad Rescue Set	blue Jeep with Chopper Squad decal and red/white boat with Surf Rescue decal	40	60	100
Chrysler Imperial Convertible	4-1/4" red or blue-green body with gray base, working hood, trunk & doors, golf bag in trunk, detailed engine, clear windshield, aqua interior, driver, chrome bumpers	44	66	110
Chubb Pathfinder Crash Tender		44	66	110
Chubb Pathfinder Crash Truck	9-1/2" red body with either "Airport Fire Brigade" or "New York Airport" decals, upper & lower body, gold water cannon unpainted & sirens, clear windshield, yellow interior, black steering wheel, chrome plastic deck, silver lights, plastic	60	90	150
Circus Cage Wagon		56	84	140
Circus Crane & Cage	red and blue trailer	400	600	1000
Circus Crane & Cage Wagon	crane truck, cage wagon and accessories	150	225	375
Circus Crane Truck		80	120	200
Circus Horse Transporter		80	120	200
Circus Human Cannonball Truck		30	45	75
Circus Land Rover & Elephant Cage	red Range Rover with blue canopy, Chipperfields Circus decal on canopy, burnt orange elephant cage on red bed trailer	90	135	250
Circus Land Rover & Trailer	yellow/red Land Rover with Pinder-Jean Richard decals	30	45	75
Circus Menagerie Transporter		120	180	350
Circus Set	vehicle and accessory set in two versions: with #426 Booking Office, 1963-65; with #503 Giraffe Truck, 1966, each set	340	510	1000
Citroen 2CV Charleston	4-1/8" long, yellow/black or maroon/black body versions	12	18	30
Citroen Alpine Rescue Safari	4" white body, light blue interior, red roof & rear hatch, yellow roof rack & skis, clear windshield, man & dog, gold die cast bobsled, Alpine Rescue decals	90	130	225
Citroen DS19 Rally	4" long, light blue body, white roof, yellow interior, four jewel headlights, Monte Carlo Rally and #75 decals	70	105	175
Citroen DS19	4" long, one-piece body in several colors, clear windows, silver lights, grille and bumpers, smooth wheels, rubber tires: colors: cream, yellow/black, red, metallic green, yellow	56	84	140

Citroen Dyane	4-1/2" metallic yellow or green body, black roof & interior, working rear hatch, clear windows, black base & tow bar, silver bumpers, grille & headlights, red taillights, marching duck & French flag decals, suspension, chrome wheels	12	18	30
Citroen ID-19 Safari	4" long, orange body with red/brown or red/green luggage on roof rack, green/brown interior, working hatch, two passengers, Wildlife Preservation decals	40	60	100
Citroen Le Dandy Coupe	4" metallic maroon body & base, yellow interior, working trunk & two doors, clear windows, plastic interior, folding seats, chrome grille & bumpers, jewel headlights, red taillights, suspension, spoked wheels, rubber tires	50	75	125
Citroen Le Dandy Coupe	4" metallic dark blue hood, sides & base, plastic aqua interior, white roof & trunk lid, clear windows, folding seats, chrome grille & bumpers, jewel headlights, red taillights, suspension, spoked wheels, rubber tires	70	105	175
Citroen SM	4-3/16" metallic lime gold with chrome wheels or mauve body with spoked wheels, pale blue interior & lifting hatch cover, working rear hatch & two doors, chrome inner drs., window frames, bumpers, grille, amber headlights, red taillights, black	16	24	40
Citroen Tour de France Car	4-1/4" red body, yellow interior & rear bed, clear windshield & headlights, driver, black plastic rack with four bicycle wheels, swiveling team manager figure with megaphone in back of car, Paramount & Tour de France decals, Whizz Wheels	40	60	100
Citroen Winter Olympics Car	4-1/8" long, white body, blue roof and hatch, blue interior, red roof rack with yellow skis, gold sled with rider, skier, gold Grenoble Olympiade decals on car roof	80	120	200
Citroen Winter Sports Safari	4" long, white body in three versions: two with Corgi Ski Club decals and either with or without roof ski rack, or one with 1964 Winter Olympics decals	56	84	140
Coast Guard Jaguar XJ12C	3-1/4" long, olive drab body either with or without suspension, Red Cross decals, clear front windows, white rear windows	18	27	45
Combine, Tractor & Trailer	set of three: #1111 combine, #50 Massey Ferguson tractor, and #51 trailer	110	165	275
Commer 3/4 Ton Ambulance	3-1/2" long, in either white or cream body, red interior, blue dome light, red Ambulance decals	36	54	90
Commer 3/4 Ton Milk Float	3-1/2" long, white cab with either light or dark blue body, one version with CO-OP decals	32	48	80
Commer 3/4 Ton Pickup	3-1/2" long, either red cab with orange canopy or yellow cab with red canopy, yellow interior in both	30	45	75
Commer 3/4 Ton Police Bus	3-1/2" long, battery operated working dome light, in several color combinations of dark or light metallic blue or green bodies	44	66	110
Commer 3/4 Ton Van	3-1/2" long, either dark blue body with Hammonds decals (1971) or white body with CO-OP decals (1970)	44	66	110
Commer 5 Ton Dropside Truck	4-5/8" long, either blue or red cab, both with cream rear body, sheet metal tow hook, smooth wheels, rubber tires	40	60	100
Commer 5 Ton Platform Truck	4-5/8" long, either yellow or metallic blue cab with silver body	40	60	100

mer Holiday Mini	3-1/2" white interior, clear windshield, silver bumpers, grille & headlights, Holiday Camp Special decal, roof rack, two working rear doors	30	45	75
Commer Military Ambulance	3-5/8" long, olive drab body, blue rear windows and dome light, driver, Red Cross decals	50	75	125
Commer Military Police Van	3-5/8" long, olive drab body, barred rear windows, white MP decals, driver	52	78	130
Commer Mobile Camera Van	3-1/2" long, metallic blue lower body and roof rack, white upper body, two working rear doors, black camera on gold tripod, cameraman	70	105	175
Commer Refrigerator Van	4-5/8" long, either light or dark blue cab, both with cream bodies and red/white/blue Wall's Ice Cream decals	90	130	225
Commuter Dragster	4-7/8" long, maroon body with Ford Commuter, Union Jack and #2 decals, cast silver engine, chrome plastic suspension and pipes, clear windshield, driver, spoke wheels	30	45	75
Construction Set	orange tractor and Mazda	32	48	80
Constructor Set	one each red and white cab bodies, with four different interchangeable rear units; van, pickup, milk truck, and ambulance	48	72	120
Cooper-Maserati Racing Car	3-3/8" long, blue body with red/white/blue Maserati and #7 decals, unpainted engine and suspension, chrome plastic steering wheel, roll bar, mirrors and pipes, driver, cast eight-spoke wheels, plastic tires	26	39	65
Cooper-Maserati Racing Car	3-3/8" long, yellow/white body with yellow/black stripe and #3 decals, driver tilts to steer car	18	27	45
Corgi Flying Club Set	blue/orange Land Rover with red dome light, blue trailer with either orange/yellow or orange/white plastic airplane	24	36	60
Corporal Missile & Erector	1959-62	240	360	600
Corporal Missile Launcher	1960-61	36	54	90
Corporal Missile on Launcher	1959-62	80	120	200
Corporal Missile Set	missile and ramp, erector vehicle and army truck	340	510	850
Corvette Sting Ray	4" metallic green or red body, yellow interior, black working hood, working headlights, clear windshield, amber roof panel, gold dash, chrome grille & bumpers, decals, gray die cast base, Golden jacks, cast wheels, plastic tires	40	60	100
Corvette Sting Ray	3-3/4" metallic silver/red body, two working headlights, clear windshield, yellow interior, silver hood panels, four jewel headlights, suspension, chrome bumpers, with spoked or shaped wheels, rubber tires	60	90	175
Corvette Sting Ray	3-3/4" long, yellow body, red interior, suspension, #13 decals	55	85	140
Corvette Sting Ray	3-5/8" long, metallic gray body with black hood, Whizz Wheels	50	75	125

Corvette Sting Ray	3-7/8" long, either dark metallic blue or metallic mauve-rose body, chrome dash, Whizz Wheels	50	75	125
Country Farm Set	#50 Massey Ferguson tractor, red hay trailer with load, fences, figures	30	45	75
Country Farm Set	same as 4-B but without hay load on trailer	30	45	75
Daimler 38 1910	1964-69	20	30	50
Daktari Set	two versions: cast wheels, 1968-73; Whizz Wheels, 1974-75, each set	60	90	150
Datsun 240Z	3-5/8" long, red body with #11 and other decals, two working doors, white interior, orange roll bar and tire rack; one version also has East Africa Rally decals	14	21	35
Datsun 240Z	3-5/8" long, white body with red hood and roof, #46 and other decals	14	21	35
David Brown Tractor	4-1/8" long, white body with black/white David Brown #1412 decals, red chassis and plastic engine	12	18	30
David Brown Tractor & Trailer	two-piece set; #55 tractor and #56 trailer	30	45	75
De Tomaso Mangusta	3-7/8" long, metallic dark green body with gold stripes and logo on hood, silver lower body, clear front windows, cream interior, amber rear windows and headlights, gray antenna, spare wheel, Whizz Wheels	26	39	65
De Tomaso Mangusta	5" white upper/light blue lower body/base, black interior, clear windows, silver engine, black grille, amber headlights, red taillights, gray antenna, spare wheel, gold stripes & black logo decal on hood, suspension, removable gray chassis	32	48	80
Decca Airfield Radar Van		120	180	350
Dick Dastardly's Racing Car	5" long, dark blue body, yellow chassis, chrome engine, red wings, Dick and Muttley figures	60	90	150
Dodge Kew Fargo Tipper	5-1/4" long, white cab and working hood, blue tipper, red interior, clear windows, black hydraulic cylinders, cast wheels, plastic tires	34	51	85
Dodge Livestock Truck	5-3/8" long, tan cab and hood, green body, working tailgate and ramps, five pigs	34	51	85
Dougal's Magic Roundabout Car	4-1/2" long, yellow body, red interior, clear windows, dog and snail, red wheels with gold trim, Magic Roundabout decals	70	105	175
Dropside Trailer	4-3/8" long, cream body, red chassis in five versions: smooth wheels 1957-61; shaped wheels, 1962-1965; white body, cream or blue chassis; or silver gray body, blue chassis, each	10	15	25
Ecurie Ecosse Racing Set	transporter with three cars in two versions: RRM, Vanwall and Lotus XI, 1961-64; BRM, Vanwall and Ferrari, 1964-66, each set	170	230	450
Ecurie Ecosse Transporter	7-3/4" long, in dark blue body with either blue or yellow lettering, or light blue body with red or yellow lettering, working tailgate and sliding door, yellow interior, shaped wheels, rubber tires	70	105	200
Emergency Set	three-vehicle set with figures and accessories, Ford Cortina Police car, Police Helicopter, Range Rover Ambulance	40	60	100

Name	Description			
gency Set	Land Rover Police Car and Police Helicopter with figures and accessories	40	60	100
44G Dropside Truck		36	54	90
ERF 44G Moorhouse Van	4-5/8" long, yellow cab, red body, Moorhouse Lemon Cheese decals	100	150	250
ERF 44G Platform Truck	4-5/8" long, light blue cab with either dark blue or white flatbed body	36	54	90
ERF Dropside Truck & Trailer	#456 truck and #101 trailer with #1488 cement sack load and #1485 plank load	60	90	150
ERF Neville Cement Tipper	3-3/4" long, yellow cab, gray tipper, cement decal, with either smooth or shaped wheels	32	48	80
ERG 64G Earth Dumper	4" long, red cab, yellow tipper, clear windows, unpainted hydraulic cylinder, spare tire, smooth wheels, rubber tires	30	45	75
Euclid Caterpillar Tractor	4-1/4" long, TC-12 lime green body with black or white rubber treads, gray plastic seat, driver figure, controls, stacks, silver grille, painted blue engine sides & Euclid decals	90	135	250
Euclid TC-12 Bulldozer	5" long, yellow body with black treads or lime green body with white treads, silver blade surface, gray plastic seat controls & stacks, silver grille & lights, painted blue engine sides, sheet metal base, rubber treads & Euclid decals	90	130	225
Euclid TC-12 Bulldozer	6-1/8" long, red or green body, metal control rod, driver, black rubber treads	90	130	225
Ferrari 206 Dino	4-1/8" long, black interior and fins, in either red body with #30 and gold or Whizz Wheels, or yellow body with #23 and gold or Whizz Wheels	24	36	60
Ferrari 308GTS	4-5/8" long, red or black body with working rear hood, black interior with tan seats, movable chrome headlights, detailed engine	14	21	35
Ferrari 308GTS Magnum	4-5/8" long, red body with solid chrome wheels	24	36	60
Ferrari 312 B2 Racing Car	4" long, red body, white fin, gold engine, chrome suspension, mirrors and wheels, Ferrari and #5 decals	16	24	40
Ferrari Berlinetta 250LM	3-3/4" red body with yellow stripe, blue windshields, chrome interior, grille & exhaust pipes, detailed engine, #4 Ferrari logo & yellow stripe decals, spoked wheels & spare, rubber tires	30	45	75
Ferrari Daytona	5" apple green body, black tow hook, red-yellow-silver black Daytona #5 & other racing decals, amber windows, headlights, black plastic interior, base, four spoke chrome wheels	14	21	35
Ferrari Daytona	4-3/4" long, white body with red roof and trunk, black interior, two working doors, amber windows and headlights, #81 and other decals	14	21	35
Ferrari Daytona & Racing Car	blue/yellow Ferrari and Surtees on yellow trailer	12	18	30
Ferrari Daytona JCB	4-3/4" long, orange body with #33, Corgi and other decals, chrome spoked wheels	20	30	50

Ferrari Racing Car	3-5/8" long, red body, chrome plastic engine, roll bar and dash, driver, silver cast base and exhaust, Ferrari and #36 decals	24	36	60
Fiat 1800	3-3/4" long, one-piece body in several colors, clear windows, plastic interior, silver lights, grille and bumpers, red taillights, smooth wheels, rubber tires, colors: blue body with light or bright yellow interior, mustard or cream body	24	36	60
Fiat 2100	3-3/4" long, light mauve body, yellow interior, purple roof, clear windows with rear blind, silver grille, license plates & bumpers, red taillights, shaped wheels, rubber tires	22	33	55
Fiat X 1/9 & Powerboat	green/white Fiat, with white/gold boat	30	45	75
Fiat X1/9	4-3/4" metallic blue body & base, white Fiat #3, multicolored lettering & stripe decals, black roof, trim, interior, rear panel, grille, bumpers & tow hook, chrome wheels & detailed engine	14	21	35
Fiat X1/9	4-1/2" metallic light green or silver body with black roof, trim & interior, two working doors, rear panel, grille, tow hook & bumpers, detailed engine, suspension, chrome wheels	14	21	35
Fire Bug	1972-73	20	30	50
Fire Engine	1975-78	16	24	40
Flying Club Set	green/white Jeep with Corgi Flying Club decals, green trailer, blue/white airplane	36	54	90
Ford 5000 Super Major Tractor	3-3/4" long, blue body/chassis with Ford Super Major 5000 decals, gray cast fenders and rear wheels, gray plastic front wheels, black plastic tires, driver	30	45	75
Ford 5000 Tractor with Scoop	3-1/8" long, blue body/chassis, gray fenders, yellow scoop arm and controls, chrome scoop, black control lines	52	78	130
Ford Aral Tank Truck		20	30	50
Ford Capri	4" orange-red or dark red body, gold wheels with red hubs, two working doors, clear windshield & headlights, black interior, folding seats, black grille, silver bumpers	14	21	35
Ford Capri 3 Litre GT		14	21	35
Ford Capri 30 S		14	21	35
Ford Capri S	4-3/4" white body, red lower body & base, red interior, clear windshield, black bumpers, grille & tow hook, chrome headlights & wheels, red taillights, #6 & other racing decals	14	21	35
Ford Capri Santa Pod Gloworm	4-3/8" long, white/blue body with red/white/blue lettering and flag decals, red chassis, amber windows, gold-based black engine, gold scoop, pipes and front suspension	18	27	45
Ford Car Transporter		20	30	50
Ford Car Transporter		20	30	50
Ford Cobra Mustang		12	18	30

Name	Description			
nsul	3-5/8" long, one-piece body in several colors, clear windows, silver grille, lights and bumpers, smooth wheels, rubber tires	45	65	110
Ford Consul Classic	3-3/4" long, cream or gold body & base, yellow interior, pink roof, clear windows, gray steering wheel, silver bumpers, grille	35	55	90
Ford Consul-Mechanical	same as model 200-A but with friction motor and blue or green body	55	85	140
Ford Cortina Estate Car	3-1/2" metallic dark blue body & base, brown & cream simulated wood panels, cream interior, chrome bumpers & grille, jewel headlights	35	55	90
Ford Cortina Estate Car	3-3/4" red body & base or metallic charcoal gray body & base, cream interior, chrome bumpers & grille, jewel headlights	35	55	90
Ford Cortina GXL	4" tan or metallic silver blue body, black roof & stripes, red plastic interior, working doors, clear windshield	30	45	75
Ford Cortina Police Car	4" white body, red or pink & black stripe labels, red interior, folding seats, blue dome light, clear windows, chrome bumpers	12	18	30
Ford Covered Semi-Trailer		15	25	40
Ford Escort 13 GL		8	12	20
Ford Escort Police Car	4-3/16" blue body & base, tan interior, white doors, blue dome lights, red Police labels, black grille & bumpers	8	12	20
Ford Esso Tank Truck	1976-81	15	25	40
Ford Express Semi-Trailer	1965-70	60	90	150
Ford Exxon Tank Truck	1976-81	15	25	40
Ford GT 70	1972-73	10	15	25
Ford Guinness Tanker	1982	20	30	50
Ford Gulf Tank Truck	1976-78	15	25	40
Ford Holmes Wrecker	1967-74	70	105	200
Ford Michelin Container Truck	1981	15	25	40
Ford Mustang Fastback	1965-66	30	45	95
Ford Mustang Fastback	1965-69	25	35	60
Ford Mustang Mach 1	4-1/4" green upper body, white lower body & base, cream interior, folding seat backs, chrome headlights & rear bumper	25	35	60
Ford Sierra	5" many versions with plastic interior, working hatch & two doors, clear windows, folding seat back, lifting hatch cover	8	12	20
Ford Sierra and Caravan Trailer	blue #299 Sierra, two-tone blue/white #490 Caravan	15	20	35
Ford Sierra Taxi		8	12	20

Ford Thames Airborne Caravan	3-3/4" long, different versions of body & plastic interior with table, white blinds, silver bumpers, grille & headlights, two doors	35	55	95
Ford Thames Wall's Ice Cream Van	4" long, light blue body, cream pillar, chimes, chrome bumpers & grille, crank at rear to operate chimes, no figures	70	105	175
Ford Thunderbird 1957	5-3/16" long, cream body, dark brown, black or orange plastic hardtop, black interior, open hood & trunk, chrome bumpers	10	15	25
Ford Thunderbird 1957	5-1/4" long, white body, black interior & plastic top, amber windows, white seats, chrome bumpers, headlights & spare wheel cover	10	15	25
Ford Thunderbird Hardtop	4-1/8" long, clear windows, silver lights, grille and bumpers, red taillights, rubber tires; light green body 1959-61	50	80	130
Ford Thunderbird Hardtop-Mechanical	4-1/8" long, same as 214-A but with friction motor and pink or light green body	70	105	175
Ford Thunderbird Roadster	4-1/8" long, clear windshield, silver seats, lights, grille and bumpers, red taillights, rubber tires, white body	50	75	125
Ford Torino Road Hog	5-3/4" orange-red body, yellow and gray chassis, gold lamps, chrome radiator shell, windows & bumpers, one-piece body	15	20	35
Ford Tractor & Conveyor	tractor, conveyor with trailer, figures and accessories	60	90	150
Ford Tractor and Beast Carrier		60	90	150
Ford Tractor with Trencher	5-5/8" long, blue body/chassis, gray fenders, cast yellow trencher arm and controls, chrome trencher, black control lines	50	75	125
Ford Transit Milk Float	5-1/2" white one-piece body, blue hood & roof, tan interior, chrome & red roof lights, open compartment door & milk cases	15	25	40
Ford Transit Tipper		10	15	25
Ford Transit Wrecker		25	35	60
Ford Wall's Ice Cream Van	3-1/4" light blue body, dark cream pillars, plastic striped rear canopy, white interior, silver bumpers, grille & headlights	50	75	150
Ford Zephyr Estate Car	3-7/8" light blue one-piece body, dark blue hood & stripes, red interior, silver bumpers, grille & headlights, red taillights	30	45	75
Ford Zephyr Patrol Car	3-3/4" white or cream body, blue & white Police/Politie/Rijkspolitie decals, red interior, blue dome light, silver bumpers	35	50	85
Fordson Power Major Halftrack Tractor	3-1/2" long, blue body/chassis, silver steering wheel, seat and grille, three versions: orange cast wheels, gray treads	90	135	225
Fordson Power Major Tractor	3-1/4" long, blue body/chassis with Fordson Power Major decals, silver steering wheel, seat, exhaust, grille and lights	45	65	110
Fordson Power Major Tractor	3-3/8" long, blue body with Fordson Power Major decals, driver, blue chassis and steering wheel, silver seat, hitch, exhaust	50	75	125

Fordson Tractor & Plowc	tractor and four-furrow plow	55	85	140
Fordson Tractor & Plow	#55 Fordson Tractor & 56 Four Furrow plow	55	85	140
Four Furrow Plow	3-5/8" long, red frame, yellow plastic parts	15	20	35
Four Furrow Plow	3-3/4" long, blue frame with chrome plastic parts	15	20	35
French Construction Set	1980	25	35	60
German Life Saving Set	red/white Land Rover and lifeboat, white trailer, German decals	30	45	75
Ghia L64 Chrysler V-8	4-1/4", different color versions, plastic interior, hood, trunk & two doors working, detailed engine, clear windshield	25	40	65
Ghia-Fiat 600 Jolly	3-1/4", light or dark blue body, red & silver canopy, red seats, two figures, windshield, chrome dash, floor, steering wheels	45	65	110
Ghia-Fiat 600 Jolly	3-1/4" long, dark yellow body, red seats, two figures and a dog, clear windshield, silver bumpers and headlights, red taillights	60	90	150
Giant Daktari Set	black/green Land Rover, tan Giraffe truck, blue/brown Dodge Livestock truck, tan figures, set	225	350	650
Giant Tower Crane		35	50	85
Glider Set	two versions: white Honda, 1981-82; yellow Honda, 1983 on, each set	30	45	75
Golden Eagle Jeep	3-3/4" three different versions, tan plastic top, chrome plastic base, bumpers & steps, chrome wheels	8	12	20
Golden Guinea Set	three vehicle set, gold plated Bentley Continental, Chevy Corvair and Ford Consul	90	135	300
GP Beach Buggy		15	20	35
Grand Prix Racing Set	four vehicle set with accessories in two versions: with #330 Porsche, 1969; with Porsche #371, 1970-72, each set	135	210	400
Grand Prix Set	#30-A, sold by mail order only	50	75	125
Green Hornet's Black Beauty	5" black body, green window/interior, two figures, working chrome grille & panels with weapons, green headlights, red taillights	175	275	500
Green Line Bus	4-7/8" green body, white interior & stripe, TDK lables, six spoked wheels	10	15	25
Half Track Rocket Launcher & Trailer	6-1/2" two rocket launchers & single trailer castings, gray plastic roll cage, man with machine gun, front wheels & hubs	20	35	55
Hardy Boys' Rolls-Royce	4-5/8" long, red body with yellow hood, roof and window frames, band figures on roof on removable green base	70	105	200
Heinkel	2-3/8" long, blue body, white interior, three-wheeler	15	30	70
Hesketh-Ford Racing Car	5-5/8" long, white body with red/white/blue Hesketh, stripe and #24 decals, chrome suspension, roll bar, mirrors and pipes	12	18	30

HGB-Angus Firestreak	6-1/4" long, chrome plastic spotlight and ladders, black hose reel, red dome light, white water cannon, in two interior versions	35	50	85
Hillman Hunter	4-1/4" blue body, gray interior, black hood, white roof, unpainted spotlights, clear windshield, red radiator screen, black equipment	50	75	125
Hillman Husky	3-1/2" long, one-piece tan or metallic blue/silver body, clear windows, silver lights, grille and bumpers, smooth wheels	40	60	100
Hillman Husky-Mechanical	3-1/2" long, same as 206-A but with friction motor, black base and dark blue, grayor cream body	50	75	125
Hillman Imp	3-1/4" metallic copper, blue, dark blue, gold & maroon one-piece bodies, with white/yellow interior, silver bumpers, headlights	30	45	75
Hillman Imp Rally	3-1/4" long, in various metallic body colors, with cream interior, Monte Carlo Rally and #107 decals	30	45	75
Honda Ballade Driving School	4-3/4" red body/base, tan interior, clear windows, tow hook, mirrors, bumpers	10	15	25
Honda Prelude	4-3/4" long, dark metallic blue body, tan interior, clear windows, folding seats, sunroof, chrome wheels	8	12	20
Hyster 800 Stacatruck	8-1/2" long, clear windows, black interior with driver	35	50	85
Incredible Hulk Mazda Pickup	5" metallic light brown body, gray or red plastic cage, black interior, green & red figure, Hulk decal on hood, chrome wheels	20	30	75
Inter-City Mini Bus	4-3/16" long, orange body with brown interior, clear windows, green/yellow/black decals, Whizz Wheels	8	12	20
International 6x6 Army Truck	5-1/2" long, olive drab body with clear windows, red/blue decals, six cast olive wheels with rubber tires	70	105	175
Iso Grifo 7 Litre	4" metallic blue body, light blue interior, black hood & stripe, clear windshield, black dash, folding seats, chrome bumpers	12	18	30
Jaguar 1952 XK120 Rally	4-3/4" long, cream body with black top and trim, red interior, Rally des Alps and #414 decals	8	12	20
Jaguar 2.4 Litre	3-7/8" long, one-piece white body with no interior 1957-59, or yellow body with red interior 1960-63, clear windows	50	80	130
Jaguar 2.4 Litre Fire Chief's Car	3-3/4" long, red body with unpainted roof signal/siren, red/white fire and shield decals on doors, in two versions	60	90	150
Jaguar 2.4 Litre-Mechanical	3-7/8" long, same as 208-A but with friction motor and metallic blue body	60	90	150
Jaguar E Type	3-3/4" maroon or metallic dark gray body, tan interior, red & clear plastic removeable hardtop, clear windshield, folded top	45	65	110
Jaguar E Type 2+2	4-3/16" long, working hood, doors and hatch, black interior with folding seats, copper engine, pipes and suspension, spoked wheels	40	60	100
Jaguar E Type 2+2	4-1/8" long, in five versions: red or yellow with nonworking doors; or with V-12 engine in yellow body or metallic yellow body--	35	55	90

Jaguar E Type Competition	3-3/4" gold or chrome plated body, black interior, blue & white stripes & black #2 decals, no top, clear windshield & headlights	45	65	110
Jaguar Mark X Saloon	4-1/4", seven different versions with working front & rear hood castings, clear windshields, plastic interior, gray steering wheel	35	55	90
Jaguar XJ12C	5-1/4" five different metallic versions, working hood & two doors, clear windows, tow hook, chrome bumpers, grille & headlights	10	15	25
Jaguar XJ12C Police Car	5-1/8" long, white body with blue and pink stripes, light bar with blue dome light, tan interior, police decals	12	18	30
Jaguar XJS	5-3/4" long, metallic burgundy body, tan interior, clear windows, working doors, spoked chrome wheels	10	15	25
Jaguar XJS Motul	5-3/4" long, black body with red/white Motul and #4, chrome wheels	8	12	20
Jaguar XJS-HE Supercat	5-1/4" black body with silver stripes & trim, red interior, dark red taillights, light gray antenna, no tow hook, clear windshield	8	12	20
Jaguar XK120 Hardtop	4-3/4" long, red body, black hardtop, working hood and trunk, detailed engine, cream interior, clear windows, chrome wheels	8	12	20
James Bond Aston Martin	3-3/4" metallic gold body, red interior, working roof hatch, clear windows, two figures, left seat ejects	70	105	225
James Bond Aston Martin	4" metallic silver body, red interior, two figures, working roof hatch, ejector seat, bullet shield and guns, chrome bumpers	100	150	275
James Bond Aston Martin	5" metallic silver body & die cast base, red interior, two figures, clear windows, passenger set raises to eject	30	45	75
James Bond Bobsled	2-7/8" long, yellow body, silver base, Bond figure, 007 decals, Whizz Wheels	60	90	175
James Bond Citroen 2CV6	4-1/4" dark yellow body & hood, red interior, clear windows, chrome headlights, red taillights, black plastic grille	15	25	50
James Bond Lotus Esprit	4-3/4" white body & base, black windshield, grille & hood panel, white plastic roof device that triggers fins & tail, rockets	30	45	95
James Bond Moon Buggy	4-3/8" long, white body with blue chassis, amber canopy, yellow tanks, red radar dish, arms and jaws, yellow wheels	190	310	525
James Bond Mustang Mach 1	4-3/8" long, red and white body with black hood	100	150	275
James Bond Set	set of three: Lotus Esprit, Space Shuttle and Aston Martin	80	120	225
James Bond Toyota 2000GT	4" long, white body, black interior with Bond and passenger, working trunk and gun rack, spoked wheels, plastic tires	125	200	375
JCB 110B Crawler Loader	6-1/2" long, white cab, yellow body, working red shovel, red interior with driver, clear windows, black treads, JCB decals	20	30	50
Jean Richard Circus Set	yellow/red Land Rover and cage trailer with Pinder-Jean Richard decals, office van and trailer, Human Cannonball truck, ring	100	150	275

Jeep & Horse Box	metallic painted Jeep and trailer	15	25	40
Jeep & Motorcycle Trailer	red working Jeep with two blue/yellow bikes on trailer	15	20	35
Jeep CJ-5	4" long, dark metallic green body, removable white top, white plastic wheels, spare tire	8	12	20
Jeep FC-150 Covered Truck	four versions: blue body, rubber tires (1965-67), yellow/brown body, rubber tires (1965-67), blue body, plastic tires	30	45	75
Jeep FC-150 Pickup	3-1/2" long, blue body, clear windows, sheet metal tow hook, in two wheel versions: smooth or shaped wheels	35	55	90
Jeep FC-150 Pickup with Conveyor Belt	7-1/2" long, red body, yellow interior, orange grille, two rubber belts, shaped wheels, black rubber tires	45	65	110
Jeep FC-150 Tower Wagon	4-5/8" long, metallic green body, yellow interior and basket with workman figure, clear windows, with either rubber or plastic wheels	40	60	100
JPS Lotus Racing Car	10-1/2" long, black body, scoop and wings with gold John Player Special, Texaco and #1 decals, gold suspension, pipes and wheels	30	45	75
Karrier Bantam Two Ton Van	4" long, blue body, red chassis and bed, clear windows, smooth wheels, rubber tires	35	55	95
Karrier Butcher Shop	3-5/8" long, white body, blue roof, butcher shop interior, Home Service decals, in two versions: with or without suspension	65	100	165
Karrier Circus Booking Office	3-5/8" long, red body, light blue roof, clear windows, circus decals, shaped wheels, rubber tires	105	165	275
Karrier Dairy Van	4-1/8" long, light blue body with Drive Safely on Milk decals, white roof, with either smooth or shaped wheels	50	75	125
Karrier Field Kitchen	3-5/8" long, olive body, white decals	60	90	150
Karrier Ice Cream Truck	3-5/8" long, cream upper, blue lower body and interior, clear windows, sliding side windows, Mister Softee decals, figure inside	90	135	225
Karrier Lucozade Van	4-1/8" long, yellow body with gray rear door, Lucozade decals, rubber tires, with either smooth or shaped wheels	70	105	175
Karrier Mobile Canteen	3-5/8" long, blue body, white interior, amber windows, roof knob rotates figure, working side panel counter	60	90	150
Karrier Mobile Grocery	3-5/8" long, light green body, grocery store interior, red/white Home Service decals, friction motor, rubber tires	70	110	185
King Tiger Heavy Tank	6-1/8" long, tan and rust body, working turret and barrel, tan rollers and treads, German decals	30	45	75
Kojak's Buick Regal	5-3/4" metallic bronze brown body, off-white interior, two doors, clear windows, chrome bumpers, grille & headlights, red taillights	25	40	85
Lamborghini Miura	3-3/4" long, silver body, black interior, yellow/purple stripes and #7 decal	30	45	75
Lamborghini Miura P400	3-3/4" long, with red or yellow body, working hood, detailed engine, clear windows, jewel headlights, bull, Whizz Wheels	40	60	100

Lancia Fulvia Zagato	3-5/8" long, metallic blue body, light blue interior, working hood and doors, folding seats, amber lights, cast wheels	25	35	60
Lancia Fulvia Zagato	3-5/8" long, orange body, black working hood and interior, Whizz Wheels	15	25	40
Land Rover & Ferrari Racer	red/tan Land Rover, yellow trailer	60	90	150
Land Rover & Horse Box	blue/white Land Rover with horse trailer in two versions: cast wheels, 1968-74; Whizz Wheels, 1975-77	50	75	125
Land Rover 109WB	5-1/4" long, working rear doors, tan interior, spare on hood, plastic tow hook	12	18	30
Land Rover and Pony Trailer	two versions: tan/cream Rover, 1958-62; tan/cream #438 Land Rover, 1963-68, each set	50	75	125
Land Rover Breakdown Truck	4-3/8" long, red body with silver boom and yellow canopy, revolving spotlight, Breakdown Service decals	35	55	90
Land Rover Breakdown Truck	4-3/8" long, red body, yellow canopy, chrome revolving spotlight, Breakdown Service decals	25	35	60
Land Rover Circus Vehicle	3-1/2" long, red body, yellow interior, blue rear and speakers, revolving clown, chimp figures, Chipperfield decals	60	90	150
Land Rover Pickup	3-3/4" long, yellow or metallic blue body, spare on hood, clear windows, sheet metal tow hook, rubber tires	45	70	120
Land Rover with Canopy	3-3/4" long, one-piece body with clear windows, plastic interior, spare on hood, issued in numerous colors	35	55	90
Lincoln Continental	5-3/4" metallic gold or blue body, black roof, maroon plastic interior, working hood, trunk & doors, clear windows, TV	60	90	150
Lions of Longleat	black/white Land Rover pickup with lion cages and accessories, two versions: cast wheels, 1969-73; Whizz Wheels, 1974, each	70	105	200
London Set	orange Mini, Policeman, London Taxi and Routemaster bus	50	75	125
London Set	London Taxi and Routemaster bus in two versions: with mounted Policeman, 1980-81; without Policeman, 1982 on, each set	25	35	60
London Set	taxi and bus with policeman, in two versions: "Corgi Toys" on bus, 1964-66; "Outspan Oranges" on bus, 1967-68, each set	55	85	140
London Transport Routemaster Bus	4-1/2" long, clear windows with driver and conductor, released with numerous advertiser logos	35	50	85
London Transport Routemaster Bus	4-7/8" long, clear windows, interior, some models have driver and conductor, released with numerous advertiser logos	25	35	60
Lotus Elan S2 Hardtop	2-1/4" long, cream interior with folding seats and tan dash, working hood, separate chrome chassis, issued in blue body	30	45	75
Lotus Elan S2 Roadster	3-3/8" long, working hood, plastic interior with folding seats, shaped wheels and rubber tires, issued in metallic blue or white	30	45	75

Lotus Eleven	2-1/4" long, clear windshield and plastic headlights, smooth wheels, rubber tires, racing decals, in several color variations	60	95	160
Lotus Elite	5-1/8" red body, white interior, two working doors, clear windshield, black dash, hood panel, grille, bumpers, base & tow hook	12	18	30
Lotus Elite 22	4-3/4" long, dark blue body with silver trim	12	18	30
Lotus Racing Car	5-5/8" long, black body and base, gold cast engine, roll bar, pipes, dash and mirrors, driver, gold cast wheels, in two versions	25	35	60
Lotus Racing Set	three versions: #3 on Elite and JPS on racer; #7 on Elite and JPS on racer; #7 on Elite and Texaco on racer, each set	30	45	75
Lotus Racing Team Set	four vehicle set in two versions, with accessories: #319 Lotus has either red or black interior, each set	30	45	75
Lotus-Climax Racing Car	3-5/8" long, green body and base with black/white #1 and yellow racing stripe decals, unpainted engine and suspension	25	35	60
Lotus-Climax Racing Car	3-5/8" long, orange/white body with black/white stripe and #8 decals, unpainted cast rear wing, cast 8-spoke wheels	15	25	40
M60 A1 Medium Tank	4-3/4" long, green/tan camo body, working turret and barrel, green rollers, white decals	30	45	75
Mack Container Truck	11-3/8" long, yellow cab, red interior, white engine, red suspension, white ACL decals	30	50	80
Mack Esso Tank Truck	10-3/4" long, white cab and tank with Esso decals, red tank chassis and fenders	20	30	50
Mack Exxon Tank Truck	10-3/4" long, white cab and tank, red tank chassis and fenders, red interior, chrome catwalk, Exxon decals	15	25	40
Mack Trans Continental Semi	10", orange cab body & semi chassis & fenders, metallic light blue semi body, unpainted trailer rests	35	55	90
Mack-Priestman Crane Truck	9" long, red truck, yellow crane cab, red interior, black engine, Hi Lift and Long Vehicle decals	50	75	125
Magic Roundabout Train	1973	70	105	225
Man From U.N.C.L.E. Oldsmobile	4-1/8" long, plastic interior, blue windows, two figures, two spotlights, dark metallic blue	90	130	250
Man From U.N.C.L.E. Oldsmobile	4-1/8" long, plastic interior, blue windows, two figures, two spotlights, cream body	130	475	550
Marcos 3 Litre	3-3/8" long, working hood, detailed engine, black interior, Marcos decal, Whizz Wheels, issued in orange or metallic blue/green	20	30	50
Marcos Matis	4-1/4" metallic red body & doors, cream interior & headlights, silver gray lower body base, bumpers, hood panel	20	35	55
Marcos Volvo 1800 GT	3-5/8" long, issued with either white or blue body, plastic interior with driver, spoked wheels, rubber tires	25	35	60
Massey Ferguson 165 Tractor	3" long, gray engine and chassis, red hood and fenders with black/white Massey Ferguson 165 decals, white grille, red cast wheels	35	55	90

Massey Ferguson 165 Tractor with Saw	3-1/2" long, red hood and fenders, gray engine and seat, cast yellow arm and control, chrome circular saw	55	85	140
Massey Ferguson 165 Tractor with Shovel	5-1/8" long, gray chassis, red hood, fenders and shovel arms, unpainted shovel and cylinder, red cast wheels, black plastic tires	45	65	110
Massey Ferguson 50B Tractor	4" long, yellow body, black interior and roof, red plastic wheels with black plastic tires	12	18	30
Massey Ferguson 65 Tractor	3" long, silver steering wheel, seat and grille, red engine hood, red wheels with black rubber tires	40	60	100
Massey Ferguson 65 Tractor And Shovel	4-3/4" long, two versions: either cream or gray chassis, each	55	85	140
Massey Ferguson Combine	6-1/2" long, red body with yellow metal blades, metal tines, black/white decals, orange wheels	70	105	175
Massey Ferguson Combine	6-1/2" long, red body, plastic blades, red wheels	60	90	150
Massey Ferguson Tipping Trailer	3-5/8" long, two versions: either yellow or gray tipper and tailgate, each	10	15	25
Massey Ferguson Tractor & Tipping Trailer		50	75	125
Massey Ferguson Tractor & Tipping Trailer	#50 MF tractor with driver, #51 trailer	50	75	125
Massey Ferguson Tractor with Fork	4-7/8" long, red cast body and shovel, arms, cream chassis, red plastic wheels, black rubber tires, Massey Ferguson 65 decals	60	90	150
Massey Ferguson Tractor with Shovel	6" long, two versions: either yellow and red or red and white body colors	20	30	50
Massey Ferguson Tractor with Shovel & Trailer	#35 MF tractor with driver and shovel, #62 trailer	30	45	75
Matra & Motorcycle Trailer	red Rancho with two yellow/blue bikes on trailer	15	20	35
Matra & Racing Car	black/yellow Rancho and yellow car with Team Corgi decals	15	25	40
Mazda 4X4 Open Truck	4-7/8" long, blue body, white roof, black windows, no interior, white plastic wheels	15	20	35
Mazda B-1600 Pickup Truck	4-7/8" long, issued in either blue and white or blue and silver bodies with working tailgate, black interior, chrome wheels	15	20	35
Mazda Camper Pickup	5-3/8" long, red truck and white camper with red interior and folding supports	15	25	40
Mazda Custom Pickup	4-7/8" long, orange body with red roof	12	18	30
Mazda Motorway Maintenance Truck	6-1/8" long, deep yellow body with red base, black interior and hydraulic cylinder, yellow basket with workman figure	18	25	45
Mazda Pickup & Dinghy	two versions: red Mazda with "Ford" decals; or with "Sea Spray" decals	25	35	60

McLaren M19A Racing Car	4-5/8" long, white body, orange stripes, chrome engine, exhaust and suspension, black mirrors, driver, Yardley McLaren #55 decals	15	25	40
McLaren M23 Racing Car	10-1/4" long, red/white body and wings with red/white/black Texaco-Marlboro #5 decals, chrome pipes, suspension and mirrors	30	45	75
Mercedes-Benz 240D	5-1/4" three different versions, working trunk, two doors, clear windows, plastic interior, two hook, chrome bumpers, grille & headlights	10	15	25
Mercedes-Benz & Caracan	truck and trailer in two versions: with blue Mercedes truck, 1975-79; with brown Mercedes, 1980-81	15	25	40
Mercedes-Benz 220SE Coupe	3-3/4" long, cream, black or dark red body, red plastic interior, clear windows, working trunk, silver bumpers, grille & plate	40	60	100
Mercedes-Benz 220SE Coupe	4" metallic maroon body, yellow plastic interior, light gray base, clear windows, silver bumpers, headlights, grille & license	40	60	100
Mercedes-Benz 220SE Coupe	4" metallic dark blue body, cream plastic interior, medium gray base, clear windows, silver bumpers, headlights, grille & license	40	60	100
Mercedes-Benz 240D Rally	5-1/8" cream or tan body, black, red & blue lettering & dirt, red plastic interior, clear windows, black radiator guard & roof	10	15	25
Mercedes-Benz 240D Taxi	5" orange body, orange interior, black roof sign with red and white Taxi labels, black on door	12	18	30
Mercedes-Benz 300SC Convertible	5" black body, black folded top, white interior, folding seat backs, detailed engine, chrome grille & wheels, lights, bumpers	8	12	20
Mercedes-Benz 300SC Hardtop	5" maroon body, tan top & interior, open hood & trunk, clear windows, folding seat backs, top with chrome side irons	8	12	20
Mercedes-Benz 300SL	5" red body & base, tan interior, open hood & two gullwing doors, black dash, detailed engine, clear windows, chrome bumpers	8	12	20
Mercedes-Benz 300SL	4-3/4" silver body, tan interior, black dash, clear windows, open hood & two gullwing doors, detailed engine, chrome bumpers	8	12	20
Mercedes-Benz 300SL Coupe	3-3/4" different body & interior versions, hardtop, clear windows, '59-60 smooth wheels no suspension, '61-65 racing stripes	45	65	110
Mercedes-Benz 300SL Roadster	3-3/4" different body & interior versions, plastic interior, smooth, shaped or cast wheels, racing stripes & number, driver	45	65	110
Mercedes-Benz 350SL	3-3/4" white body, spoke wheels or metallic dark blue body solid wheels, pale blue interior, folding seats, detailed engine	15	25	40
Mercedes-Benz 600 Pullman	4-1/4" metallic maroon body, cream interior & steering wheel, clear windshields, chrome grille, trim & bumpers	40	60	100
Mercedes-Benz Ambulance	5-3/4" three different versions, white interior, open rear & two doors, blue windows & dome lights, chrome bumpers, grille & headlights	15	20	35

Mercedes-Benz Ambulance	5-3/4" white body & base, red stripes & taillights, Red Cross & black & white ambulance labels, open rear door, white interior	15	20	35
Mercedes-Benz C-111	4" orange main body with black lower & base, black interior, vents, front & rear grilles, silver headlights, red taillights	12	18	30
Mercedes-Benz Fire Chief	5" light red body, black base, tan plastic interior, blue dome light, white Notruf 112 decals, red taillights, no tow hook	15	25	40
Mercedes-Benz Police Car	5" white body with two different hood versions, brown interior, polizei or police lettering, blue dome light	12	18	30
Mercedes-Benz Refrigerator		12	18	30
Mercedes-Benz Refrigerator	8" yellow cab & tailgate, red semi-trailer, two-piece lowering tailgate & yellow spare wheel base, red interior, clear window	12	18	30
Mercedes-Benz Semi-Trailer	1983	12	18	30
Mercedes-Benz Semi-Trailer Van	8-1/4" black cab & plastic semi trailer, white chassis & airscreen, red doors, red-blue & yellow stripes, white Corgi lettering	12	18	30
Mercedes-Benz Tanker	7-1/4" tan cab, plastic tank body, black chassis, black & red Guinness labels, with chrome or black plastic catwalk, clear windows	12	18	30
Mercedes-Benz Tanker	7-1/4" two different versions, cab & tank, chassis, chrome or black plastic catwalk, red/white/green 7-Up labels	12	18	30
Mercedes-Benz Unimog & Dumper	6-3/4" yellow cab & tipper, red fenders & tipper chassis, charcoal gray cab chassis, black plastic mirrors or without	25	35	60
Mercedes-Benz Unimog 406	3-3/4" yellow body, red front fenders & bumpers, metallic charcoal gray chassis with olive or tan rear plastic covers, red interior	18	25	45
Mercedes-Faun Street Sweeper	5" orange body with light orange or brown figure, red interior, black chassis & unpainted brushing housing & arm castings	15	25	40
Metropolis Police Car	6" metallic blue body, off white interior, white roof/stripes, two working doors, clear windows, chrome bumpers, grille & headlights	20	30	50
MG Maestro	4-1/2" yellow body, black trim, opaque black windows, black plastic grille, bumpers, spoiler, trim & battery hatch, clear headlights	15	20	35
MGA	3-3/4" metallic light brown body, all white interior, black dash, clear windshield, silver bumpers, grille & headlight decals	60	90	150
MGB GT	3-1/2" dark red body, pale blue interior, open hatch & two doors, jewel headlights, chrome grille & bumpers, orange taillights	50	75	125
MGC GT	3-1/2" bright yellow body & base, black interior, hood & hatch, folding seats, luggage, jewel headlights, red taillights	50	75	125

MGC GT	3-1/2" red body, black hood & base, black interior, open hatch & two doors, folding seat backs, luggage, orange taillights	50	75	125
Midland Red Express Coach	5-1/2" red one-piece body, black roof with shape or smooth wheels, yellow interior, clear windows, silver grille & headlights	70	105	175
Military Set	set of three, Tiger tank, Bell Helicopter, Saladin Armored Car	60	90	150
Milk Truck & Trailer	blue/white milk truck with trailer	60	90	150
Mini Camping Set	cream Mini, with red/blue tent, grille and figures	25	40	65
Mini-Marcos GT850	2-1/8" white body, red-white-blue racing stripe & #7 labels, clear headlights, Whizz Wheels	20	30	50
Mini-Marcos GT850	3-1/4" metallic maroon body, white name & trim decals, cream interior, open hood & doors, clear windows & headlights	30	45	75
Minissima	2-1/4" cream upper body, metallic lime green lower body with black stripe centered, black interior, clear windows, headlights	15	20	35
Monkeemobile	4-3/4" red body/base, white roof, yellow interior, clear windows, four figures, chrome grille, headlights, engine, orange taillights	145	225	400
Monte Carlo Rally Set	three vehicle set, Citroen, Mini and Rover rally cars	275	425	800
Morris Cowley	3-1/8" long, one-piece body in several colors, clear windows, silver lights, grille and bumper, smooth wheels, rubber tires	45	65	110
Morris Cowley-Mechanical	3-1/8" long, same as 202-A but with friction motor, available in off-white or green body	55	85	140
Morris Marina	3-3/4" metallic dark red or lime green body, cream interior, working hood & two doors, clear windshield, chrome grille & bumpers	15	25	40
Morris Mini-Cooper	2-3/4" yellow or blue body either body & base and/or hood, white roof and/or hood, two versions, red plastic interior, jewel headlights	25	40	70
Morris Mini-Cooper	2-7/8" red body & base, white roof, yellow interior, chrome spotlight, No. 37 & Monte Carlo Rally decals	55	85	140
Morris Mini-Cooper Deluxe	2-3/4" black body/base, red roof, yellow & black wicker work decals on sides & rear, yellow interior, gray steering wheel, jewel headlights	45	65	110
Morris Mini-Minor	2-7/8" long, one-piece body in several colors, plastic interior, silver lights, grille and bumpers, red taillights, Whizz Wheels	30	45	75
Morris Mini-Minor	2-3/4" three to four different versions with shaped and/or smooth wheels, plastic interior, silver bumpers, grille & headlights	40	60	100
Motorway Ambulance	4" white body, dark blue interior, red-white-black labels, dark blue windows, clear headlights, red die cast base & bumpers	10	15	25
Mr. McHenry's Trike	1972-74	70	105	175

Mustang Organ Grinder Dragster	4" long, yellow body with green/yellow name, #39 and racing stripe decals, black base, green windshield, red interior, roll bar	20	30	50
National Express Bus		8	12	20
Noddy's Car	3-3/4" yellow body, red fenders & base, Chubby, Golliwogg & Noddy figures, chrome bumpers & grille castings, black grille	107	165	300
Noddy's Car	3-3/4" yellow body, red chassis, Chubby inside 1970; 3-1/2" 1975-1977 Noddy alone, closed trunk with spare tire	60	90	175
NSU Sport Prinz	3-1/4" metallic burgundy or maroon body, yellow interior, one-piece body, silver bumpers, headlights & trim, shaped wheels	30	45	75
Off Road Set	#5 decal on Jeep, blue boat	15	20	35
Olds Toronado & Speedboat	blue Toronado, blue/yellow boat with swordfish decals	60	90	150
Oldsmobile 88 Staff Car	4-1/4" drab olive body, four figures, white decals	50	75	125
Oldsmobile Sheriff's Car	4-1/4" long, black upper body with white sides, red interior with red dome light & County Sheriff decals on doors, single body casting	50	75	125
Oldsmobile Super 88	4-1/4" long, three versions: light blue, light or dark metallic blue body with white stripes, red interior, single body casting	40	60	100
Oldsmobile Toronado	4-1/8" metallic peacock blue body, cream interior, one-piece body, clear windshield, chrome bumpers, grille, headlight covers	35	55	90
Oldsmobile Toronado	4-3/16" metallic copper red one-piece body, cream interior, Golden jacks, gray tow hook, clear windows, bumpers, grille, headlights	35	55	90
Opel Senator Doctor's Car	1980-81	10	15	25
Open Top Disneyland Bus	4-3/4" yellow body, red interior & stripe, Disneyland labels, eight spoked wheels or orange body, white interior & stripe	30	50	95
OSI DAF City Car	2-3/4" orange/red body, light cream interior, textured black roof, sliding left door, working hood, hatch & two right doors	18	25	45
Penguinmobile	3-3/4" black & white lettering on orange-yellow-blue decals, gold body panels, seats, air scoop, chrome engine	20	30	65
Pennyburn Workmen's Trailer	3-1/8" long, blue body w/working lids, red plastic interior, chrome tools, red cast wheels, plastic tires	15	20	35
Peugeot 505 STI	4-7/8" cream body & base, red interior, blue-red-white Taxi labels, black grille, bumpers, tow hook, chrome headlights & wheels	8	12	20
Peugeot 505 Taxi	4-7/8" long, cream body, red interior, red/white/blue taxi decals	8	12	20
Platform Trailer	4-3/8" long, in five versions: silver body, blue chassis; silver body, yellow chassis; blue body, red chassis, blue body, yellow chassis	10	15	25

Plymouth Sports Suburban	4-1/4" long, dark cream body, tan roof, red interior, die cast base, red axle, silver bumpers, trim and grille and rubber tires	40	60	100
Plymouth Sports Suburban	4-1/4" pale blue body with silver trim, red roof, yellow interior, gray die cast base without rear axle bulge, shaped wheels	40	60	100
Plymouth Suburban Mail Car	4-1/4" white upper, blue lower body with red stripes, gray die cast base without rear axle bulge, silver bumpers & grille	55	85	140
Police Land Rover	5" white body, red & blue police stripes, black lettering, open rear door, opaque black windows, blue dome light, roof light	15	25	40
Police Land Rover & Horse Box	white Land Rover with police decals and mounted policeman	30	45	75
Police Vigilant Range Rover	4" white body, red interior, black shutters, blue dome light, two chrome & amber spotlights, black grille, silver headlights	25	35	60
Pontiac Firebird	4" metallic silver body & base, red interior, black hood, stripes & convertible top, doors open, clear windows, folding seats	50	75	125
Pony Club Set	brown/white Land Rover with Corgi Pony Club decals, horse box, horse and rider	30	45	75
Popeye's Paddle Wagon	4-7/8" yellow body, red chassis, blue rear fenders, bronze & yellow stacks, white plastic deck, blue lifeboat with Swee' Pea	165	280	525
Popeye's Paddle Wagon Jr.		70	105	200
Porsche 917	4-1/4" red or blue body, black or gray base, blue or amber tinted windows & headlights, open rear hood, headlights	15	20	35
Porsche 92 Turbo	4-1/2" black body with gold trim, yellow interior, four chrome headlights, clear windshield, taillight-license plate decal, black	15	20	35
Porsche 924	4-1/2" bright orange body, dark red interior, black plastic grille, multicolored stripes, swivel roof spotlight	10	15	25
Porsche 924	4-7/8" red or metallic light brown body, dark red interior, two doors open & rear window, chrome headlights, black plastic grille	10	15	25
Porsche 924 Police Car	4-1/4" white body with different hood & doors versions, blue & chrome light, Polizei white on green panels or Police labels	15	25	40
Porsche Carrera 6	3-7/8" white body, red or blue trim, blue or amber tinted engine covers, black interior, clear windshield & canopy, red jewel taillights	30	45	75
Porsche Carrera 6	3-3/4" white upper body, red front hood, doors, upper fins & base, black interior, purple rear window, tinted engine cover	25	35	60
Porsche Targa 911S	3-1/2" three different versions, black roof with or without stripe, orange interior, open hood & two doors, chrome engine & bumpers	25	35	60
Porsche Targa Police Car	3-1/2" white body & base, red doors & hood, black roof & plastic interior also comes with an orange interior, unpainted siren	25	35	60

Porsche-Audi 917	4-3/4" white body, red & black no. 6, L & M, Porsche Audi & stripe labels or orange body, orange two-tone green white no. 6	15	20	35
Priestman Cub Crane	9" orange body, red chassis & two-piece bucket, unpainted bucket arms, lower boom, knobs, gears & drum castings, clear window	50	75	125
Priestman Cub Power Shovel	6" orange upper body & panel, yellow lower body, lock rod & chassis, rubber or plastic treads, pulley panel, gray boom	40	60	100
Priestman Shovel & Carrier	cub shovel & low loader machinery carrier	90	135	225
Professionals Ford Capri	5" metallic silver body & base, red interior, black spoiler, grille, bumpers, tow hook & trim, blue windows, chrome wheels	30	45	75
Psychedelic Ford Mustang	3-3/4" light blue body & base, aqua interior, red-orange-yellow No. 20 & flower decals, cast eight spoke wheels, plastic tire	30	45	75
Public Address Land Rover	4" green body, yellow plastic rear body & loudspeakers, red interior, clear windows, silver bumper, grille & headlights	50	75	125
Quartermaster Dragster	5-3/4" long, dark metallic green upper body with green/yellow/black #5 and Quartermaster decals, light green lower body	30	45	75
RAC Land Rover	3-3/4" three versions of body, plastic interior & rear cover, RAC & Radio Rescue decals	60	90	150
Radio Luxembourg Dragster	5-3/4" long, blue body with yellow/white/blue John Wolfe Racing, Radio Luxembourg and #5 decals, silver engine	30	45	75
Radio Roadshow Van	4-3/4" white body, red plastic roof & rear interior, opaque black windows, red-white-black Radio Tele Luxembourg labels, gray	25	35	60
RAF Land Rover	3-3/4" blue body & cover, one-piece body, sheet metal rear cover, RAF rondel decal, with or without suspension, silver bumper	60	90	150
RAF Land Rover & Bloodhound	set of three standard colored, Massey Ferguson Tractor, Bloodhound Missile, Ramp & Trolley	150	240	400
RAF Land Rover & Thunderbird	Standard colors, #350 Thunderbird Missileon Trolley & 351 R.A.F. Land Rover	100	150	250
Rambler Marlin Fastback	4-1/8" red or blue body, black roof & trim, cream interior, clear windshield, folding seats, chrome bumpers, grille & headlights	35	55	90
Rambler Marlin with Kayak & Trailer	blue Marlin with roof rack, blue/white trailer	100	150	250
Range Rover Ambulance	4" two different versions of body sides, red interior, raised roof, open upper & lower doors, black shutters, blue dome light	20	30	50
Raygo Rascal Roller	4-7/8" dark yellow body, base & mounting, green interior & engine, orange & silver roller mounting & castings, clear windshield	15	25	40
Red Wheelie Motorcycle	4" long, red plastic body and fender with black/white/yellow decals, black handlebars, kickstand and seat, chrome engine, pipes	10	15	25

Reliant Bond Rug 700 E.S.	2-1/2" bright orange or lime green body, off white seats, black trim, silver headlights, red taillights	15	25	40
Renault 11 GTL	4-1/4" light tan body & base, red interior, open doors & rear hatch, lifting hatch cover, folding seats, grille	15	25	40
Renault 16	3-3/4" metallic maroon body, dark yellow interior, chrome base, grille & bumpers, clear windows, hatch cover/Renault decal	25	35	60
Renault 16TS	3-7/8" long, metallic blue body with Renault decal on working hatch, clear windows, detailed engine, yellow interior	25	35	60
Renault 5 Police Car	3-7/8" white body, red interior, blue dome light, black hood, hatch & doors with white Police labels, orange taillights	15	20	35
Renault 5 Turbo	3-3/4" bright yellow body, red plastic interior, black roof & hood, working hatch & two doors, black dash, chrome rear engine	12	18	30
Renault 5 Turbo	4" white body, red roof, red & blue trim painted on, No. 5 lettering, blue & white label on windshield	12	18	30
Renault 5TS	3-3/4" metallic golden orange body, black trim, tan plasic interior, working hatch & two doors, clear windows & headlights	12	18	30
Renault 5TS	3-3/4" light blue body, red plastic interior, dark blue roof, dome light, S.O.S. Medicine lettering, working hatch & two doors	12	18	30
Renault 5TS Fire Chief	3-3/4" red body, tan interior, amber headlights, gray antenna, black/white Sapeurs Pompiers decals, blue dome light	15	25	40
Renault Alpine 5TS	3-3/4" dark blue body, off white interior, red & chrome trim, clear windows & headlights, gray base & bumpers, black grille	15	25	40
Renault Floride	3-5/8" long, one-piece body, clear windows, silver bumper, grille, lights and plates, red taillights, rubber tires	35	55	95
Renegade Jeep	4" dark blue body with no top, white interior, base & bumper, white plastic wheels & rear mounted spare, Renegade	8	12	20
Renegade Jeep with Hood	4" yellow body with removeable hood, red interior, base, bumper, white plastic wheels, side mounted spare, Renegade, number 8	8	12	20
Riley Pathfinder	4" long, red or dark blue one-piece body, clear windows, silver lights, grille and bumpers, smooth wheels, rubber tires	45	65	110
Riley Pathfinder Police Car	4" long, black body with blue/white Police lettering, unpainted roof sign, gray antenna	50	75	125
Riley Pathfinder-Mechanical	4" long with friction motor and either red or blue body	50	75	125
Riot Police Quad Tractor	3-3/4" white body & chassis, brown interior, red roof with white panel, gold water cannons, gold spotlight with amber lense	15	20	35
Road Repair Unit	10" dark yellow Land Rover with battery hatch & trailer with red plastic interior with sign & open panels, stripe & Roadwork	15	25	40

Rocket Age Set	set of eight standard including colored Thunderbird Missile on Trolley, R.A.F. Land Rover, R.A.F. Staff Car, Radar Scanner, Decca Radar	315	470	850
Rocket Launcher & Trailer	1975-80	25	35	60
Roger Clark's Capri	4" white body, black hood, grille & interior, open doors, folding seats, chrome bumpers, clear headlights, red taillights	12	18	30
Rolls-Royce Corniche	5-1/2" different versions with light brown interior, working hood, trunk & two doors, clear windows, folding seats, chrome bumpers	10	15	25
Rolls-Royce Silver Ghost	4-1/2" silver body/hood, charcoal & silver chassis, bronze interior, gold lights, box & tank, clear windows, dash lights, radiator	15	25	40
Rolls-Royce Silver Shadow	4-3/4" metallic white upper/dusty blue lower body, working hood, trunk & two doors, clear windows, folding seats, chrome bumpers	30	45	75
Rolls-Royce Silver Shadow	4-3/4" metallic silver upper/metallic blue lower body, light brown interior, hole in trunk for spare tire mounting	25	40	65
Rolls-Royce Silver Shadow	4-3/4" metallic silver upper/metallic blue lower body, light brown interior, no hole in trunk for spare tire	25	40	65
Rolls-Royce Silver Shadow	4-3/4" metallic blue body, bright blue interior, working hood, trunk & two doors, clear windows, folding seats, spare wheel	25	40	65
Routemaster Bus-Promotionals	4-7/8" different body & interior versions promotional	15	25	40
Rover 2000	3-3/4" metallic blue with red interior or maroon body with yellow interior, gray steering wheel, clear windshields	30	45	75
Rover 2000 Rally	3-3/4" two different versions, metallic dark red body, white roof, shaped wheels, No. 136 & Monte Carlo Rally decal	50	75	125
Rover 2000TC	3-3/4" metallic olive green or maroon one-piece body, light brown interior, chrome bumpers/grille, jewel headlights, red taillights	30	45	75
Rover 2000TC	3-3/4" metallic purple body, light orange interior, black grille, one-piece body, amber windows, chrome bumpers & headlights	25	35	60
Rover 3500	5-1/4" three different body & interior versions, plastic interior, open hood, hatch & two doors, lifting hatch cover	8	12	20
Rover 3500 Police Car	5-1/4" white body, light red interior, red stripes, white plastic roof sign, blue dome light, red & blue Police & badge label	8	12	20
Rover 3500 Triplex	5-1/4" white sides & hatch, blue roof & hood, red plastic interior & trim, detailed engine, red-white-black no. 1	8	12	20
Rover 90	3-7/8" long, one-piece body in several colors, silver headlights, grille and bumpers, smooth wheels, rubber tires; colors available	50	75	125
Rover 90-Mechanical	3-7/8" long with friction motor and red, green, gray or metallic green body	60	90	150

Safari Land Rover & Trailer	black/white Land Rover in two versions: with chrome wheels, 1976; with red wheels, 1977-80	20	30	50
Saint's Jaguar XJS	5-1/4" white body, red interior, black trim, Saint figure hood label, open doors, black grille, bumpers & tow hook, chrome headlights	30	45	75
Saint's Volvo P-1800	3-5/8" long, one-piece white body with red Saint decals on hood, gray base, clear windows, black interior with driver	55	85	175
Saint's Volvo P-1800	3-3/4" three versions of white body with silver trim & different colored Saint decals on hood, driver, one-piece body	55	85	175
Saladin Armored Car	3-1/4" drab olive body, swiveling turret & raising barrel castings, black plastic barrel end & tires, olive cast wheels	30	45	75
Scammell Carrimore Tri-deck Car Transporter	11" orange cab chassis & lower deck, white cab & middle deck, blue top deck (three decks), red interior, black hydraulic cylinders	35	55	95
Scammell Circus Crane Truck	8" red upper cab & silver rear body, light blue crane base & winch crank housing, red interior & tow hook, jewel headlights	175	275	450
Scammell Coop Semi-Trailer Truck	9" white cab & fenders, light blue semi-trailer, red interior, gray bumper base, jewel headlights, black hitch lever, spare wheel	135	210	350
Scammell Ferrymasters Semi-Trailer Truck	9-1/4" long, white cab, red interior, yellow chassis, black fenders, clear windows, jewel headlights, cast wheels, plastic tires	60	90	150
Scania Bulk Carrier	5-5/8" long, white cab, blue and white silos, ladders and catwalk, amber windows, blue British Sugar decals, Whizz Wheels	6	9	15
Scania Bulk Carrier	5-5/8" long, white cab, orange and white silos, clear windows, orange screen, black/orange Spillers Flour decals	6	9	15
Scania Container Truck	5-1/2" long, yellow truck and box with red Ryder Truck rental decals, clear windows, black exhaust stack, red rear doors	6	9	15
Scania Container Truck	5-1/2" long, blue cab with blue and white box and rear doors, white deck, Securicor Parcels Decals, in 2 rear door colors	6	9	15
Scania Container Truck	5-1/2" long, white cab and box with BRS Truck Rental decals, blue windows, red screen, roof and rear doors	6	9	15
Scania Dump Truck	5-3/4" long, white cab with green tipper, black/green Barratt decals, black exhaust and hydraulic cylinders, spoked Whizz Wheels	6	9	15
Scania Dump Truck	5-3/4" long, yellow truck and tipper with black Wimpey decals, in two versions: either clear or green windows	6	9	15
Security Van	4" long, black body, blue windows and dome light, yellow/black Security decals, Whizz Wheels	6	9	15
Service Ramp	accessory	30	45	75
Shadow-Ford Racing Car	5-5/8" long, black body and base with white/black #17, UOP and American flag decals, cast chrome suspension and pipes	10	15	25

Shadow-Ford Racing Car	5-5/8" long, white body, red stripes, driver, chrome plastic pipes, mirrors and steering wheel, in two versions	10	15	25
Shell or BP Garage	gas station/garage with pumps and other accessories in two versions: Shell or B.P., each set	295	450	750
Shelvoke & Drewry Garbage Truck	5-7/8" long, orange cab, silver body with City Sanitation decals, black interior, grille and bumpers, clear windows	15	25	40
Silver Jubilee Landau	Landua with four horses, two footmen, two riders, Queen and Prince figures, and Corgi dog, in two versions	15	25	40
Silver Jubilee London Transport Bus	4-7/8" long, silver body with red interior, no passengers, decals read "Woolworth Welcomes the World" and "The Queen's Silver	12	18	30
Silver Streak Jet Dragster	6-1/4" long, metallic blue body with sponsor and flag decals on tank, silver engine, orange plastic jet and nose cone	12	18	30
Silverstone Racing Layout	seven vehicle set with accessories; Vanwall, Lotus IX, Aston Martin, Mercedes 300SL, BRM, Ford Thunderbird, Land Rover Truck	400	600	1200
Simca 1000	3-1/2" chrome plated body, #8 & red-white-blue stripe decals, one-piece body, clear windshield, red interior	30	45	75
Simon Snorkel Fire Engine	10-1/2" long, red body with yellow interior, blue windows and dome lights, chrome deck, black hose reels and hydraulic cylinders	30	45	75
Simon Snorkel Fire Engine	9-7/8" long, red body with yellow interior, two snorkle arms, rotating base, five firemen in cab and one more in basket	35	55	90
Skyscraper Tower Crane	9-1/8" tall, red body with yellow chassis and booms, gold hook, gray loads of block, black/white Skyscraper decals	30	45	75
Spider-Bike	4-1/2" medium blue body, one-piece body, dark blue plastic front body & seat, blue & red Spider-Man figure, amber windshield	40	60	100
Spider-Buggy	5-1/8" red body, blue hood, clear windows, dark blue dash, seat & crane, chrome base with bumper & steps. silver headlights	50	75	125
Spider-Copter	5-5/8" long, blue body with Spider-Man decals, red plastic legs, tongue and tail rotor, black windows and main rotor	30	45	85
Spider-Man Set	set of three: Spider-Bike, Spider-Copter and Spider-Buggy	80	120	225
Standard Vanguard	3-5/8" long, one-piece red and white body, clear windows, silver lights, grille and bumpers, smooth wheels, rubber tires	50	75	125
Standard Vanguard RAF Staff Car	3-3/4" long, blue body with friction motor, RAF decals	55	85	140
Standard Vanguard-Mechanical	3-5/8" long, with friction motor and red/off-white body with black or gray base, or red/gray body	55	85	140
Starsky & Hutch Ford Torino	5-3/4" red one-piece body, white trim, light yellow interior, clear windows, chrome bumpers, grille & headlights, orange taillights	50	75	100
STP Patrick Eagle Racing Car	5-5/8" long, red body with red/white/black STP and #20 decals, chrome lower engine and suspension, black plastic upper engine	20	30	50

Stromberg Jet Ranger Helicopter	5-5/8" long, black body with yellow trim and interior, clear windows, black plastic rotors, white/blue decals	30	45	85
Studebaker Golden Hawk	4-1/8" long, one-piece body in several colors, clear windows, silver lights, grille and bumpers, smooth wheels, rubber tires	55	85	140
Studebaker Golden Hawk-Mechanical	4-1/8" long, with friction motor and white body with gold trim	70	105	175
Stunt Motorcycle	3" long, made for Corgi Rockets race track, gold cycle, blue rider with yellow helmet, clear windshield, plastic tires	70	105	175
SU-100 Medium Tank	5-5/8" long, olive and cream camo upper body, gray lower, working hatch and barrel, black treads, red star and #103 decals	30	50	80
Sunbeam Imp Police Car	3-1/4" white or light blue body, tan interior, driver, black or white hood & lower doors, dome light, Police decals, cast wheels	25	40	65
Sunbeam Imp Rally	3-3/8" long, metallic blue body with white stripes, Monte Carlo Rally and #77 decals, cast wheels	20	35	55
Super Karts	two karts, orange and blue, Whizz Wheels in front, slicks on rear, silver and gold drivers	12	18	30
Superman Set	set of three: Supermobile, Daily Planet Helicopter and Metropolis Police Car	70	120	225
Supermobile	5-1/2" blue body, red, chrome or gray fists, red interior, clear canopy, driver, chrome arms with removeable "striking fists"	30	45	75
Supervan	4-5/8" long, silver van with Superman decals, working rear doors, chrome spoked wheels	15	25	50
Surtees TS9 Racing Car	4-5/8" long, black upper engine, chrome lower engine, pipes and exhaust, driver, Brook Bond Oxo-Rob Walker decals	12	18	30
Surtees TS9B Racing Car	4-3/8" long, red body with white stripes and wing, black plastic lower engine, driver, chrome upper engine, pipes, suspension	12	18	30
Talbot-Matra Rancho	4-3/4" long, working tailgate and hatch, clear windows, plastic interior, black bumpers, grille and tow hook, in several colors	10	15	25
Tandem Disc Harrow	3-5/8" long, yellow main frame, red upper frame, working wheels linkage, unpainted linkage and cast discs, black plastic tires	15	20	35
Tarzan Set	metallic green Land Rover with trailer, cage and other accessories	90	135	275
Thunderbird Bermuda Taxi	4" white body with blue, yellow, green plastic canopy with red fringe, yellow interior, driver, yellow & black labels	50	75	125
Thunderbird Missile & Trolley	5-1/2" ice blue or silver missile, RAF blue trolley, red rubber nose cone, plastic tow bar, steering front & rear axles	55	85	165
Thwaites Tusker Skip Dumper	3-1/8" yellow body, chassis & tipper, driver & seat, hydraulic cylinder, red wheels, black tires two sizes, name labels	10	15	25

Tiger Mark I Tank	6" tan & green camouflage finish, German emblem, swiveling turret & raising barrel castings, black plastic barrel end, antenna	30	45	75
Tipping Farm Trailer	5-1/8" long, cast chassis and tailgate, red plastic tipper and wheels, black tires, in two versions	10	15	25
Tipping Farm Trailer	4-1/4" long, red working tipper and tailgates, yellow chassis, red plastic wheels, black tires	10	15	25
Tour de France Set	Renault with Paramount Film roof sign, rear platform with cameraman and black camera on tripod, plus bicycle and rider	70	105	200
Tour de France Set	with white Peugeot	25	40	75
Touring Caravan	4-3/4" white body with blue trim, white plastic open roof & door, pale blue interior, red plastic hitch & awning	15	25	40
Tower Wagon & Lamp Standard	red Jeep Tower wagon with yellow basket, workman figure	40	60	100
Toyota 2000 GT	4" metallic dark blue or purple body, cream interior, one-piece body, red gear shift & antenna, two red & two amber taillights	15	25	40
Tractor & Beast Carrier	Fordson tractor, figures & beast carrier	65	100	165
Tractor with Shovel & Trailer	standard colors, No. 69 Massey Ferguson Tractor & 62 Tipping Trailer	65	100	165
Tractor, Trailer & Field Gun	10-3/4" tractor body & chassis, trailer body, base & opening doors, gun chassis & raising barrel castings, brown plastic interior	30	50	80
Transporter & Six Cars	Ford transporter with six cars, Mini DeLuxe, Mini Rally, Mini, Rover, Sunbeam Imp, Ford Cortina Estate Car	250	395	700
Transporter & Six Cars	Scammell transporter with six cars, Mini DeLuxe, Mini, Mini Rally, The Saint's Volvo, Sunbeam Imp, MGC GT	270	415	750
Triumph Acclaim Driving School	4-3/4" dark yellow body with black trim, black roof mounted steering wheel steers front wheels, clear windows, mirrors, bumpers	15	25	40
Triumph Acclaim Driving School	4-3/4" yellow or red body/base, Corgi Motor School decals, black roof mounted steering wheel steers front wheels, clear windows	15	25	40
Triumph Acclaim HLS	4-3/4" metallic peacock blue body/base, black trim, light brown interior, clear windows, mirrors, bumpers, vents, tow hook	12	18	30
Triumph Herald Coupe	3-1/2" long, blue or gold top and lower body, white upper body, red interior, clear windows, silver bumpers, grille, headlights	35	50	85
Triumph TR2	3-1/4" cream body with red seats, light green body with white or cream seats, one-piece body, clear windshield, silver grille	70	105	175
Triumph TR3	2-1/4" metallic olive or cream body, red seats, one-piece body, clear windshield, silver grille, bumpers & headlights	60	90	150
Trojan Heinkel	2-1/2" long, issued in mauve, red or orange body, plastic interior, silver bumpers & headlights, red taillights, suspension	35	55	95

Trojan Heinkel	2-1/2" long, red body, yellow plastic interior, clear windows, silver bumpers & headlights, red taillights, suspension	35	55	95
Trojan Heinkel	2-1/2" long, orange body, yellow plastic interior, clear windows, silver bumpers & headlights, red taillights, suspension	35	55	95
Twin Packs and 2601		6	9	15
Tyrrell P34 Racing Car	4-3/8" long, dark blue body and wings with yellow stripes, #4 and white Elf and Union Jack decals, chrome plastic engine	20	30	55
Tyrrell P34 Racing Car	without yellow decals	20	30	55
Tyrrell-Ford Racing Car	4-5/8" long, dark blue body with blue/black/white Elf and #1 decals, chrome suspension, pipes, mirrors, driver	18	25	45
Unimog Dump Truck	3-3/4" blue cab, yellow tipper, fenders & bumpers, metallic charcoal gray chassis, red interior, black mirrors, gray tow hook	20	30	50
Unimog Dump Truck	4" yellow cab, chassis, rear frame & blue tipper, fenders & bumpers, red interior, no mirrors, gray tow hook, hydraulic cylinders	20	30	50
Unimog Dumper & Priestman Cub Shovel	standard colors, #1145 Mercedes-Benz unimog with Dumper & 1128 Priestman Cub Shovel	70	105	175
Unimog with Snowplow (Mercedes-Benz)	6" four different body versions, red interior, cab, rear body, fender-plow mounting, lower & charcoal upper chassis, rear fenders	30	45	75
U.S. Racing Buggy	3-3/4" long, white body with red/white/blue stars, stripes and USA #7 decals, red base, gold engine, red plastic panels	18	25	45
Vanwall Racing Car	3-3/4" long, clear windshield, unpainted dash, silver pipes and decals, smooth wheels, rubber tires, in three versions: green body	35	55	90
Vauxhall Velox	3-3/4" long, one-piece body in several colors, clear windows, silver lights, grille and bumpers, smooth wheels, rubber tires	50	75	125
Vauxhall Velox-Mechanical	3-3/4" long, with friction motor; orange or red body	60	90	150
Vegas Ford Thunderbird	5-1/4" orange/red body & base, black interior & grille, open hood & trunk, amber windshield, white seats, driver, chrome bumper	25	40	65
VM Polo Mail Car		25	35	60
Volkswagen 1200	3-1/2" seven different versions, plastic interior, one-piece body, silver headlights, red taillights, die cast base & bumpers	20	30	50
Volkswagen 1200 Driving School	3-1/2" metallic red or blue body, yellow interior, gold roof mounted steering wheel that steers, silver headlights, red taillights	25	35	60
Volkswagen 1200 Police Car	3-1/2" two different body versions made for Germany, Netherlands & Switzerland, blue dome light in chrome collar	40	60	100
Volkswagen 1200 Rally	3-1/2" light blue body, off-white plastic interior, silver headlights, red tailights, suspension, Whizz Wheels	20	30	50

Volkswagen 1200	3-1/2" dark yellow body, white roof, red interior & dome light, unpainted base & bumpers, black & white ADAC Strassenwacht	60	90	150
Volkswagen Breakdown Van	4" tan or white body, red interior & equipment boxes, clear windshield, chrome tools, spare wheels, red VW emblem, no lettering	50	75	125
Volkswagen Delivery Van	3-1/4" white upper & red lower body, plastic red or yellow interior, silver bumpers & headlights, red VW emblem, shaped wheels	55	85	140
Volkswagen Driving School	3-1/2" metallic blue body, yellow interior, gold roof mounted steering wheel that steers, silver headlights, red taillights	25	40	70
Volkswagen East African Safari	3-1/2" light red body, brown interior, working front & rear hood, clear windows, spare wheel on roof steers front wheels, jewel headlights	90	135	225
Volkswagen Kombi Bus	3-3/4" off green upper & olive green lower body, red interior, silver bumpers & headlights, red VW emblem, shaped wheels	50	75	125
Volkswagen Military Personnel Carrier	3-1/2" drab olive body, white decals, driver	55	85	140
Volkswagen Pickup	3-1/2" dark yellow body, red interior & rear plastic cover, silver bumpers & headlights, red VW emblem, shaped wheels	45	65	110
Volkswagen Police Car/Foreign Issues	3-1/2" five different versions, one-piece body, red interior, dome light, silver headlights, red taillights, clear windows	60	90	150
Volkswagen Tobler Van	3-1/2" light blue body, plastic interior, silver bumpers, Trans-o-lite headlights & roof panel, shaped wheels, rubber tires	55	85	140
Volvo Concrete Mixer	8-1/4" yellow or orange cab, red or white mixer with yellow & black stripes, rear chassis, chrome chute & unpainted hitch casings	30	45	75
Volvo P-1800	3-1/2" one-piece body with six versions, clear windows, plastic interior, shaped wheels, rubber tires	40	60	100
VW 1500 Karmann-Ghia	3-1/2" three color versions, plastic interior and taillights, front & rear working hoods, clear windshields, silver bumpers	35	55	90
VW Polo	3-3/4" apple green or bright yellow body, black DBP & posthorn (German Post Office) decals, off white interior, black dash	25	40	65
VW Polo	3-3/4" metallic light brown body, off-white interior, black dash, clear windows, silver bumpers, grille & headlights	12	18	30
VW Polo Auto Club Car		15	25	40
VW Polo German Auto Club Car	3-1/2" yellow body, off-white interior, black dash, silver bumpers, grille & headlights, white roof, yellow dome light	25	35	60
VW Polo Police Car	3-1/2" white body, green hood & doors, black dash, silver bumpers, grille & headlights, white roof, blue dome light	15	25	40
VW Polo Turbo	3-3/4" cream body, red interior with red & orange trim, working hatch & two door castings, clear windshield, black plastic dash	12	18	30

VW Racing Tender & Cooper	white VW with racing decals, blue Cooper	50	75	125
VW Racing Tender & Cooper Maserati	two versions: tan or white VW truck, each set	50	75	125
Warner & Swasey Crane	8-1/2" yellow cab & body, blue chassis, blue/yellow stripe decals, red interior, black steering wheel, silver knob, gold hook	30	45	75
White Wheelie Motorcycle	4" long, white body with black/white police decals	15	20	35
Wild Honey Dragster	3" long, yellow body with red/yellow Wild Honey and Jaguar Powered decals, green windows and roof, black grille, driver, Whizz Wheels	25	40	65

Dinky

Cars

Name	Description	Good	Ex	Mint
36A	Armstrong Siddeley, blue or brown	85	130	225
76	Austin A105	65	90	150
106/140A	Austin Atlantic Convertible, blue	65	90	150
	Austin Devon	65	90	150
342	Austin Mini-Moke	20	30	55
131	Cadillac Eldorado	60	95	155
32/30A	Chrysler Airflow	130	250	450
F550	Chrysler Saratoga	70	100	190
F535/24T	Citroen 2 CV	50	70	90
F522/24C	Citroen DS-19	60	90	135
F545	DeSoto Diplomat, green	70	100	190
F545	DeSoto Diplomat, orange	60	85	125
191	Dodge Royal	65	90	150
27D/344	Estate Car	45	70	115
212	Ford Cortina Rally Car	35	55	75
148	Ford Fairlane, pale green	30	55	80
148	Ford Fairlane, South African issue, bright blue	150	300	700
170	Ford Sedan	65	90	150

		Good	Ex	Mint
57/005	Ford Thunderbird (Hong Kong)	40	70	100
F565	Ford Thunderbird, South African Issue, blue	120	250	600
171	Hudson Sedan	65	90	150
238	Jaguar D-Type	60	85	125
157	Jaguar XK 120, green, yellow, red	50	95	135
157	Jaguar XK 120, turquoise, cerise	80	125	250
157	Jaguar XK 120, white	120	200	400
157	Jaguar XK 120, yellow/gray	80	125	250
241	Lotus Racing Car	20	30	50
231	Maserati Race Car	45	75	110
	Morris Oxford	40	75	100
161	Mustang Fastback	35	55	75
132	Packard Convertible	100	175	250
F545	Panhard PL17	45	80	120
F521/24B	Peugeot 403	50	90	135
115	Plymouth Fury Sports	50	75	100
	Plymouth Station Wagon	60	100	200
F524/24E	Renault Dauphine	60	85	125
30B	Rolls Royce (1940s Version)	60	85	125
198	Rolls Royce Phantom V	50	75	100
145	Singer Vogue	50	75	100
153	Standard Vanguard	60	85	125
F24Y/540	Studebaker Commander	65	90	150
166	Sunbeam Rapier	30	70	140
24C	Town Sedan	85	130	200
105	Triumph TR-2, gray	60	85	135
105	Triumph TR-2, yellow	75	120	200
164	Vauxhall Cresta	65	90	150
129	Volkswagen 1300 Sedan	50	75	100
187	VW Karman Ghia	45	80	125

Emergency Vehicles

Name	Description	Good	Ex	Mint

		Good	Ex	Mint
30F	Ambulance	100	160	275
F501	Citroen DS19 Police	75	100	175
F25D/562	Citroen Fire Van	80	110	250
555/955	Commer Fire Engine	60	85	135
F32D/899	Delahaye Fire Truck	120	190	375
195	Fire Chief Land Rover	35	50	85
F551	Ford Taunus Police	65	90	150
255	Mersey Tunnel Police	60	85	135
244	Plymouth Police Car	25	35	50
268	Range Rover Ambulance	25	35	50
25H/25	Streamlined Fire Engine (Post-War)	75	100	175
263	Superior Criterion Ambulance	50	75	100
956	Turntable Fire Escape (Bedford)	75	100	175
251	USA Police Car (Pontiac)	35	50	85
278	Vauxhall Victor Ambulance	55	85	115

Trucks

Name	Description	Good	Ex	Mint
974	A.E.C. Hoyner Transporter	60	90	130
471	Austin Van "Nestles"	60	110	175
472	Austin Van "Raleigh"	60	110	175
470	Austin Van "Shell/BP"	60	110	175
14A/400	B.E.V. Truck	15	30	70
482	Bedford Van "Dinky Toys"	60	115	200
F898	Berliet Transformer Carrier	100	200	450
923	Big Bedford "Heinz" (Baked Beans)	100	165	300
408/922	Big Bedford (blue/yellow)	90	135	210
408/922	Big Bedford (maroon/fawn)	80	120	185
449	Chevrolet El Camino	35	65	100
F561	Citroen "Cibie" Delivery Van	90	150	350
F586	Citroen Milk Truck	145	275	600
F35A/582	Citroen Wrecker	75	120	250
571/971	Coles Mobile Crane	40	70	110

25B	Covered Wagon ("Carter Paterson")	150	300	750
25B	Covered Wagon (green, gray)	65	115	160
28N	Delivery Van ("Atco", type 2)	200	375	850
28N	Delivery Van ("Atco", type 3)	135	200	350
28E	Delivery Van ("Ensign", type 1)	300	500	1000
28B	Delivery Van ("Pickfords", type 1)	300	500	1000
28B	Delivery Van ("Pickfords", type 2)	200	375	600
30W/421	Electric Articulated Vehicle	60	85	120
941	Foden "Mobilgas" Tanker	145	350	750
942	Foden "Regent" Tanker	135	300	550
503/903	Foden Flat Truck w/ Tailboard 1, gray/blue	140	210	450
503/903	Foden Flat Truck w/ Tailboard 1, red/black	140	210	450
503/903	Foden Flat Truck w/ Tailboard 2, blue/orange	90	150	275
417	Ford Transit Van	15	20	30
25R	Forward Control Wagon	45	65	90
514	Guy Van "Lyons"	275	550	1600
514	Guy Van "Spratts"	135	300	575
431	Guy Warrior 4 Ton	150	270	450
449/451	Johnston Road Sweeper	25	50	75
419/533	Leland Comet Cement Truck	85	150	250
944	Leland Tanker "Shell/BP"	125	215	450
	Leyland Tanker "Corn Products"	700	1200	3000
25F	Market Gardeners Wagon (yellow)	65	115	160
280	Midland Bank	60	85	120
986	Mighty Antar with Propeller	125	215	400
273	Mini Mino Van ("R.A.C.")	65	115	150
274	Mini Minor Van (Joseph Mason Paints)	150	300	500
260	Morris Royal Mail	65	90	150
22C	Motor Truck (red, green, blue)	80	120	200
22C	Motor Truck (red/blue)	150	350	650
F32C	Panhard ("Esso")	75	120	170
F32AJ	Panhard ("Kodak")	140	250	450
F32AB	Panhard ("SNCF")	100	165	280

		Good	Ex	Mint
25D	Petrol Wagon ("Power")	150	300	500
982/582	Pullmore Car Transporter	75	125	175
F561	Renault Estafette	65	90	150
F571	Saviem Race Horse Van	125	225	400
F33C/579	Simca Glass Truck (gray/green)	75	120	170
F33C/579	Simca Glass Truck (yellow/green)	100	150	250
30P/440	Studebaker Tanker ("Mobilgas")	80	120	200
	Studebaker Tanker ("Castrol")	125	275	400
422/30R	Thames Flat Truck	45	75	110
31B/451	Trojan ("Dunlop")	70	110	185
F38A/895	Unic Bucket Truck	75	120	225
F36A/897	Willeme Log Truck	75	120	200
F36B/896	Willeme Semi	85	130	225

Doepke

Name	Description	Good	Ex	Mint
Adams Road Grader	26" long, orange, #2006	115	190	290
Adams Road Grader	26" long, yellow, #2006	165	240	340
American LaFrance Aerial Ladder Truck	33-1/2" long, red, #2008	195	275	350
American LaFrance Improved Aerial Ladder Truck	33-1/2" long, red, with outriggers and cast aluminum ladder, #2014	225	310	385
American LaFrance Pumper	19" long, red, #2010	225	310	395
American LaFrance Searchlight Truck	white with battery-operated search light, #2023	950	1200	1800
Barber-Greene Bucket Loader	on tracks, 18" tall, early model w/swivel chute, green, #2001	330	410	525
Barber-Greene Bucket Loader	on tracks, 18" tall, later model w/out swivel chute, green, #2001	225	300	425
Barber-Greene Bucket Loader	on tracks; 18" tall, later model w/out swivel chute, orange, #2001	275	350	475
Barber-Greene Bucket Loader	on wheels, 22" long, green, #2013	250	350	475
Bulldozer	15" long, yellow, #2012	375	450	550
Clark Airport Tractor and Trailers Set	26-1/2" long; three pieces: red tractor, green trailer, yellow trailer, #2015	325	400	500
Euclid Truck	27" long, orange, #2009	175	250	330
Euclid Truck	27" long, forest green, #2009	200	275	350
Euclid Truck	27" long, olive green, #2009	225	300	395

Heiliner Scraper	29" long, red, #2011	220	300	395
Jaeger Concrete Mixer	15" long, yellow w/black drum, #2002	225	310	450
Jaguar	18" long, kit or built, light blue or red, #2018	395	495	565
MG Auto	15-1/2" long, kit, aluminum body; red, yellow, or gray primer, #2017	325	410	495
Unit Crane	11" long, without boom, orange, with finger wheel, #2007	225	300	375
Unit Crane	11" long, without boom, orange, w/out finger wheel, #2007	195	275	350
Wooldridge Earth Hauler	25", yellow, #2000	165	230	350

Auburn race car with goggled driver, rubber, 10 inches long. EXC-$100

Hot Wheels 1932 Ford Vicky, #6250, 1969. EXC-$50

Hot Wheels

Name		Description	Year	VG	EXC
9649	'31 Doozie	orange, blackwall	1977	8	15
9649	'31 Doozie	orange, redline	1977	15	60
	'32 Ford Delivery	white/pink, Early Times logo, blackwalls	1993	15	30
4367	'40 Ford Two-Door	black with white hubs, Real Rider	1983	15	40
9647	'56 Hi Tail Hauler	orange, blackwall	1977	10	35
9647	'56 Hi Tail Hauler	orange, redline	1977	15	60
9638	'57 Chevy	red, blackwall	1977	10	30
9638	'57 Chevy	red, redline	1977	20	85
9522	'57 T-Bird	black with white hubs, Real Rider	1986	30	150
4352	3 Window '34	black, Real Rider	1984	50	160
	A-OK	red, Real Rider	1981	75	275
	Alien	blue	1988	10	20
6968	Alive '55	assorted	1973	75	500
6968	Alive '55	blue	1974	90	350
6968	Alive '55	green	1974	50	110
9210	Alive '55	chrome, blackwall	1977	15	30
9210	Alive '55	chrome, redline	1977	15	55
6451	Ambulance	assorted	1970	30	50
9118	American Hauler	blue	1976	20	50
9089	American Tipper	red	1976	20	50
7662	American Victory	light blue	1975	20	60
6460	AMX/2	assorted	1971	30	100
9243	Aw Shoot	olive	1976	15	25
7670	Backwoods Bomb	green, redline or blackwall	1977	30	120
7670	Backwoods Bomb	light blue	1975	40	125
8258	Baja Bruiser	blue, redline or blackwall	1977	25	85
8258	Baja Bruiser	light green	1976	300	1000
8258	Baja Bruiser	orange	1974	30	75
8258	Baja Bruiser	yellow, blue in tampo	1974	200	900
8258	Baja Bruiser	yellow, magenta in tampo	1974	200	900
6217	Beatnik Bandit	assorted	1968	15	45
	Black Passion	black	1990	15	45
6406	Boss Hoss	assorted	1971	75	175
6499	Boss Hoss	chrome, Club Kit	1970	50	160
6264	Brabham-Repco F1	assorted	1969	10	25
1690	Bronco 4-Wheeler	Toys R Us	1981	50	120
6178	Bugeye	assorted	1971	30	75
6976	Buzz Off	assorted	1973	75	400

No.	Name	Description	Year		
6976	Buzz Off	blue	1974	30	90
6976	Buzz Off	gold plated, redline or blackwall	1977	15	30
6187	Bye Focal	assorted	1971	90	375
2196	Bywayman	blue, red interior	1989	40	50
2509	Bywayman	Toys R Us	1979	50	100
	Cadillac Seville	gold, Mexican, Real Rider	1987	50	100
	Cadillac Seville	gray, French, Real Rider	1983	40	100
2879	Captain America	white, Scene Machine	1979	40	100
6420	Carabo	assorted	1970	20	60
7617	Carabo	light green	1974	25	70
7617	Carabo	yellow	1974	400	1200
6452	Cement Mixer	assorted	1970	20	45
6256	Chapparal 2G	assorted	1969	15	35
7671	Chevy Monza 2+2	orange	1975	40	110
9202	Chevy Monza 2+2	light green	1975	200	600
7665	Chief's Special Cruiser	red	1975	30	75
7665	Chief's Special Cruiser	red, blackwall	1977	10	20
7665	Chief's Special Cruiser	red, redline	1977	25	65
3303	Circus Cats	white 60	1981	50	120
6251	Classic '31 Ford Woody	assorted	1969	20	70
6250	Classic '32 Ford Vicky	assorted	1969	20	50
6253	Classic '36 Ford Coupe	assorted	1969	15	50
6253	Classic '36 Ford Coupe	blue	1969	10	25
6252	Classic '57 T-Bird	assorted	1969	25	70
2529	Classic Caddy	red/white/blue, Museum Exhibit car	1992	15	35
	Classic Cobra	blue with white hubs, Real Rider	1985	40	80
6404	Classic Nomad	assorted	1970	30	110
6466	Cockney Cab	assorted	1971	30	100
6266	Continental Mark III	assorted	1969	20	60
9120	Cool One	plum, blackwall	1977	20	40
9241	Corvette Stingray	red	1976	30	80
9506	Corvette Stingray	chrome	1976	20	50
9506	Corvette Stingray	chrome, blackwall set only	1977	55	0
6267	Custom AMX	assorted	1969	25	80
6211	Custom Barracuda	assorted	1968	35	325
6208	Custom Camaro	assorted	1968	50	375
6208	Custom Camaro	white enamel	1968	300	2000
6268	Custom Charger	assorted	1969	50	190
6215	Custom Corvette	assorted	1968	50	250
6205	Custom Cougar	assorted	1968	60	275
6218	Custom El Dorado	assorted	1968	25	100
6212	Custom Firebird	assorted	1968	45	220
6213	Custom Fleetside	assorted	1968	60	250
6206	Custom Mustang	assorted	1968	75	425
6206	Custom Mustang	assorted with open hood scoops or ribbed windows	1968	400	1200
6269	Custom Police Cruiser	assorted	1969	55	200
6207	Custom T-Bird	assorted	1968	50	165

6220	Custom VW Bug	assorted	1968	15	60
3255	Datsun 200SX	maroon, Canada	1982	75	175
6401	Demon	assorted	1970	15	35
6210	Deora	assorted	1968	60	375
5880	Double Header	assorted	1973	120	450
6975	Double Vision	assorted	1973	110	400
6967	Dune Daddy	assorted	1973	110	400
6967	Dune Daddy	light green	1975	25	75
6967	Dune Daddy	orange	1975	175	450
8273	El Rey Special	dark blue	1974	225	450
8273	El Rey Special	green	1974	40	75
8273	El Rey Special	light blue	1974	200	650
8273	El Rey Special	light green	1974	95	300
7650	Emergency Squad	red	1975	15	50
6471	Evil Weevil	assorted	1971	40	85
6417	Ferrari 312P	assorted	1970	20	30
6973	Ferrari 312P	assorted	1973	300	1100
6973	Ferrari 312P	red	1974	40	80
6021	Ferrari 512-S	assorted	1972	75	250
6469	Fire Chief Cruiser	red	1970	10	25
6454	Fire Engine	red	1970	25	60
	Flat Out 442	green, Canada	1984	75	120
6214	Ford J-Car	assorted	1968	10	60
6257	Ford MK IV	assorted	1969	10	35
9119	Formula 5000	white	1976	20	45
9511	Formula 5000	chrome	1976	30	65
6018	Fuel Tanker	assorted	1971	60	175
6005	Funny Money	gray	1972	60	325
7621	Funny Money	gray, blackwall	1977	20	65
7621	Funny Money	gray, redline	1977	25	75
7621	Funny Money	magenta	1974	30	80
9645	GMC Motorhome	orange, blackwall	1977	10	25
9645	GMC Motorhome	orange, redline	1977	200	600
	Gold Passion	gold, Toy Fair promo	1992	40	100
	Good Humor Truck	white	1986	55	125
	Goodyear Blimp	chrome, Mattel promo	1992	65	0
6461	Grass Hopper	assorted	1971	25	55
7621	Grass Hopper	light green	1974	30	90
7622	Grass Hopper	light green, no engine	1975	90	350
	Greased Gremlin	red, Mexican, Real Rider	1987	100	300
7652	Gremlin Grinder	green	1975	25	60
9201	Gremlin Grinder	chrome, blackwall	1977	15	30
1789	GT Racer	blue	1989	25	60
9090	Gun Bucket	olive	1976	25	60
9090	Gun Bucket	olive, blackwall	1977	25	60
7664	Gun Slinger	olive	1975	25	50
7664	Gun Slinger	olive, blackwall	1976	15	30
6458	Hairy Hauler	assorted	1971	20	50

	Hammer Down	red set only	1980	125	0
6189	Heavy Chevy	chrome, Club Kit	1970	50	175
6408	Heavy Chevy	assorted	1970	25	55
7619	Heavy Chevy	light green	1974	200	750
7619	Heavy Chevy	yellow	1974	75	175
9212	Heavy Chevy	chrome, redline or blackwall	1977	40	120
6979	Hiway Robber	assorted	1973	75	250
6175	Hood	assorted	1971	15	90
	Hot Bird	blue	1980	40	100
	Hot Bird	brown	1980	45	120
6219	Hot Heap	assorted	1968	10	35
2881	Human Torch	black	1979	10	25
6184	Ice T	yellow	1971	40	200
6980	Ice T	assorted	1973	200	650
6980	Ice T	light green	1974	30	75
6980	Ice T	light green, blackwall	1977	20	35
6980	Ice T	yellow with hood tampo	1974	200	525
2850	Incredible Hulk Van	white, Scene Machine	1979	45	100
6263	Indy Eagle	assorted	1969	10	25
6263	Indy Eagle	gold	1969	50	200
9186	Inferno	yellow	1976	30	60
6421	Jack Rabbit Special	white	1970	10	55
6421	Jack-in-the-Box Promotion	white, Jack rabbit w/decals	1970	225	0
6179	Jet Threat	assorted	1971	45	160
8235	Jet Threat II	magenta	1976	35	80
9183	Khaki Kooler	olive	1976	15	30
6411	King Kuda	assorted	1970	25	100
6411	King Kuda	chrome, Club Kit	1970	30	120
8272	Large Charge	green	1975	25	60
9643	Letter Getter	white, blackwall	1977	5	10
9643	Letter Getter	white, redline	1977	175	550
6412	Light My Firebird	assorted	1970	20	55
6254	Lola GT 70	assorted	1969	10	30
6262	Lotus Turbine	assorted	1969	10	30
9185	Lowdown	gold plated, redline or blackwall	1977	15	30
9185	Lowdown	light blue	1976	30	75
6423	Mantis	assorted	1970	15	40
6277	Masterati Mistral	assorted	1969	50	125
9184	Maxi Taxi	yellow	1976	25	60
9184	Maxi Taxi	yellow, blackwall	1977	20	60
6255	McClaren M6A	assorted	1969	10	40
6275	Mercedes 280SL	assorted	1969	10	40
6962	Mercedes 280SL	assorted	1973	100	450
6169	Mercedes C-111	assorted	1972	80	250
6978	Mercedes C-111	assorted	1973	300	1200
6978	Mercedes C-111	red	1974	40	90
6414	Mighty Maverick	assorted	1970	35	85

7653	Mighty Maverick	blue	1975	30	65
9209	Mighty Maverick	chrome, blackwall	1977	25	50
9209	Mighty Maverick	light green	1975	200	400
6456	Mod-Quad	assorted	1970	15	40
6970	Mongoose	red/blue	1973	400	1400
6410	Mongoose Funny Car	red	1970	50	160
5954	Mongoose II	metallic blue	1971	75	350
5952	Mongoose Rail Dragster	blue, two pack	1971	75	600
7660	Monte Carlo Stocker	yellow	1975	45	90
7660	Monte Carlo Stocker	yellow, blackwall	1977	20	50
7668	Motocross I	red	1975	50	160
2853	Motorcross Team Van	red, Scene Machine	1979	50	125
	Movin' On	white set only	1980	125	0
6455	Moving Van	assorted	1970	50	125
7664	Mustang Stocker	white	1975	400	1200
7664	Mustang Stocker	yellow with magenta tampo	1975	90	300
9203	Mustang Stocker	chrome	1976	40	90
9203	Mustang Stocker	chrome, redline or blackwall	1977	40	90
9203	Mustang Stocker	yellow with red in tampo	1975	300	900
5185	Mutt Mobile	assorted	1971	75	175
3927	NASCAR Stocker	white, NASCAR/Mountain Dew base	1983	90	165
9244	Neet Streeter	blue	1976	20	60
9244	Neet Streeter	blue, blackwall	1977	15	30
9510	Neet Streeter	chrome	1976	20	40
9510	Neet Streeter	chrome, blackwall set only	1977	40	0
6405	Nitty Gritty Kitty	assorted	1970	25	65
6000	Noodle Head	assorted	1971	40	150
6981	Odd Job	assorted	1973	100	600
9642	Odd Rod	plum, blackwall or redline	1977	200	400
9642	Odd Rod	yellow, blackwall	1977	20	40
9642	Odd Rod	yellow, redline	1977	30	50
1695	Old Number 5	red, no louvers	1982	10	20
6467	Olds 442	assorted	1971	275	625
5881	Open Fire		1972	100	400
6402	Paddy Wagon	blue	1970	15	30
6966	Paddy Wagon	blue	1973	30	120
6966	Paddy Wagon	blue, blackwall	1977	10	20
7661	Paramedic	white	1975	25	55
7661	Paramedic	yellow	1976	25	45
7661	Paramedic	yellow, blackwall or redline	1977	25	45
6419	Peepin' Bomb	assorted	1970	10	25
2023	Pepsi Challenger	yellow funny car	1982	15	20
6183	Pit Crew Car	white	1971	50	450
9240	Poison Pinto	green, blackwall	1977	10	20
9240	Poison Pinto	light green	1976	25	60
9508	Poison Pinto	chrome	1976	20	40
9508	Poison Pinto	chrome, blackwall set only	1977	50	0
6963	Police Cruiser	white	1973	250	600

6963	Police Cruiser	white	1974	35	90
6963	Police Cruiser	white with blue light	1977	30	65
6963	Police Cruiser	white, blackwall	1977	25	45
6972	Porsche 911	orange	1975	25	60
7648	Porsche 911	black, six pack blackwall	1977	175	350
7648	Porsche 911	yellow	1975	40	75
9206	Porsche 911	chrome, redline or blackwall	1977	20	40
6416	Porsche 917	assorted	1970	15	40
6972	Porsche 917	assorted	1973	300	950
6972	Porsche 917	orange	1974	40	75
6972	Porsche 917	orange, blackwall	1977	15	25
6972	Porsche 917	red	1974	175	500
6459	Power Pad	assorted	1970	25	65
6965	Prowler	assorted	1973	200	1000
6965	Prowler	light green	1974	500	1000
6965	Prowler	orange	1974	35	75
9207	Prowler	chrome, blackwall	1977	35	70
6216	Python	assorted	1968	10	55
2620	Race Ace	white	1986	15	30
6194	Racer Rig	red/white	1971	100	375
	Racing Team Van	yellow, Scene Machine	1981	40	60
7659	Ramblin' Cruiser	white without phone number	1977	15	20
7659	Ramblin' Wrecker	white	1975	20	45
7659	Ramblin' Wrecker	white, blackwall	1977	10	20
7666	Ranger Rig	green	1975	20	65
7616	Rash I	blue	1974	300	800
7616	Rash I	green	1974	35	65
5699	Rear Engine Mongoose	red	1972	200	600
5856	Rear Engine Snake	yellow	1972	200	600
6400	Red Baron	red	1970	15	40
6964	Red Baron	red	1973	30	200
6964	Red Baron	red, blackwall	1977	10	20
	Red Passion	red	1994	10	20
3304	Rescue Squad	red, Scene Machine	1982	50	90
7615	Road King Truck	yellow set only	1974	400	1000
9088	Rock Buster	yellow	1976	20	35
9088	Rock Buster	yellow, blackwall	1977	10	15
9507	Rock Buster	chrome	1976	15	30
9507	Rock Buster	chrome, blackwall set only	1977	45	0
6186	Rocket Bye Baby	assorted	1971	60	200
8259	Rodger Dodger	blue	1974	200	550
8259	Rodger Dodger	gold plated, blackwall or redline	1977	25	70
8259	Rodger Dodger	magenta	1974	40	90
6276	Rolls-Royce Silver Shadow	assorted	1969	25	45
	Ruby Red Passion	red	1992	25	45
6468	S'Cool Bus	yellow	1971	175	750
2854	S.W.A.T. Van	blue, Scene Machine	1979	70	110

6403	Sand Crab	assorted	1970	10	40
7651	Sand Drifter	green	1975	150	375
7651	Sand Drifter	yellow	1975	20	50
6974	Sand Witch	assorted	1973	100	400
6193	Scooper	assorted	1971	100	325
6413	Seasider	assorted	1970	50	120
9644	Second Wind	white, blackwall or redline	1977	35	75
6265	Shelby Turbine	assorted	1969	10	25
6176	Short Order	assorted	1971	35	100
9646	Show Hoss II	yellow, blackwall	1977	35	60
9646	Show Hoss II	yellow, redline	1977	300	600
6982	Show-Off	assorted	1973	140	400
6022	Sidekick	assorted	1972	80	200
6209	Silhouette	assorted	1968	20	90
8261	Sir Rodney Roadster	yellow, blackwall	1977	25	40
8261	Sir Sidney Roadster	light green	1974	325	650
8261	Sir Sidney Roadster	orange/brown	1974	375	700
8261	Sir Sidney Roadster	yellow	1974	25	65
6003	Six Shooter	assorted	1971	75	225
6436	Sky Show Fleetside (Aero Launcher)	assorted	1970	400	850
6969	Snake	white/yellow	1973	600	1500
5951	Snake Dragster	white, two-pack	1971	75	0
6409	Snake Funny Car	assorted	1970	60	300
5953	Snake II	white	1971	60	275
6020	Snorkel	assorted	1971	60	150
2855	Space Van	gray, Scene Machine	1979	45	100
6006	Special Delivery	blue	1971	45	150
2852	Spider-Man	black	1979	10	30
2852	Spider-Man Van	white, Scene Machine	1979	50	125
6261	Splittin' Image	assorted	1969	10	35
9641	Spoiler Sport	light green, blackwall	1977	5	10
9641	Spoiler Sport	light green, redline	1977	15	25
9521	Staff Car	olive, blackwall	1977	500	750
9521	Staff Car	olive, six-pack only	1977	400	750
8260	Steam Roller	white	1974	25	70
8260	Steam Roller	white with seven stars	1974	100	300
9208	Steam Roller	chrome with seven stars	1977	100	300
9208	Steam Roller	chrome, redline or blackwall	1977	20	40
7669	Street Eater	black	1975	30	50
9242	Street Rodder	black	1976	40	85
9242	Street Rodder	black, blackwall	1977	20	45
6971	Street Snorter	assorted	1973	110	400
6188	Strip Teaser	assorted	1971	65	200
6418	Sugar Caddy	assorted	1971	20	70
9505	Super Chromes	chrome, blackwall six-pack	1977	375	0
7649	Super Van	black, blackwall	1977	15	25
7649	Super Van	blue	1975	650	0

7649	Super Van	plum	1975	90	250
7649	Super Van	Toys-R-Us	1975	100	350
9205	Super Van	chrome	1976	20	40
6004	Superfine Turbine	assorted	1973	300	1100
6007	Sweet "16"	assorted	1973	90	375
6422	Swingin' Wing	assorted	1970	15	40
6177	T-4-2	assorted	1971	35	165
9648	T-Totaller	black, blackwall	1977	10	30
9648	T-Totaller	black, Red Line, six-pack only	1977	500	1000
9648	T-Totaller	brown, blackwall	1977	10	30
6019	Team Trailer	white/red	1971	95	225
2882	Thing, The	dark blue	1979	15	35
2880	Thor	yellow	1979	10	30
9793	Thrill Driver Torino	red/white, blackwall, set of two	1977	275	0
6407	TNT-Bird	assorted	1970	25	70
7630	Top Eliminator	blue	1974	50	165
7630	Top Eliminator	gold plated, redline or blackwall	1977	25	45
6260	Torero	assorted	1969	10	60
7647	Torino Stocker	gold plated, redline or blackwall	1977	30	70
7647	Torino Stocker	red	1975	35	70
7655	Tough Customer	olive	1975	15	55
6450	Tow Truck	assorted	1970	30	80
6424	Tri-Baby	assorted	1970	15	40
	Turbo Mustang	blue	1984	35	65
6259	Turbofire	assorted	1969	10	45
6258	Twinmill	assorted	1969	10	35
8240	Twinmill II	orange	1976	10	35
8240	Twinmill II	orange, blackwall	1977	10	25
9502	Twinmill II	chrome, blackwall set only	1977	45	0
9509	Twinmill II	chrome	1976	20	45
7654	Vega Bomb	orange, blackwall	1977	25	55
7658	Vega Bomb	green	1975	250	800
7658	Vega Bomb	orange	1975	40	85
7620	Volkswagen	orange with bug on roof	1974	30	60
7620	Volkswagen	orange with stripes on roof	1974	100	400
6274	Volkswagen Beach Bomb	surf boards in rear window	1969	4500	0
6274	Volkswagen Beach Bomb	surf boards on side raised panels	1969	50	275
	VW Bug	pink, Real Rider	1993	15	35
7654	Warpath	white	1975	50	110
6192	Waste Wagon	assorted	1971	90	325
6001	What-4	assorted	1971	50	150
6457	Whip Creamer	assorted	1970	15	40
7618	Winnipeg	yellow	1974	90	300
6977	Xploder	assorted	1973	100	500
9639	Z Whiz	blue	1982	20	55
9639	Z Whiz	gray, blackwall	1977	10	20
9639	Z Whiz	gray, redline	1977	25	55
9639	Z Whiz	white, redline	1977	1500	0

Hubley

Cars

Make	Description	Good	Ex	Mint
Auto and Trailer	cast iron, 6-3/4" long, 1939	175	235	295
Auto and Trailer	cast iron, sedan 7-1/4" long, trailer 7-1/8" long, 1936	185	245	315
Buick Convertible	opening top, 6-1/2" long	50	65	90
Buick Convertible	top down, 6-1/2" long	45	60	80
Cadillac	black rubber tires, die cast with tin bottom plate	25	40	70
Car Carrier With Four Cars	cast iron, 10" long	300	475	675
Chrysler Airflow	6" long	145	200	350
Chrysler Airflow	battery-operated lights, cast iron, 1934	1250	1900	2750
Chrysler Airflow	cast iron, 4-1/2" long	110	195	325
Coupe	cast iron, 9-1/2" long, 1928	900	1400	1800
Coupe	cast iron, 8-1/2" long, 1928	600	1100	1500
Coupe	cast iron, 7" long, 1928	400	650	800
Ford Convertible	cast iron, V/8, 1930s	65	100	185
Ford Coupe	cast iron, V-8, 1930s	65	100	185
Ford Model-T	movable parts	100	150	200
Ford Sedan	cast iron, V-8, 1930s	65	100	185
Ford Town Car	cast iron, V-8, 1930s	65	100	185
Limousine	cast iron, 7" long, 1918	250	325	400
Lincoln Zephyr	1937	250	350	450
Mr. Magoo Car	old timer car, battery-operated, 9" long, 1961	75	115	150
Open Touring Car	cast iron, 7-1/2" long, 1911	675	900	1250
Packard Roadster	9-1/2" long, 1930	90	145	250
Packard Straight 8	hood raises, detailed cast motor, cast iron, 11" long, 1927	7500	10000	15000
Race Car #22	cast iron, 7-1/2" long	40	55	85
Race Car #2241	7" long, 1930s	50	75	100
Racer	white rubber wheels, cast iron, 7" long	200	300	400
Racer	cast iron, 10-3/4" long, 1931	75	150	250
Racer	nickel-plated driver, cast iron, 4-3/4" long, 1960s	75	115	150
Racer	red with black wheels, silver grille and driver, 7-1/2" long	35	55	75
Racer #12	die cast, prewar	60	95	125
Racer #629	7" long, 1939	50	75	135
Roadster	cast iron, 7-1/2" long, 1920	75	150	225
Sedan	cast iron, 7" long, 1920s	175	265	350

		Good	Ex	Mint
Service Car	5" long, 1930s	75	115	150
Speedster	cast iron, 7" long, 1911	125	225	350
Station Wagon	die cast	50	75	100
Streamlined Racer	cast iron, 5" long	70	125	140
Studebaker	take-apart, 5" long	400	600	800
Tinytown Station Wagon and Boat Trailer		45	70	90
Touring Car	woman and dog seated in back, driver in front, 10" long, 1920	650	1000	1450
Yellow Cab	with luggage rack, cast iron, 8" long, 1940	325	500	700

Emergency Vehicles

Make	Description	Good	Ex	Mint
Ahrens-Fox Fire Engine	cast iron, 11-1/2" long, 1932	5000	6500	8000
Auto Fire Engine	cast iron, 15" long, 1912	4200	5500	7000
Fire Engine	blue and green, large rear wheels with smaller front wheels, cast iron, 10-3/4" long, 1920"s	4500	5750	7500
Fire Engine	cast iron, 14-1/2" long, 1932	1575	2250	3000
Fire Truck	5" long, 1930s	75	100	150
Fire Truck No. 468		60	95	125
Hook and Ladder Fire Truck	rubber wheels, die cast, 18" long	150	250	500
Hook and Ladder Truck	cast iron, 8" long	100	125	200
Hook and Ladder Truck	cast iron, 23" long, 1912	1850	3000	4500
Hook and Ladder Truck	cast iron, 16-1/2" long, 1926	850	1200	1700
Ladder Fire Truck	cast iron, 5-1/2" long	40	60	80
Ladder Truck	14" long, 1940s	150	275	500
Police Patrol	with three policemen, cast iron, 11" long, 1919	900	1450	2500
Pumper Fire Truck	plastic, 1950s	25	45	65
Seven Man Fire Patrol	cast iron, 15" long, 1912	3575	5700	7500
Special Ladder Truck	cast iron, 13" long, 1938	465	575	975

Trucks

Make	Description	Good	Ex	Mint
Auto Dump Coal Wagon	cast iron, 16-1/4" long, 1920	800	1200	1500
Auto Express with Roof	cast iron, 9-1/2" long, 1910	500	875	1200
Auto Truck	spoke wheels, cast iron, 10" long, 1918	600	1200	1650
Auto Truck	five-ton truck, cast iron, 17-1/2" long, 1920	1000	1650	2250
Bell Telephone Truck	12" long, 1940	50	75	100
Bell Telephone Truck	spoke wheels, cast iron, 5-1/2" long, 1930	225	335	450
Bell Telephone Truck	white tires, winch works, cast iron, 10" long, 1930	500	1000	1500
Bell Telephone Truck	no driver, white tires, cast iron, 3-3/4" long, 1930	150	225	300
Bell Telephone Truck	white tires, cast iron, 7" long, 1930	300	400	500
Borden's Milk Truck	cast iron, 7-1/2" long, 1930	1650	2850	4250
Compressor Truck	1953 Ford	60	90	120

		Good	Ex	Mint
Delivery Van	cast iron, 4-1/2" long, 1932	365	475	675
Dump Truck	cast iron, 7-1/2" long	225	335	450
Dump Truck	white rubber tires, 4-1/2" long, 1930s	100	150	200
Dump Truck	plastic, 1950s	25	35	55
Gas Tanker	5-1/2" long	115	225	295
General Shovel Truck	dual rear wheels, cast iron, 10" long, 1931	500	750	1000
Ingersoll-Rand Compressor	cast iron, 8-1/4" long, 1933	3250	6500	10000
Lifesaver Truck	cast iron, 4-1/4" long	350	475	700
Long Bed Dump Truck	series 510, Ford, cast iron	110	175	300
Mack Dump Truck	cast iron, 11" long, 1928	600	800	1450
Merchants Delivery Truck	cast iron, 6-1/4" long, 1925	400	600	850
Milk Truck	cast iron, 3-3/4" long, 1930	115	200	295
Nucar Transport	with four vehicles, cast iron, 16" long, 1932	675	1200	1500
Open Bed Auto Express	cast iron, 9-1/2" long, 1910	725	1200	1700
Panama Shovel Truck	Mack truck, cast iron, 13" long, 1934	750	1500	2000
Railway Express Truck	cast iron	135	225	275
Shovel Truck	metal, 10" long	250	375	500
Stake Bed Truck	cast iron, 3" long	75	115	150
Stake Truck	die cast, 7" long, 1950s	75	115	150
Stake Truck	white rubber tires, 7" long, 1930s	85	130	175
Stake Truck	white cab, blue stake bed, 12" long	100	150	200
Stockyard Truck #851	with three pigs	60	95	165
Tanker	cast iron, 7" long, 1940s	85	130	175
Tow Truck	Ford, cast metal, 7" long, 1950s	50	65	165
Tow Truck	9" long	135	225	275
Truckmixer	Ford, mixer cylinder rotates when truck moves, cast iron, 8" long, 1932	50	85	185
Wrecker	whitewall tires, green/white, 11-1/2" long	25	50	75
Wrecker	cast iron, 5" long	60	95	125
Wrecker	6" long	70	125	145
Wrecker	red, die cast, 9-1/2" long, 1940"s	60	95	165

Marx

Cars

Make	Description	Good	Ex	Mint
Amos 'N' Andy Fresh Air Taxi Cab	tin litho, wind-up, 8" long, 1930	650	875	1600
Army Car	battery-operated	65	100	200
Army Staff Car	litho steel, tin wind-up, 1930s	125	200	425

Army Staff Car	with flasher and siren, tin wind-up, 11" long, 1940s	75	125	400
Big Lizzie Car	tin wind-up, 7-1/4" long, 1930s	75	125	235
Blondie's Jalopy	tin litho, 16" long, 1941	325	500	850
Boat Tail Racer #3	tin wind-up, 5" long, 1930s	40	55	200
Bouncing Benny Car	pull toy, 7" long, 1939	325	500	750
Bumper Auto	large bumpers front and rear, tin wind-up, 1939	60	100	225
Cadillac Coupe	8-1/2" long, 1931	175	275	400
Cadillac Coupe	trunk w/tools on luggage carrier, tin wind-up, 11" long, 1931	200	300	525
Camera Car	heavy gauge steel car, 9-1/2" long, 1939	850	1300	1900
Careful Johnnie	plastic driver, 6-1/2" long, 1950s	100	150	350
Charlie McCarthy "Benzine Buggy" Car	with white wheels, tin wind-up, 7" long, 1938	450	625	950
Charlie McCarthy "Benzine Buggy" Car	with red wheels, tin wind-up, 7" long, 1938	600	900	1450
Charlie McCarthy and Mortimer Snerd Private Car	tin wind-up, 16" long, 1939	600	900	1500
Charlie McCarthy Private Car	wind-up, 1935	1450	2200	3500
College Boy Car	blue car with yellow trim, tin wind-up, 8" long, 1930s	300	450	525
Convertible Roadster	nickel-plated tin, 11" long, 1930s	175	275	395
Coo Coo Car	8" long, tin wind-up, 1931	375	575	825
Crazy Dan Car	tin wind-up, 6" long, 1930s	140	225	395
Dagwood the Driver	8" long, tin wind-up, 1941	200	300	900
Dan Dipsy Car	nodder, tin wind-up, 5-3/4" long, 1950s	250	375	450
Dick Tracy Police Car	9" long	150	225	350
Dick Tracy Police Station Riot Car	friction, sparkling, 7-1/2" long, 1946	130	200	375
Dick Tracy Squad Car	yellow flashing light, tin litho, wind-up, 11" long, 1940s	250	375	525
Dick Tracy Squad Car	battery-operated, tin litho, 11-1/4" long, 1949	170	275	475
Dick Tracy Squad Car	friction, 20" long, 1948	125	170	300
Dippy Dumper	Brutus or Popeye, celluloid figure, tin wind-up, 9", 1930s	350	525	900
Disney Parade Roadster	tin litho, wind-up, 1950s	100	150	900
Donald Duck Disney Dipsy Car	plastic Donald, tin wind-up, 5-3/4" long, 1953	425	650	895
Donald Duck Go-Kart	plastic and metal, friction, rubber tires, 1960s	75	130	325
Donald the Driver	plastic Donald, tin car, wind-up, 6-1/2" long, 1950s	200	300	595
Dora Dipsy Car	nodder, tin wind-up, 5-3/4" long, 1953	400	600	725
Dottie the Driver	nodder, tin wind-up, 6-1/2" long, 1950s	150	225	450
Drive-Up Self Car	turns left, right or straight, 1940	100	150	225
Driver Training Car	tin wind-up, 1930s	80	120	225
Electric Convertible	tin and plastic, 20" long	65	100	295
Falcon	plastic bubble top, black rubber tires	50	75	175
Funny Fire Fighters	7" long, tin wind-up, 1941	800	1200	1600

Funny Flivver Car	tin litho, wind-up, 7" long, 1926	275	425	675
G-Man Pursuit Car	sparks, 14-1/2" long, 1935	190	285	750
Gang Buster Car	tin wind-up, 14-1/2" long, 1938	200	300	800
Giant King Racer	dark blue, tin wind-up, 12-1/4" long, 1928	250	375	725
Hot Rod #23	friction motor, tin, 8" long, 1967	45	75	90
Huckleberry Hound Car	friction	125	200	250
International Agent Car	tin wind-up	30	55	125
International Agent Car	friction, tin litho, 1966	60	100	195
Jaguar	battery-operated, 13" long	225	325	450
Jalopy	tin driver, friction, 1950s	125	200	250
Jalopy Car	tin driver, motor sparks, crank, wind-up	140	225	280
Jolly Joe Jeep	tin litho, 5-3/4" long, 1950s	150	225	375
Joy Riders Crazy Car	tin litho, wind-up, 8" long, 1928	340	500	675
Jumping Jeep	tin litho, 5-3/4" long, 1947	210	325	425
King Racer	yellow body, red trim, tin wind-up, 8-1/2" long, 1925	375	575	750
King Racer	yellow with black outlines, 8-1/2" long, 1925	250	430	575
Komical Kop	black car, tin litho, wind-up, 7-1/2" long, 1930s	450	675	900
Leaping Lizzie Car	tin wind-up, 7" long, 1927	250	375	500
Learn To Drive Car	wind-up	110	165	225
Lonesome Pine Trailer and Convertible Sedan	22" long, 1936	375	600	795
Machine Gun on Car	hand crank activation on gun, 3" long	75	130	225
Magic George and Car	litho, 1940s	170	250	350
Mechanical Speed Racer	tin wind-up, 12" long, 1948	125	200	275
Mickey Mouse Disney Dipsy Car	plastic Mickey, tin wind-up, 5-3/4" long, 1953	425	655	875
Mickey the Driver	plastic Mickey, tin car, wind-up, 6-1/2" long, 1950s	170	250	450
Midget Racer "Midget Special" #2	miniature car, clockwork-powered, 5" long, 1930s	125	200	250
Midget Racer "Midget Special" #7	miniature car, tin wind-up, 5" long, 1930s	125	200	250
Milton Berle Crazy Car	tin litho, wind-up, 6" long, 1950s	250	375	595
Mortimer Snerd's Tricky Auto	tin litho, wind-up, 7-1/2" long, 1939	400	600	750
Mystery Car	press down activation, 9" long, 1936	125	200	275
Mystery Taxi	press down activation, steel, 9" long, 1938	160	250	375
Nutty Mad Car	blue car with goggled driver, friction, hard plastic, 1960s	75	130	200
Nutty Mad Car	red tin car, vinyl driver, friction, 4" long, 1960s	100	150	225
Nutty Mad Car	with driver, battery-operated, 1960s	100	150	225
Old Jalopy	tin wind-up, driver, "Old Jalopy" on hood, 7" long, 1950	225	325	425
Parade Roadster	with Disney characters, tin litho, wind-up, 11" long, 1950	225	325	900
Peter Rabbit Eccentric Car	tin wind-up, 5-1/2" long, 1950s	250	375	500
Queen of the Campus	with four college students' heads, 1950	250	400	525

Race 'N Road Speedway	HO scale racing set, 1950s	60	100	125
Racer #12	tin litho, wind-up, 16" long, 1942	225	325	625
Racer #3	miniature car, tin wind-up, 5" long	75	125	195
Racer #4	miniature car, tin wind-up, 5" long	75	125	195
Racer #5	miniature car, tin wind-up, 5" long, 1948	75	125	195
Racer #61	miniature car, tin wind-up, 4-3/4" long, 1930	75	125	195
Racer #7	miniature car, tin wind-up, 5" long, 1948	75	125	195
Racing Car	two man team, tin litho, wind-up, 12" long, 1940	125	200	425
Racing Car	plastic driver, tin wind-up, 27" long, 1950	100	175	450
Roadster	11-1/2" long, 1949	100	150	225
Roadster and Cannon Ball Keeper	wind-up, 9" long	175	250	350
Roadster Convertible with Trailer and Racer	mechanical, 1950	125	200	275
Rocket Racer	tin litho, 1935	275	425	550
Rolls-Royce	black plastic, friction, 6" long, 1955	40	60	80
Royal Coupe	tin litho, wind-up, 9" long, 1930	175	275	375
Secret Sam Agent 012 Car	tin litho, friction, 5" long, 1960s	40	65	165
Sedan	battery-operated, plastic, 9-1/2" long	175	275	350
Sheriff Sam and His Whoopee Car	plastic, tin wind-up, 5-3/4" long, 1949	200	300	475
Siren Police Car	15" long, 1930s	75	125	395
Smokey Sam the Wild Fireman Car	6-1/2" long, 1950	125	200	395
Smokey Stover Whoopee Car	1940s	175	275	525
Snoopy Gus Wild Fireman	7" long, 1926	500	750	1150
Speed Cop	two 4" all tin wind-up cars, track, 1930s	175	275	795
Speed King Racer	tin litho, wind-up, 16" long, 1929	325	500	650
Speed Racer	13" long, 1937	250	375	500
Speedway Coupe	tin wind-up, battery-operated headlights, 8" long, 1938	200	300	400
Speedway Set	two wind-up sedans, figure eight track, 1937	250	375	500
Sports Coupe	tin, 15" long, 1930s	125	200	250
Station Wagon	green with woodgrain pattern, wind-up, 7" long, 1950	50	75	250
Station Wagon	litho family of four with dogs on back windows, 6-3/4" long	60	100	275
Station Wagon	light purple with woodgrain pattern, wind-up, 7-1/2" long	60	100	275
Station Wagon	friction, 11" long, 1950	125	200	325
Streamline Speedway	two tin wind-up racing cars, 1936	175	275	395
Stutz Roadster	driver, 15" long, wind-up, 1928	325	500	750
Super Hot Rod	"777" on rear door, 11" long, 1940s	200	300	400
Super Streamlined Racer	tin wind-up, 17" long, 1950s	125	200	400
The Marvel Car, Reversible Coupe	tin wind-up, 1938	125	200	400
Tricky Safety Car	6-1/2" long, 1950	100	150	200

Make	Description	Good	Ex	Mint
Tricky Taxi	black/white version, tin wind-up, 4-1/2" long, 1935	160	250	375
Tricky Taxi	red, black, and white, tin wind-up, 4-1/2" long, 1940s	175	275	375
Uncle Wiggly, He Goes A Ridin' Car	rabbit driving, tin wind-up, 7-1/2" long, 1935	425	650	850
Walt Disney Television Car	friction, 7-1/2" long, 1950s	125	200	425
Western Auto Track	steel, 24" long	75	125	225
Whoopee Car	witty slogans, tin litho, wind-up, 7-1/2" long, 1930s	375	580	775
Whoopee Cowboy Car	bucking car, cowboy driver, tin wind-up, 7-1/2" long, 1930s	400	600	800
Woody Sedan	tin friction, 7-1/2" long	60	100	225
Yellow Taxi	wind-up, 7" long, 1927	275	425	575
Yogi Bear Car	friction, 1962	50	85	195

Emergency Vehicles

Make	Description	Good	Ex	Mint
Ambulance	tin litho, 11" long	125	175	375
Ambulance	13-1/2" long, 1937	225	350	650
Ambulance with Siren	tin wind-up	100	150	400
Army Ambulance	13-1/2" long, 1930s	250	375	750
Boat Tail Racer #2	litho, 13" long, 1948	125	200	425
Chief-Fire Department No. 1 Truck	friction, 1948	60	90	195
Chrome Racer	miniature racer, 5" long, 1937	85	125	250
City Hospital Mack Ambulance	tin litho, wind-up, 10" long, 1927	190	280	500
Electric Car	runs on electric power, license #A7132, 1933	225	325	500
Electric Car	wind-up, 1933	175	250	475
Fire Chief Car	working lights, 16" long	125	200	295
Fire Chief Car	wind-up, 6-1/2" long, 1949	75	125	275
Fire Chief Car	battery-operated headlights, wind-up, 11" long, 1950	100	150	325
Fire Chief Car	friction, loud fire siren, 8" long, 1936	150	250	425
Fire Chief Car with Bell	10-1/2" long, 1940	175	250	450
Fire Engine	sheet iron, 9" long, 1920s	100	175	335
Fire Truck	battery-operated, two celluloid firemen, 12" long	50	75	300
Fire Truck	friction, all metal, 14" long, 1945	90	135	295
Giant King Racer	pale yellow, tin wind-up, 12-1/2" long, 1928	225	325	575
Giant King Racer	red, 13" long, 1941	200	300	550
Giant Mechanical Racer	tin litho, 12-3/4" long, 1948	100	175	350
H.Q. - Staff Car	14-1/2" long, 1930s	325	500	750
Hook and Ladder Fire Truck	three tin litho firemen, 13-1/2" long	90	135	225
Hook and Ladder Fire Truck	plastic ladder on top, 24" long, 1950	90	135	225
Plastic Racer	6" long, 1948	50	75	150
Racer with Plastic Driver	tin litho car, 16" long, 1950	150	225	375

Make	Description	Good	Ex	Mint
Rocket-Shaped Racer #12	1930s	275	425	600
Siren Fire Chief Car	red car with siren, 1934	225	325	495
Siren Fire Chief Truck	battery-operated, 15" long, 1930s	100	175	325
Tricky Fire Chief Car	4-1/2" long, 1930s	250	375	625
V.F.D. Emergency Squad	with ladder, metal, electrically powered, 14" long, 1940s	70	125	200
V.F.D. Fire Engine	with hoses and siren, 14" long, 1940s	120	180	295
V.F.D. Hook and Ladder Fire Truck	33" long, 1950	140	225	325
War Department Ambulance	1930s	100	150	695

Trucks

Make	Description	Good	Ex	Mint
A & P Supermarket Truck	pressed steel, rubber tires, litho, 19" long	50	100	275
Aero Oil Co. Mack Truck	tin litho, friction, 5-1/2" long, 1930	125	200	350
Air Force Truck	32" long	75	125	300
American Railroad Express Agency Inc. Truck	open cab, 7" long, 1930s	100	150	325
American Truck Co. Mack Truck	friction, 5" long	100	150	225
Armored Trucking Co. Mack Truck	black cab, yellow printing, wind-up, 9-3/4" long	200	300	400
Armored Trucking Co. Truck	tin litho, wind-up, 10" long, 1927	100	150	325
Army Truck	tin, 12" long, 1950	60	90	150
Army Truck	20" long	50	75	125
Army Truck	canvas top, 20" long, 1940s	150	225	325
Army Truck	olive drab truck, 4-1/2" long, 1930s	125	200	350
Army Truck with Rear Benches and Canopy	olive drab paint, 10" long	75	125	225
Artillery Set	three-piece set, 1930	100	150	225
Auto Carrier	two yellow plastic cars, two ramp tracks, 14" long, 1950	125	200	295
Auto Mack Truck	yellow/red, 12" long, 1950	50	75	175
Auto Transport Mack Truck and Trailer	dark blue cab, dark green trailer, wind-up, 11-1/2" long, 1932	150	225	375
Auto Transport Mack Truck and Trailer	medium blue cab, friction, 11-1/2" long, 1932	150	225	425
Auto Transport Mack Truck and Trailer	dark blue cab, wind-up, 11-1/2" long, 1932	150	225	400
Auto Transport Truck	pressed steel, with two plastic cars, 14" long, 1940	75	125	225
Auto Transport Truck	with two tin litho cars, 34" long, 1950s	60	90	200
Auto Transport Truck	with three wind-up cars, 22-3/4" long, 1931	250	375	525
Auto Transport Truck	with three racing coupes, 22" long, 1933	250	375	525
Auto Transport Truck	double decker transport truck, 24-1/2" long, 1935	275	425	575
Auto Transport Truck	with dump truck, roadster and coupe, 30 1/2" long, 1938	275	425	575

Item	Description			
Auto Transport Truck	with three cars, 21" long, 1940	250	375	575
Auto Transport Truck	21" long, 1947	175	250	400
Auto Transport Truck	with two plastic sedans, wooden wheels, 13-3/4" long, 1950	75	130	225
Auto Transwalk Truck	with three cars, 1930s	175	250	395
Bamberger Mack Truck	dark green, wind-up, 5" long, 1920s	200	300	525
Big Load Van Co. Hauler and Trailer	with little cartons of products, 12-3/4" long, 1927	200	300	525
Big Load Van Co. Mack Truck	wind-up, 13" long, 1928	225	350	600
Big Shot Cannon Truck	battery-operated, 23" long, 1960s	150	250	325
Cannon Army Mack Truck	9" long, 1930s	175	250	325
Carpenter's Truck	stake bed truck, pressed steel, 14" long, 1940s	175	250	350
Carrier with Three Racers	tin litho, wind-up, 22-3/4" long, 1930	150	225	425
Cement Mixer Truck	red cab, tin finish mixing barrel, 6" long, 1930s	100	150	300
City Coal Co. Mack Dump Truck	14" long, 1934	225	350	525
City Delivery Van	yellow steel truck, 11" long	140	210	280
City Sanitation Dept. "Help Keep Your City Clean" Truck	12-3/4" long, 1940	60	90	250
Coal Truck	battery-operated, automatic dump, forward and reverse, tin	75	125	175
Coal Truck	1st version, red cab, litho blue and yellow dumper, 12" long	140	225	280
Coal Truck	2nd version, light blue truck, 12" long	140	225	280
Coal Truck	3rd version, Lumar Co. truck, 10" long, 1939	150	250	310
Coca-Cola Truck	tin, 17" long, 1940s	125	200	250
Coca-Cola Truck	yellow, 20" long, 1950	150	225	300
Coca-Cola Truck	stamped steel, 20" long, 1940s	175	250	350
Coca-Cola Truck	red steel, 11-1/2" long, 1940s	100	175	250
Contractors and Builders Truck	10" long	125	200	250
Curtiss Candy Truck	red plastic truck, 10" long, 1950	125	200	250
Dairy Farm Pickup Truck	22" long	60	100	150
Delivery Truck	blue truck, 4" long, 1940	100	175	225
Deluxe Delivery Truck	with six delivery boxes, stamped steel, 13-1/4" long, 1948	100	150	200
Deluxe Trailer Truck	tin and plastic, 14" long, 1950s	70	100	145
Dodge Salerno Engineering Department Truck		600	900	1200
Dump Truck	4-1/2" long, 1930s	100	175	325
Dump Truck	motor, tin friction, 12" long, 1950s	50	75	100
Dump Truck	red cab, gray bumper, yellow bed, 18" long, 1950	100	150	200
Dump Truck	6" long, 1930s	100	150	250
Dump Truck	red cab, green body, 6-1/4" long	50	75	100
Dump Truck	yellow cab, blue bumper, red bed, 18" long, 1950	100	150	200
Emergency Service Truck	friction, tin	125	200	275

Emergency Service Truck	friction, tin, searchlight behind car and siren	150	225	300
Firestone Truck	metal, 14" long, 1950s	50	75	150
Ford Heavy Duty Express Truck	cab with canopy, 1950s	60	100	175
Gas Truck	green truck, 4" long, 1940	60	90	165
Giant Reversing Tractor Truck	with tools, tin wind-up, 14" long, 1950s	75	130	350
Gravel Truck	1st version, pressed steel cab, red tin dumper, 10" long, 1930	100	150	250
Gravel Truck	2nd version, metal, 8-1/2" long, 1940s	75	125	200
Gravel Truck	3rd version, metal with "Gravel Mixer" drum, 10" long, 1930s	100	150	250
Grocery Truck	cardboard boxes, tinplate and plastic, 14-1/2" long	90	150	225
Guided Missile Truck	blue, red and yellow body, friction, 16" long, 1958	75	125	225
Highway Express Truck	pressed steel	95	150	185
Highway Express Truck	tin, tin tires, 16" long, 1940s	50	75	185
Highway Express Truck	"Nationwide Delivery," 1950s	100	150	225
Highway Express Van Truck	metal, 15-1/2" long, 1940s	100	150	225
Jalopy Pickup Truck	tin wind-up, 7" long	60	90	175
Jeep	11" long, 1946-50	75	130	200
Jeepster	mechanical, plastic	110	165	250
Lazy Day Dairy Farm Pickup Truck and Trailer	22" long	45	75	275
Lincoln Transfer and Storage Co. Mack Truck	wheels have cut-out spokes, tin litho, wind-up, 13" long, 1928	350	525	750
Lone Eagle Oil Co. Mack Truck	bright blue cab, green tank, wind-up, 12" long, 1930	225	350	550
Lumar Contractors Scoop/Dump Truck	17-1/2" long, 1940s	75	125	200
Lumar Lines and Gasoline Set	1948	250	375	725
Lumar Lines Truck	red cab, aluminum finished trailer, 14" long	125	200	300
Lumar Motor Transport Truck	litho, 13" long, 1942	75	130	250
Machinery Moving Truck		60	90	200
Mack Army Truck	pressed steel, wind-up, 7-1/2" long	70	100	250
Mack Army Truck	friction, 5" long, 1930	125	200	350
Mack Army Truck	khaki brown body, wind-up, 10-1/2" long	125	225	400
Mack Army Truck	13-1/2" long, 1929	225	350	600
Mack Dump Truck	dark red cab, medium blue bed, wind-up, 10" long, 1928	150	225	475
Mack Dump Truck	medium blue truck, wind-up, 13" long, 1934	200	300	525
Mack Dump Truck	silver cab, medium blue dump, wind-up, 12-3/4" long, 1936	225	355	525
Mack Dump Truck	no driver, 19" long, 1930	300	450	650
Mack Dump Truck	tin litho, wind-up, 13-1/2" long, 1926	225	350	575
Mack Railroad Express Truck #7	tin, 1930s	75	125	450
Mack Towing Truck	dark green cab, wind-up, 8" long, 1926	175	275	450

Mack U.S. Mail Truck	black body, wind-up, 9-1/2" long	250	375	500
Magnetic Crane and Truck	1950	175	275	350
Mammoth Truck Train	truck with five trailers, 1930s	150	250	450
Meadowbrook Dairy Truck	14" long, 1940	150	275	375
Mechanical Sand Dump Truck	steel, 1940s	100	150	275
Medical Corps Ambulance Truck	olive drab paint, 1940s	100	150	275
Merchants Transfer Mack Truck	red open-stake truck, 10" long	225	350	450
Merchants Transfer Mack Truck	13-1/3" long, 1928	250	375	600
Military Cannon Truck	olive drab paint, cannon shoots marbles, 10" long, 1939	125	200	250
Milk Truck	white truck, 4" long, 1940	60	90	120
Miniature Mayflower Moving Van	operating lights	60	90	125
Motor Market Truck	10" long, 1939	100	175	225
Navy Jeep	wind-up	50	75	100
North American Van Lines Tractor Trailer	wind-up, 13" long, 1940s	100	175	225
Panel Wagon Truck		30	55	75
Pet Shop Truck	plastic, six compartments with six vinyl dogs, 11" long	125	200	250
Pickup Truck	blue/yellow with wood tires, 9" long, 1940s	50	75	150
Polar Ice Co. Ice Truck	13" long, 1940s	100	175	275
Police Patrol Mack Truck	wind-up, 10" long	200	300	475
Popeye Dippy Dumper Truck	Popeye is celluloid, tin wind-up	325	500	800
Pure Milk Dairy Truck	glass bottles, pressed steel, 1940	55	80	250
Railway Express Agency Truck	green closed van truck, 1940s	90	135	300
Range Rider	tin wind-up, 1930s	250	375	500
RCA Television Service Truck	plastic Ford panel truck, 8-1/2" long, 1948-50	150	225	300
Reversing Road Roller	tin wind-up	60	100	125
Road Builder Tank	1950	125	200	250
Rocker Dump Truck	17-1/2" long	60	90	120
Roy Rogers and Trigger Cattle Truck	metal, 15" long, 1950s	60	100	225
Royal Oil Co. Mack Truck	dark red cab, medium green tank, wind-up, 8-1/4" long, 1927	200	300	500
Royal Van Co. Mack Truck	1927	250	375	600
Royal Van Co. Mack Truck	red cab, tin litho and paint, wind-up, 9" long, 1928	210	315	550
Run Right To Read's Truck	14" long, 1940	125	200	250
Sand and Gravel Truck	"Builder's Supply Co.," tin wind-up, 1920	150	225	400
Sand Truck	tin litho, 12-1/2" long, 1940s	125	200	275
Sand Truck	9" long, 1948	100	150	200
Sand-Gravel Dump Truck	tin litho, 12" long, 1950	150	225	300

Sand-Gravel Dump Truck	blue cab, yellow dump with "Gravel" on side, tin, 1930s	140	225	285
Sanitation Truck	1940s	135	200	270
Searchlight Truck	pressed steel, 9-3/4" long, 1930s	160	250	325
Side Dump Truck	1940	90	130	275
Side Dump Truck	10" long, 1930s	140	225	280
Side Dump Truck and Trailer	15" long, 1935	150	225	300
Sinclair Tanker	tin, 14" long, 1940s	150	225	300
Stake Bed Truck	rubber stamped chicken on one side of truck, bunny on other	100	150	200
Stake Bed Truck	pressed steel, wooden wheels, 7" long, 1936	60	90	200
Stake Bed Truck	red cab, green stake bed, 20" long, 1947	100	150	200
Stake Bed Truck	medium blue cab, red stake bed, 10" long, 1940	75	130	185
Stake Bed Truck	red cab, yellow and red trailer, 14" long	100	150	200
Stake Bed Truck	red cab, blue stake bed, 6" long, 1930s	75	125	150
Stake Bed Truck and Trailer	red truck, silver stake bed	125	200	250
Streamline Mechanical Hauler, Van, and Tank Truck Combo	heavy gauge steel, 10 3/8" long, 1936	170	275	350
Sunshine Fruit Growers Truck	red cab, yellow/white trailer with blue roof, 14" long	100	150	225
Tipper Dump Truck	wind-up, 9-3/4" long, 1950	75	130	175
Tow Truck	aluminum finsih, tin litho wind-up, 6-1/4" long	75	125	150
Tow Truck	aluminum finish, wind-up, 6-1/4" long	95	150	190
Tow Truck	10" long, 1935	125	200	250
Tow Truck	red cab, yellow towing unit, 6" long, 1930s	137	200	275
Toyland Dairy Truck	10" long	140	210	280
Toyland's Farm Products Mack Milk Truck	with 12 wooden milk bottles, 10-1/4" long, 1931	200	300	400
Toytown Express Truck	plastic cab	45	70	95
Tractor Trailer with Dumpster	blue/yellow hauler, tan dumpster	125	200	250
Truck Train	stake hauler and five trailers, 41" long, 1933	250	400	525
Truck Train	stake hauler and four trailers, 41" long, 1938	350	550	725
Truck with Electric Lights	15" long, 1930s	110	165	300
Truck with Electric Lights	battery-operated lights, 10" long, 1935	125	200	375
Truck with Searchlight	toolbox behind cab, 10" long, 1930s	150	225	400
U.S. Air Force Willy's Jeep	tin body, plastic figures	70	100	140
U.S. Army Jeep with Trailer		100	150	200
U.S. Mail Truck	metal, 14" long, 1950s	225	350	450
U.S. Trucking Co. Mack Truck	dark maroon cab, friction, 5-1/2" long, 1930	100	150	200
Van Truck	plastic, 10" long, 1950s	40	60	80
Western Auto Truck	steel, 25" long	60	90	125
Willy's Jeep	steel, 12" long, 1938	125	200	250
Willy's Jeep and Trailer	1940s	100	160	215
Wrecker Truck	1930s	145	225	290

Matchbox

No.	Name	Description	Good	VG	EXC
47-A	1 Ton Trojan Van	red body, no windows, 2-1/4" long, 1958	25	35	45
73-A	10 Ton Pressure Refueller	bluish gray body, six gray plastic wheels, 2-5/8" long, 1959	20	25	35
4-H	1957 Chevy	metallic rose body, chrome interior, large five arch rear wheels, 2-15/16" long, 1979	2	8	12
42-G	1957 Ford T-Bird	red convertible, white interior, silver grille and trunk mounted spare, 1982	3	5	6
30-B	6-Wheel Crane Truck	silver body, orange crane, metal or plastic hook, gray wheels, 2-5/8" long, 1961	20	30	40
30-D	8-Wheel Crane Truck	red body, yellow plastic hook, five spoke thin wheels, 3" long, 1970	5	7	10
30-C	8-Wheel Crane Truck	green body, orange crane, red or yellow hook, eight black wheels on four axles, 3" long, 1965	15	20	25
51-C	8-Wheel Tipper	blue tinted windows, eight black plastic wheels, 3" long, 1969	7	10	15
51-D	8-Wheel Tipper	yellow cab, silver/gray tipper, blue windows, five spoke thin wheels, 3" long, 1970	4	6	8
65-E	Airport Coach	white top and roof, metallic blue bottom, amber windows, yellow interior, comes with varying airline logo decals, 3" long, 1977	5	10	15
51-A	Albion Chieftan	yellow body, tan and light tan bags, small round decal on doors, 2-1/2" long, 1958	10	20	25
75-D	Alfa Carabo	pink body, ivory interior, black trunk, five spoke wide wheels, 3" long, 1971	3	4	5
61-B	Alvis Stalwart	white body, yellow plastic removable canopy, green windows, six plastic wheels, 2-5/8" long, 1966	20	30	50
69-E	Armored Truck	red body, white plastic roof, silver/gray base and grille, "Wells Fargo" on sides, 2-13/16" long, 1978	3	5	8
50-E	Articulated Truck	purple tinted windows, small wide wheels, five spoke wide wheels, 2-3/4" long, 1973	6	8	12
30-G	Articulated Truck	blue cab, white grille, silver/gray dumper, five spoke accent wheels, 3" long, 1981	3	5	6
53-A	Aston Martin DB2 Saloon	metallic light green, 2-1/2" long, 1958	20	30	40
19-C	Aston Martin Racing Car	metallic green, metal steering wheel and wire wheels, black plastic tires, 2-1/2" long, 1961	10	30	45
15-B	Atlantic Tractor Super	orange body, tow hook, spare wheel behind cab on body, 2-5/8" long, 1959	15	30	40
16-A	Atlantic Trailer	tan body, six metal wheels, tan tow bar, 3-1/8" long, 1956	15	25	35
16-B	Atlantic Trailer	orange body, eight gray plastic wheels with knobby treads, 3-1/4" long, 1957	15	50	80
32-G	Atlas Extractor	red/orange body, gray platform, turret and treads, black wheels, 3" long 1981	2	4	6
23-E	Atlas Truck	metallic blue cab, silver interior, orange dumper, red and yellow labels on doors, 3" long, 1975	6	8	10

23-G	Audi Quattro	white body, red and black print sides, clear windows, "Audi Sport" on doors, 1982	2	3	5
71-A	Austin 200 Gallon Water Truck	olive green body, four black plastic wheels, 2-3/8" long, 1959	10	25	30
36-A	Austin A50	silver grille, with or without silver rear bumper, no windows, 2-3/8" long, 1957	15	20	30
29-B	Austin A55 Cambridge Sedan	two-tone green, light green roof and rear top half of body, dark metallic green hood and lower body, 2-3/4" long, 1961	10	20	25
68-A	Austin MK II Radio Truck	olive green body, four black plastic wheels, 2-3/8" long, 1959	20	25	30
17-B	Austin Taxi Cab	maroon body, 2-1/4" long, 1960	35	50	70
1-D	Aveling Barford Road Roller	green body, canopy, tow hook, 2-5/8" long, 1962	7	10	15
43-B	Aveling Barford Tractor Shovel	yellow body, yellow or red driver, four large plastic wheels, 2-5/8" long, 1962	10	15	25
16-E	Badger Exploration Truck	metallic red body, silver grille, 2-1/4" long, 1974	3	4	6
13-F	Baja Dune Buggy	metallic green, orange interior, silver motor, 2-5/8" long, 1971	3	4	6
58-A	BEA Coach	blue body, four wheels with small knobby treads, 2-1/2" long, 1958	20	25	35
30-E	Beach Buggy	pink, yellow paint splatters, clear windows, 2-1/2" long, 1970	3	4	6
47-E	Beach Hopper	dark metallic blue body, hot pink splattered over body, bright orange interior, tan driver, 2-5/8" long, 1974	3	4	5
14-C	Bedford Ambulance	white body, silver trim, two rear doors open, 2-5/8" long, 1962	15	60	80
28-A	Bedford Compressor Truck	silver front and rear grilles, metal wheels, 1-3/4" long, 1956	15	35	45
42-A	Bedford Evening News Van	yellow/orange body, silver grille, 2-1/4" long, 1957	15	35	45
27-A	Bedford Low Loader	light blue cab, dark blue trailer, silver grille and side gas tanks, four metal wheels on cab, two metal wheels on trailer, 3-1/8" long, 1956	100	350	450
27-B	Bedford Low Loader	green cab, tan trailer, silver grille, four gray wheels on cab, two wheels on trailer, 3-3/4" long, 1959	20	55	75
29-A	Bedford Milk Delivery Van	tan body, white bottle load, 2-1/4" long, 1956	15	25	30
17-A	Bedford Removals Van	maroon body, peaked roof, gold grille, 2-1/8" long, 1956	35	115	150
40-A	Bedford Tipper Truck	red cab, silver grille, two front wheels, four dual rear wheels, 2-1/8" long, 1957	25	40	50
3-B	Bedford Ton Tipper	gray cab, gray wheels, dual rear wheels, 2-1/2" long, 1961	10	15	20
13-A	Bedford Wreck Truck	tan body, red metal crane and hook, 2" long, 1955	30	40	55
13-B	Bedford Wreck Truck	tan body, red metal crane and hook, crane attached to rear axle, 2-1/8" long, 1958	30	45	60
23-A	Berkeley Cavalier Trailer	decal on lower right rear of trailer, metal wheels, flat tow hook, 2-1/2" long, 1956	10	30	40
26-E	Big Banger	red body, blue windows, small front wheels, large rear wheels, 3" long, 1972	4	6	8
12-F	Big Bull	orange body, green plow blade, base and sides, chrome seat and engine, orange rollers, 2-1/2" long, 1975	4	6	8

22-F	Blaze Buster	red body, silver interior, yellow label, five spoke slicks, 3" long, 1975	4	6	8
61-C	Blue Shark	metallic dark blue, white driver, clear glass, four spoke wide wheels, 3" long, 1971	3	4	6
23-B	Bluebird Dauphine Trailer	green with gray plastic wheels, decal on lower right rear of trailer, door on left rear side opens, 2-1/2" long, 1960	45	135	200
56-C	BMC 1800 Pininfarina	clear windows, ivory interior, five spoke wheels, 2-3/4" long, 1970	7	10	15
45-D	BMW 3.0 CSL	orange body, yellow interior, 2-7/8" long, 1976	3	5	7
53-B	BMW M1	silver gray metallic body with plastic hood, red interior, black stripes and "52" on sides, 2-15/16" long, 1981	2	4	5
9-C	Boat and Trailer	white hull, blue deck, clear windows, five spoke wheels on trailer, 3-1/4" long, 1966	4	6	15
9-D	Boat and Trailer	white hull, blue deck, clear windows, five spoke wheels on trailer, 3-1/4" long, 1970	3	5	20
72-E	Bomag Road Roller	yellow body, base and wheel hubs, black plastic roller, 2-15/16" long, 1979	2	4	6
44-E	Boss Mustang	yellow body, amber windows, silver interior, clover leaf wide wheels, 2-7/8" long, 1972	3	4	6
25-C	BP Petrol Tanker	yellow hinged cab, white tanker body, six black plastic wheels, 3" long, 1964	8	15	20
52-B	BRM Racing Car	blue or red body, white plastic driver, yellow wheels, 2-5/8" long, 1965	10	20	25
54-C	Cadillac Ambulance	white body, blue tinted windows, white interior, red cross labels on sides, 2-3/8" long, 1970	5	7	20
27-C	Cadillac Sedan	with or without silver grille, clear windows, white roof, silver wheels, 2-3/4" long, 1960	15	30	40
38-G	Camper	red body, off white camper, unpainted base, 3" long 1980	3	5	7
8-A	Caterpillar Tractor	driver has same color hat as body, metal rollers, rubber treads, crimped axles, 1-1/2" long, 1955	40	60	80
8-B	Caterpillar Tractor	yellow body and driver, large smoke stack, metal rollers, rubber treads, crimped axles, 1-5/8" long, 1959	20	35	45
8-C	Caterpillar Tractor	yellow body and driver, large smoke stack, metal rollers, rubber treads, rounded axles, 1-7/8" long, 1961	10	15	25
8-D	Caterpillar Tractor	yellow body, no driver, plastic rollers, rubber treads, rounded axles, 2" long, 1964	10	15	20
37-D	Cattle Truck	yellow body, gray plastic box with fold down rear door, black plastic wheels, green tinted windows, 2-1/4" long, 1966	7	10	15
37-E	Cattle Truck	gray plastic box, white plastic cattle inside, five spoke thin wheels, green tinted windows, 2-1/2" long, 1970	5	7	20
71-F	Cattle Truck	metallic brown body, yellow/orange cattle carrier, 3" long, 1976	4	6	7
25-H	Celica GT	blue body, black base, white racing stripes and "78" on roof and doors, 2-15/16" long, 1978	3	7	12
25-J	Celica GT	yellow body, blue interior, red "Yellow Fever" on hood, side racing stripes, clear windows, large rear wheels, 1982	2	4	6
3-A	Cement Mixer	blue body and rotating barrel, orange metal wheels, 1-5/8" long, 1953	25	35	45
19-G	Cement Truck	red body, yellow plastic barrel with red stripes, large wide arch wheels, 3" long, 1976	4	5	7

41-F	Chevrolet Ambulance	white body, blue windows and dome light, gray interior, 2-15/16" long, 1978	4	7	10
57-B	Chevrolet Impala	pale blue roof, metallic blue body, green tinted windows, 2-3/4" long, 1961	20	25	35
20-C	Chevrolet Impala Taxi Cab	orange/yellow or bright yellow body, ivory or red interior and driver, 3" long, 1965	10	15	20
44-G	Chevy 4x4 Van	green body and windows, white "Ridin High" with horse and fence on sides, 1982	2	3	5
34-G	Chevy Pro Stocker	white body, red interior, clear front and side windows, frosted rear window, 3" long, 1981	2	3	5
68-E	Chevy Van	orange body, unpainted base and grille, large rear wheels, 3" long, 1979	3	5	7
49-D	Chop Suey Motorcycle	metallic dark red body, yellow bull's head on front handle bars, 2-3/4" long, 1973	5	7	10
12-G	Citroen CX	metallic body, silver base and lights, blue plastic hatch door, 3" long, 1979	4	8	12
66-A	Citroen DS 19	light or dark yellow body, with or without silver grille, four plastic wheels, 2-1/2" long, 1959	10	30	40
51-E	Citroen SM	clear windows, frosted rear windows, five spoke wheels, 3" long, 1972	3	4	6
65-C	Claas Combine Harvester	red body, yellow plastic rotating blades and front wheels, black plastic front tires, solid rear wheels, 3" long, 1967	7	10	15
39-D	Clipper	metallic dark pink, amber windows, bright yellow interior, 3" long, 1973	3	4	5
11-H	Cobra Mustang	orange body, "The Boss" on doors, 1982	2	3	5
37-B	Coca-Cola Lorry	orange/yellow body, uneven case load, open base, metal rear fenders, 2-1/4" long, 1957	25	75	140
37-C	Coca-Cola Lorry	yellow body of various shades, even case load, silver wheels, black base, 2-1/4" long, 1960	25	55	125
51-F	Combine Harvester	red body, black painted base, yellow plastic grain chute, 2-3/4" long, 1978	3	5	8
69-A	Commer 30 CWT Van	silver grille, sliding left side door, four plastic wheels, yellow "Nestle's" decal on upper rear panel, 2-1/4" long, 1959	10	30	40
47-B	Commer Ice Cream Canteen	metallic blue body, cream or white plastic interior with man holding ice cream cone, black plastic wheels, 1963	60	95	100
21-C	Commer Milk Truck	pale green body, clear or green tinted windows, ivory or cream bottle load, 2-1/4" long, 1961	20	30	40
50-A	Commer Pickup Truck	with or without silver grille and bumpers, four wheels, 2-1/2" long, 1958	35	55	75
62-G	Corvette	metallic red body, unpainted base, gray interior, 1979	2	4	6
40-F	Corvette T Roof	white body and interior, black "09" on door, red and black racing stripes, 1982	2	3	5
26-G	Cosmic Blues	white body, blue "COSMIC BLUES" and stars on sides, 2-7/8" long, 1970	2	3	4
74-E	Cougar Village	metallic green body, yellow interior, unpainted base, 3-1/16" long, 1978	3	4	6
41-A	D-Type Jaguar	dark green body, tan driver, open air scoop, 2-13/16" long, 1957	15	30	55
41-B	D-Type Jaguar	dark green body, tan driver, silver wheels, open and closed air scoop, 2-7/16" long, 1960	50	100	150
58-C	D.A.F. Girder Truck	cream body shades, green tinted windows, six black wheels, red plastic girders, 3" long, 1968	7	10	15
58-D	D.A.F. Girder Truck	green windows, five spoke thin wheels, red plastic girders, 2-7/8" long, 1970	5	7	20

47-C	DAF Tipper Container Truck	aqua or silver cab, yellow tipper box with light gray or dark gray plastic roof, 3" long, 1968	6	8	12
47-D	DAF Tipper Container Truck	silver cab, yellow tipper box, five spoke thin wheels, 3" long, 1970	4	6	20
14-A	Daimler Ambulance	cream body, silver trim, no number cast on body, "AMBULANCE" cast on sides, 1-7/8" long, 1956	20	35	45
14-B	Daimler Ambulance	silver trim, "AMBULANCE" cast on sides, red cross on roof, 2-5/8" long, 1958	40	65	85
74-B	Daimler Bus	double deck, white plastic interior, four black plastic wheels, 3" long, 1966	10	15	20
74-C	Daimler Bus	double deck, white plastic interior, five spoke thin wheels, 3" long, 1970	7	10	20
67-E	Datsun 260Z 2+2	metallic burgundy body, black base and grille, yellow interior, 3" long, 1978	3	4	6
24-G	Datsun 280ZX	black body and base, clear windows, five spoke wheels, 2-7/8" long, 1979	2	3	5
33-E	Datsun or 126X	yellow body, amber windows, silver interior, 3" long, 1973	5	8	10
9-A	Dennis Fire Escape Engine	red body, metal wheels, no front bumper, 2-1/4" long, 1955	10	20	30
20-F	Desert Dawg Jeep 4x4	white body, red top and stripes, white "Jeep" and yellow, red and green, "Desert Dawg" decal, 1982	2	3	5
1-A	Diesel Road Roller	dark green body, flat canopy, tow hook, driver, 1-7/8" long, 1953	15	25	35
1-H	Dodge Challenger	red body, white plastic top, silver interior, wide five spoke wheels, 2-15/16" long, 1976	3	5	8
63-G	Dodge Challenger	green body, black base, bumpers and grille, clear windows, 2-7/8" long, 1980	3	5	7
52-C	Dodge Charger	clear windows, black interior, five spoke wide wheels, 2-7/8" long, 1970	4	6	8
63-C	Dodge Crane Truck	yellow body, green windows, six black plastic wheels, rotating crane cab, 3"long, 1968	7	10	15
63-D	Dodge Crane Truck	yellow body, green windows, four spoke wide wheels, yellow plastic hook, 2-3/4" long, 1970	5	7	20
70-D	Dodge Dragster	pink body, clear windows, silver interior, five spoke wide front wheels, 3" long, 1971	7	10	15
13-D	Dodge Wreck Truck	green cab and crane, yellow body, green windows, 3" long, 1965	300	500	700
13-E	Dodge Wreck Truck	yellow cab, rear body, red plastic hook, green windows, 3" long, 1970	10	15	40
43-E	Dragon Wheels Volkswagen	light green body, amber windows, silver interior, orange on black "Dragon Wheels" on sides, large rear wheels, 2-13/16" long, 1972	5	7	9
58-B	Drott Excavator	red or orange body, movable front shovel, green rubber treads, 2-5/8" long, 1962	35	50	70
2-A	Dumper	green body, red dumper, gold trim, thin driver, green painted wheels, 1-5/8" long, 1953	35	50	70
2-B	Dumper	green body, red dumper, no trim color, fat driver, 1-7/8" long, 1957	20	30	40
48-C	Dumper Truck	red body, green tinted windows, 3" long, 1966	10	20	25
48-D	Dumper Truck	bright blue cab, yellow body, green windows, 3" long, 1970	5	7	25
25-A	Dunlop Truck	dark blue body, silver grille, 2-1/8" long, 1956	10	20	25
57-E	Eccles Trailer Caravan	orange roof, green plastic interior, five spoke thin wheels, 3" long, 1970	5	7	10
20-B	ERF 686 Truck	dark blue body, silver radiator, eight plastic silver wheels, No. 20 cast on black base, 2-5/8" long, 1959	25	45	60

6-C	Euclid Quarry Truck	yellow body, three round axles, two front black plastic wheels, two solid rear dual wheels, 2-5/8" long, 1964	15	25	30
6-B	Euclid Quarry Truck	yellow body, four ribs on dumper sides, plastic wheels, 2-1/2" long, 1957	10	20	25
35-D	Fandango	white body, red interior, chrome rear engine, large five spoke rear wheels, 3" long, 1975	3	5	8
58-F	Faun Dump Truck	yellow cab and dumper, black base, 2-7/8" long, 1976	5	10	15
70-F	Ferrari 308 GTB	red body and base, black plastic interior, side stripe, 2-15/16" long, 1981	2	3	5
75-B	Ferrari Berlinetta	metallic green body of various shades, ivory interior and tow hook, four wire or silver plastic wheels, 3" long, 1965	10	20	25
75-C	Ferrari Berlinetta	ivory interior, five spoke thin wheels, 2-3/4" long, 1970	5	7	25
73-B	Ferrari F1 Racing Car	light and dark red body, plastic driver, white and yellow "73" decal on sides, 2-5/8" long, 1962	15	25	40
61-A	Ferret Scout Car	olive green, tan driver faces front or back, four black plastic wheels, 2-1/4" long, 1959	10	20	25
56-B	Fiat 1500	silver grille, red interior and tow hook, brown or tan luggage on roof, 2-1/2" long, 1965	10	15	20
9-G	Fiat Abarth	white body, red interior, 1982	2	3	5
18-E	Field Car	yellow body, tan plastic roof, ivory interior and tow hook, green plastic tires, 2-5/8" long, 1969	50	145	200
18-F	Field Car	yellow body, tan roof, red wheels, ivory interior and tow hook, 2-5/8" long, 1970	5	7	20
29-C	Fire Pumper Truck	red body, metal grille, white plastic hose and ladders, 3" long, 1966	3	7	20
29-D	Fire Pumper Truck	red body, metal grille, white plastic hose and ladders, 3" long, 1970	2	5	20
53-G	Flareside Pick-up	blue body, white interior, grille and pipes, clear windshield, lettered with "326", "Baja Bouncer" and "B.F. Goodrich", 1982	2	4	5
11-F	Flying Bug	metallic red, gray windows, small five spoke front wheels, large five spoke rear wheels, 2-7/8" long, 1972	5	7	10
63-B	Foamite Fire Fighting Crash Tender	red body, six black plastic wheels, white plastic hose and ladder on roof, 2-1/4" long, 1964	10	15	40
21-D	Foden Concrete Truck	orange/yellow body and rotating barrel, green tinted windows, eight plastic wheels, 3" long, 1968	3	5	15
21-E	Foden Concrete Truck	red body, orange barrel, green base and windows five spoke wheels, 2-7/8" long, 1970	2	10	20
26-A	Foden Ready Mix Concrete Truck	orange body and rotating barrel, silver or gold grille, four silver plastic wheels, 1-3/4" long, 1956	50	100	140
26-B	Foden Ready Mix Concrete Truck	orange body, gray plastic rotating barrel, with or without silver grille, six gray wheels, 2-1/4" long, 1961	60	130	180
7-B	Ford Anglia	blue body, green tinted windows, 2-5/8" long, 1961	10	15	30
54-D	Ford Capri	ivory interior and tow hook, clear windows, five spoke wide wheels, 3" long, 1971	3	4	6
45-B	Ford Corsair with Boat	pale yellow body, red interior and tow hook, green roof rack with green plastic boat, 2-3/8" long, 1965	10	15	20
25-E	Ford Cortina	clear windows, ivory interior and tow hook, thin five spoke wheels, 2-3/4" long, 1970	3	6	10
55-H	Ford Cortina	metallic gold/green body, unpainted base and grille, wide multispoke wheels, 3-1/16" long, 1979	3	4	5
55-I	Ford Cortina	metallic tan body, yellow interior, blue racing stripes, 1982	2	4	6

25-D	Ford Cortina G.T.	light brown body in various shade, ivory interior and tow hook, 2-7/8" long, 1968	4	7	10
31-A	Ford Customline Station Wagon	yellow body, no windows, with or without red painted tail lights, 2-5/8" long, 1957	20	30	40
9-F	Ford Escort RS2000	white body, black base and grille, tan interior, wide multispoke wheels, 3" long, 1978	3	5	7
59-B	Ford Fairlane Fire Chief's Car	red body, ivory interior, clear windows, four plastic wheels, 2-5/8" long, 1963	35	75	125
55-B	Ford Fairlane Police Car	silver grille, ivory interior, clear windows, four plastic wheels, 2-5/8" long, 1963	20	55	100
31-B	Ford Fairlane Station Wagon	green or clear windows, with or without red painted tail lights, 2-3/4" long, 1960	10	30	35
59-C	Ford Galaxie Fire Chief's Car	red body, ivory interior, driver and tow hook, clear windows, four black plastic wheels, 2-7/8" long, 1966	5	10	40
59-D	Ford Galaxie Fire Chief's Car	red body, ivory interior and tow hook, clear windows, four spoke thin wheels, 2-7/8" long, 1970	3	7	30
55-C	Ford Galaxie Police Car	white body, ivory interior, driver and tow hook, clear windows, 2-7/8" long, 1966	10	15	30
45-C	Ford Group 6	metallic green body, ivory interior, clear windows, five spoke wide wheels, 3" long, 1970	5	7	10
41-C	Ford GT	white or yellow body, red interior, clear windows, yellow or red plastic wheels, 2-5/8" long, 1965	20	30	40
41-D	Ford GT	white body, red interior, clear windows, five spoke wheels, 2-5/8" long, 1970	5	7	20
71-C	Ford Heavy Wreck Truck	red cab, white bumper, amber or green windows, 3" long, 1968	25	75	100
71-D	Ford Heavy Wreck Truck	red cab, white body, green windows and dome light, four spoke wide wheels, 3" long, 1970	15	25	30
8-F	Ford Mustang	wide five spoke wheels, interior and tow hook same color, 2-7/8" long, 1970	10	25	50
8-E	Ford Mustang Fastback	white body, red interior, clear windows, 2-7/8" long, 1966	7	10	30
6-E	Ford Pick up	red body, white removable canopy, five spoke wheels, 2-3/4" long, 1970	5	7	15
6-D	Ford Pick up	red body, white removable plastic canopy, four black plastic wheels, 2-3/4" long, 1968	10	15	20
30-A	Ford Prefect	blue body, metal wheels, silver grille, black tow hook, 2-1/4" long, 1956	20	60	90
7-C	Ford Refuse Truck	orange cab, gray plastic dumper, silver metal loader, 3" long, 1966	7	10	15
7-D	Ford Refuse Truck	gray plastic body, silver metal dumper, 3" long, 1970	6	8	15
63-A	Ford Service Ambulance	olive green body, four plastic wheels, round white circle on sides with red cross, 2-1/2" long, 1959	15	20	45
70-A	Ford Thames Estate Car	yellow upper, bluish/green lower, four plastic wheels, 2-1/8" long, 1959	10	15	30
59-A	Ford Thames Van	silver grille, four plastic knobby wheels, 2-1/8" long, 1958	35	75	110
75-A	Ford Thunderbird	cream top half, pink bottom half, green tinted windows, 2-5/8" long, 1960	25	35	45
61-D	Ford Wreck Truck	red body, black base and grille, frosted amber windows, 3" long, 1978	3	5	7
33-B	Ford Zephyr 6MKIII	blue/green body shades, clear windows, ivory interior, 2-5/8" long, 1963	15	20	30

53-D	Ford Zodiac	clear windows, ivory interior, five spoke wheels, 2-3/4" long, 1970	5	7	15
39-A	Ford Zodiac Convertible	peach/pink body shades, tan driver, metal wheels, silver grille, 2-5/8" long, 1957	35	65	90
53-C	Ford Zodiac MK IV	metallic silver blue body, clear windows, ivory interior, four black plastic wheels, 2-3/4" long, 1968	7	10	15
33-A	Ford Zodiac MKII Sedan	with or without silver grille, with or without red painted tail lights, 2-5/8" long, 1957	20	30	45
72-A	Fordson Tractor	blue body with tow hook, 2" long, 1959	10	20	25
15-F	Fork Lift Truck	red body, yellow hoist, 2-1/2" long, 1972	3	4	6
34-E	Formula 1 Racing Car	metallic pink, white driver, clear glass, wide four spoke wheels, 2-7/8" long, 1971	7	10	15
36-F	Formula 5000	orange body, silver rear engine, large clover leaf rear slicks, 3" long, 1975	5	7	10
28-H	Formula Racing Car	gold body, silver engine and pipes, white driver and "Champion", black "8" on front and sides, large clover leaf rear wheels, 1982	2	3	5
22-E	Freeman Inter-City Commuter	clear windows, ivory interior, five spoke wide wheels, 3" long, 1970	5	7	10
63-E	Freeway Gas Truck	red cab, purple tinted windows, small wide wheels on front, clover leaf design, 3" long, 1973	10	15	20
62-A	General Service Lorry	olive green body, six black wheels, 2-5/8" long, 1959	15	25	30
44-D	GMC Refrigerator Truck	red ribbed roof cab, turquoise box with gray plastic rear door that opens, green windows, 1967	7	10	20
44-D	GMC Refrigerator Truck	green windows, four spoke wheels, gray plastic rear door, 2-13/16" long, 1970	5	7	15
26-C	GMC Tipper Truck	red tipping cab, silver tipper body with swinging door, four wheels, 2-5/8" long, 1968	5	7	20
26-D	GMC Tipper Truck	red cab, silver/gray tipper body, four spoke wide wheels, 2-1/2" long, 1970	10	15	20
66-C	Greyhound Bus	silver body, white plastic interior, clear or dark amber windows, six black plastic wheels, 3" long, 1967	25	35	45
66-D	Greyhound Bus	silver body, white interior, amber windows, five spoke thin wheels, 3" long, 1970	5	10	20
70-B	Grit Spreader Truck	dark red cab, four black plastic wheels, 2-5/8" long, 1966	5	7	15
70-C	Grit Spreader Truck	red cab, yellow body, green windows, gray plastic rear pull, 2-5/8" long, 1970	6	8	15
4-F	Gruesome Twosome	metallic gold body, wide five spoke wheels, 2-7/8" long, 1971	5	7	10
23-F	GT 350	white body, blue stripes on hood, roof and rear deck, 2-7/8" long, 1970	3	4	5
7-E	Hairy Hustler	metallic bronze, silver interior, five spoke front wheels, clover leaf rear wheels, 2-7/8" long, 1971	5	7	10
50-G	Harley-Davidson Motorcycle	silver/brown metallic frame and tank, chrome engine and pipes, brown rider, 2-11/16" long, 1980	2	3	7
66-B	Harley-Davidson Motorcycle/Sidecar	metallic bronze body, three wire wheels, 2-5/8" long, 1962	20	45	75
69-B	Hatra Tractor Shovel	orange or yellow movable shovel arms, four plastic tires, 3" long, 1965	20	30	40
40-C	Hay Trailer	blue body with tow bar, yellow plastic racks, yellow plastic wheels, 3-3/4" long, 1967	5	10	15
55-G	Hellraiser	white body, unpainted base and grille, silver rear engine, 3" long, 1975	3	5	7
15-G	Hi Ho Silver	metallic pearl gray body, 2-1/2" long, 1971	7	10	15

56-D	Hi-Tailer	white body, silver engine and windshield, wide five spoke front wheels, wide clover leaf rear wheels, 3" long, 1974	4	6	8
43-A	Hillman Minx	with or without silver grille, with or without red painted tail lights, 2-5/8" long, 1958	15	20	30
38-C	Honda Motorcycle and Trailer	metallic blue/green cycle with wire wheels, black plastic tires, orange trailer, 2-7/8" long, 1967	10	15	20
38-D	Honda Motorcycle and Trailer	yellow trailer with five spoke thin wheels, 2-7/8" long, 1970	5	7	20
18-G	Hondarora Motorcycle	red frame and fenders chrome bars, fork, engine, black seat, 2-3/8" long, 1975	5	15	25
17-E	Horse Box	blue tinted windows, five spoke thin wheels, white plastic horses inside box, 2-3/4" long, 1970	5	10	15
40-E	Horse Box	orange cab, off white van with tan plastic door, small wheels, 2-13/16" long, 1977	4	5	7
17-D	Horse Box, Ergomatic Cab	red cab, green plastic box, gray side door, 1969	10	15	20
7-A	Horse Drawn Milk Float	orange body, white driver and bottle load, brown horse with white mane and hoofs, 2-1/4" long, 1954	25	55	90
46-G	Hot Chocolate	metallic brown front lid and sides, black roof, 2-13/16" long, 1972	3	4	5
67-d	Hot Rocker	metallic lime/green body, white interior and tow hook, five spoke wide wheels, 3" long, 1973	3	5	7
36-E	Hot Rod Draguar	metallic red body, clear canopy, wide five spoke wheels, 2-13/16" long, 1970	4	6	8
2-G	Hovercraft	metallic green top, tan base, silver engine, yellow windows, 3-1/8" long, 1976	4	8	12
72-D	Hovercraft	white body, black bottom and base, red props, 3" long, 1972	4	7	10
17-C	Hoveringham Tipper	red body, orange dumper, 2-7/8" long, 1963	7	10	25
42-C	Iron Fairy Crane	red body, yellow/orange crane, black plastic wheels, yellow plastic single cable hook, 3" long, 1969	7	10	30
42-D	Iron Fairy Crane	four spoke wheels, yellow plastic hook, 3" long, 1970	25	35	50
14-D	Iso Grifo	blue body, light blue interior and tow hook, clear windows, 3" long, 1968	5	7	15
14-E	Iso Grifo	five spoke wheels, clear windows, 3" long, 1969	5	10	15
65-A	Jaguar 3.4 Litre Saloon	silver grille, silver or black bumpers, four gray plastic wheels, 2-1/2" long, 1959	7	10	15
65-B	Jaguar 3.8 Litre Sedan	red body shades, green tinted windows, four plastic wheels, 2-5/8" long, 1962	5	7	30
28-C	Jaguar Mark 10	light brown body, off white interior, working hood, gray motor and wheels, 2-3/4" long, 1964	35	65	90
32-A	Jaguar XK 140 Coupe	with or without silver grille, with or without red painted tail lights, 2-3/8" long, 1957	20	30	40
32-B	Jaguar XKE	metallic red body, ivory interior, clear or tinted windows, 2-5/8" long, 1962	15	20	35
38-F	Jeep	olive green body, black base and interior, wide five spoke reverse accent wheels, no hubs, 2-3/8" long, 1976	5	8	12
5-H	Jeep 4x4 Golden Eagle	brown body, wide four spoke wheels, eagle decal on hood, 1982	2	5	8
72-B	Jeep CJ5	yellow body, red plastic interior/tow hook, four yellow wheels, black plastic tires, 2-3/8", 1966	10	15	20
72-C	Jeep CJ5	red interior and tow hook, eight spoke wheels 2-3/8" long, 1970	5	7	10
53-F	Jeep CJ6	red body, unpainted base, bumper and winch, five spoke rear accent wheels, 2-15/16" long, 1977	2	3	5

71-B	Jeep Gladiator Pickup Truck	red body, clear windows, green or white interior, four black plastic wheels, fine treads, 2-5/8" long, 1964	18	25	30
2-F	Jeep Hot Rod	cream seats and tow hook, large wide four spoke wheels, 2-5/16" long, 1971	7	10	15
50-B	John Deere Tractor	green body and tow hook, yellow plastic wheels, 2-1/8" long, 1964	10	20	30
51-B	John Deere Trailer	green tipping body with tow bar, two small yellow wheels, three plastic barrels, 2-5/8" long, 1964	20	35	50
11-C	Jumbo Crane	yellow body, black plastic wheels, 3" long, 1965	5	10	15
71-E	Jumbo Jet Motorcycle	dark metallic blue body, red elephant head on handle bars, wide wheels, 2-3/4" long, 1973	4	6	8
38-A	Karrier Refuse Collector	silver grille headlights and bumper, 2-3/8" long, 1957	15	25	30
50-C	Kennel Truck	metallic green body, clear or blue tinted canopy, four plastic dogs, 2-3/4" long, 1969	5	15	40
50-D	Kennel Truck	green windows, light blue tinted canopy, four plastic dogs, 2-3/4" long, 1970	5	15	45
45-E	Kenworth Caboner Aerodyne	white body with blue and brown side stripes, silver grille, tanks and pipes, 1982	2	3	5
41-G	Kenworth Conventional Aerodyne	red cab and chassis, silver tanks and pipes, black and white stripes on cab, 1982	2	3	5
27-F	Lamborghini Countach	yellow body, silver interior and motor, five spoke wheels, 2-7/8" long, 1973	5	7	10
20-D	Lamborghini Marzel	amber windows, ivory interior, 2-3/4" long, 1969	15	20	35
33-C	Lamborghini Miura	metal grille, silver plastic wheels, red or white interior, clear or frosted back window, 2-3/4" long, 1969	10	15	20
33-D	Lamborghini Miura	clear windows, frosted rear window, five spoke wheels, 2-3/4" long, 1970	25	40	50
36-B	Lambretta TV 175 Motor Scooter and Sidecar	metallic green, three wheels, 2" long, 1961	25	35	45
12-A	Land Rover	olive green body, tan driver, metal wheels, 1-3/4" long, 1955	20	25	35
12-B	Land Rover	olive green body, no driver, tow hook, 2-1/4" long, 1959	35	55	75
57-C	Land Rover Fire Truck	red body, blue tinted windows, white plastic ladder on roof, 2-1/2" long, 1966	10	15	25
57-D	Land Rover Fire Truck	red body, blue tinted windows, white plastic removable ladder, 2-1/2" long, 1970	5	7	20
32-C	Leyland Petrol Tanker	green cab, white tank body, blue tinted windows, eight plastic wheels, 3" long, 1968	25	40	50
32-D	Leyland Petrol Tanker	green cab, white tank body, blue tinted windows, five spoke thin wheels, 3" long, 1970	10	20	50
40-B	Leyland Royal Tiger Coach	silver/gray body, green tinted windows four plastic wheels, 3" long, 1961	10	15	20
31-C	Lincoln Continental	clear windows, ivory interior, black plastic wheels, 2-7/8" long, 1964	10	15	20
31-D	Lincoln Continental	clear windows, ivory interior, five spoke wheels, 2-3/4" long, 1970	5	10	30
28-G	Lincoln Continental MK-V	red body, tan interior, 3" long, 1979	10	15	20
5-C	London Bus	red body, silver grille and headlights, 2-9/16" long, 1961	10	20	25
5-A	London Bus	red body, gold grille, metal wheels, 2" long, 1954	20	45	65

5-D	London Bus	red body, white plastic seats, black plastic wheels, 2-3/4" long, 1965	5	10	30
5-B	London Bus	red body, 2-1/4" long, 1957	20	45	65
	London E Class Tramcar	red, cream roof; News of the World decals	25	60	90
56-A	London Trolley Bus	red body, two trolley poles on top of roof, six wheels, 2-5/8" long, 1958	45	70	90
17-F	Londoner Bus	red body, white interior, five spoke wide wheels, 3" long, 1972	10	15	20
21-A	Long Distance Coach	light green body, black base, "London to Glasgow" orange decal on sides, 2-1/4" long, 1956	10	20	25
21-B	Long Distance Coach	green body, black base, No. 21 cast on baseplate, "London to Glasgow" orange decal on sides, 2-5/8" long, 1958	20	60	45
5-E	Lotus Europa	metallic blue body, clear windows, ivory interior and tow hook, 2-7/8" long, 1969	5	7	10
19-D	Lotus Racing Car	white driver, large rear wheels, 2-3/4" long, 1966	10	15	20
19-E	Lotus Racing Car	metallic purple, white driver, five spoke wide wheels with clover leaf design, 2-3/4" long, 1970	5	10	15
60-D	Lotus Super Seven	butterscotch, clear windshield, black interior and trunk, four spoke wide wheels, 2-7/8" long,1971	5	7	10
49-A	M3 Army Personnel Carrier	olive green body, gray rubber treads, 2-1/2" long, 1958	15	25	30
28-D	Mack Dump Truck	orange body, green windows, four large plastic wheels, 2-5/8" long, 1968	4	7	15
28-E	Mack Dump Truck	pea green body, green windows, large ballon wheels with clover leaf design, 2-5/8" long, 1970	2	5	15
35-A	Marshall Horse Box	red cab, brown horse box, silver grille, three rear windows in box, 2" long, 1957	20	25	35
52-A	Maserati 4 Cl. T/1948	red or yellow body, cream or white driver with or without circle on left shoulder, 2-3/8" long, 1958	10	17	25
32-E	Maserati Bora	metallic burgundy, clear windows, bright yellow interior, wide five spoke wheels, 3" long, 1972	5	7	10
4-A	Massey Harris Tractor	red body with rear fenders, tan driver, four spoke metal front wheels, 1954	30	40	55
4-B	Massey Harris Tractor	red body, no fenders, tan driver, solid metal front wheels, hollow inside rear wheels, 1-5/8" long, 1957	25	40	50
72-F	Maxi Taxi	yellow body, black "MAXI TAXI" on roof, five spoke wheels, 3" long, 1973	2	3	4
66-E	Mazda RX 500	orange body, purple windows, silver rear engine, five spoke wide wheels, 3" long, 1971	3	4	5
31-G	Mazda RX-7	white body, black base, burgundy stripe, black "RX-7", 3" long, 1979	3	4	5
31-H	Mazda RX-7	gray body with sunroof, black interior, 1982	15	25	35
10-A	Mechanical Horse and Trailer	red cab with three metal wheels, gray trailer with two metal wheels, 2-3/8" long, 1955	15	25	35
10-B	Mechanical Horse and Trailer	red cab, ribbed bed in trailer, metal front wheels on cab, 2-15/16" long, 1958	25	35	45
53-B	Mercedes-Benz 220 SE	silver grille, clear windows, ivory interior, four wheels, 2-3/4" long, 1963	15	25	30
27-D	Mercedes-Benz 230 SL	unpainted metal grille, red plastic interior and tow hook, black plastic wheels, 3" long, 1966	5	10	20
27-E	Mercedes-Benz 230 SL	metal grille, blue tinted windshield, five spoke wheels, 2-7/8" long, 1970	5	10	20

Number	Model	Description			
46-C	Mercedes-Benz 300 SE	clear windows, ivory interior, black plastic wheels, 2-7/8" long, 1968	5	10	20
46-D	Mercedes-Benz 300 SE	clear windows, ivory interior, five spoke thin wheels, 2-7/8" long, 1970	5	10	20
6-F	Mercedes-Benz 350 SL	orange body, black plastic convertible top, light yellow interior, 3" long, 1973	5	10	20
56-E	Mercedes-Benz 450 SEL	metallic blue body, unpainted base and grille, 3" long, 1979	3	4	5
3-D	Mercedes-Benz Ambulance	ivory interior, Red Cross label on side doors, 2-7/8" long, 1970	5	10	15
3-C	Mercedes-Benz Ambulance	varying body colors, white interior and stretcher, blue windows and dome light, metal grille, black plastic wheels, 2-7/8" long, 1968	5	7	15
68-B	Mercedes-Benz Coach	white plastic top half, white plastic interior, clear windows, four black plastic wheels, 2-7/8" long, 1965	30	40	55
42-F	Mercedes-Benz Container Truck	red body, black base and grille, removable ivory container with red top and back door, six wheels, 3" long, 1977	4	5	7
1-F	Mercedes-Benz Lorry	metallic gold, removable orange or yellow canopy, 3" long, 1970	4	6	8
1-E	Mercedes-Benz Lorry	pale green body, removable orange plastic canopy, 3" long, 1967	5	7	15
56-F	Mercedes-Benz Taxi	tan plastic interior, unpainted base, clear plastic windows, red "Taxi" sign on roof, 3" long, 1980	3	4	5
2-D	Mercedes-Benz Trailer	pale green body, removable orange canopy, tow hook, black plastic wheels, 3 1/2" long, 1968	5	7	15
2-E	Mercedes-Benz Trailer	metallic gold body, removable canopy, rotating tow bar, 3-1/4" long, 1970	3	5	15
49-B	Mercedes-Benz Umimog	silver grille, four black plastic tires, 2-1/2" long, 1967	10	15	20
62-C	Mercury Cougar	metallic lime green body shades, red plastic interior and tow hook, silver wheels, 3" long, 1968	7	10	15
62-D	Mercury Cougar	red interior and tow hook, five spoke thin wheels, 3" long, 1970	3	5	15
62-E	Mercury Cougar "Rat Rod"	red interior and tow hook, small five spoke front wheels, larger five spoke wide rear windows, 3" long, 1970	4	6	8
59-E	Mercury Fire Chief's Car	red body, ivory interior, two occupants, clear windows, five spoke wide wheels, 3" long, 1971	5	7	20
55-D	Mercury Police Car	white body, ivory interior with two figures, clear windows, four silver wheels with black plastic tires, 3" long, 1968	10	15	40
55-E	Mercury Police Car	white body, ivory interior, two occupants, five spoke thin wheels, 3" long, 1970	5	7	15
55-F	Mercury Police Station Wagon	white body, ivory interior, no occupants, five spoke wide wheels, 3" long, 1971	5	7	10
73-C	Mercury Station Wagon	metallic lime green body shades, ivory interior with dogs in rear, 3-1/8" long, 1968	7	10	15
73-D	Mercury Station Wagon	red body, ribbed rear roof, ivory interior with two dogs, 3" long, 1970	3	5	10
73-E	Mercury Station Wagon	red body, ribbed rear roof, ivory interior with two dogs, 3" long, 1972	3	5	7
35-C	Merryweather Fire Engine	metallic red body, blue windows, white removable ladder on roof, five spoke thin wheels, 3" long, 1969	5	7	10

48-A	Meteor Sports Boat and Trailer	metal boat with tan deck and blue hull, black metal trailer with tow bar, 2-3/8" long, 1958	30	45	60
19-B	MG Midget	silver or gold grilles, tan driver, 2-1/4" long, 1958	20	45	75
19-A	MG Midget	white body, tan driver, red seats, spare tire on trunk, 2" long, 1956	30	60	75
64-B	MG-1100	green body, ivory interior, driver, dog and tow hook, clear windows, four black plastic wheels, 2-5/8" long, 1966	5	7	15
64-C	MG-1100	ivory interior and tow hook, one occupant and dog, clear windows, 2-5/8" long, 1970	7	10	15
19-B	MGA Sports Car	white body variation, silver wheels, tan driver, silver or gold grilles, 2-1/4" long, 1958	50	95	125
51-G	Midnight Magic	black body, silver stripes on hood, five spoke front wheels, clover leaf rear windows, 1972	2	3	4
14-F	Mini Haha	red body, pink driver, silver engine, large spoke rear slicks, 2-3/8" long, 1975	5	9	12
74-A	Mobile Refreshment Canteen	cream, white, or silver body, upper side door opens with interior utensils, "Refreshment" on front side, 2-5/8" long, 1959	15	40	65
1-G	Mod Rod	yellow body, tinted windows, red or black wheels, 2-7/8" long, 1971	10	15	20
25-F	Mod Tractor	metallic purple, orange/yellow seat and tow hook, 2-1/8" long, 1972	10	15	20
73-G	Model A Ford	off white body, black base, green fenders and running boards, 1979	2	3	5
3-E	Monteverdi Hai	dark orange body, blue tinted windows, ivory interior, 2-7/8" long, 1973	3	6	8
60-A	Morris J2 Pickup	blue body, open windshield and side door windows, four plastic wheels, 2-1/4" long, 1958	15	25	30
46-A	Morris Minor 1000	dark green body, metal wheels, no windows, 2" long, 1958	20	30	45
2-C	Muirhill Dumper	red cab, green dumper, black plastic wheels, 2-1/6" long, 1961	10	20	25
54-G	NASA Tracking Vehicle	white body, silver radar screen, red windows, blue "Space Shuttle Command Center", red "NASA" on roof, 1982	2	3	5
36-C	Opel Diplomat	metallic light gold body, white interior and tow hook, clear windows, black plastic wheels, 2-3/5" long, 1966	10	15	20
36-D	Opel Diplomat	ivory interior and tow hook, clear windows, five spoke thin wheels, 2-7/8" long, 1970	5	7	15
74-F	Orange Peel	white body, wide orange and black stripe and black "ORANGE PEEL" on each side, 3" long, 1971	3	4	5
47-F	Pannier Tank Loco	green body, black base and insert, six large plastic wheels, 3" long, 1979	3	5	7
8-H	Pantera	white body, blue base, red/brown interior, five spoke rear slicks, 3" long, 1975	35	45	60
54-E	Personnel Carrier	olive green body, green windows, black base and grille, tan men and benches, 3" long, 1976	4	5	7
43-G	Perterbilt Conventional	black cab and chassis, silver grille, fenders and tanks, red and white side stripes, six wheels, 3" long, 1982	2	3	5
19-H	Peterbilt Cement Truck	green body, orange barrel, "Big Pete" decal on hood, 1982	2	3	5
30-H	Peterbilt Quarry Truck	yellow body, gray dumper, silver tanks, "Dirty Dumper" on sides, six wheels, 1982	2	4	6
56-G	Peterbilt Tanker	blue cab, white tank with red "Milk's the One", silver tanks, grille, and pipes, 1982	15	25	40

48-E	Pi-Eyed Piper	metallic blue body, amber windows, small front wheels, large rear wheels, 2-7/8" long, 1972	5	7	10
46-B	Pickford Removal Van	green body, with or without silver grilles, 2-5/8" long, 1960	15	30	50
10-D	Pipe Truck	red body, gray pipes, "Leyland" or "Ergomatic" on front base, eight black plastic wheels, 2-7/8", 1966	7	10	15
10-E	Pipe Truck	black pipe racks, eight five spoke thin wheels, 2-7/8" long, 1970	4	6	15
10-F	Piston Popper	metallic blue body, white interior, 2-7/8" long, 1973	4	6	8
60-F	Piston Popper	yellow body, red windows, silver engine, labels top and sides, large rear wheels, 1982	2	3	5
59-F	Planet Scout	metallic green top, green bottom and base, silver interior, grille and roof panels, large multispoke rear wheels, 2-3/4" long 1975	4	5	7
10-G	Plymouth Gran Fury Police Car	white body w/black detailing, "Police" on doors, white interior, 3" long, 1979	3	4	5
52-D	Police Launch	white deck, blue hull and men, 3" long, 1976	2	4	6
33-F	Police Motorcyclist	white frame, seat and bags, silver engine and pipes, wire wheels, 2-1/2" long, 1977	5	7	10
20-E	Police Patrol	white body, "Police" on orange side stripe, orange interior, 2-7/8" long, 1975	6	8	12
39-B	Pontiac Convertible	purple body, with or without silver grille, cream or ivory interior, silver wheels, 2-3/4" long, 1962	30	50	75
4-G	Pontiac Firebird	metallic blue body, silver interior, slick tires, 2-7/8" long, 1975	2	7	12
22-C	Pontiac Grand Prix Sports Coupe	light gray interior and tow hook, clear windows, four black plastic wheels, 3" long, 1964	6	9	12
22-D	Pontiac Grand Prix Sports Coupe	light gray interior, clear windows, five spoke thin wheels, 3" long, 1970	2	4	6
16-G	Pontiac Trans Am	white body, red interior, clear windows, blue eagle decal, 1982	2	3	4
35-F	Pontiac Trans Am T Roof	black body, red interior, yellow "Turbo" on doors, yellow eagle on hood, 1982	2	3	5
43-C	Pony Trailer	yellow body, clear windows, gray plastic rear fold-down door, four plastic wheels, 2-5/8" long, 1968	7	10	15
43-D	Pony Trailer	yellow body, clear windows, gray rear door, five spoke thin wheels, 2-5/8" long, 1970	3	5	15
68-C	Porsche 910	amber windows, ivory interior, five spoke wheels, 2-7/8" long, 1970	7	10	15
59-G	Porsche 928	metallic brown body, black base, wide five spoke wheels, 3" long, 1980	3	5	6
3-F	Porsche Turbo	metallic brown body, black base, yellow interior, wide five arch wheels, 3" long, 1978	4	7	10
15-A	Prime Mover	silver trim on grille and tank, tow hook same color as body, 2-1/8" long, 1956	20	35	50
6-A	Quarry Truck	orange cab, gray dumper with six vertical ribs, metal wheels, 2-1/8" long, 1954	15	30	50
29-E	Racing Mini	clear windows, five spoke wide wheels, 2-1/4" long, 1970	5	7	10
44-F	Railway Passenger Car	cream plastic upper and roof, red metal lower, black base, 3-1/16" long, 1978	3	5	7
14-G	Rallye Royal	metallic pearl gray body, black plastic interior, five spoke wide wheels, 2-7/8" long, 1973	3	4	5
48-G	Red Rider	red body, white "Red Rider" and flames on sides, 2-7/8" long, 1972	2	3	4
15-C	Refuse Truck	blue body, gray dumper with opening door, 2-1/2" long, 1963	10	15	20

Number	Name	Description			
36-G	Refuse Truck	red metallic body, silver/gray base, orange plastic container, 3" long, 1980	2	3	4
62-F	Renault 17TL	white interior, green tinted windows, green "9" in yellow and black circle, 3" long, 1974	5	7	10
21-G	Renault 5TL	yellow body and removable rear hatch, tan interior, silver base and grille, 2 11/16" long, 1978	4	9	15
1-I	Revin' Rebel	orange body, blue top, black interior, large five spoke rear wheels, 1982	2	3	5
19-F	Road Dragster	ivory interior, silver plastic motor, 2-7/8" long, 1970	3	4	6
1-B	Road Roller	pale green body, canopy, tow hook, dark tan or light tan driver, 2-1/4" long, 1953	25	45	65
1-C	Road Roller	light green or dark green body, canopy, metal rollers, tow bar, driver, 2-3/8" long, 1958	20	25	35
21-F	Road Roller	yellow body, red seat, black plastic rollers, 2-5/8" long, 1973	7	10	15
11-A	Road Tanker	green body, flat base between cab and body, gold trim on front grille, gas tanks, metal wheels, no number cast, 2" long, 1955	60	265	360
11-B	Road Tanker	red body, gas tanks, "11" on baseplate, black plastic wheels, 2-1/2" long, 1958	20	55	80
44-B	Rolls-Royce Phantom V	clear windows, ivory interior, black plastic wheels, 2-7/8" long, 1964	15	20	30
44-A	Rolls-Royce Silver Cloud	metallic blue body, no windows, with or without silver grille, 2-5/8" long, 1958	15	20	25
24-C	Rolls-Royce Silver Shadow	metallic red body, ivory interior, clear windows, silver hub caps or solid silver wheels, 3" long, 1967	10	15	20
24-D	Rolls-Royce Silver Shadow	ivory interior, clear windows, five spoke wheels, 3" long, 1970	5	7	20
69-C	Rolls-Royce Silver Shadow Coupe	amber windshield, five spoke wheels, 3" long, 1969	5	7	10
39-E	Rolls-Royce Silver Shadow II	metallic silver gray body, red interior, clear windshield, 3-1/16" long, 1979	3	5	7
7-G	Rompin' Rabbit	white body, red windows, yellow lettered "Rompin Rabbit" on side, 1982	2	3	5
54-B	S & S Cadillac Ambulance	white body, blue tinted windows, white interior, red cross decal on front doors, 2-7/8" long, 1965	10	15	30
65-D	Saab Sonnet	metallic blue body, amber windows, light orange interior and hood, five spoke wide wheels, 2-3/4" long, 1973	5	7	10
12-C	Safari Land Rover	clear windows, white plastic interior and tow hook, black plastic wheels, 2-1/3" long, 1965	7	10	20
12-D	Safari Land Rover	metallic gold, clear windows, tan luggage, five spoke thin wheels, 2-13/16" long, 1970	10	20	30
67-A	Saladin Armoured Car	olive green body, rotating gun turret, six black plastic wheels, 2-1/2" long, 1959	15	20	25
48-F	Sambron Jacklift	yellow body, black base and insert, no window, orange and yellow fork and boom combinations, 3-1/16" long, 1977	4	7	10
54-A	Saracen Personnel Carrier	olive green body, six black plastic wheels, 2-1/4" long, 1958	10	17	25
11-D	Scaffolding Truck	silver body, green tinted windows, black plastic wheels, 2-1/2" long, 1969	4	7	25
11-E	Scaffolding Truck	silver/gray body, green tinted windows, yellow pipes, 2-7/8" long, 1969	5	10	25
64-A	Scammel Breakdown Truck	olive green, double cable hook, six black plastic wheels, 2-1/2" long, 1959	15	25	30

16-C	Scammel Mountaineer Dump Truck/Snow Plow	gray cab, orange dumper body, six plastic wheels, 3" long, 1964	10	20	25
5-F	Seafire Boat	white deck, blue hull, silver engine, red pipes, 2-15/16" long, 1975	6	8	10
75-F	Seasprite Helicopter	white body, red base, black blades, 1977	3	5	7
12-E	Setra Coach	clear windows, ivory interior, five spoke thin wheels, 3" long, 1970	5	7	10
29-F	Shovel Nose Tractor	yellow body and base, red plastic shovel, silver engine, 2-7/8" long, 1976	8	15	20
24-F	Shunter	metallic green body, red base, tan instruments, no window, 3" long, 1978	3	5	7
26-F	Site Dumper	yellow body and dumper, black base, 2-5/8" long, 1976	2	3	5
60-B	Site Hut Truck	blue body, blue windows, four black plastic wheels, 2-1/2" long, 1966	7	10	15
60-C	Site Hut Truck	blue cab, blue windows, five spoke thin wheels, 2-1/2" long, 1970	5	7	15
41-E	Siva Spider	metallic red body, cream interior, clear windows, wide five spoke wheels, 3" long, 1972	5	7	10
37-G	Skip Truck	red body, yellow plastic bucket, light amber windows, silver interior, 2-11/16" long, 1976	3	5	7
64-D	Slingshot Dragster	pink body, white driver, five spoke thin front wheels, eight spoke wide rear wheels, 3" long, 1971	7	10	15
13-G	Snorkel Fire Engine	red body, yellow plastic snorkel and fireman, 3" long, 1977	3	5	7
35-B	Snowtrac Tractor	red body, silver painted grille, green windows, white rubber treads, 2-3/8" long, 1964	10	15	20
37-F	Soopa Coopa	metallic blue, amber windows, yellow interior, 2-7/8" long, 1972	3	4	5
48-B	Sports Boat and Trailer	plastic boat, red or white deck, hulls in red, white or cream, gold or silver motors, blue metal two-wheel trailers, boat 2-3/8" long, trailer 2-5/8" long, 1961	35	65	80
4-E	Stake Truck	cab colors vary, 2-7/8" long, 1970	5	7	15
4-D	Stake Truck	yellow cab, green tinted windows, 2-7/8" long, 1967	5	10	30
20-A	Stake Truck	gold trim on front grille and side gas tanks, ribbed bed, metal wheels, 2-3/8" long, 1956	50	75	100
38-E	Stingeroo Cycle	metallic purple body, ivory horse head at rear of seat, five spoke wide rear wheels, 3" long, 1973	4	6	8
46-E	Stretcha Fetcha	white body, blue windows, pale yellow interior, 2" long, 1972	6	8	12
28-F	Stroat Armored Truck	metallic gold body, brown plastic observer coming out of turret, five spoke wide wheels, 2-5/8" long, 1974	8	15	25
42-B	Studebaker Lark Wagonaire	blue body, sliding rear roof panel, white plastic interior and tow hook, 3" long, 1965	10	15	20
10-C	Sugar Container Truck	blue body, eight gray plastic wheels, "Tate & Lyle" decals on sides and rear, 2-5/8" long, 1961	30	55	75
37-H	Sun Burner	black body, red and yellow flames on hood and sides, 3" long, 1972	2	3	4
30-F	Swamp Rat	green deck, yellow plastic hull, tan soldier, black engine and prop, 3" long, 1976	2	4	6
27-G	Swing Wing Jet	red top and fins, white belly and retractable wings, 3" long, 1981	2	3	5
53-E	Tanzara	orange body, silver interior, small front wheels, larger rear wheels, 3" long, 1972	3	4	5
24-E	Team Matchbox	white driver, silver motor, wide clover leaf wheels, 2-7/8" long, 1973	15	20	25

62-B	Television Service Van	cream body, green tinted windows with roof window, four plastic wheels, 2-1/2" long, 1963	25	40	50
28-B	Thames Trader Compressor Truck	yellow body, black wheels, 2-3/4" long, 1959	20	25	35
13-C	Thames Wreck Truck	red body, bumper and parking lights, 2-1/2" long, 1961	15	25	30
74-D	Toe Joe	metallic lime green body, yellow interior, five spoke wide wheels, 2-3/4" long, 1972	3	4	6
23-C	Trailer Caravan	yellow or pink body with white roof, blue removable interior, 2-7/8" long, 1965	4	7	15
4-C	Triumph Motorcycle and Sidecar	silver/blue body, wire wheels, 2-1/8" long, 1960	25	40	60
42-E	Tyre Fryer	metallic red body, cream interior, clear windows, wide five spoke wheels, 3" long, 1972	3	4	6
5-G	U.S. Mail Jeep	blue body, white base and bumpers, black plastic seat, white canopy, wide five-arch rear wheels, 2-3/8" long, 1978	5	10	15
34-F	Vantastic	orange body, white base and interior, silver engine, large rear slicks, 2-7/8" long, 1975	4	7	9
22-B	Vauxhall Cresta	with or without silver grille, tow hook, plastic wheels, 2-5/8" long, 1958	20	40	60
40-D	Vauxhall Guildsman	pink body, light green windows, light cream interior and tow hook, wide five spoke wheels, 3" long, 1971	3	4	5
22-A	Vauxhall Sedan	dark red body, cream or off white roof, tow hook, 2-1/2" long, 1956	15	30	45
38-B	Vauxhall Victor Estate Car	yellow body, red or green interior, clear windows, 2-5/8" long, 1963	10	18	25
45-A	Vauxhall Victor Saloon	yellow body, with or without green tinted windows, with or without silver grille, 2-3/8" long, 1958	10	15	25
31-E	Volks Dragon	red body, purple tinted windows, 2-1/2" long, 1971	3	4	5
25-B	Volkswagen 1200 Sedan	silver-blue body, clear or tinted windows, 2-1/2" long, 1960	20	40	55
15-D	Volkswagen 1500 Saloon	off white body and interior, clear windows, "137" on doors, 2-7/8" long, 1968	10	20	30
15-E	Volkswagen 1500 Saloon	clear windows, "137" on doors, red decal on front, 2-7/8" long, 1968	7	15	20
67-B	Volkswagen 1600 TL	ivory interior, four black plastic tires, 2-3/4" long, 1967	10	15	20
67-C	Volkswagen 1600 TL	ivory interior, clear windows, five spoke wheels, 2-5/8" long, 1970	5	10	20
23-D	Volkswagen Camper	orange top, clear windows, five spoke wheels, 2-1/8" long, 1970	5	7	10
34-C	Volkswagen Camper Car	silver body, orange interior, black plastic wheels, raised roof, six windows, 2-5/8" long, 1967	15	20	30
34-D	Volkswagen Camper Car	silver body, orange interior, black plastic wheels, short raised sun roof, 2-5/8" long, 1968	10	20	25
7-F	Volkswagen Golf	green body, black base and grille, 2-7/8" long, 1976	4	8	12
34-B	Volkswagen Microvan	light green body, dark green interior, flat roof window tinted green, 2 3/5" long, 1962	20	30	40
34-A	Volkswagen Microvan	blue body, gray wheels, "Matchbox Inter-national Express" on sides, 2-1/4" long, 1957	30	40	50
73-F	Weasel	metallic green body, large five spoke slicks, 2-7/8" long, 1974	3	4	6

24-A	Weatherhill Hydraulic Excavator	metal wheels, "Weatherhill Hydraulic" decal on rear, 2-3/8" long, 1956	20	25	35
24-B	Weatherhill Hydraulic Excavator	yellow body, small and medium front wheels, large rear wheels, 2-5/8" long, 1959	10	15	20
57-F	Wild Life Truck	yellow body, red windows, light tinted blue canopy, 2-3/4" long, 1973	3	4	6
57-A	Wolseley 1500	with or without grilles, four wheels, 2-1/8" long, 1958	20	30	35
58-E	Woosh-n-Push	yellow body, red interior, large rear wheels, 2-7/8" long, 1972	3	4	5
35-E	Zoo Truck	1981	4	7	10

Nylint

Cars

Name	Description	Good	Ex	Mint
Howdy Doody Pump Mobile	8-1/2" long	250	450	650

Emergency Vehicles

Name	Description	Good	Ex	Mint
Ladder Truck	post war, 30" long	100	175	250

Trucks

Name	Description	Good	Ex	Mint
Guided Missile Launcher	1957	75	125	175
Tournahauler	dark green, tractor with enclosed cab, platform trailer, slid-out ramps, 41-1/2" long with ramp extended, 1955	125	150	250
U-Haul Ford Truck and Trailer	with twin I-Beam suspension	125	187	250

Smith-Miller

Emergency Vehicles

Name	Description	Good	Ex	Mint
"L" Mack Aerial Ladder	red w/gold lettering; polished aluminum surface, SMFD decals on hood and trailer sides, six-wheeler, 1950	375	475	795

Trucks

Name	Description	Good	Ex	Mint
"B" Mack Associated Truck Lines	red cab, polished aluminum trailer, decals on trailer sides, six-wheel tractor, eight-wheel trailer, 1954	500	850	1200
"B" Mack Blue Diamond Dump	all white truck with blue decals, hydraulic piston, 10-wheeler, 1954	600	950	1300
"B" Mack Lumber Truck	yellow cab and timber deck, three rollers, loading bar and two chains, six-wheeler, load of nine timbers, 1954	450	650	1000
"B" Mack Orange Dump Truck	construction orange all over, no decals, hydraulic piston, 10-wheeler, 1954	650	1150	1650
"B" Mack P.I.E.	red cab, polished trailer, six-wheel tractor, eight-wheel trailer, 1954	375	600	850
"B" Mack Searchlight	dark red paint schemes, fully rotating and elevating searchlight, battery-operated, 1954	500	775	1100
"B" Mack Silver Streak	yellow cab, unpainted, unpolished trailer sides, "Silver Streak" decal on both sides, six-wheel tractor, eight-wheel trailer, 1954	450	775	1050
"B" Mack Watson Bros.	yellow cab, polished aluminum trailer, decals on trailer sides and cab doors, 10-wheel tractor, eight-wheel trailer, 1954	650	1100	1500
"L" Mack Army Materials Truck	Army green, flatbed with dark green canvas, 10-wheeler, load of three wood barrels, two boards, large and small crate, 1952	375	500	750
"L" Mack Army Personnel Carrier	all Army green, wood sides, Army seal on door panels, military star on roof, 10-wheeler, 1952	375	500	750
"L" Mack Bekins Van	white, covered with "Bekins" decals, six-wheel tractor, four-wheel trailer, 1953	1000	1650	2000
"L" Mack Blue Diamond Dump	white cab, white dump bed, blue fenders and chassis, hydraulically operated, 10-wheeler, 1952	425	750	1050
"L" Mack International Paper Co.	white tractor cab, "International Paper Co." decals, six wheel tractor, four wheel trailer, 1952	375	650	900
"L" Mack Lyon Van	silver gray cab, dark blue fenders and frame, silver gray van box with blue "Lyon" decal, six-wheeler, 1950	425	800	1100
"L" Mack Material Truck	light metallic green cab, dark green fenders and frame, wood flatbed, six-wheeler, load of two barrels and six timbers, 1950	400	600	875
"L" Mack Merchandise Van	red cab, black fenders and frame, "Smith-Miller" decals on both sides of van box, double rear doors, six-wheeler, 1951	425	695	1000
"L" Mack Mobil Tandem Tanker	all red cab, "Mobilgas" and "Mobiloil" decals on tank sides, six-wheel tractor, six-wheel trailer, 1952	450	725	1000
"L" Mack Orange Hydraulic Dump	orange cab, orange dump bed, hydraulic, 10-wheeler, may or may not have "Blue Diamond" decals, 1952	850	1500	1950
"L" Mack Orange Materials Truck	all orange, flatbed with canvas, 10-wheeler, load of three barrels, two boards, large and small crate, 1952	400	650	900
"L" Mack P.I.E.	all red tractor, polished aluminum trailer, "P.I.E." decals on sides and front, six wheel tractor, eight-wheel trailer, 1950	395	550	850
"L" Mack Sibley Van	dark green cab, black fenders and frame, dark green van box with "Sibley's" decal in yellow on both sides, six-wheeler, 1950	850	1375	1850
"L" Mack Tandem Timber	red/black cab, six-wheeler, load of six wood lumber rollers, two loading bars, four chains and 18 or 24 boards, 1950	400	550	725
"L" Mack Tandem Timber	two-tone green cab, six-wheeler, load of six wood lumber rollers, two loading bars, four chains, and 18 timbers, 1953	400	550	725
"L" Mack Telephone Truck	all dark or two-tone green truck, "Bell Telephone System" decals on truck sides, six-wheeler, 1952	475	750	975
"L" Mack West Coast Fast Freight	silver with red/black or silver cab and chassis, "West Coast-Fast Freight" decals on sides of box, six-wheeler, 1952	475	775	1000

Chevrolet Arden Milk Truck	red cab, white wood body, four-wheeler, 1945	275	465	800
Chevrolet Bekins Van	blue die cast cab, all white trailer, 14-wheeler, 1945	275	350	750
Chevrolet Coca-Cola Truck	red cab, wood body painted red, four-wheeler, 1945	300	600	850
Chevrolet Flatbed Tractor-Trailer	unpainted wood trailer, unpainted polished cab, 14-wheeler, 1945	250	300	500
Chevrolet Heinz Grocery Truck	yellow cab, load of four waxed cases, 1946	225	325	475
Chevrolet Livestock Truck	polished, unpainted tractor cab and trailer, 1946	175	275	375
Chevrolet Lumber	green cab, load of 60 polished boards and two chains, 1946	150	195	275
Chevrolet Lyons Van	blue cab, silver trailer, 1946	165	325	500
Chevrolet Material Truck	green cab, no side rails, load of three barrels, two cases and 18 boards, 1946	135	185	225
Chevrolet Stake	yellow tractor cab	185	250	425
Chevrolet Trans-continental Vanliner	blue tractor cab, white trailer, "Bekins" logos and decals on trailer sides, 1946	200	350	495
Chevrolet Union Ice Truck	blue cab, white body, load of eight waxed blocks of ice, 1946	300	495	800
Ford Bekins Van	red sand-cast tractor, gray sheet metal trailer, 14-wheeler, 1944	275	500	750
Ford Coca-Cola Truck	red sandcast cab, wood body painted red, four-wheeler, 1944	400	650	900
GMC Arden Milk Truck	red cab, white painted wood body with red stakes, four-wheeler, 1947	200	425	650
GMC Bank of America Truck	dark brownish green cab and box, 'Bank of America' decal on box sides, four-wheeler, 1949	115	165	275
GMC Be Mac Tractor-Trailer	red cab, plain aluminum frame, "Be Mac Transport Co." in white letters on door panels, 14-wheeler, 1949	250	350	700
GMC Bekins Vanliner	blue cab, metal trailer painted white, 14-wheeler, 1947	175	275	425
GMC Coca-Cola Truck	red cab, yellow wood body, four-wheeler, load of 16 Coca-Cola cases, 1947	400	675	895
GMC Coca-Cola Truck	all yellow truck, red Coca-Cola decals, five spoke hubs, four-wheeler, load of six cases each with 24 plastic bottles, 1954	275	450	750
GMC Drive-O	red cab, red dump body, runs forward and backward with handturned control at end of 5-1/2 ft. cable, six-wheeler, 1949	175	300	450
GMC Dump Truck	all red truck, six-wheeler, 1950	150	200	285
GMC Emergency Tow Truck	white cab, red body and boom, 'Emergency Towing Service' on body side panels, four-wheeler, 1953	185	250	400
GMC Furniture Mart	blue cab, off-white body, "Furniture Mart, Complete Home Furnishings" markings on body sides, four-wheeler, 1953	135	275	295
GMC Heinz Grocery Truck	yellow cab, wood body, six-wheeler, 1947	250	325	450
GMC Highway Freighter Tractor-Trailer	red tractor cab, hardwood bed on trailer with full length wood fences, "Fruehauf" decal on trailer, 14-wheeler, 1948	150	210	325
GMC Kraft Foods	yellow cab, yellow steel box, large "Kraft" decal on both sides, four-wheeler, 1948	200	300	450
GMC Lumber Tractor-Trailer	metallic blue cab and trailer, three rollers and two chains, 14-wheeler, 1949	185	250	350

GMC Lumber Truck	green cab, six-wheeler, 1947	165	215	300
GMC Lyons Van Tractor-Trailer	blue tractor cab, "Lyons Van" decals on both sides, fold down rear door, 14-wheeler, 1948	165	250	400
GMC Machinery Hauler	construction orange cab and lowboy trailer, "Fruehauf" decal on gooseneck, 13-wheeler, 1949	150	225	335
GMC Machinery Hauler	construction orange cab and lowboy trailer, "Fruehauf" decal on gooseneck, 13-wheeler, 1949	150	225	335
GMC Machinery Hauler	construction orange, two loading ramps, 10-wheeler, 1953	200	295	425
GMC Marshall Field's & Company Tractor-Trailer	dark green cab and trailer, double rear doors, never had Smith-Miller decals, 10-wheeler, 1949	295	395	500
GMC Material Truck	green cab, wood body, six-wheeler, load of three barrels, three cases and 18 boards, 1947	115	150	250
GMC Material Truck	yellow cab, natural finish hardwood bed and sides, four-wheeler, load of four barrels and two timbers, 1949	125	175	265
GMC Mobilgas Tanker	red cab and tanker trailer, large "Mobilgas", "Mobiloil" emblems on sides and rear panel of tanker, 14-wheeler, 1949	135	225	400
GMC Oil Truck	orange cab, rear body unpainted, six-wheeler, load of three barrels, 1947	115	185	265
GMC P.I.E.	red cab, polished aluminum box trailer, double rear doors, "P.I.E." decals on sides and front panels, 14-wheeler, 1949	150	265	350
GMC People's First National Bank and Trust Company	dark brownish green cab and box, "People's First National Bank & Trust Co." decals on box sides, 1951	165	250	385
GMC Rack Truck	red or yellow cab, natural finish wood deck, red stake sides, six-wheeler, 1948	135	200	325
GMC Redwood Logger Tractor-Trailer	green or maroon cab, unpainted aluminum trailer with four hardwood stakes, load of three cardboard logs, 1948	365	585	700
GMC Rexall Drug Truck	orange cab and closed steel box body, "Rexall" logo on both sides and on front panel of box, four-wheeler, 1948	500	750	1000
GMC Scoop Dump	rack and pinion dump with a scoop, five spoke wheels, six-wheeler, 1954	275	350	575
GMC Searchlight Truck	four wheel truck pulling four wheel trailer, color schemes vary, "Hollywood Film Ad" on truck body side panels, 1953	300	415	695
GMC Silver Streak	unpainted polished cab and trailer, wrap around sides and shield, some had tail gate, 1950	140	200	300
GMC Sunkist Special Tractor-Trailer	cherry/maroon tractor cab, natural mahogany trailer bed, 14-wheeler, 1947	165	275	475
GMC Super Cargo Tractor-Trailer	silver gray tractor cab, hardwood bed on trailer with red wraparound side rails, 14-wheeler, load of 10 barrels, 1948	150	225	395
GMC Timber Giant	green or maroon cab, unpainted aluminum trailer with four hardwood stakes, load of three cardboard logs, 1948	175	285	495
GMC Tow Truck	white cab, red body and boom, five spoke cast hubs, "Emergency Towing Service" on body side panels, four-wheeler, 1954	95	135	200
GMC Transcontinental Tractor-Trailer	red tractor cab, hardwood bed on trailer with full length wood fences, "Fruehauf" decal on trailer, 14-wheeler, 1948	150	210	325
GMC Triton Oil Truck	blue cab, mahogany body unpainted, six-wheeler, load of three Triton Oil drums (banks) and side chains, 1947	115	185	265
GMC U.S. Treasury Truck	gray cab and box, "U.S. Treasury" insignia and markings on box sides, four-wheeler, 1952	235	325	475

Tonka

Emergency Vehicles

Name	Description	Good	Ex	Mint
Fire Department Rescue Van		60	150	275
Fire Jeep	1963-64	100	200	325
Hydraulic Aerial Ladder	1957	100	200	400
Ladder Truck	1954	135	225	450
Ladder Truck	1959; white	175	325	600
Suburban Pumper	1957	135	200	375
Suburban Pumper	1959; white w/red hydrant	150	250	425
T.F.D. Tanker	1958; white w/red decals	275	425	800
U.S.A.F. Ambulance		100	160	250

Trucks

Name	Description	Good	Ex	Mint
Ace Hardware Semi Truck	1955; red w/decals	200	425	850
Airport Service Truck	1962	125	225	300
Allied Van Lines	1953; orange w/black lettering	100	200	350
Army Troop Carrier	1964	75	150	250
Big Mike with V-Plow	1957; orange with Hi-Way Dept. decals	300	500	850
Car Hauler	1961; yellow	150	250	400
Cargo King	1956	75	150	250
Carnation Milk Van	1955; white w/decals	125	225	400
Cement Truck	1960; red	100	200	300
Coast to Coast Stores Truck	red cab	100	170	295
Cross Country Freight Semi Truck	1955; white w/red logo	160	225	475
Deluxe Fisherman	1960; with boat and trailer	100	200	400
Deluxe Fisherman	1960; with houseboat and trailer	135	225	425
Deluxe Sportsman	1958; with boat and trailer	160	225	375
Dump Truck		85	135	200
Dump Truck	1955-57	75	125	250
Dump Truck and Sandloader	1961	100	200	300
Eibert Coffee Van	1954	150	340	575
Gambles Pickup Truck	1955-63; white	100	200	300

Gambles Semi Truck	1956; white		190	270	450
Gasoline Tanker	1957; red		200	400	850
Gasoline Tanker	1958; orange		250	450	900
Grain Hauler	1952-53; red cab		65	175	250
Green Giant Transport Truck	1953; white w/green lettering		100	200	400
Green Giant Utility Truck	1953; white w/green decals		100	160	300
Hi-Way Dump Truck	1956		100	150	300
Hydraulic Dump Truck	1957		100	175	250
Hydraulic Land Rover	1959; orange		200	500	1000
Livestock Van	1952-53; red		75	150	275
Log Hauler	red cab w/logs		100	150	250
Minute Maid Box Van	1955; white w/decals		200	400	675
Parcel Delivery Van	1954; brown		100	200	400
Pickup Truck	1955		150	250	350
Pickup Truck w/Camper	1963		80	195	300
Pickup Truck/Stake Trailer	1957; with animal		150	225	400
Ramp Hoist	1963		175	250	550
Rescue Squad Van	1960-61; white w/red accents		100	250	500
Sanitary Service Truck	1959		190	350	750
Sportsman Pickup Truck	1959; tan w/boat on top		125	225	300
Standard Tanker	1961; "Standard" on side		200	450	700
Star-Kist Tuna Box Van	1954; red cab; blue body		200	500	700
Steel Carrier	1950-53; orange or yellow cab; green body		125	180	265
Thunderbird Express Semi Truck	1959; red or white		100	200	400
Tonka Air Express	1959; black w/decals		175	265	400
Tonka Express	1950; green cab; red box with decals		100	300	500
Tonka Farms Stock Rack Truck	1957		150	225	400
Tonka Marine Service	1961		125	350	500
Tonka Service Van	1961; light blue		95	200	280
Tonka Toy Transport Truck	1949; red w/silver roof		150	225	325
Tractor and Carry-All	1949-50		100	200	300
Utility Truck	1950-53; several colors		100	175	200
Wrecker Truck	1949-53; blue		100	175	225

Tootsietoy

Cars

Name	Description	Good	Ex	Mint
Andy Gump Car	1932; Funnies series	75	300	500
Armored Car	"U.S. Army" on sides, camouflage, black tires, 1938-41	25	35	65
Auburn Roadster	red, white rubber wheels	15	35	50
Austin-Healy	light brown roadster; 6" long, 1956	20	30	60
Baggage Car		10	15	30
Bluebird Daytona Race Car		20	35	65
Boat Tail Roadster	red roadster, 6" long	20	35	55
Buick Brougham	tan/black	20	35	70
Buick Coupe	blue with white wheels, 1924	30	42	65
Buick Coupe	4"	20	35	50
Buick Estate Wagon	yellow and maroon with black wheels, 6" long, 1948	20	30	50
Buick Experimental Car	blue with black wheels, detailed tin bottom, 6" long, 1954	25	50	85
Buick LaSabre	red open top, black wheels, 6" long, 1951	25	45	70
Buick Roadmaster	blue with black wheels, four-door, 1949	25	40	65
Buick Roadster	yellow open top, black wheels, 4" long, 1938	25	45	65
Buick Sedan	6" long	25	35	55
Buick Special	4" long, 1947	15	25	50
Buick Station Wagon	green with yellow top, black wheels, 6" long, 1954	20	30	45
Buick Tourer	red with white wheels, 1925	25	45	70
Buick Touring Car		50	75	110
Cadillac	HO series, blue car/white top, 2" long, 1960	10	20	30
Cadillac 60	red-orange with black wheels, four-door, 1948	20	35	60
Cadillac 62	red-orange with white top, black wheels, four-door, 6" long, 1954	20	35	120
Cadillac Brougham		40	60	85
Cadillac Coupe	blue/tan, black wheels	40	60	85
Cadillac Sedan	white rubber wheels	40	60	85
Cadillac Touring Car	1926	50	90	120
Chevrolet Brougham		40	60	85
Chevrolet Coupe		20	35	90
Chevrolet Roadster		20	35	90
Chevrolet Sedan		20	35	75
Chevrolet Touring Car		60	150	200

Chevrolet Bel Air	yellow with black wheels, 3" long, 1955	15	30	50
Chevrolet Coupe	green with black wheels, 3"	20	35	55
Chevrolet Fastback	blue with black wheels, 3" long, 1950	15	20	35
Chevrolet Ambulance	4"	15	20	35
Chrysler Convertible	blue-green with black wheels, 4" long, 1960	15	25	35
Chrysler Experimental Roadster	orange open top, black wheels	25	40	60
Chrysler New Yorker	blue with black wheels, four-door, 6" long, 1953	25	35	55
Chrysler Windsor Convertible	green with black wheels, 4" long, 1941	20	30	45
Chrysler Windsor Convertible	black wheels, 6" long, 1950	50	90	120
Classic Series 1906 Cadillac or Studebaker	green and black, spoke wheels	10	15	25
Classic Series 1907 Stanley Steamer	yellow and black, spoke wheels, 1960-65	10	15	25
Classic Series 1912 Ford Model T	black with red seats, spoke wheels	10	15	25
Classic Series 1919 Stutz Bearcat	black and red, solid wheels	10	15	25
Classic Series 1929 Ford Model A	blue and black, black tread wheels, 1960-65	10	15	25
Corvair	red, 4" long, 1960s	30	55	75
Corvette Roadster	blue open top, black wheels, 4" long, 1954-55	15	20	35
Coupe	miniature	20	25	40
DeSoto Airflow	green with white wheels	20	35	60
Doodlebug	same as Buick Special	50	75	100
Ferrari Racer	red with gold driver, black wheels, 6" long, 1956	30	40	65
Ford	red with open top, black wheels, 6" long, 1940	15	25	40
Ford B Hotrod	1931	15	20	40
Ford Convertible Coupe	1934	30	50	70
Ford Convertible Sedan	red with black wheels, 3" long, 1949	10	20	35
Ford Coupe	powder blue with tan top, white wheels, 1934	30	50	75
Ford Coupe	blue or red with white wheels, 1935	25	35	45
Ford Customline	blue with black wheels, 1955	15	20	30
Ford Fairlane 500 Convertible	red with black wheels, 3" long, 1957	10	15	30
Ford Falcon	red with black wheels, 3" long, 1960	10	15	30
Ford LTD	blue with black wheels, 4" long, 1969	15	20	35
Ford Mainliner	red with black wheels, four-door, 3" long, 1952	10	20	30
Ford Model A Coupe	blue with white wheels	25	35	50
Ford Model A Sedan	green with black wheels	25	35	50
Ford Ranch Wagon	green with yellow top, four-door, 4" long, 1954	15	25	35
Ford Ranch Wagon	red with yellow top, four-door, 3" long, 1954	15	20	35
Ford Roadster	powder blue with open top, white wheels	25	40	60
Ford Sedan	1934	35	50	70
Ford Sedan	powder blue with white solid wheels, 1935	25	35	50

Model	Description			
Ford Sedan	lime green with black wheels, four-door, 3" long, 1949	15	20	35
Ford Station Wagon	powder blue with white top, black wheels, 6" long, 1959	15	20	35
Ford Station Wagon	blue with black wheels, 3" long, 1960	10	15	25
Ford Station Wagon	red with white top, black wheels, four-door, 6" long, 1962	25	40	55
Ford Tourer	open top, red with silver spoke wheels	20	30	45
Ford V-8 Hotrod	red with open top, black wheels, open silver motor, 6" long, 1940	15	25	35
Ford w/Trailer	blue sedan, white rubber wheels	50	75	130
Graham Convertible Coupe	rear spare tire, rubber wheels, 1933-35	50	125	175
Graham Convertible Coupe	side spare tire, rubber wheels, 1933-35	50	125	175
Graham Convertible Sedan	rear spare tire, rubber wheels, 1933-35	50	125	175
Graham Convertible Sedan	side spare tire, rubber wheels, 1933-35	50	125	175
Graham Coupe	rear spare tire, rubber wheels, 1933-35	50	115	150
Graham Coupe	side spare tire, rubber wheels, 1933-35	50	115	150
Graham Roadster	rear spare tire, rubber wheels, 1933-35	50	115	150
Graham Roadster	side spare tire, rubber wheels, 1933-35	50	115	150
Graham Sedan	rear spare tire, rubber wheels, 1933-35	50	115	150
Graham Sedan	side spare tire, rubber wheels, 1933-35	50	115	150
Graham Towncar	rear spare tire, rubber wheels, 1933-35	50	115	150
Graham Towncar	side spare tire, 1933-35	50	115	140
Insurance Patrol	miniature	15	25	35
International Station Wagon	4" long, rubber wheels, 1940s	25	45	50
International Station Wagon	red/yellow, white wheels, 1939-41	15	25	50
International Station Wagon	red/yellow, 3" long	15	25	50
International Station Wagon	orange with black wheels, postwar	15	20	30
Jaguar Type D	green with black wheels, 3" long, 1957	10	15	25
Jaguar XK 120 Roadster	green open top, black wheels, 3" long	10	15	25
Jaguar XK 140 Coupe	blue with black wheels, 6" long	20	30	50
Kaiser Sedan	blue with black wheels, 6" long, 1947	25	45	55
KO Ice	1932; Funnies series	100	325	425
Lancia Racer	dark green with black wheels, 6" long, 1956	30	50	75
Large Bluebird Racer	green with yellow solid wheels	20	40	60
LaSalle Convertible	rubber wheels	80	200	300
LaSalle Convertible Sedan	rubber wheels	80	200	300
LaSalle Coupe	rubber wheels	100	200	300
LaSalle Sedan	red with black rubber wheels, 3" long	15	20	30
LaSalle Sedan	rubber wheels	140	200	275
Limousine	blue with silver spoke wheels; prewar	20	40	65
Lincoln	prewar; red with white rubber wheels, four-door	110	400	500
Lincoln Capri	red with yellow top, black wheels, two-door, 6" long	20	35	50
Mercedes 190 SL Coupe	powder blue with black wheels, 6" long, 1956	15	25	40
Mercury	red with black wheels, four-door, 4" long, 1952	15	20	40

Item	Description			
Mercury Custom	blue with black wheels, four-door, 4" long, 1949	15	30	40
Mercury Fire Chief Car	red with black wheels, 4" long, 1949	25	35	50
MG TF Roadster	red open top, black wheels, 6" long, 1954	15	25	45
MG TF Roadster	blue open top, black wheels, 3" long, 1954	15	20	35
Model T Pick-up	3", black, spoked metal wheels	25	40	50
Moon Mullins Police Car	1932; Funnies series	130	200	425
Nash Metropolitan Convertible	red with black tires, 1954	25	35	60
Observation Car		10	15	30
Offenhauser Racer	dark blue with black wheels, 4" long, 1947	10	20	35
Oldsmobile 88 Convertible	yellow with black wheels, 4" long, 1949	15	25	35
Oldsmobile 88 Convertible	bright green with black wheels, 6" long, 1959	20	25	40
Oldsmobile 98	white body with blue top, skirted fenders, black wheels, 4" long, 1955	20	25	40
Oldsmobile 98	red body with yellow top, open fenders, black wheels, 4" long, 1955	20	25	45
Oldsmobile 98 Staff Car		20	25	45
Oldsmobile Brougham		25	35	50
Oldsmobile Coupe		25	35	50
Oldsmobile Roadster	orange/black, white wheels, 1924	25	45	75
Oldsmobile Sedan		25	35	50
Oldsmobile Touring		25	35	50
Open Touring	green convertible, white wheels, 3"	25	35	45
Packard	white body with blue top, black wheels, four-door, 6" long, 1956	25	35	45
Plymouth	dark blue with black wheels, two-door, 3" long, 1957	10	15	20
Plymouth Sedan	blue with black wheels, four-door, 3" long, 1950	15	20	30
Pontiac Fire Chief	red with black wheels, 4" long, 1950	20	35	50
Pontiac Sedan	green with black wheels, two-door, 4" long, 1950	15	25	45
Pontiac Star Chief	red with black wheels, four-door, 4" long, 1959	15	25	40
Porsche Roadster	red with open top, black wheels, two-door, 6" long, 1956	20	25	40
Pullman Car		10	15	30
Racer	miniature	25	40	50
Racer	orange with black wheels, 3" long, 1950s	10	15	30
Rambler Wagon	dark green w/yellow top, black wheels, yellow interior, 1960s	15	25	35
Rambler Wagon	blue with black wheels, 4" long, 1960	15	25	35
Roadster		50	100	140
Roadster	miniature	15	25	40
Sedan		50	100	135
Sedan	miniature	20	25	40
Small Racer	blue with driver, white wheels, 1927	50	110	175
Smitty	1932; Funnies series	170	250	500
Station Wagon	red w/tan upper, 3"	15	35	55
Studebaker Coupe	green with black wheels, 3" long, 1947	25	35	50

Name	Description	Good	Ex	Mint
Studebaker Lark Convertible	lime green with black wheels, 3" long, 1960	10	15	25
Tank Car	miniature	20	25	40
Thunderbird Coupe	powder blue with black wheels, 4" long, 1955	15	30	40
Thunderbird Coupe	blue with black wheels, 3" long, 1955	15	20	30
Torpedo Coupe	gray; prewar	20	25	45
Torpedo Sedan	red	20	30	50
Triumph TR 3 Roadster	black wheels, 3" long, 1956	10	20	35
Uncle Walt	1932; Funnies series	150	300	450
Uncle Willie	1932; Funnies series	150	300	450
VW Bug	metallic gold with black tread wheels, 6" long, 1960	15	25	30
VW Bug	lime green with black tread wheels, 3" long, 1960	10	20	35
Yellow Cab Sedan	green with white wheels, 1921	10	20	30

Emergency Vehicles

Name	Description	Good	Ex	Mint
American LaFrance Pumper	red, 3" long, 1954	15	20	35
Chevrolet Ambulance	army green, red cross on roof top, army star on top of hood, 4" long, 1950	15	25	50
Chevrolet Ambulance	yellow, red cross on top, 4" long, 1950	15	25	40
Fire Hook and Ladder	red/blue with side ladders	25	40	50
Fire Water Tower Truck	blue/orange, red water tower	30	60	80
Ford Wrecker	3" long, 1935, brown, white rubber wheels	30	50	65
Graham Ambulance	white with red cross on sides	40	95	125
Graham Wrecker	red/black; rubber wheels	50	110	150
Hook and Ladder	with driver; white rubber wheels, 1937-41	40	60	75
Hook and Ladder	red and silver; white rubber wheels	50	75	90
Hook and Ladder	#1040	20	25	40
Hose Car	with driver and figure standing by water gun; 1937-41	35	50	80
Hose Wagon	red with silver hose, white rubber wheels, 3" long, prewar	25	30	45
Hose Wagon	red, black rubber wheels, postwar	20	25	40
Insurance Patrol	red, white wheels, prewar	25	30	45
Insurance Patrol	red, black rubber wheels, postwar	20	25	40
Insurance Patrol	with driver	25	40	60
Jumbo Wrecker	6" long, 1941	25	40	60
Lincoln Wrecker	sedan w/wrecker hook	200	425	600
Mack L-Line Fire Pumper	red with ladders on sides	35	65	75
Mack L-Line Hook and Ladder	red with silver ladder	35	65	75

Trucks

Name	Description	Good	Ex	Mint
Army Half Truck	1941	30	55	75

Army Jeep	windshield up, 6" long, 1950s	15	25	40
Army Jeep CJ3	extended back, windshield down, 4" long, 1950	10	15	35
Army Jeep CJ3	no windshield, 3" long, 1950	10	15	40
Army Supply Truck	with driver	25	40	55
Box Truck	red w/white wheels, 3" long	15	20	30
Buick Delivery Van		25	35	50
Cadillac Delivery Van		25	35	50
Chevrolet Delivery Van		25	35	50
Chevrolet Cameo Pickup	green with black wheels, 4" long, 1956	15	25	40
Chevrolet El Camino	red	20	25	40
Chevrolet El Camino Camper and Boat	blue body with red camper, black/white boat on top of camper	25	35	45
Chevrolet Panel Truck	light green with black wheels, 4" long, 1950	25	30	40
Chevrolet Panel Truck	green, 3" long, 1950	10	20	30
Chevrolet Panel Truck	green, front fenders opened, 3" long, 1950s	15	20	35
Civilian Jeep	burnt orange, open top, black wheels, 3" long, 1950	10	15	30
Civilian Jeep	red, open top, black wheels, 4" long, 1950	15	20	35
Civilian Jeep	blue with black tread wheels, 6" long, 1960	15	20	35
CJ3 Army Jeep	open top, no steering wheel cast on dashboard, 3" long, 1950	10	15	30
CJ5 Jeep	red with black tread wheels, windshield up, 6" long, 1960s	15	20	30
CJ5 Jeep	red with black tread wheels, windshield up, 6" long, 1950s	15	25	35
Coast to Coast Van	9" long	40	75	100
Commercial Tire Van	"Commercial Tire & Supply Co."; white rubber wheels; prewar	70	150	200
Diamond T K5 Dump Truck	yellow cab and chassis, green dump body, 6" long	25	35	50
Diamond T K5 Semi	red tractor and light green closed trailer	25	45	55
Diamond T K5 Stake Truck	orange, open sides, 6" long, 1940	25	35	55
Diamond T K5 Stake Truck	orange, closed sides, 6" long, 1940	25	35	55
Diamond T Metro Van	powder blue, 6" long	35	75	100
Diamond T Tow Truck	red with silver tow bar	25	35	55
Dodge D100 Panel	green and yellow, 6" long	25	40	55
Dodge Pickup	lime green, 4" long	20	30	40
Federal Bakery Van	black with cream wheels, 1924	50	85	110
Federal Florist Van	black with cream wheels, 1924	75	175	220
Federal Grocery Van	black with cream wheels, 1924	45	70	100
Federal Laundry Van	black with cream wheels, 1924	50	85	110
Federal Market Van	black with cream wheels, 1924	55	85	110
Federal Milk Van	black with cream wheels, 1924	55	85	110
Ford C600 Oil Tanker	bright yellow, 3" long	10	15	20
Ford C600 Oil Tanker	red, 6" long, 1962	15	30	40
Ford Econoline Pickup	red, 1962	15	25	35
Ford F1 Pickup	orange, closed tailgate, 3" long, 1949	15	20	35
Ford F1 Pickup	orange, open tailgate, 3" long, 1949	15	20	35

Item	Description			
Ford F6 Oil	orange, 4" long, 1949	10	15	25
Ford F6 Oil Tanker	red with Texaco, Sinclair, Shell or Standard on sides, 6" long, 1949	25	50	100
Ford F6 Pickup	red, 4" long, 1949	15	25	40
Ford F600 Army Anti-Aircraft Gun	tractor-trailer flatbed, guns on flatbed	20	30	45
Ford F600 Army Radar	tractor-trailer flatbed, yellow radar unit on flatbed, 6" long, 1955	20	30	45
Ford F600 Army Stake Truck	tractor-trailer box, army star on top of trailer box roof and "U.S. Army" on sides, 6" long, 1955	25	40	55
Ford F600 Stake Truck	light green, 6" long, 1955	15	25	35
Ford Pickup	3", beige; 1935; white rubber wheels	25	40	55
Ford Shell Oil Truck		45	60	85
Ford Styleside Pickup	orange, 3" long, 1957	10	15	30
Ford Texaco Oil Truck		45	60	85
Hudson Pickup	red, 4" long, 1947	25	40	55
International Bottle Truck	lime green	30	45	65
International Car Transport Truck	red tractor, orange double-deck trailer with cars	35	50	70
International Gooseneck Trailer	orange tractor and flatbed trailer	30	40	55
International K1 Panel Truck	blue, 4" long	20	30	55
International K1 Oil Truck	green, comes with oil brands on sides, 6" long	20	30	45
International RC180 Grain Semi	green tractor and red trailer	30	50	70
International Sinclair Oil Truck	6" long	35	75	100
International Standard Oil Truck	6" long	35	75	100
Jeepster	bright yellow with open top, black wheels, 3" long, 1947	10	15	35
Jumbo Pickup	6" long, green w/black wheels, 1936-41	25	35	50
Mack Anti-Aircraft Gun		25	40	55
Mack B-Line Cement Truck	red truck with yellow cement mixer, 1955	20	35	55
Mack B-Line Oil Tanker	red tractor and trailer, "Mobil"	20	35	55
Mack B-Line Stake Trailer	red tractor, orange closed trailer, 1955	20	35	55
Mack Coal Truck	"City Fuel Company," 10 wheels	60	120	175
Mack Coal Truck	orange cab with blue bed, four wheels, 1925	90	100	250
Mack Coal Truck	red cab with black bed, 1928	60	120	160
Mack Dairy Tanker	1930s; two-piece cab; Tootsietoy Dairies	75	100	225
Mack L-Line Dump Truck	yellow cab and chassis, light green dump body, 6" long, 1947	20	35	55
Mack L-Line Semi and Stake Trailer	red tractor and trailer	50	95	125
Mack L-Line Semi-Trailer	red tractor cab, silver semi-trailer, "Gerard Motor Express" on sides	60	115	145
Mack L-Line Stake Truck	red with silver bed inside	25	35	55
Mack L-Line Tow Truck	red with silver tow bar	25	35	55

Mack Log Hauler	red cab, trailer with load of logs, 1940s	50	95	135
Mack Mail Truck	red cab with light brown box, "U.S. Mail Airmail Service" on sides, 3" long, 1920s	40	70	100
Mack Milk Truck	"Tootsietoy Dairy," one-piece cab	50	110	175
Mack Oil Tanker	"DOMACO" on side of tanker	60	100	155
Mack Oil Truck	red cab with orange tanker, 1925	25	40	55
Mack Railway Express	1930s; Wrigley's Gum	55	115	165
Mack Searchlight Truck	1931-41	25	40	55
Mack Stake Trailer-Truck	enclosed cab, open stake trailer, 'Express' on sides of trailer	50	90	120
Mack Stake Truck	orange cab with red stake bed, 1925	25	40	60
Mack Trailer-Truck	open cab	50	85	110
Mack Transport	red, open cab with flatbed trailer	60	150	200
Mack Transport	yellow, 1941, with three cars at angle	150	500	700
Mack Van Trailer-Truck	enclosed cab and box trailer	50	100	140
Mack Wrigley's Spearmint Gum Truck	4", green with white rubber wheels, red hubs	70	150	225
Model T Pickup	3" long, 1914	30	50	75
Oil Tanker	green with white wheels; prewar	15	25	35
Oil Tanker	blue and silver, two caps on top of tanker, 3" long	20	30	40
Oil Tanker	orange, four caps on top of tanker, 3" long, postwar	20	25	40
Oil Tanker	blue, three caps on top, 2" long, 1932	20	25	50
Oldsmobile Delivery Van		25	35	50
Shell Oil Truck	yellow/silver, 6", white rubber wheels	50	85	120
Sinclair Oil Truck	6" long; green/silver	50	85	120
Special Delivery	1936	20	25	40
Stake Truck	miniature	25	40	55
Standard Oil Truck	red/silver; 6", white rubber wheels	80	100	150
Texaco Oil Truck	red/silver; 6", white rubber wheels	55	85	120
Tootsietoy Dairy	semi trailer truck	75	110	140
Tootsietoy Oil Tanker	red cab, silver tanker, "Tootsietoy Line" on side, 1950s	60	95	125
Wrigley's Box Van	with or without decal, 1940s	45	60	75

Williams, A.C.

Cars

Name	Description	Good	Ex	Mint
1930s Chrysler Convertible Coupe	6", operating rumble seat	300	400	500
1930s Chrysler Roadster	5"	100	200	300

Name	Description	Good	Ex	Mint
1930s Coupe	5", rubber tires, turned metal wheels, twin sidemount spare tires	150	250	350
1930s Sedan	5", rubber tires, turned metal wheels, twin sidemount spare tires	150	250	350
1930s Sedan	6-1/2", rubber tires, turned metal wheels, twin sidemount spare tires	250	350	450
Dream Car	cast iron, 4-7/8" long, 1930	75	150	250
Ford Model A Fordor Sedan	6", nickel-plated cast spoke wheels	600	900	1200
Ford Roadster	1936	450	550	650
Lincoln Touring Cars	spoked wheels, cast iron, 8-3/4" long, 1924	400	600	800
Racer	yellow, cast iron, 8-1/2" long, 1932	300	450	600
Taxi	cast iron, 5-1/4" long, 1920	200	350	500
Touring Cars	disc wheels, cast iron, 9-1/8" long, 1922	400	600	800
Touring Cars	solid wheels, cast iron, 11-3/4" long, 1917	500	750	1200

Trucks

Name	Description	Good	Ex	Mint
Austin Transport Set	with three vehicles, cast iron, 12-1/2" long, 1930	500	850	1250
Car Carrier w/Three Austin Cars	12"	800	1200	1600
Coast to Coast Cartage Semi Stake Trailer	10", nickel plated stamped steel spoke wheels	400	600	800
Coast to Coast Cartage Semi Stake Trailer	6-1/2"	100	150	200
Interchangeable Delivery Truck	cast iron, 7-1/4" long, 1932	175	250	350
Mack Bulldog Gasoline Tank Truck	7", nickel plated cast spoke wheels	300	450	600
Mack Bulldog Gasoline Tank Truck	5", nickel plated stamped steel spoke wheels	125	175	225
Mack Bulldog Stake Truck	4-3/4", nickel plated stamped steel spoke wheels	100	150	200
Moving Van	cast iron, 4-3/4" long 1930	150	225	300
Pickup Truck	cast iron, 4-3/4" long, 1926	100	150	200

Winross

Name	Description	Good	Ex	Mint
AACA Hershey Region Fall Meet	sleeper single axle (White 7000 cab) tanker, (incentive)	95	100	125
AACA Hershey Region Fall Meet	long nose single axle (White 9000 cab), stk., wind screen doubles (incentive)	95	100	125

AACA Library and Research Center	FL/T stk. aerodynamic wind screen	60	65	75
ACME Printing	long nose tandem axle (White 9000)	30	45	50
Adirondack Beverage Co.	Ford cab (Ford C1 9000), long nose tandem axle, stacks, wind screen	20	25	35
Almond Joy	Ford cab (Ford C1 9000), long nose tandem axle, stacks, other side Mounds	45	50	60
Alpo	long nose tandem axle (White 9000 cab)	30	45	50
Amana	sleeper tandem axle (White 7000 cab)	35	45	50
American Red Cross	International 8300/T stacks Hanover top logo not Winross 1/600	55	65	75
Amoco Mileage Caravan	sleeper single axle (White 7000 cab) blue cab swing dolly	75	80	90
Anderson Windows	Internationl 8300/T stacks	50	60	65
Andes Candies	Mack cab (Mack Ultra-liner), sleeper tandem axle (White 7000 cab), wind screen, reefer	40	50	60
Antique Car Show (Hershey)	International 8300/T stacks	55	65	75
Antique Car Show (Hershey)	Ford cab (Ford C1 9000), long nose tandem axle stacks, drop bed	55	65	75
Avis Truck Rental	cab over single axle (White 5000 cab)	25	35	45
Bicentennial Trail Issue	long nose tandem axle (White 9000 cab)	40	50	60
Bon Ton Potato Chips	Ford cab (Ford C1 9000), long nose single axle, black tanks, old suspension	90	100	125
Bon Ton Potato Chips	Ford cab (Ford C1 9000), long nose single axle, chrome tanks	35	45	55
Borden	milk tanker, screw replaces the rivet in the ear of the floor trailer, with ladder	80	90	110
Borden	Credit & Sales sleeper tandem axle (White 7000 cab), plastic dolly	35	40	50
Bowman Trans.	long nose tandem axle (White 9000 cab), stacks, wind screen	90	100	125
Bubble Yum	cab over single axle (White 5000 cab), red, plastic dolly	55	65	75
Bud Light (Fox Dist.)	Ford cab (Ford C1 9000), long nose tandem axle, stacks	90	100	125
Budd Movers	sleeper tandem axle (White 7000 cab), stacks, drop bed	135	175	200
Busch	Ford cab (Ford C1 9000), long nose tandem axle, stacks, wind screen (Hauck & Sons)	80	90	100
Butternut Coffee	sleeper tandem axle (White 7000 cab), stacks	25	35	45
California Raisins	Ford cab (Ford C1 9000), long nose tandem axle, stacks	60	70	80
Campbell's Soup	Mack cab (Mack Ultra-liner), sleeper tandem axle (White 7000 cab), aerodynamic wind screen, tanker Tomato Juice	70	80	90
Cerro Cooper	sleeper tandem axle (White 7000 cab), stacks	30	40	50
Cherry Hill Orchard	Ford cab (Ford C1 9000), long nose tandem axle, stack, full fairing T-Bird reefer	45	55	65
Cherry Hill Orchard	Mack cab (Mack Ultra-liner), sleeper tandem axle (White 7000 cab), aerodynamic wind screen, full fairing T-Bird reefer	45	55	65
Cola-Cola	long nose single axle (White 9000 cab) unpainted doors	100	125	150
Cola-Cola	long nose single axle (White 9000 cab) red plain doors	100	125	150
Cola-Cola	Ford Aeromax 120 cab, aerodynamic conventional sleeper, tandem axle, stacks, Dearborn Convention	175	200	300

Coleman's Ice Cream	Ford cab (Ford C1 9000), long nose tandem axle, stack, aerodynamic wind screen tool box sleeper	40	50	60
Colorado Beef	long nose single axle and long nose tandem axle (White 9000 cab) and stacks	30	40	50
Coors	Ford cab (Ford C1 9000), long nose tandem axle, stack, full fairing drop bed "Bill Elliott"	185	200	250
Coors	Ford Aeromax 120 cab, an aerodynamic conventional sleeper, stack	55	65	75
Corning	sleeper tandem axle (white 7000 cab), "Lots for You" (both sides shown)	30	40	50
Cracker Jack	silk screen, plastic dolly	200	250	300
Dairymen	Ford cab (Ford C1 9000), stack, tanker	90	100	125
Dannon Yogurt	cab over single axle with Beatrice logo	25	30	35
Diamond Crystal Salt	silk screen	50	55	60
Diefenbach's Potato Chips	Ford cab (Ford C1 9000), long nose tandem axle, stack, 25th Anniversary	40	50	60
Domino's	Kenworth T800, tandem axle, stack, T-Bird reefer	40	50	60
Downy's Honey Butter	Ford cab (Ford C1 9000), long nose tandem axle, stack, T-Bird reefer, chassis cylinder (fuel tank for a reefer)	40	50	60
Eastman Kodak	long nose tandem axle (White 9000 cab), metal dolly, Kodak logo	55	65	75
Eastman Kodak	Mack ultra-liner cab, sleeper tandem axle (White 7000 cab), stacks, drop bed, (racing team)	350	400	500
Eastwood Company	Ford Aeromax 120 cab, an aerodynamic conventional sleeper, long nose tandem axle, stack, wind screen, doubles	40	50	60
Eastwood Company	Ford cab (Ford C1 9000), long nose tandem axle, stack, turbo wind screen (Motor Sports)	55	65	75
Eastwood Company	Kenworth T800, tandem axle, stack, turbo wind screen, parabolic shape, straight truck	55	65	75
Emergency Fire	1500 cab light or dark red	100	125	150
Emergency Fire	3000 cab white	300	325	350
Evergreen Juice Co.	Mack cab (Mack Ultra-liner), sleeper tandem axle (White 7000 cab), stack	30	40	50
Firestone	International 8300, tandem axle	55	65	75
Florigold (Sealed Sweet)	sleeper tandem axle	55	65	75
Ford, Story of	Ford Aeromax 120 cab, tandem axle, stack, yellow cab (#1), 1905	150	175	200
Fourth of July	Ford cab (Ford C1 9000), long nose tandem axle, stack, aerodynamic wind screen	55	65	75
Foxx Paper (fictional company)	3000 cab, 32' flat bed with side boards and simulated paper roll load	20	25	30
Georgia Pacific	Mack cab (Mack Ultra-liner), sleeper tandem axle (White 7000 cab), stack, wind screen, drop bed	250	300	350
Girl Scout Cookies	Ford cab (Ford C1 9000), long nose tandem axle, stack	55	65	75
Glade Spinfresh	long nose single axle (White 9000 cab)	25	30	35
Good & Plenty Candy	International 8300, tandem axle, stack	30	40	50
Good Poultry Services	Ford cab (Ford C1 9000), long nose tandem axle, stack, wind screen, tanker	30	40	50
Goodwill	Ford cab (Ford C1 9000), long nose single axle, stack	30	40	50
Goodwrench	International 8300, tandem axle, stack, drop bed #3 Dale Earnhart with cars	100	125	150
Graebel	sleeper tandem axle (White 7000 cab), stack, wind screen, drop bed (Movers)	75	85	100

Graebel	sleeper tandem axle (White 7000 cab), stack, wind screen, drop bed (Van Line)	30	35	45
Great American Van Lines	single tandem axle (White 7000 cab), stack, drop bed	70	75	90
H & H Excavating	Ford cab (Ford C1 9000), long nose tandem axle, stack	30	40	50
H & R Block	Mack cab (Mack Ultra-liner), sleeper tandem axle (White 7000 cab), stack	30	40	50
Halls	long nose tandem axle, plastic dolly, smooth front trailer	90	100	125
Hanover Brands	silk screen, swing dolly (both sides)	125	150	200
Hanover Transfer Co.	International 8300, tandem axle, stack	70	85	100
Hardee's	Mack cab (Mack Ultra-liner), sleeper tandem axle (White 7000 cab), stack, reefer, under chassis cylinder (fuel tank for a reefer)	65	70	80
Hawaiian Punch	sleeper tandem axle (White 7000 cab), wind screen	100	125	150
Hershey's Chocolate	sleeper single axle (White 7000 cab), foil tanker	100	125	150
Hershey's Chocolate	Ford cab (Ford C1 9000), long nose tandem axle, stack, red cab foil tanker	100	125	150
Hershey's Chocolate	Kenworth T800, tandem axle, stack, Strawberry Syrup tanker	75	85	100
Hershey's Chocolate	Ford cab (Ford C1 9000), long nose tandem axle, stack, aerodynamic wind screen, milk tanker	75	85	100
Hertz	long nose single axle (White 9000 cab), 32' wheel, dolly cast doors	75	85	100
Hess Mills (Purina Chows)	Ford cab (Ford C1 9000), long nose tandem axle, stack. vert. brush tanker	40	50	60
Hostess Cake	Ford cab (Ford C1 9000), long nose tandem axle, stack, wind screen, other side Wonder	60	70	80
Iceland Seafood	sleeper single axle (White 7000 cab)	70	80	90
Iola Car Show	long nose single axle (White 9000 cab)	20	25	30
Iola Car Show	cab over single axle (White 5000 cab)	20	25	30
James River Corp.	Mack cab (Mack Ultra-liner), sleeper tandem axle (White 7000 cab), stack, wind screen	35	45	55
Jeno's Pizza	sleeper single axle (White 7000 cab), pin, plastic dolly	50	55	60
Johnson Wax	sleeper tandem axle (White 7000 cab), vert. brush tanker "Innobulk"	25	30	40
Juice Bowl	sleeper tandem axle (White 7000 cab), wind screen	45	55	65
Kraft	International 8300, tandem axle, stack, T-Bird reefer, "America Spells Cheese" top logo	60	70	80
Lancaster Farm Toy Show	Ford cab (Ford C1 9000), long nose tandem axle, stack, met, maroon, flatbed with J.D. farm equipment	150	175	200
Lancaster Farm Toy Show	Ford cab (Ford C1 9000), long nose tandem axle, stack, met, slate blue, flatbed with J.D. farm equipment	150	175	200
Lancaster Farm Toy Show	Ford cab (Ford C1 9000), long nose tandem axle, stack, met, brown, flatbed with J.D. farm equipment	150	175	200
Lancaster Farm Toy Show	Mack cab (Ultra-liner), sleeper tandem axle, red cab, flatbed with Ford farm tractor	150	175	200
Lancaster Farm Toy Show	Mack cab (Ultra-liner), sleeper tandem axle, brown cab, flatbed with J.D. farm equipment	150	175	200
Lancaster Farm Toy Show	Mack cab (Ultra-liner), sleeper tandem axle, blue cab, flatbed with International farm tractor	150	175	200
Lea & Perrins	sleeper tandem axle (White 7000 cab)	25	30	40
Leinenkugel Brewery	Ford cab (Ford C1 9000), long nose tandem axle, stack	35	45	55

Name	Description			
Londonderry Fire Co.	Ford cab (Ford C1 9000), long nose tandem axle, stack, vert. brush tanker	40	50	60
Lysol	long nose single axle (White 9000 cab)	25	30	40
Mack Trucks "Story of Mack Trucks Set #1"	Mack cab (Mack Ultra-liner), sleeper tandem axle (White 7000 cab), stack 1893 new & old suspension	125	150	175
Mack Trucks "Story of Mack Trucks Set #1"	Mack cab (Mack Ultra-liner). sleeper tandem axle (White 7000 cab), stack 1905 new & old suspension	125	150	175
Mack Trucks "Story of Mack Trucks Set #1"	Mack cab (Mack Ultra-liner). sleeper tandem axle (White 7000 cab), stack 1909 new & old suspension	125	150	175
Martin's Potato Chips	Ford cab (Ford C1 9000), long nose single axle, stack, aerodynamic wind screen, white cab	35	45	55
Maxwell House (Sterling Martin)	Ford Aeromax 120 cab, an aerodynamic conventional sleeper	55	65	75
McDonald's	sleeper tandem axle (White 7000 cab), Martin Brower, T-Bird reefer	40	50	60
Michelob Fox District	Ford cab (Ford C1 9000), long nose tandem axle, stack, tanker	100	110	125
Monfort	sleeper tandem axle (White 7000 cab)	100	110	125
Morton Salt	sleeper single axle (White 7000 cab)	70	80	90
Mountain Dew	International 8300, tandem axle, stack	35	45	55
Mrs. Paul's	International 8300, tandem axle, stack, tanker	60	70	80
Mt. Joy Co-op	Ford cab (Ford C1 9000), long nost tandem axle, foil tanker with graphics	70	85	100
Nabisco	sleeper single axle (White 7000 cab), Jr. Mints-Chuckles both sides shown	85	95	110
National Private Trucking Association	Ford cab (Ford C1 9000), long nose tandem axle, stack	20	25	30
National Toy Show	long nose single axle, Ford "F" Series, Ford cab with pop-up hood, two tractors both sides and cabs	75	85	100
Nestle's Quik	sleeper tandem axle (White 7000 cab), vert. brush	70	80	90
Old Milwaukee	long nose single axle (White 9000 cab), metal dolly, black chassis	70	80	90
Old Style (Heileman Brewery)	sleeper tandem axle (White 7000 cab), plastic dolly, one shield	55	65	75
Old Toyland Shows	long nose single axle (White 9000 cab), stacks, white cab both sides shown	25	30	35
Owens Corning Fiberglass	sleeper single axle (White 7000 cab), vert. brush tanker	40	50	60
P.I.E. Nationwide	long nose tandem axle (White 9000 cab), wind screen	55	65	75
P.I.E. Nationwide	Ford cab, long nose single axle, wind screen, stacks, doubles, with Olympic rings	300	350	400
Pennsylvania Pump Primers	Ford cab (Ford C1 9000), long nose tandem axle, stack, tool box #1	30	40	50
Pepsi	screw replaces the rivet in the rear of the floor of the trailer, plastic dolly	150	175	200
Pepsi	International 8300, tandem axle, stack, special edition	150	175	200
Pillsbury	sleeper tandem axle (White 7000 cab), Hungry Jack/Crescent Rolls	80	90	100
Prince Spaghetti	long nose single axle (White 9000 cab)	55	65	75
Quaker Oats	Mack cab (Mack Ultra-liner), sleeper tandem axle (White 7000 cab), stack, Kankakee Distribution Center	30	40	50
Quaker State	sleeper single axle (White 7000 cab), swing dolly	100	150	200
RCA	long nose tandem axle (White 9000 cab), stack, "Home Video"	80	85	100

Reading Railroad	long nose tandem axle (White 9000 cab), no stack	65	70	80
Reading Railroad	long nose tandem axle (White 9000 cab), one stack	85	90	100
Red Ball Movers	sleeper tandem axle (White 7000 cab), van red, metal dolly	80	90	100
Red Hawk Racing	Ford Aeromax 120 cab, an aerodynamic conventional sleeper, stack, tandem axle, double bed, Jeff McClure	90	100	120
Reese's	long nose tandem axle (White 9000 cab), cab logo, foil tanker, (peanut butter cups)	35	45	55
Rochester Smelting	long nose tandem axle (White 9000 cab), metal dolly, flat bed with block load	150	175	200
Sakrete	screw replaces the rivet in the rear of the floor of the trailer	85	95	100
Schmidt's Beer	long nose tandem axle (White 9000 cab)	100	125	150
Seven Up	sleeper single axle (White 7000 cab), red wheels, red metal dolly	90	100	125
Shasta	sleeper single axle (White 7000 cab)	30	35	45
Silver Spring Fire Co.	Mack cab (Mack Ultra-liner), sleeper tandem axle (White 7000 cab), stack, tanker	40	50	60
Simon Candy	Mack cab (Mack Ultra-liner), sleeper tandem axle (White 7000 cab), stack, full fairing clear sided doubles; with candy	55	65	75
Snyder's of Hanover	Mack cab (Mack Ultra-liner), sleeper single axle (White 7000 cab), stack	90	100	110
Sony	Mack cab (Mack Ultra-liner), sleeper tandem axle (White 7000 cab), stack, wind screen	60	65	75
Spickler's	Ford cab (Ford C1 9000), long nose tandem axle, stack, vert. brush, tanker	45	55	65
Stephens Boat Works (fictional company)	long nose single axle (White 9000 cab), blue 32'	150	175	200
Sunoco	Ford cab (Ford C1 9000), long nose tandem axle, stack, full fairing drop bed "Ultra Racing Team" (Marlin) plain	125	150	175
Sunoco	Ford Aeromax 120 cab, an aerodynamic conventional sleeper, tandem axle, stack, drop bed, Terry Labonte	200	250	300
SuperAmerica	long nose tandem axle (White 9000 cab), tanker	30	35	45
Superbubble	sleeper tandem axle (White 7000 cab)	25	30	35
Timberline	sleeper tandem axle (White 7000 cab), stack	35	45	55
TMI (Three Mile Island)	sleeper tandem axle (White 7000 cab), stack, wind screen, flat bed, nuc. waste load, each numbered	100	125	150
Toledo Toy Show	International 8300, tandem axle, stack	25	30	40
Totinos	sleeper tandem axle (White 7000 cab), stack, T-Bird reefer	35	40	50
Transport for Christ (Mobile Chapel)	Mack cab (Mack Ultra-liner), sleeper tandem axle (White 7000 cab), stack, wind screen	35	40	50
Transport Topics	long nose tandem axle (White 9000 cab), tanker, swing dolly	90	100	125
Tyson Foods	sleeper tandem axle (White 7000 cab), wind screen, reefer, "America's Choice"	80	90	110
U.S. Brands	sleeper tandem axle (White 7000 cab), wind screen	25	35	45
U.S. Gypsum	sleeper tandem axle (White 7000 cab), blue with red letters	55	65	75
U.S. Mail	cab over single axle (White 5000 cab), "Zip" blue metal dolly	55	65	75
U.S. Steel	long nose tandem axle (White 9000 cab), long wheel base cab, green, 32' flat bed, silver I-beam	90	100	125
Union Carbide	sleeper tandem axle (White 7000 cab), vert. brush, tanker	55	65	75

Unique Garden Center	sleeper tandem axle (White 7000 cab), stack, reefer	25	30	40
United Auto Workers (UAW)	Ford cab (Ford C1 9000), long nose tandem axle, stack (America Works)	65	70	75
United Way	Ford cab (Ford C1 9000), long nose tandem axle, stack, tanker (Collector Model 1 of 500)	30	40	50
Warner-Lambert	Ford cab (Ford C1 9000), long nose tandem axle, aerodynamic wind screen, "Efferdent" on side	25	30	35
Watergate	cab over single axle (White 5000 cab)	20	25	30
Weaver Chicken	sleeper tandem axle (White 7000 cab), white metal dolly "Country Style"	80	90	110
Westmans 32' Transport Tanker	3000 cab with wheels, blue with red, logo on trailer, wheel dolly	175	200	250
Westmans 32' Transport Tanker	long nose single axle (White 9000 cab), white trailer, red letters, wheel dolly	150	175	200
White Oak Mills	sleeper tandem axle (White 7000 cab), stack, tanker with catwalk	90	100	110
Wilbur Chocolate	Ford cab (Ford C1 9000), long nose tandem axle, stack, aerodynamic wind screen, T-Bird reefer, "Wilbur Buds"	60	65	75
Winross at Dyersville	Ford Aeromax 120 cab, an aerodynamic conventional sleeper, stack, Erie Canal	65	70	75
Winross at Hershey	Ford cab (Ford C1 9000), long nose tandem axle, stack, aerodynamic wind screen, blue cab	30	40	50
Winross at Hershey	Mack cab (Mack Ultra-liner), sleeper tandem axle (White 7000 cab), aerodynamic wind screen, green cab	30	40	50
Winross at Hershey	International 8300, tandem axle, Hershey Commemorative	40	45	50
Winross at Hershey	Mack cab (Mack Ultra-liner), sleeper tandem axle (White 7000 cab), aerodynamic wind screen, farm scene	30	40	50
Winross at Hershey	Ford Aeromax 120 cab, an aerodynamic conventional sleeper, stack, tandem axle, quilts	75	80	90
Winross at Hershey	Ford Aeromax 120 cab, an aerodynamic conventional sleeper, tandem axle	75	80	90
Winross at Hershey	Ford Aeromax 120 cab, an aerodynamic conventional sleeper, tandem axle, stack, quilts, different shade pink wind screen (Collectors Series)	40	45	50
Winross at Hershey	Mack cab (Mack Ultra-liner), tandem axle, chrome stacks, aerodynamic wind screen, car restoration	30	40	50
Winross at Hershey	Mack cab (Mack Ultra-liner), tandem axle, gray stacks, aerodynamic wind screen, car restoration, Collector Series	30	40	50
Winross at Hershey	Kenworth T800, tandem axle, tent scene	30	40	50
Winross at Rochester	Kenworth T800, tandem axle, stack, Erie Canal	30	40	50
Winross Hospitality Day	Mack cab (Mack Ultra-liner), tandem axle, stack, wind screen, blue cab, "You've Got a Friend in PA"	50	55	60
Winston Motor Sports	Ford Aeromax 120 cab, an aerodynamic conventional sleeper, stack, 20-year anniversary	45	50	55
Wonder Bread	Ford cab (C1 9000), long nose tandem axle, stack, wind screen, other side "Hostess"	70	75	80
Wyler's	sleeper single axle (White 7000 cab), pin, plastic dolly, "Realemon" on both sides	25	30	40
Y & S Candies	Mack cab (Mack Ultra-liner), sleeper tandem axle (White 7000 cab), stack, wind screen	55	65	75
Yellow Freight System	screw replaces the rivet in the rear of the floor of the trailer, rib trailer, plastic dolly	25	30	40
Yoplait Yogurt	sleeper tandem axle (White 7000 cab), stack, wind screen, reefer, trailer edged white	30	40	50

		Good	Ex	Mint
Zeager Bros. Inc.	Ford cab (C1 9000), long nose tandem axle, stack, flat bed with two lumber stacks	100	125	150
Zembo Temple	Ford cab (C1 9000), long nose tandem axle, stack, wind screen, white wheels	85	95	100

Wyandotte

Cars

Name	Description	Good	Ex	Mint
Air Speed Coupe	5-7/8" long, rubber wheels	40	75	95
Coupe	6-1/2" long, wood or rubber wheels	40	75	90
Rocket Racer	6" long	50	75	100
Soap Box Derby Racer	6-1/4"	45	100	150
Station Wagon	woodgrain and passenger lithography; 21" long	200	300	450
Zephyr Racer	10" long	75	125	150
Zephyr Roadster	13-3/8" long; rubber wheels	400	600	750

Emergency Vehicles

Name	Description	Good	Ex	Mint
Ambulance	6", wood wheels	45	70	90
Ambulance	11-1/4" long; Red Cross and "Wyandotte Toys" on side	75	150	185

Trucks

Name	Description	Good	Ex	Mint
Circus Truck and Wagon	19" long; red/yellow; w/cardboard animals	650	950	1400
Contractors' Truck	11-1/4" long; metal wheels; w/miniature wheelbarrow	70	125	175
Engineer Corps Truck	17-1/2" long; wood wheels; marked "Army Engineer Corps"	75	130	190
Gasoline Truck	21" long; rubber wheels	100	200	300
Hook 'n Ladder Truck	10-1/4" long, detachable ladders, rubber wheels	90	130	160
Ice Truck	11-1/2" long, wood wheels	100	190	250
Medical Corps Truck	11-3/4" long; metal wheels; "U.S.A. Medical Corps" on side	90	175	250
Milk Truck	11-1/2" long, wood wheels	100	190	250
Semi-Trailer Dump Truck	17-3/8" long; rubber wheels	60	90	150
Stake Truck	6-3/4" long, rubber or wood wheels	35	65	80

Buddy L 1927 coach bus with opening front doors and 22 chair seats. EXC-$9,000

Doepke's Jaguar XK120 roadster #2018 from 1955. EXC-$565

Smith-Miller's 1950 Mack Model L Pacific Intermountain Express tractor-trailer from 1954, 27-1/2 inches long, red cab and polished aluminum trailer. This toy originally sold for $19.95. EXC-$850

Smith-Miller's Mack Model L Bekins Van Lines Co. white tractor-trailer from 1953, 27-1/2 inches long. This toy cost $15.95 when new. EXC-$2,000

Doepke Model #2017 MG-TD roadster. EXC-$495

Wyandotte Toys tin woodie with retractable hardtop and opening trunk lid. EXC-$400

Corgi Toys Dodge Kew Fargo Tipper truck. EXC-$85

Corgi Toys #233 Heinkel three-wheeler. EXC-$70

Corgi Toys MGA roadster. EXC-$150

Corgi Toys VW 1500 Karmann Ghia. EXC-$90

Dinky Toys #24C Citroen DS-19. EXC-$135

Dinky Toys #170 Ford Sedan. EXC-$150

Dinky Toys #132 Packard convertible. EXC-$250

Dinky Toys Plymouth Station Wagon. EXC-$200

Dinky Toys #164 Vauxhall Cresta. EXC-$150

Dinky Toys Volkswagen 1300 Sedan. EXC-$100

Dinky Toys Studebaker Castrol Tanker. EXC-$400

Tootsietoy Chevrolet Cameo Carrier from 1956. EXC-$40

Arcade "Red Baby" International truck with dump bed and driver, 10-1/4" long, 1923. EXC-$1,000

Buddy L Fast Freight truck with open top cargo trailer, 20" long, 1948. EXC-$200

Marx City Sanitation Dept. truck, "Help Keep Your City Clean", tin litho, 12-3/4" long, circa 1948. EXC-$250

Marx Super Hot Rod #777, with box, tin, with driver, with electric flashing engine block, 11" long, circa 1949. EXC-$400

Marx Electric Marx Mobile child's ride-on convertible, battery operated, tin and plastic, circa 1950s. EXC-$175

Matchbox Superfast 72-unit Deluxe Collector's Case, 1970. EXC-$30

Matchbox #4 1957 Chevy, 2-15/16" long, 1979. EXC-$12

Matchbox #21 Commer Bottle Float (milk truck), 2-1/4" long, 1961. EXC-$40

Matchbox #71 Jeep Gladiator pickup, 2-5/8" long, 1964. EXC-$30

Matchbox Superfast
#20 Lamborghini
Marcel, 2-3/4" long,
1969. EXC-$35

Wyandotte
"Sunshine Dairy"
truck, pressed
steel, full color
lithography, circa
1938. EXC-$225

Wyandotte
"Wrecker Car"
truck, pressed
steel, with
operational boom
cable, circa 1948.
EXC-$145

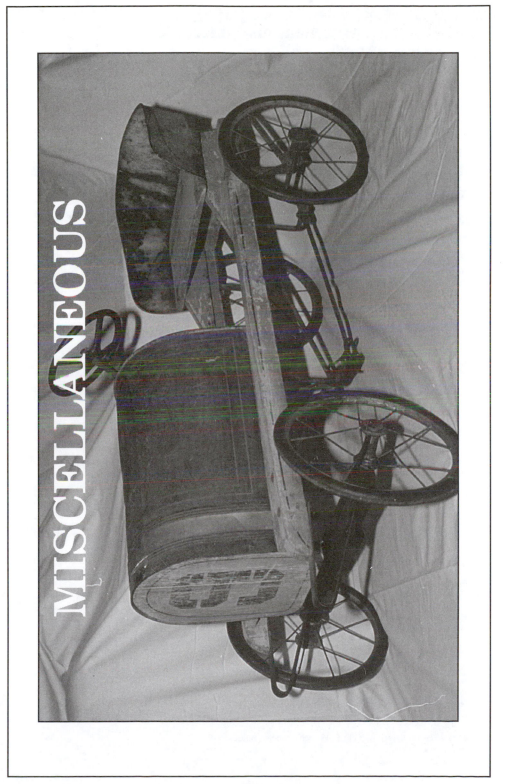

MISCELLANEOUS

Miscellaneous Collectibles

Description	Good	Very Good	Excellent
Cadillac screw-on hubcap	16	26	40
Dodge screw-on hubcap	4	6	10
Dort screw-on hubcap	8	13	20
Essex screw-on hubcap	4	6	10
Ford screw-on hubcap	4	6	10
Krit screw-on hubcap	6	10	15
Maxwell screw-on hubcap	6	10	15
Minerva screw-on hubcap	14	23	35
Nash screw-on hubcap	4	6	10
Oakland screw-on hubcap	4	6	10
Packard screw-on hubcap	16	26	40
Pierce-Arrow screw-on hubcap	16	26	40
Studebaker screw-on hubcap	6	10	15
Stutz screw-on hubcap	16	26	40
Velie screw-on hubcap	6	10	15
AC Fire Ring Spark Plug lighted wall clock, plastic, 16-inch diameter, orange-black-yellow-creme	125	175	225
Buick two-sided cast iron newstand paper weight, reads "Newsiest Buick Yet"/"Big News Is Buick" on opposing sides, 7 x 3 inches, circa 1937	45	65	90
Cadillac cigar box, paper litho cover on cardboard, 2-1/2 x 9 x 5-1/2 inches, red-blue-gold-black	125	160	185
Chrysler neon dealership sign, blue, 1940s	400	650	1000
Crosley "Time For Crosley" wall clock, 15-inch diameter, red-white-blue	125	200	275
Firestone Battery cigarette box, 3 x 3-1/2 x 2-1/4 inches, shaped like battery	5	15	20
Ford Sales and Service, Parts and Accessories lighted wall clock, octagonal	175	290	450
Fwd Truck watch fob, "America's foremost Heavy-Duty Truck"	10	20	25
Greyhound bus salt & pepper shakers, 1 x 1 x 2-1/2 inches, Japanese, creme-silver-blue	25	45	60
Hupmobile Sales & Service wall clock, 15-inch diameter, wood with glass face, orange and black	150	275	325
Miracle Power lighted wall clock, 12-inch diameter, blue-yellow-orange-black	25	65	90

Pan automobile watch fob, 1-1/2-inch diameter disc with Pan car on top	85	95	115
Pennzoil "Sound Your Z" wall clock, 20-inch diameter, orange and black, Pam Clock Co.	160	210	250
Plymouth neon dealership sign, 21-1/2 x 24-1/2 inches, shaped like flag, white and red	200	290	350
Pontiac copper ashtray, shaped like arrowhead, reads "Pontiac - Chief of the Sixes"	25	35	50
Portable Ford charcoal grille, 8 x 11-1/4 x 7 inches, pressed metal, with two boxes of Ford briquets	160	210	250
Triumph motorcycle "Fun Time" wall clock, 16-inch diameter, plastic, blue-black-white	200	290	350
Tydol Gasoline lighted wall clock, 15-inch diameter, white and black	150	215	275
Volkswagen candy jar with cork stopper, 6 x 5-1/2 inches, amber colored glass	15	35	50
Walker Mufflers wall clock, shaped like a muffler, white-silver-blue-red	25	75	150
Willard Batteries lighted free-standing clock, reverse glass face, 22 x 15 inches, red-white-black	250	380	475
Woman's leather handbag with 1956 Ford convertible graphics, tan-red-green-black	15	35	50
Antique clothing, Burberry style dust wrapper	14	23	35
Antique clothing, Burberry style motorcycle slip-on and pullover	12	19	30
Antique clothing, Esso service station uniform shirt, gray and white pinstripe	14	23	35
Antique clothing, Ulster overcoat	14	23	35
Antique clothing, Burberry suit	18	29	45
Duncan parking meter, two-hour limit	10	16	25
Double parking meter, 12-hour limit	8	13	20
Glass globe paperweight on base inscribed Romy Hammes Tractor Sales, interior scene shows 3 tractors	75	85	100
Hand-shaped automobile stop light, neon, w/ mounting bracket for rear bumper	300	350	400
1930s parking meter	15	25	50
1950s Duncan model D-2 parking meter (made into lamp)	14	23	35
1965 parking meter	4	6	10
1932 Hudson four-door sedan quarter-scale auto show display car, cast aluminum	5,500	12,500	22,500
1956 Club de Mer factory concept car styling model, silver with red interior	3,500	8,500	13,000

Description			
1957 Oldsmobile Super 88 Fiesta dealership True Match Color Selector transparency	100	300	600
1958 Oldsmobile Super 88 dealership True Match Color Selector transparency	75	250	450
1959 Oldsmobile dealership True Match Color Selector transparency	70	200	375
1958 Pontiac dealer showroom catalog, tri-fold, hardcover	200	290	350

Lunch Boxes

Description	Good	Very Good	Excellent
Adam-12 lunch box, tin, Aladdin Industries, 1973	65	75	90
Dragstrip lunch box, tin, Aladdin Industries	55	65	80
Racing Wheels lunch box, tin, King-Seeley Thermos Co.	55	65	80

Shaving Mugs

Description	Good	Very Good	Excellent
Shaving mug with 1902 Oldsmobile illustration	10	16	25
Shaving mug with 1902 Crestmobile illustration	10	16	25
Shaving mug with 1904 Winton illustration	10	16	25
Shaving mug with 1904 Peerless illustration	10	16	25
Shaving mug with 1906 Royal Tourist illustration	10	16	25
Shaving mug with 1909 Winton truck illustration	10	16	25
Shaving mug with 1910 Peerless illustration	10	16	25
Shaving mug with 1911 Locomobile illustration	10	16	25
Shaving mug with 1913 Haynes illustration	10	16	25
Shaving mug with 1914 Hupmobile illustration	10	16	25
Shaving mug with 1915 Star auto illustration	10	16	25
Shaving mug with 1915 Chevrolet bakery truck illustration	10	16	25
Shaving mug with 1916 Cadillac illustration	10	16	25
Shaving mug with 1917 Chevrolet illustration	10	16	25
Shaving mug that belonged to auto body man named "DeRosa;" shows car body being painted	600	1000	1500
Shaving mug that belonged to auto mechanic; shows mechanic working on car	390	650	1000

Shaving mug with name "J. Field"	500	845	1300
Shaving mug depicting old car	10	16	25
Shaving mug showing sedan owned by Mr. Scheid	500	845	1300
Shaving mug showing touring car owned by Mr. Zahn	500	845	1300
Shaving mug showing an old truck	12	19	30
Shaving mug showing auto engine	8	13	20
Shaving mug showing runabout owned by Mr. Rushworth	600	1000	1500
Shaving mug showing runabout owned by Mr. Young	600	1000	1500
Shaving mug showing old car	12	19	30
Shaving mug showing panel van	12	19	30
Shaving mug showing panel van	12	19	30
Shaving mug showing canopied express truck	14	23	85
Shaving mug showing large touring car owned by Mr. Nostrand	500	800	1200
Shaving mug showing large touring car owned by Mr. Merit	500	800	1200
Shaving mug showing car owned by Mr. Mitterich	500	800	1200
Shaving mug showing car owned by Mr. Quigley	500	800	1200
Shaving mug showing non-auto transportation scene	12	19	30

Automotive Postage Stamps

Description	Good	Very Good	Excellent
1893 Duryea, 32-cent U.S. stamp issued in 1995	.20	.40	.60
1894 Haynes, 32-cent U.S. stamp issued in 1995	.20	.40	.60
1898 Columbia, 32-cent U.S. stamp issued in 1995	.20	.40	.60
1899 Winton, 32-cent U.S. stamp issued in 1995	.20	.40	.60
1901 White, 32-cent U.S. stamp issued in 1995	.20	.40	.60
1901 issue of electric automobile in Washington, four-cent U.S. stamp	85	100	130
1901 issue of electric automobile in Washington (stamp has inverted center with car upside down), four-cent U.S. stamp	10,000	14,000	17,000
1904 issue of "Automobile Service" (depicting a Ford?), 15-cent U.S. parcel postage stamp	40	60	85
1909 Model T Ford (on Henry Ford stamp), 12-cent U.S. stamp issued in 1968	.08	.15	.25
1909 Stanley Steamer, 12-cent U.S. stamp issued in 1985	.08	.15	.25

"1911 Racing Car" (Marmon Wasp), 17-1/2-cent U.S. stamp issued in 1987	.10	.18	.30
1917 electric automobile, 17-cent U.S. stamp issued in 1981	.12	.20	.35
1928 Locomobile, 25-cent U.S. stamp issued in 1988	.15	.25	.50
1929 Pierce-Arrow, 25-cent U.S. stamp issued in 1988	.15	.25	.50
1931 Cord, 25-cent U.S. stamp issued in 1988	.15	.25	.50
1932 Packard, 25-cent U.S. stamp issued in 1988	.15	.25	.50
1933 Stutz Bearcat, 11-cent U.S. stamp issued in 1985	.08	.15	.25
1935 Duesenberg SJ, 25-cent U.S. stamp issued in 1988	.15	.25	.50
"Automobiles of 1902 and 1952", three-cent U.S. stamp, 50th Anniversary of American Automobile Association issued in 1952	.07	.10	.15
1971 German postage stamps, set of four stamps honoring Berlin-to-Pottsdam Race. Depict Opel rocket car, Auto Union, Mercedes SSK, and racing scene	.75	1	2

Automotive Coins, Medals and Tokens

Description	Good	Very Good	Excellent
Chevrolet Detroit American Legion Convention key ring medal (a trio of legion members on front, eagle landing on bowtie logo on back), 1931	1	3	5
Ford 50th Anniversary medal (Henry, Edsel and Henry II on front, 50 years of progress message on back), 1953	3	7	10
Ford Ypsilanti Plant "40 Years of Progress" medal (Ford logo on front, assembly plant on back), 1972	2	5	8
Hudson "40 Years of Engineering Leadership" medal (1949 Hudson on front, 1909 Hudson on back), 1949	1	3	5
General Motors/Pontiac "Chief of the Sixes" medal	2	5	8
United Auto Workers Union Flint Sit Down Strike commemorative medal, 1987	1	3	5
Lucky Piece token for Farley's 76 service station	1	3	5
Good Luck token for Jones Whitaker "The House of Chevrolet"	1	3	5
Good Luck token for Joie Chitwood World Champion Dare Devils touring thrill show (Indian on front, automobile launching off ramp on back)	2	5	8
Chevrolet maintenance promotion medal "You Get The Dime, Now Go After The Whole Dollar"	3	7	10
Rambler "The New Standard Of Basic Excellence" promotional medal	1	3	5
1892 Columbus Buggy Company token (issued at Colombian Exposition in Chicago, Illinois)	16	26	40

Description	Good	Very Good	Excellent
1910 Parry automobile, token	7	12	18
1933 Ford Chicago World's Fair "Century of Progress" souvenir medal honoring "30 Years of Progress" on Ford Motor Company's 30th Anniversary (shows 1933 Ford grille on front/V-8 logo on back)	6	10	15
1934 Chrysler Corporation, medal, Airflow; "A Century of Progress in a Decade." (1924 Chrysler on back - 10th anniversary of Chrysler)	4	6	10
1934 Ford Chicago World's Fair "Century of Progress" souvenir medal (shows V-8 emblems on both sides)	6	10	15
1935 Pontiac token. Indian head and "silver streaks"	6	10	15
Mid-1930s Dodge Truck Division token with sales pitch imprint	8	13	20
1940 Oldsmobile token. Front of 1940 Oldsmobile on obverse. Says "America's biggest money's worth: 1940 Olds" on reverse. Believed to be scarce.	5	8	12
1940 Buick encased silver dollar. Believed rare	50	100	150
1941 Buick encased silver dollar. Believed rare	50	100	150
1954 General Motors "Motorama" spinner token	3	5	7
1954-1955 General Motors "50 Millionth Car" commemorative medal. Issue dated Nov. 23, 1954. (Pictures the 1955 Chevrolet Bel Air two-door hardtop)	4	6	10
1955 General Motors "Motorama" spinner token	3	5	7
1956 Chrysler Corporation, medal "Forward Look," (arrowhead logo on one side; brand names of Chrysler marques listed on other side	6	10	15
1956 General Motors "Motorama" spinner token	3	5	7
1959 Chevrolet, "Best of '59 Jubilee," commemorative token. Back is stamped "Chevy Showboat, Greenbrier, White Sulfur Springs, W.V.)	3	5	7
1963 Mercury "Silver Anniversary" commemorative medal (chrome-plated)	15	20	30
1966 AMC, aluminum token, obverse reads "Sensible Spectaculars;" and reverse says "Rambler Extra Value Features Make Your Rambler Dollar a Bigger Dollar." Has car names on one side. Only known AMC promotional medal	3	5	7
Madison Mint .999 fine silver ingot illustrating Stanley Steamer roadster	15	20	30
Auburn-Cord-Duesenberg four token issue (modern commemorative)	15	20	30

Whiskey Decanters

Description	Good	Very Good	Excellent
Garnier bottle, circa-1912 touring car	15	30	45

Decanter, circa-1912 Rolls- Royce Silver Ghost Town Car	15	30	45
Jewel Tea Company, antique delivery wagon, (1974 issue)	25	50	75
1970 Jim Beam whiskey decanter, 1911 Marmon Wasp, honored first Indianapolis 500	50	75	100
1970 Jim Beam whiskey decanter, Mint 400, "World's Greatest Off-Road Race"	30	55	80
1972 Jim Beam whiskey decanter, "Beam on Wheels" series. 1902 Curved Dash Oldsmobile (honored 75th anniversary of Oldsmobile)	25	50	75
1973 Jim Beam whiskey decanter, "Beam on Wheels," Volkswagen Bug (Red)	15	30	45
1973 Jim Beam whiskey decanter, "Beam on Wheels," Volkswagen Bug (Blue)	15	30	45
1974 Jim Beam whiskey decanter, 1913 Model T Ford runabout (black)	20	35	50
1974 Jim Beam whiskey decanter, 1913 Model T Ford runabout (green)	20	35	50
1975 Jim Beam whiskey decanter, Bobby Unser's Indianapolis 500 Olsenite Eagle	25	50	75
1976 Jim Beam whiskey decanter, Sports Car Club of America	10	15	20
1976 whiskey decanter, ceramic, 1907 Thomas-Flyer 6-70 Model K Flyabout; replica of 1908 New York-to-Paris Great Race winner (blue)	25	45	65
1976 whiskey decanter, ceramic, 1907 Thomas-Flyer 6-70 Model K Flyabout; replica of 1908 New York-to-Paris Great Race winner (white)	25	45	65
1977 whiskey decanter, ceramic, 1914 Stutz, monocle windshield, (yellow and black)	25	45	65
1977 whiskey decanter, ceramic, 1914 Stutz, monocle windshield, (gray and black)	25	45	65
1977 whiskey decanter, ceramic, 1913 Cadillac	20	35	50
1977 Jim Beam whiskey decanter, AC Spark Plug Company	15	30	45
1978 Jim Beam whiskey decanter. 1978 Corvette (25th Anniversary of the Chevrolet Corvette)	75	125	175
1978 Jim Beam whiskey decanter, Mr. Goodwrench	15	30	45
1978 Jim Beam whiskey decanter, Delco Freedom Battery	10	15	20
1978 Jim Beam whiskey decanter, 1957 Chevrolet Bel Air	25	50	75
1978 Jim Beam whiskey decanter, 1903 Ford Model A runabout (red with black trim)	20	35	50
1978 Jim Beam whiskey decanter, 1903 Ford Model A runabout (black with red)	20	35	50

	Good	Very Good	Excellent
1981 Jim Beam whiskey decanter, Ford Model A Fire Chief's car, red	50	75	125
1981 Jim Beam whiskey decanter, Ford Model A Fire Chief's car, yellow (100 made for Jim Beam salesmen)	375	550	800
1981 Jim Beam whiskey decanter, Ford Model A Fire Chief's car, black (25 made for Jim Beam sales people who hit their quotas)	500	850	1200
1981 Jim Beam whiskey decanter, Ford Model A four-door phaeton light blue	25	45	65
1981 Jim Beam whiskey decanter, Ford Model A four-door phaeton, dark blue, Police Car	50	75	100
1981 Jim Beam whiskey decanter, 1928-1929 Ford Model A pickup	75	100	150
1981 Jim Beam whiskey decanter, 1930 Ford Model A Police Paddy Wagon	50	75	125
1981 Jim Beam whiskey decanter, 1934 Duesenberg Model J Town Car (blue body with white top)	50	75	100
1982 Jim Beam whiskey decanter, 1934 Duesenberg Model J Town Car, commemorates 27th annual Auburn-Cord-Duesenberg Fest in Auburn, Indiana, Labor Day Weekend 1982, (midnight blue body)	50	75	125

Advertising Signs & Badges

Description	Good	Very Good	Excellent
Teens, AAA, brass radiator badge	20	33	50
1920s, AAA, radiator badge, poured glass or porcelain	50	75	100
1920s Rickenbacker two-way porcelain dealership service sign, "A Car Worthy Of Its Name", 24 x 15 inches	2000	2250	2500
1925 season Automobile Blue Book Hotel sign, porcelain, 20 x 25 inches	390	650	1000
1930s, AAA, stamped die-cast badge	16	26	40
1930s Buick Valve In Head Authorized Sales & Service dealership sign, porcelain, 36-inch diameter, red-white-blue	390	650	1000
1930s Chrysler/Plymouth dealership service sign, porcelain	90	170	250
1931 Nash Motor Car Company, porcelain dealership sign	390	650	1000
1931 Packard Motor Car Company, porcelain dealership sign	450	780	1200
1950s Oldsmobile dealership service sign, tin	400	750	1100
1950s, AAA, porcelain sign	30	50	75
1950s, AAA, stick-on decal	2	3	5
1962 Avanti by Studebaker silk wall banner, 24 x 36 inches	60	100	150

	Good	Very Good	Excellent
AAA, porcelain sign(s), with state name(s)	50	75	125
American Motors, porcelain dealership sign	40	65	100
FoMoCo Genuine Ford Parts dealership service sign, tin, 18-inch diameter, two sided, red and white	25	50	75
Mopar Parts And Accessories sign, tin, 16-1/2 x 59 inches, red-creme-brown	190	250	300
Oakland Motor Car Company (became Pontiac), porcelain dealership sign	75	150	175
Pontiac, porcelain dealership sign (round with Indian head)	155	260	400

Pedal Cars

Description	Good	Very Good	Excellent
Gendron pedal car, Cadillac (standard)	1560	2600	4000
Gendron pedal car, Cadillac (deluxe)	1755	2925	4500
Gendron pedal car, 1927 Jordan	3200	5000	7500
Gendron pedal car, 1937 Pontiac w/ silver streaks	1500	2400	3700
Gendron pedal vehicle, 1938 Tri-motor airplane	2340	3900	6000
Gendron pedal car, 1938 Packard roadster	1835	3055	4700
Gendron pedal car, 1938 Pierce Arrow	3200	5000	7500
1918 pedal car, Automobile #9 racer	1700	2450	3200
1920s pedal car, Star Auto Racer	330	555	850
1920s pedal car, Dodge Racer	350	585	900
1920s pedal car, Green Auto Racer	350	585	900
1920s pedal car, Speed King Racer	350	585	900
1920s pedal car, Dan Patch "Big Racer"	400	700	1000
1920s pedal car, Studebaker roadster	650	1100	1800
1923 pedal car, Packard, American National Toy Co.	780	1300	2000
1923 pedal car, Packard Tandem Drive Touring, American National Toy Co.	3120	5200	8000
1925 pedal car, Paige, American National Toy Co.	2100	3600	5700
1935 pedal car, Lincoln Roadster, American National Toy Co.	5000	9000	13000
1930s pedal vehicle, Mack Bulldog fire engine with ladders	750	2200	4500
1930s pedal car, Ford roadster with V-8 engine	1200	1800	2900
1939 pedal car, Lincoln-Zephyr, Steelcraft	750	2200	4500

Description	Good	Very Good	Excellent
1940s pedal car, Arcade taxi, yellow with black and gray trim	225	350	500
1941 pedal car, Chrysler, Steelcraft	1200	1800	2900
1941 pedal car, Station Wagon, Garton	650	1100	1800
1949 pedal car, Murray-Ohio, "James Dean" Mercury	250	400	650
1950 pedal car, Murray Champion with Ball Bearing Drive	235	375	600
1950s pedal car, (Giordini Italian), "Juan Fangio" Grand Prix racer	780	1300	2000
1950 pedal car, Austin J-40 with Dunlop Cord tires and battery pack for working lights, lifting hood and trunk, green	850	1075	1350
1950 pedal car, F-530 Comet, Steelcraft, w/ windshield	330	550	850
1954 pedal car, Buick Torpedo, Murray	1200	1800	2900
1954 pedal car, Station Wagon, BMC	330	550	850
1956 child's car, Pontiac fiberglass body, electric lights. Designed by Jack K. Stuart	1850	3000	4500
1957 pedal car, Hot Rod 99, Garton, orange with black trim	780	1300	2000
1957 pedal car, Kidillac, Garton	850	1075	1350
1957 pedal car, Ranch Wagon, Garton	330	550	850
1957 child's car, Mercury Junior	225	370	575
1958 pedal car, Murray Speedway Pace Car 500	330	550	850
1963 pedal car, Murray Fireball Racer	200	325	450
1965 pedal car, Ford Mustang, AMF	330	550	850
1966 pedal car, Dragster, AMF	200	325	450
1969 pedal car, Pontiac GTO, AMF	200	325	450

Kid And Juvenile Cars

Description	Good	Very Good	Excellent
Citroen juvenile car (electric)	2145	3575	5500
1958 DeSoto juvenile car	9000	12000	15000
Shaw cyclecar	585	975	1500
1932 Syco Sales Company Juvenile car	585	975	1500

Airflow Toys and Collectibles

Description	Good	Very Good	Excellent
1934 toy car, Cor-Cor, Chrysler Airflow (green)	585	975	1500
1934 toy car, Cor-Cor, Chrysler Airflow (maroon)	585	975	1500
1934 toy car, Cor-Cor, Chrysler Airflow (bright red)	600	1000	1550
1934 toy car, Kingsbury, Chrysler Airflow, 14 inches long	295	490	750
1935 toy car, Kingsbury, Chrysler Airflow, 14 inches long	255	425	650
1936 toy car, Kingsbury, Chrysler Airflow, 14 inches long	255	425	650
1937 toy car, Kingsbury, Chrysler Airflow, 14 inches long	295	490	750
Toy car. Airflow four-door sedan. Steel. Painted red. All-white tires. Has bright metal waterfall grille and front bumper. Three air vents on side of hood. No skirted fenders.	165	275	425
Toy car. Airflow four-door sedan. Painted red-orange with dark green fenders. Both front and rear fenders skirted. Metal. Dark green door/hood seams and silver hood vents painted on body. Bright metal waterfall grille and front bumper. Criss-cross pattern painted on the running boards.	49	82	125
Toy car. Airflow two-door coupe. Red-orange with dark blue fenders. Front and rear fenders full skirted. Light blue hood. Spare tire painted on rear deck lid in light and dark blue. Orange spare tire center.	49	82	125
Toy car. Airflow four-door sedan. Metal. Painted all dark green. Fully skirted front/rear fenders.	40	65	100
Toy car. Airflow two-door coupe. Sheet metal. Silver body. Black fenders and front and rear bumpers. Rear fenders fully enclosed. Bright metal waterfall grille.	60	98	150
Toy car. Airflow two-door coupe. Sheet metal. Medium blue body. Dark blue fenders and front/rear bumpers. Same as above, but different grille. Rear fenders fully enclosed. Bright metal waterfall grille.	70	115	175
Toy Car. Airflow two-door coupe. Slush metal. Painted silver gray. White balloon tires. No skirted fenders. Body details engraved in metal.	65	110	165
Toy car. Airflow two-door coupe. Metal. Painted red. Fully skirted front and rear fenders. Bright metal grille and front bumper. Key hole for key-wind mechanism on left side.	55	90	140
Model car. Airflow. Four-door sedan. Metal. Painted off-white with black top insert. Bright metal waterfall grille, headlights, bumpers and trim. Rear mounted spare tire. Fully skirted rear fender.	585	975	1500
Toy truck or bus. Airflow. Molded rubber. Painted blue. Fully skirted rear wheels. Black rubber tires.	40	65	100
Toy teardrop (Airflow) trailer. Metal. Painted red. Full skirted fenders. Black rubber tires.	1050	1755	2700

Toy bus. Airflow styling. Silver. "Greyhound" embossed on sides. Slush metal. Protruding molded headlights and hood ornament. Fully skirted rear fenders. White rubber tires.

30	50	75

Toy tractor and three-compartment tanker-trailer. "Airflow" styling. Metal. Painted green. White rubber tires.

30	50	75

Toy truck. "Airflow" like styling. Sheet metal. Painted red. Bright metal grille, bullet headlights and veed front bumper. Fully enclosed front/rear fenders. Black rubber tires.

30	50	75

Model truck. Shell Airflow tanker. Painted chrome yellow with red Shell lettering. Bright metal grille, wheels, windshield frame and bumpers. Approximately nine inches long. Fully enclosed rear fenders. Black rubber tires. (Modern)

20	33	50

Toy truck. Airflow tanker. Sheet metal. Painted bright red. Four- compartment tanker body with ribs on top. Fin on front of hood. Bright metal waterfall grille, headlights and double-bar front bumper. Fully enclosed front/rear fenders. Black rubber tires.

60	100	150

Toy truck. Airflow tanker. Sheet metal. Painted medium-dark green. Has Sinclair Gasoline markings on sides. Three-compartment tanker body. No ribs on top of tank body. Snub-nose cab. Bright metal front grille, headlights and single-bar, fluted and veed, front bumper. Fully enclosed front/rear fenders. Black rubber tires.

60	100	150

Toy truck. Airflow-like styling. One-piece, but resembles fifth-wheel style house trailer. Molded rubber. Painted mostly medium blue with top of trailer in chrome yellow. Fully enclosed front and rear fenders on "cab" and rear on "trailer." Black rubber tires.

20	33	50

Toy fire truck. Airflow type styling. Hook and ladder with open cab. Painted red with yellow aerial ladder. Silver painted waterfall grille. Open fenders. Black rubber tires.

23	40	60

Pedal car. Airflow styling. Late 1930s. Red and cream. Has separate "catwalk" grilles on each side and parking "lamps" on tops of fenders.

1300	2500	3500

Pedal car. Fire truck. Chrysler Airflow. Red with white trim. Ladder rails with wooden ladders. Bell.

1440	2400	3700

Kid's ride-on toy truck. Dodge Airflow. Seat on rear dump box and T-handle juts out of cab. Metal. Painted bright red. Fully enclosed front and rear fenders with bright metal "wing" ornaments. Has bright metal grille, headlamps and bumper. White wheel discs and black rubber tires.

80	130	200

Small coaster wagon. Airflow-like styling. Metal. Painted red. Silver-painted front waterfall grille. Black rubber tires.

30	50	75

Small "Comet" coaster wagon. Airflow-like styling. Metal. Painted dark green with black "Comet" lettering. Black tiller. Black rubber tires.

350	585	900

Small "Comet" coaster wagon. Airflow-like styling. Metal. Painted light green with no "Comet" lettering. Pink tongue. Black tiller. Yellow wheels. (Possibly incorrect finish).

390	650	1000

Description	Good	Very Good	Excellent
Coaster wagon. Has four "Airflow" style fenders. Red wagon body. Black fenders, tongue, and tiller. White tires.	390	650	1000
Coaster wagon. Has four "Airflow" style fenders. Red wagon body. Yellow fenders, tongue, and tiller. Black tires.	390	650	1000
Coaster wagon. Has four red "Airflow" style fenders with silver "wing" decorations. Red wagon body with yellow speedlines and lettering graphics. Red tongue, and tiller. Silver wheels with black rubber tires.	390	650	1000
Flash Strat-O-Wagon coaster wagon. Has four "Airflow" style fenders. Red wagon body with red, blue, white and yellow rocketship graphics. Body is basically teardrop shaped with flat fins extending from rear. Four streamlined black fenders. Black axles and tiller.	450	780	1200
Large coaster wagon. Airflow styling. Red with white trim. Black tiller. Has small "headlights" in front. Curved-horizontal grille impression. Skirted front and rear fenders. Red spoke wheels and whitewall tires.	450	780	1200
Large coaster wagon. Airflow style. Green with cream trim. Black tiller. Has small "headlights" in front. Waterfall grille. Skirted front/rear fenders. Cream spoke wheels and whitewall tires.	400	600	1000
1938 Edw. K. Tyron Co. (Philadelphia) No. 710 Streamlined Pedal Bike. Has Airflow- like styling. 22 inches long overall. Seat height is 10-1/2 inches. Red and cream. Front wheel eight inches; rear five inches. One-half inch rubber tires. Black rubber pedals, One-piece body. Came six-in-carton to dealers. Weight 10 pounds. Originally cost $1.60 each (wholesale)	450	780	1200
Baby buggy. "Airflow" styled chrome-plated fenders. Blue plaid fabric. Chrome hubcaps. Black rubber tires.	120	195	300
Auto jack. Airflow-like styling. Painted bright orange-red. Rear section has fin-like shape.	43	72	110

Automotive Action Games/Slot Car Sets

Description	Good	Very Good	Excellent
American Flyer Stock Car Race motorized action game, #19060, A.C. Gilbert Co.	20	35	45
Atlas HO Motoring Official's Stand, circa 1960s	10	20	30
DX Getaway Chase Game, Sunray DX Oil Co., circa 1960s	30	40	50

Automotive Prewar Board Games

Name	Year	Company	Good	VG	Exc
Auto Game, The	1906	Milton Bradley	60	80	100
Auto Race Electro Game	1929	Knapp Electric &Novelty	125	170	210

Name	Year	Company	Good	VG	Exc
Auto Race Game	1925	Milton Bradley	125	190	275
Auto Race Jr.	1925	All-Fair	125	150	200
Auto Race/Army/Navy/Game Hunt (four game set)	1920s	Wilder	110	145	180
Auto Race, Game Of	1920s	Orotech	105	140	175
Automobile Race, Game Of The	1904	McLoughlin Bros.	500	750	1000
Brownie Auto Race	1920s	Jeanette Toy & Novelty	115	155	195
Calling All Cars	1938	Parker Bros.	45	60	75
Champion Road Race	1934	Champion Spark Plugs	100	135	165
Cross Country Racer	1940	Automatic Toy	45	60	75
Cross Country Racer (w/ wind-up cars)	1940s		75	100	130
Flip It, Auto Race & Transcontinental Tour	1920s	Deluxe Game	35	65	90
Grande Auto Race	1920s	Atkins	50	75	100
Huggin' The Rail	1939	Selchow & Righter	50	75	100
Indianapolis 500 Mile Race Game	1938	Shaw	350	465	575
International Automobile Race	1903	Parker Bros.	875	1165	1450
Junior Motor Race	1925	Wolverine	40	55	70
Midget Auto Race	1930s	Cracker Jack	10	15	20
Midget Speedway, Game Of	1942	Whitman	55	75	90
Moon Mullins Automobile Race	1927	Milton Bradley	60	105	150
Motor Cycle Game	1905	Milton Bradley	300	450	600
Motor Race	1922	Wolverine	90	120	150
Road Race/Air Race (two game set)	1928	Wilder	145	200	250
Roll-O-Motor Speedway	1922	Supply Sales	65	95	110
Speedem Junior Auto Race Game	1929	All Fair	70	130	175
Speedway Motor Race	1920s	Smith, Kline & French	145	205	250
Sto-Auto Race	1920s	Stough	65	90	110

Automotive Postwar Board Games

Name	Year	Company	Good	VG	Exc
77 Sunset Strip	1960	Lowell	35	50	75
77 Sunset Strip	1960	Warner	40	65	100

Assembly Line, The Game of	1953	Selchow & Righter	25	65	85
Calling All Cars	1950s	Parker Bros.	25	45	50
Cannonball Run, The	1981	Cadaco	5	15	25
Car Travel Game	1958	Milton Bradley	5	15	25
Cars 'n Trucks Build-A-Game	1961	Ideal	15	45	80
Circle Racer Board Game	1988	Sport Games USA	5	10	15
Daytona 500 Race Game	1989	Milton Bradley	10	15	25
Driver Ed	1973	Cadaco	5	10	20
Dukes of Hazzard	1981	Ideal	5	10	15
Electric Sports Car Race	1959	Tudor	35	60	90
Empire Auto Races	1950s	Empire Plastics	20	30	50
Famous 500 Mile Race	1988	N/A	10	15	20
Formula One Car Race Game	1968	Parker Bros.	15	40	60
Four Lane Road Racing	1963	Transogram	15	45	65
Hot Rod	1953	Harett-Gilmar	30	50	75
Hot Wheels Game	1982	Whitman	10	15	20
Hot Wheels Wipe-Out Game	1968	Mattel	30	50	75
Indianapolis 500 75th Running Race Game	1991	International Games	10	15	20
International Grand Prix	1975	Cadaco	30	50	75
Interstate Highway	1963	Selchow & Righter	15	50	75
Knight Rider	1983	Parker Bros.	10	15	20
LeMans	1961	Avalon Hill	25	40	65
Matchbox Traffic Game	1960s	N/A	25	45	70
Pole Position	1983	Parker Bros.	10	15	20
Power 4 Car Racing Game	1960s	Manning	15	50	75
Raceway	1950s	B&B Toy	30	50	75
Route 66 Game	1960	Transogram	75	125	200
Rules of the Road	1977	Cadaco	5	15	25
Shifty Gear Game	1962	Schaper	5	15	25
Speedway, Big Bopper Game	1961	Ideal	35	60	90
Stock Car Race	1950s	Gardner	30	50	75
Stock Car Racing Game	1956	Whitman	30	50	75

Stock Car Racing Game (w/ Petty and Yarborough)	1981	Ribbit Toy	15	30	45
Stock Car Speedway, Game of	1965	Johnstone	55	90	135
Supercar Road Race	1962	Standard Toycraft	40	65	105
Supercar To The Rescue Game	1962	Milton Bradley	35	60	95
Test Driver Game, The	1956	Milton Bradley	25	75	125
That's Truckin'	1976	Showker	10	20	35
Thunder Road	1986	Milton Bradley	10	15	25
Tru-Action Electric Sports Car Race	1959	Tudor	20	50	75
USAC Auto Racing	1980	Avalon Hill	15	35	60
Vallco Pro Drag Racing Game	1975	Zyla	15	25	35
Wacky Races Game	1970s	Milton Bradley	15	25	40

Hudson Collectibles

(Photos and information courtesy of Jim and Sandy Boyle)

Description	Good	Very Good	Excellent
Picture of factory, 41 x 32 inches, Hudson Motor Car Company, Detroit 14, Michigan. Inserts of Hudson's own body plant, gear and axle plant, original Hudson factory 1909, Hudson Motors Ltd., London, England, Hudson Motors of Canada, Ltd., Tilbury, Ontario	65	100	200
Letter opener - 8-2/3 inches long - This Time It's Hudson, 1948	25	35	45
Baseball bat - Let's go to bat for business and sell the all new Hudson for '54, 1954, 15 inches long	20	45	60
Bamboo banner - Hudson Championship 6 - Record breaking 150 stock car victories, 36 x 53 inches, 1955	150	200	300
Bamboo banner - The Standout New 220 Horsepower Hornet V8 for 1956, 36 x 55 inches, 1956	100	150	250
Bamboo banner - Standout V-line styling - totally new 1956 Hudsons, 36 x 55 inches, 1956	150	200	300
Yard stick - 55 inches - Lay this ruler across the front seat of a 1937 Hudson or Terraplane and close both doors--then try it with any other car, 1937	20	35	45
Hudson accessory lamp display stand, 1949	200	450	650
Hudson Protective Lubrication Coupons, 1950	10	20	30
Hudson custom grille guard, 1948-1953	35	65	135
Hudson Liquid Glaze Duo-Kit, 1950	20	45	55
Hudson vanity mirror, 1951	10	30	45

Hudson Kleenex dispenser, 1952	15	35	50
Hudson Twin Bed Air Mat, 1955	50	175	350
Hudson license plate frame, 1952	15	45	65
T.D.C. Stereo Viewer with 42 slides in carrying case, 1952	100	200	375
Award plaque, May 1950	45	75	125
Hudson plastic salt and pepper shaker, 1946	15	35	45
Remington 6V and 110V Blue Streak electric shaver AC/DC shaver with brochure, 1948	90	175	350
Hudson Engine Tune-Up oil can, four-ounce metal can, 1948	12.50	25	35
Hudson Lacquer, metal can with paper label, quart, 1948-1954	18	30	45
Hudson and Terraplane Tune-Up Kit in leather pouch, 1935	65	80	135
Safety swinging stop light, 1936	85	135	200
Brass Terraplane and Hudson axle-flex dealer display, 1935	45	65	110
Hudson Motor Oil one-quart glass bottle, with paper label, circa 1940	100	130	170
Hudson boat, plane, and auto compass in original box, 1948	25	50	75
Hudson polishing cloth in original Christmas box, 1948	20	35	50
Hudson Shop and Owner's Supplies, tin sign, 1946	75	150	250
1/16th scale Hudson plastic four-door sedan model, 1948, available in dark blue/medium blue, dark green/medium green, dark red/medium red	300	550	750
1/16th scale green plastic police car with siren made by Marx, complete with box, 1948-1949	150	350	450
1/16th scale red plastic fire chief car by Marx, 1948-1949	125	300	400
1/16th scale plastic model Hudson four-door sedan red on one side/clear on other side with literature demonstration booklet, 1948	350	675	850
Sheet music - "This Time It's Hudson", two variations of covers, 1948	35	55	80
Neon signs: "This Time It's Hudson", 1948	200	400	550
"Hudson Rambler", 1955	150	350	500
"Terraplane", 1933	250	500	650
Hudson Touch-up Lacquer metal rack with 48 three-ounce metal cans, 1948-1954	450	700	850
Hudsonite clutch compound, one-third pint (approximately 36 manufacturers), 1910-1957	10	25	35
Tin advertising pin - Ask me for a Hudson "Revelation" ride, 1949	20	30	50
1/25th scale metal model made by Master Caster, 1948-1951 sedan	75	125	250

1/25th scale metal model made by Master Caster, 1948-1951 coupe	80	150	300
Tin cereal promotional item, shows red Hudson logo, 1952	5	15	20
Porcelain-enameled neon tube light, vertical double-faced sign, 11 foot, 1946-1957	650	1,000	1,500
Porcelain-enameled neon lighted, horizontal double-faced sign, 6 foot, 1946-1957	550	600	1,200
Horizontal single-faced porcelain-enameled neon lighted sign, 6 foot, 1946-1957	300	500	700
Merit award thermos bottle, Hudson Motor Car Company, 1936	75	125	180
Literature display stand with contents, Hudson for '55, 1955	250	450	850
Lapel pin - "This Time It's Hudson", 1948	15	35	75
Lapel pin - "Ride the green line of safety in a new 1939 Hudson", 1939	25	55	80
Lapel pin - "Hudson Service Manager", 1952	45	85	110
Lapel pin - "Hudson Twenty Years"	75	110	150
Matchbooks, double-pack, Hudson for '51, 1951	15	30	45
Hudson Service Merchandiser, July 1949-June 1956	7	10 (per issue)	15
Terraplane-Hudson Service Magazine, December 1933-September 1935. Changed to *Hudson-Terra-plane Service Magazine*, October 1935-September 1937. Changed to *Hudson Service Magazine*, October 1937-July 1940. Changed to *Service* (monthly magazine), August 1940-March 1945	15	35 (per issue)	65
Dealers album in leather carrying case - Hudson for 1954, 1954	250	450	750
Fold-out dealers album - New 1942 Hudson, 1942	200	375	575
Fold-out dealers album - New Hudson for 1948, 1948	200	375	575
The Corte-Scope viewer with 60 viewing cards of Hudson factory and cars, 1915	150	275	475

Hudson Petroliana

By John O'Halloran

Hudson used clutch oil to cushion the cork clutch discs on all its cars from 1909 through the "stepdown" models, ending in 1954. The 1953-1954 Jets had dry discs, as did the Nash model when equipped with stickshift.

I have 18 different types of Hudson clutch oil containers, including two of recent issue. There have probably been several hundred varieties of clutch oil throughout the years, especially when considering the different sizes of containers.

Before 1930, Hudson clutches used a half-pint of oil. The 1930 and 1931 cars called for a quarter-pint, and all Hudsons after 1931 used a third-pint of oil.

Examples of early large cans of clutch oil are rare. Hudson Motor Co. continued to bottle the larger half-pint containers through the "stepdown" model years for the early cars, and these later large containers are also hard to find.

Hudson's brand name for its product was Hudsonite. This type of container still turns up regularly at swap meets, and in Very Good condition – if it's full – is worth $5.00. Vendors frequently ask more, but it would be difficult to recoup an investment of more than $5.00. Hudsonite cans in lesser condition are not as desirable; not worth more than $3.00.

A glass bottled Hudsonite is much less common than the can. A fully labeled bottle is worth at least $10.00. There exists American Motors-labeled Hudsonite, which is a post-merger product. The screw-top container is less common than the flat-top can.

The Terraplane-vintage Hudsonite is also rare. Any example of this container in decent condition would easily bring $20.00 minimum.

Most cans of non-Hudson Hudsonite are worth $3.00 in excellent condition, due to the fact that these containers are still plentiful from vendors.

An interesting aside to these clutch oil containers are two rare Hudson-related collectibles in my collection, one being a 1937 Terraplane 55-inch yardstick and the other a 1950 Hudson dealer's plaque.

My sister found the yardstick in the rafters of an old house she moved into 20 years ago. The yardsticks came in three varieties and less than a dozen are known to exist. Its value is inestimable.

I obtained the dealer's plaque in 1979, and it was the first of its kind that I'd seen. Without any difficulty, this item would bring $100.

Several examples of the flat-top containers of clutch oil used for Hudson automobiles prior to 1954. (John O'Halloran collection)

A rare 1937 Terraplane 55-inch yardstick used to "Measure the things you can SEE (Style - Size - Roominess - Luxury). (John O'Halloran collection)

Examples of the larger screw-top containers of clutch fluid used for Hudson automobiles prior to 1954. (John O'Halloran collection)

Hudson Collectibles

All information and photos courtesy
of the Janice & Dick Prasher collection.

Bamboo banner for "The Standout New 220
Horsepower Hornet V-8" for 1956. Banner
is 36x55 inches and features brown, yellow,
and gold lettering on bamboo. EXC-$250

A one-quart glass bottle of
Hudson Motor Oil with screw-
cap top and paper label, circa
1940. EXC-$170

Tin sign from 1946 that reads: Hudson Shop and Owners' Supplies. EXC-$250.

Ford pedal car representing mid-1930s roadster. EXC-$2,900

Plymouth Speedway Pace Car pedal car representing 1958 convertible.
EXC-$850

1918 Automobile racer #9 pedal car. This unrestored version is missing its headlights, windshield, and horn. The original price on this pedal car was $10. EXC-$3,200

1920s Dodge Racer pedal car with Moto Meter on dogbone base and front bumper. EXC-$900

1957 Garton Kidillac pedal car. EXC-$1,350

1950s Murray Champion pedal car with Ball Bearing Drive. EXC-$600

1950 Steelcraft F-530 Comet pedal car. EXC-$850

1959 Garton Hot Rod 99 pedal car. The original price on this pedal car was $13.95. EXC-$2,000

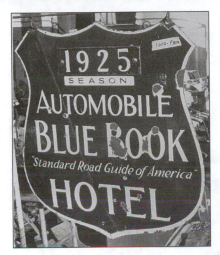

Automobile Blue Book Hotel sign from the 1925 season. EXC-$1,000

A Chrysler neon sign from the 1940s. It has a light blue hue. EXC-$975

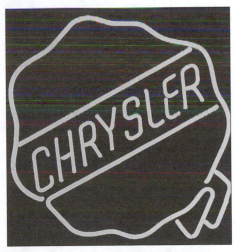

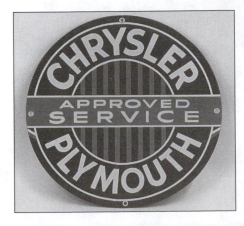

Chrysler - Plymouth Approved Service porcelain sign from the 1930s. EXC-$250

1932 Hudson four-door sedan quarter-scale auto show display vehicle made from cast aluminum. EXC-$22,500

1956 Club de Mer factory concept car styling model. EXC-$13,000

Miscellaneous

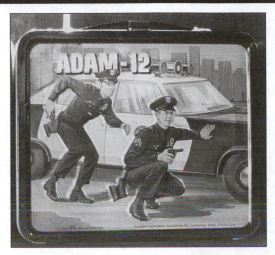

Adam-12 lunch box from TV show of same name, Aladdin Industries, 1973. EXC-$90

Drag Strip lunch box, Aladdin Industries. EXC-$80

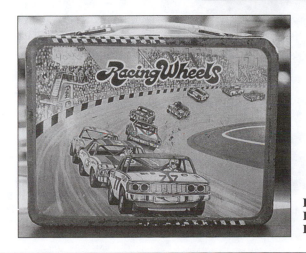

Racing Wheels lunch box, King-Seeley Thermos Co. EXC-$80

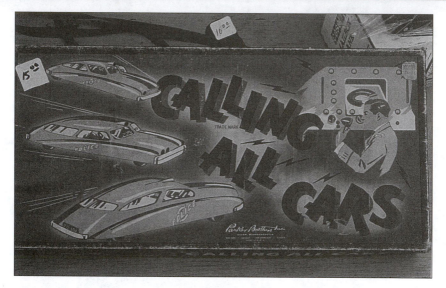

Calling All Cars board game, Parker Bros., 1938. EXC-$75

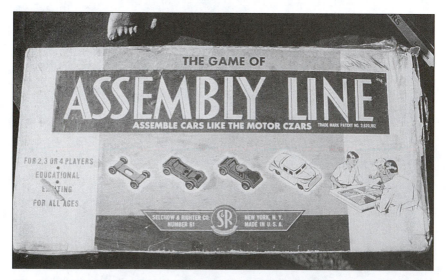

The Game Of Assembly Line board game, Selchow & Righter Co., 1953. EXC-$85

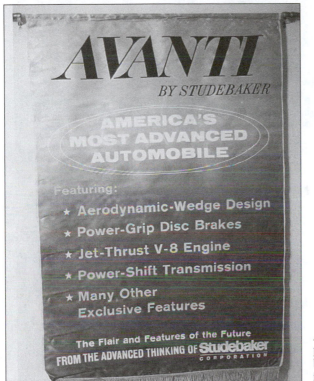

Avanti By Studebaker promotional silk wall banner, 24 x 36 inches, 1962. EXC-$150

Rickenbacker two-sided, porcelain dealership service sign - "A Car Worthy Of Its Name", circa 1920s. EXC-$2,500

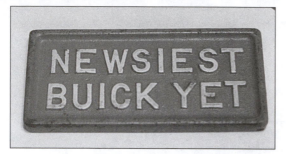

Buick cast iron two-sided newsstand paperweight, 7 x 3 inches, circa 1937. EXC-$90

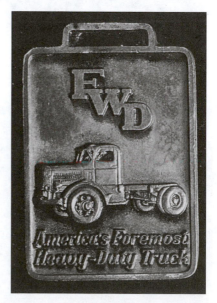

A pair of watch fobs: (left) Pan automobile, circa 1920, (right) FWD "America's Foremost Heavy-Duty Truck, circa 1952. Pan - EXC-$115. FWD - EXC-$25

Miscellaneous

Pontiac "Chief of the Sixes" copper ashtray, shaped like arrowhead. EXC-$50

Glass globe paperweight on base inscribed "Romy Hammes Tractor Sales" with interior scene of 3 tractors. EXC-$100

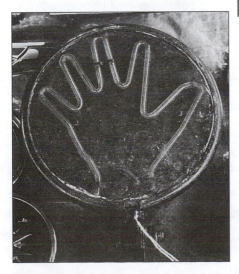

Hand-shaped, electric stoplight with mounting bracket for rear bumper, circa 1920. EXC-$400

American Flyer Stock Car Race motorized game from The A.C. Gilbert Co. of New Haven, Conn. EXC-$45

Atlas HO Motoring Official's Stand, circa 1960s. EXC-$30

DX Getaway chase game, battery operated, Sunray DX Oil Co., circa 1960s. EXC-$50

Chevrolet Detroit American Legion Convention key ring medal from 1931. EXC-$5

1934 Chrysler Airflow medal - "A Century Of Progress In A Decade" 10th Anniversary of Chrysler. EXC-$10

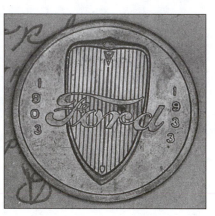

1933 Chicago World's Fair Ford 30th Anniversary medal - "Thirty Years Of Progress". EXC-$15

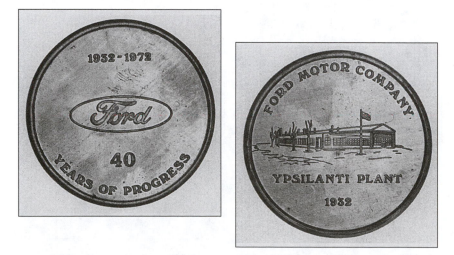

Commemorative medal for "40 Years Of Progress" at Ford Motor Co.'s Ypsilanti (Mich.) assembly plant. EXC-$8

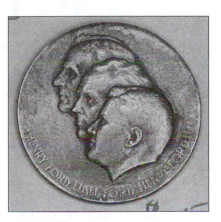

**Ford 50ᵗʰ Anniversary medal - "50 Years Forward On The American Road".
EXC-$10**

**1949 Hudson 40ᵗʰ Anniversary medal - "40 Years Of Engineering Leadership".
EXC-$5**

General Motors/Pontiac "Chief of the Sixes" promotional medal. EXC-$8

Commemorative medal for 50th Anniversary of United Automobile Workers Union Local 659 Flint (Mich.) Sit Down Strike in 1937. EXC-$5

Lucky Piece token for Farley's 76 service station. EXC-$5

Good Luck token for Jones Whitaker "The House of Chevrolet". EXC-$5

Good Luck token for Joie Chitwood World Champion Dare Devils touring thrill show. EXC-$8

Rambler promotional medal - "The New Standard Of Basic Excellence". EXC-$5

Chevrolet maintenance promotional medal - "You Get The Dime, Now Go After The Whole Dollar". EXC-$10